The Nature and Treatment of Anxiety Disorders

. . . .

C. BARR TAYLOR, M.D.
BRUCE ARNOW, Ph.D.

THE FREE PRESS
A Division of Macmillan, Inc.
NEW YORK

Collier Macmillan Publishers
LONDON

The Free Press
A Division of Macmillan, Inc.
866 Third Avenue, New York, N.Y. 10022

Collier Macmillan Canada, Inc.

Printed in the United States of America

printing number

2 3 4 5 6 7 8 9 10

Library of Congress Cataloging-in-Publication Data

Taylor, C. Barr (Craig Barr)
    The nature and treatment of anxiety disorders.

    Bibliography: p.
    Includes index.
    1. Anxiety. 2. Phobias. I. Arnow, Bruce Alan.
II. Title [DNLM: 1. Anxiety Disorders. WM 172 T239n]
RC531.T39 1988   616.85′223   88–3611
ISBN 0–02–932981–7

This book is not intended as a substitute for medical advice of
physicians. The reader should regularly consult a physician
in matters relating to his or her health and particularly in
respect of any symptoms which may require diagnosis or
medical attention.

Dedicated with love and appreciation to our wives,
SUESAN AND BETH

Contents

· · · · · · · · · ·

v

Preface

· · · · · · · · · ·

This is a book about understanding and treating patients whose primary complaint involves an anxiety disorder. Over the past five years, together with our colleagues at the Stanford University Anxiety Disorders Clinic, we have treated over 500 such patients either through our outpatient clinic or through our ongoing research program. We have collected extensive information on over 1,000 additional patients, many of whom had undertaken previous treatment for their difficulties without benefit. Our experience with this group of patients has led us to conclude that although effective clinical interventions for such difficulties have been developed over the past 20 years, they are not widely practiced.

There appear to be many reasons for this, not the least of which is that effective treatment of many anxiety disorders often requires a combination, or "package," of clinical procedures, whose components fall into different subspecialties. For example, individuals with agoraphobia often respond best to a combination of medication, in vivo exposure therapy, and cognitive therapy. While these interventions should not be considered mutually exclusive, few therapists combine them. Psychiatrists, who may be knowledgeable about the role of medication in the treatment of anxiety, rarely have the time or interest to master the delivery of exposure-based therapy. Psychologists and social workers may specialize in cognitive and/or behavioral therapies but are unable to prescribe medication. Moreover, the techniques for treating anxiety disorder patients were developed within a research literature in which presentation of therapy procedures is often brief. Thus, there are few accounts regarding the "nuts and bolts" of carrying out treatment.

We describe, in detail, a symptom-focused approach to the treatment of anxiety disorders, in many cases carried out by a multidisciplinary team. The purpose of such treatment is, at a minimum, to reduce the intensity and frequency of the presenting symptoms; in some cases, such problems will resolve entirely. Depending upon the type of anxiety disorder presented, our approach often begins with psychopharmacology combined with cognitive behavioral therapy and other directive therapies. Later, after the presenting complaint has been addressed, treatment may evolve to include family, marital, or psychodynamic therapy as appropriate.

We believe that anxiety is best understood and treated from a bio-psychosocial perspective which assumes that various biological, psychological, and social factors interact to produce a patient's unique manifestations of anxiety. The biological factors include the patient's genetic endowment, drug and medication use, illnesses, and vulnerability to stress and separation. The psychological factors include the patient's learning history and experience and a variety of other cognitive factors, including perception and appraisal patterns. The social factors include the patient's family, work, and recreational and cultural environment. Each of these factors plays a role in the final expression of symptoms in any patient.

In chapter 1 we present an overview of the nature of anxiety, followed in chapter 2 by a survey of the major theories attempting to account for it. We struggled with the question of whether to present theories relevant to the phenomenon of anxiety in one general chapter or disperse the discussion among the various chapters discussing specific anxiety disorders. We compromised by presenting some of the more general theories in chapter 2 and including ideas specific to particular disorders in later chapters.

Anxiety is a feature of many psychiatric difficulties including certain personality disorders and substance abuse. Devising an effective treatment plan begins with accurate diagnosis. Chapter 3 covers diagnostic issues and includes a flow chart to assist the clinician in making a proper diagnosis. We pay particular attention to helping the clinician distinguish between certain anxiety disorders and other psychiatric problems whose symptoms may resemble the former but require different treatment.

We present an overview of our approach to treating anxiety disorders in chapter 4. After that, we go on to examine the nature and treatment of specific anxiety disorders in chapters 5 through 10. Within space limitations, we attempted to present as much detail as possible on treatment procedures in each of these chapters, as well as information on clinical features, incidence and prevalence, differential diagnosis, assessment, and studies regarding treatment outcome.

The final two chapters summarize the psychopharmacology of agents used to treat anxiety disorders and some of the medical problems that can cause anxiety. Appendixes 1 and 2 contain the basic assessment instruments we use in our clinic, and Appendix 3, written by Mary Brouillard, and Michael Telch, Ph.D., presents the protocol developed in our research program for the group treatment of agoraphobia.

Although obsessive compulsive disorder and post-traumatic stress disorder are both considered anxiety disorders, we did not include chapters dealing with them. In the case of obsessive compulsive disorder, we felt we had little to add to treatment approaches that have been well described by others. Moreover, we have found the nature of this disturbance to be quite different from the other anxiety disorders described in this book. We have not discussed post-traumatic stress disorder for similar reasons.

Many of our colleagues have contributed to the ideas, techniques, and production of this book. We particularly want to acknowledge the help of the members of the Anxiety Disorder Clinic and Research group: W. S. Agras, M.D., Paul Bayon, Mary Brouillard, Duncan Clark, Ph.D., M.D., Sylvia Davies, Anke Ehlers, Ph.D., Leslie Fried, Karl Goodkin, Ph.D., M.D., Chris Hayward, M.D., Roy King, Ph.D., M.D., John Madden, Ph.D., Richard Maddock, M.D. (who was particularly helpful for chapter 11), Jurgen Margraf, Ph.D., Tom Merluzzi, Ph.D., Tom Nagy, Ph.D., Susan Raeburn, Ph.D., Elise Rossiter, Ph.D., Tom Roth, M.D., Jaavid Sheikh, M.D., Christy Telch, Ph.D., and Michael Telch, Ph.D. We are grateful for the very able technical and editorial assistance provided by Jennie Dishotsky, Margarite Galvan, Sherry Wright-Smith, Yuki Matsuyoshi, and Kathleen Murphy. Special thanks to Beth Sherman and Celia Knight for their help in preparing the final manuscript. Finally, we want to thank our editor, Laura Wolff, for her help and encouragement.

ONE
· · · · · · · · ·

What Is Anxiety?

· · · · · · · · · ·

> It comes over me all at once. First of all it is like something pressing
> on my eyes. My head gets so heavy, there's a dreadful buzzing and I
> feel so giddy that I almost fall over. Then there's something crushing
> my chest so that I can't get my breath. . . . My throat's closed
> together as though I were going to choke. . . . I always think I'm
> going to die. I'm brave as a rule and go about everything by
> myself—into the cellar and all over the mountain. But on a day
> when that happens I don't dare go anywhere. . . .
>
> Freud's description of Katherina (1966)

Anxiety is a universal emotion. In mild form it is experienced at one
time or another by everyone; in more extreme form it leads to fears of
impending death or catastrophe. The feeling of anxiety may occur
without physical symptoms, or it may be accompanied by numerous
overwhelming symptoms affecting many organ systems; it may cause
no change in behavior, or it may lead to immobilization or chronic
avoidance. The unpleasantness—and universality—of the symptoms
are evidenced by the fact that over 80 million prescriptions for antianxiety drugs are dispensed in the United States each year. Despite
its importance, the nature of anxiety remains elusive. Darwin conceptualized anxiety as an instinct; the learning theorist Hull saw
anxiety as a drive. For Freud, the problem of *angst*, which is usually
translated from the German as anxiety, is a "nodal point . . . a riddle
of which the solution must cast a flood of light upon our whole mental life" (Freud, 1943, p. 341). For the existentialist Rollo May (1950),
anxiety "is described on the philosophical level as the realization
that one may cease to exist as a self . . . i.e., the threat of mean-
inglessness" (p. 193). On the other hand, for Eysenck (1979), anxiety
is a conditioned fear response whose nature can be understood with-

1

out reference to its subjective components. There are many other aspects of anxiety that have been noted by the numerous clinicians and researchers who have attempted to understand and define it. Although the nature and even the definition of anxiety remain elusive and controversial, the many different approaches to anxiety have generated a number of practical treatment ideas and approaches, which, when systematically applied, may bring relief to most patients. The aim of the book is to help the clinician understand both the nature of anxiety and the numerous approaches to its treatment. In this chapter we will discuss the phenomenology and definitions of anxiety.

DEFINING ANXIETY: SEMANTIC DIFFICULTIES

Anxiety, like other emotions, is difficult to describe. The words used to describe it only approximate our inner experience and may lead to confusion. Any examination of the phenomenology of anxiety is colored by the lexicon in which it is conducted. The English word *anxiety* comes from the Latin word *anxietas* and/or *anxius*. These words contain the root *Angh*, which appears in Greek and in the *Thesauraus Latinae Linguae* in words meaning "to press tight," "to strangle," "to be weighed down with griefs." In the *Oxford English Dictionary* anxiety means: "1. uneasiness about some uncertain event, 2. solicitous desire to effect some purpose, 3. a condition of agitation and depression, with a sensation of lightness and distress in the precordial region." Jablensky (1985) notes that the English word "anxiety" does not cover the same semantic space as the French *anxiete* or the Spanish *ansiedad* although they all derive from a common root. In French, *angoisse* is used as a near-synonym for anxiety but connotes more strongly the physical sensations accompanying the experience and may be closer to the English "anguish" than to "anxiety." And the German word *angst* implies, besides "anxiety" and "anguish," "agony, dread, fear, fright, terror, consternation, alarm and apprehension." English-speaking patients will use words like "edgy," "uneasy," "nervous," "tense," "anxious," "fearful," "scared," "frightened," "alarmed," "terrified," "jittery," and "jumpy" to describe their experience.

These semantic difficulties have led to a variety of definitions. Confusion over definition occurs because some of the definitions refer to the emotions while others refer to clinical symdromes. The delineation of clinical syndromes is particularly problematic.

After an extensive review of many of the historical and current definitions of anxiety, Lewis (1970) developed the following list of characteristics common to most definitions of clinical anxiety: (1) it is an emotional state with the subjectively experienced quality of fear or a closely related emotion; (2) the emotion is unpleasant; (3) it is directed towards the future; (4) there is either no recognizable threat, or the threat is by reasonable standards, quite out of proportion to the emotion it seemingly evokes; (5) there are subjective bodily discomforts during the period of the anxiety; (6) there are manifest bodily disturbances.

These characteristics are congruent with our clinical experience. In line with Lader (1972) and Lewis (1970), we define anxiety as follows:

> It is a feeling of uneasiness and apprehension about some undefined threat. The threat is often physical with intimations of bodily harm or death, or psychological with threats to self-esteem and well-being. The feeling is diffuse and ineffable, and the indefinable nature of the feeling gives it its peculiarly unpleasant and intolerable quality.

If the threat *can* be identified, we refer to the feeling as *fear*.

The term *stress* is often equated with anxiety. Lay people, in particular, use the terms anxiety, stress and tension interchangeably. There is little agreement in the scientific community as to the definition and nature of stress, and the term is best avoided as it only causes confusion. On the other hand, it is sometimes useful to refer to a stressor, a stimulus, or event, that causes psychological and/or physiologic change, and to refer to the change as the stress response.

It is often difficult to draw a line between normal and clinical anxiety. The definition of clinical anxiety is an operational one, determined mostly by how the anxiety affects the patient. If the patient is impaired by the anxiety, seeks treatment, or engages in self-destructive behaviors to control it, the anxiety should be considered clinical. Clinical anxiety can be usefully subdivided, into specific anxiety disorders, as we will see later. Anxiety may be "free-floating" or occur episodically as panic attacks; these two types may co-exist. Anxiety has subjective, behavioral, physiologic, and cognitive dimensions which we will now discuss in more detail.

THE SUBJECTIVE DIMENSION

The subjective component of anxiety refers to patients' descriptions and interpretations of their symptoms. How patients present and interpret their symptoms often determines both the focus and course of treatment. Patients will sometimes present with anxiety as their chief complaint although more commonly patients present with a variety of physiological symptoms, like heart palpitations (associated

TABLE 1.1

*Typical Terms Used
to Describe Anxiety*

Tense	Shaky	On edge
Panicky	Anxious	Worried
Terrified	Wound-up	Scared
Jittery	Apprehensive	High-strung
Nervous		Fearful

with fear of dying). A list of terms commonly used by patients to describe anxiety is presented in Table 1.1.

McNair and Lorr (1964) employed sophisticated statistical methods to chart the relationships among certain affective terms (like those listed in Table 1.1 and many others commonly used to describe other emotions). They found that affective words clustered into seven basic descriptions of moods: anxiety–tension, anger, depression, vigor, fatigue, friendliness, and confusion. Other investigators found that moods could be factored into two dimensions: arousal–quiescence and pleasure–displeasure. Russell (1980) found that affective words could be arrayed in a circle (see Figure 1.1) in which the horizontal line is drawn between displeasure and pleasure and the vertical line is drawn between arousal and quiescence. The terms used to describe fear/tension/anxiety fall into the right lower quadrant.

This two-factor model is problematic: anger and fear situations, for instance, are both associated with high arousal and low pleasure (Mehrabian and Russell, 1974). To distinguish between these emotions, a third factor—dominance—was introduced, to reflect the sense of environmental control. From this semantic perspective, fear and anxiety are states of high arousal, negative valence, and low dominance or control (Lang, 1985).

Although patients typically use the terms discussed above to describe their anxiety, more often than not, they will seek help for problems caused by the anxiety or for symptoms associated with specific anxiety disorders. Agoraphobics for example, most frequently seek treatment when their avoidance of day-to-day tasks becomes intolerable either to themselves or to those close to them. Patients with generalized anxiety disorder or social phobia who use excessive amounts of alcohol to reduce their anguish may present to the therapist or be referred for treatment of alcohol abuse. Patients with panic attacks will often present with many of the symptoms reported in Freud's description of Katherina (Freud & Breuer, 1966). Two of our patients describe typical panic attacks in this way:

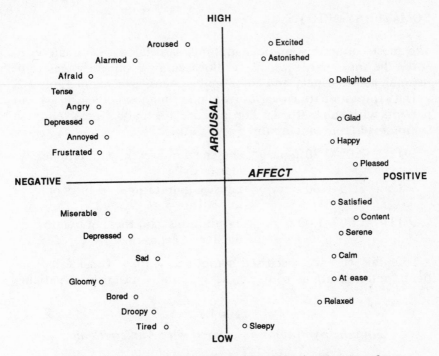

Figure 1.1 **Multidimensional Scaling for 28 Affect Words**

Statistical methods were used to array words on two dimensions. The horizontal line represents affect with increasing negative affect to the left and increasing positive affect to the right. The vertical line represents level of arousal with little arousal on the bottom increasing to high arousal at the top.

I usually start out feeling like I am short of breath, then I start to get warm and about the same time the dizziness and the nausea kicks in, and, if it's a real good one . . . then I start feeling like I'm detached from my body and, you know, I'm going to fall down or/um/like I'm outside my body and don't have control over my motor functions—can't walk and talk.

I start feeling my muscles, especially my neck tense up, my mouth gets dry, my heart starts beating a lot faster, my palms will get sweaty, I get a feeling, varying on how intense it is, between dizziness and almost vertigo. At times, not all the time, I'll get stomach cramps and . . . I can't get my thoughts together. . . . I may be somewhere and not even remember how to get out the room.

SOMATIC SYMPTOMS

The most common somatic symptoms associated with anxiety involve the muscular, sensory, cardiovascular, respiratory, gastrointestinal, genitourinary and autonomic system, as listed in Table 1.2.

The symptom pattern varies from one time to another, at least in patients with panic attacks. For instance, one patient reported these symptoms accompanying three panic attacks:

9/12	2:05–2:30 p.m.	shortness of breath, palpitations, fear of dying
9/12	5:15–6:30 p.m.	nausea, palpitations, feelings of unreality
9/13	12:05–1:00 p.m.	palpitations, shortness of breath, dizziness, headache

Thus far we have discussed symptoms without considering patients' interpretations of what the symptoms mean. How patients

TABLE 1.2

Somatic Symptoms Associated with Anxiety/Panic

System	Symptoms
Muscular-skeletal	Pains and aches, twitchings, stiffness, myoclonic jerks, grinding of teeth, unsteady voice, increased muscular tone, spasms, tremors, restlessness, wobbling legs, clumsiness
Sensory	Tinnitus, blurring of vision, hot and cold flashes, feelings of weakness, prickling sensation, flushed face, pale face, sweating, itching
Cardiovascular	Tachycardia, palpitations, pain in chest, throbbing of vessels, fainting feelings, skipped beat
Respiratory	Pressure or constriction in chest, choking feelings, sighing, dyspnea
Gastrointestinal	Difficulty in swallowing, flatulence, abdominal pain, burning sensations, abdominal discomfort, nausea, vomiting, looseness of bowels, loss of weight, loss of appetite, constipation
Genitourinary	Frequency of urination, urgency of urination, amenorrhea, menorhagia, premature ejaculation, loss of libido
Autonomic	Dry mouth, flushing, pallor, tendency to sweat, giddiness, tension headache, raising of hair

interpret the symptoms critically influences the extent of anguish and impairment and their decisions regarding where to seek help. How patients describe their symptoms will affect how they will be treated by a physician or psychotherapist; such descriptions will also influence patients' estimate of the effectiveness of treatment.

THE COGNITIVE DIMENSION

The relationship between cognitive appraisal and anxiety has received considerable attention in recent years. Various systematic investigations have found that cognitions like "I am going to die of a heart attack," "I may lose control of myself and injure someone," "I can't cope," "I'll make a fool of myself" are common among these patients. The most frequently encountered themes refer to death, disease, social rejection, or failure. Beck and Emery (1984) believe that such cognitions generally precede the onset or exacerbation of experienced anxiety and that the amount of anxiety is proportional to (1) the degree of plausibility (to the patient) of the hypothetical danger, (2) the patient's notion of the severity of harm from the danger, and (3) his estimate of the likelihood that the dreaded event will occur. Beck has since elaborated the cognitive symptoms of anxiety into three categories as shown in Table 1.3.

In an attempt to validate Beck's model of anxiety, Hibbert (1984) undertook an extensive structured interview with 25 patients suffering from generalized anxiety or panic disorder. The interview opened with a standard question about the patient's thought content when anxious: "I would like you to try to tell me what thoughts have been going through your mind when you have been anxious or something has been making you anxious in the past three weeks." Subjects were asked to recall the circumstances at the time they felt anxious and what thoughts they could remember. All of the patients with panic attacks (17 out of 25) identified anxiety-related thoughts; the most important ideas among patients with panic attacks centered around fear of physical, psychological, or social disaster occurring during such attacks. The thoughts of those without panic attacks were much less dramatic. The more severe the anxiety, the more intrusive, credible, and persistent were the cognitions to the patient.

A recent study in our laboratory extended Hibbert's findings. Like Hibbert, we found that panic patients are likely to have thoughts related to loss of control, death, and illness at times of anxiety. Also, like Hibbert (1984) (and inconsistent with Beck's theory), we found most subjects reporting that a bodily sensation precedes the cognition (Zucker et al., submitted). The following typical descriptions

TABLE 1.3

**Cognitive Symptoms
in Anxiety Disorders**

---

1. Sensory-Perceptual

Hazy, cloudy, foggy, dazed
Objects seem blurred/distant
Environment seems different/unreal
Feeling of unreality
Self-conscious
Hypervigilant

2. Thinking Difficulties

Can't recall important things
Confused
Unable to control thinking
Difficulty in concentration
Distractability
Blocking
Difficulty in reasoning
Loss of objectivity and perspective

3. Conceptual

Cognitive distortion
Fear of losing control
Fear of not being able to cope
Fear of physical injury/death
Fear of going crazy/mental disorder
Fear of negative evaluations
Frightening visual images
Repetitive fearful ideation
Obsessive thoughts

SOURCE: Modified from *Anxiety Disorders and Phobias: A Cognitive Perspective*, by Aaron T. Beck and Gary Emery with Ruth L. Greenberg. Copyright © 1985 by Aaron T. Beck, M.D., and Gary Emery, Ph.D.

illustrate this sequence and demonstrate the anguish endured by many of these patients:

It (a typical anxiety episode) generally starts with a slight nausea and mainly like an upset stomach . . . And then a feeling of fear, intense fear, of I don't know exactly what and then I . . . I need to be alone or occasionally I need to be around someone. . . . The other thing is that there's a lot of thoughts, you know, thinking that I'm going to snap suddenly, finding at times extremely difficult to get through it, just a fear that I'm possibly not going to make it through this time. . . . Sometimes I'm almost afraid that I might hurt someone because I might lose control.

Usually I'll be doing something, for instance, one day I had a real mild panic attack just standing around talking to some other people, and they'll mention one word. . . . Immediately when the word or episode or whatever is mentioned . . . I'll just withdraw into myself and start fighting anxiety, going "Well why is talking about math bothering me now? You know, I don't have a test coming up." . . . I try to talk myself out of it . . . which sometimes helps. . . . But generally I'll feel hot and the heat will come and go for up to like a half hour and if it continues I'll start getting nauseated, and the nausea will come and go. And then I get kind of shaking and I can't concentrate on anything. My mind just keeps hoppin' and skipping all around, . . . and, of course, I get worried that I'm going to vomit at an inappropriate time, and I might not be able to get away from people where they can't see it.

Whether or not thoughts cause, exacerbate or maintain anxiety and panic remains unclear; however, the cognitive themes discussed above are common in patients with panic disorder. Reducing frequency and intensity of panic attacks is an important goal of therapy.

Beck and Emery (1985) note that anxiety disorders are accompanied by thinking disorders as well as dysfunctional thoughts. Thinking disorders in anxious patients include difficulty with attention, concentration, and vigilance, and loss of objectivity. The second patient above described such a thinking disorder ("I can't concentrate on anything. My mind just keeps hoppin' and skipping all around"). Anxious patients are prone to stimulus generalization and catastrophizing; they assume that situations similar to one where they experienced panic will produce panic again and they expect such symptoms to produce dire consequences. They also display selective abstraction and loss of perspective: anxious patients pay attention to the possible harmful effects of a situation but not to the helpful or beneficial ones. Such patients also classify situations dichotomously—as safe or unsafe—rather than in gradations of safety. All of these "thinking disorders" are fruitful targets of treatment.

The cognitive symptoms and thinking disorder patterns we have discussed thus far are relatively easy to identify in patients. A more subtle problem—and one that has been studied less—is "worry." Worry is phenomenologically close to many of the affective characteristics of anxiety. The presence of "excessive worry" is one of the main criteria used to differentiate among anxiety states, yet the concept is both difficult to define and describe. There is a continuum

TABLE 1.4

Cognitive Anxiety Log

Time	Main Thought/Concern	Anxiety Level (0–10)	Activity
12:30 P.M.	Worried about how nervous I will be giving a speech next Monday	8	Driving
1:00 P.M.	Evaluation of how much client's account is worth	7	Working at desk
1:30 P.M.	Nervous about how to fill out log correctly	6	Working at desk
2:00 P.M.	Recalling recent periods of anxiety	8	Working at desk

between normal worry—focused on realistic events—and worry about unrealistic life circumstances (e.g., about possible misfortune to a child who is in no danger.) Yet the worry reported by patients may be dramatic. The following record was reported by one patient, a 35-year-old accountant, who complained of continuous excessive worry. He was asked to record what he was thinking on the half hour all day. The content of a typical segment of his diary can be seen in Table 1.4.

According to his diary, during the four times he was asked to write down his main thought/concern, he was worried once about a future event, another time about his current activity, and a third time about an anxiety episode in the past. Worry is an important component of anxiety, and the pattern of worry appearing in this man's diary is typical of patients presenting with anxiety.

PHYSIOLOGIC AND BIOCHEMICAL DIMENSIONS

As we will see, extensive research has revealed many complicated interactions among the various physiologic and biochemical aspects of anxiety, yet threat-fear-fight/flight, as described by Cannon (1929) remains a core feature. Figure 1.2 illustrates the basic phenomenon. A threatening situation may cause release of various hormones and lead to increases in sympathetic and parasympathetic nervous system activity.

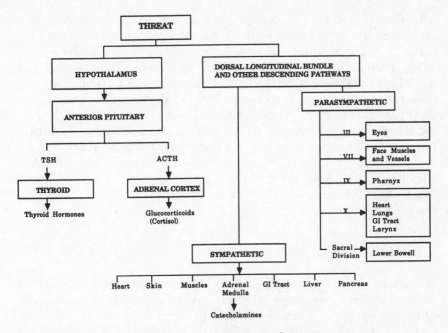

Figure 1.2 Physiology of Fear

This diagram represents the basic peripheral physiologic reaction to threat. Threat leads to increased hypothalamic activity influencing the release of thyroid secreting hormone (TSH) and adrenocortical hormone (ACTH) from the anterior pituitary. TSH causes the thyroid to release thyroid hormones; ACTH causes the adrenal cortex to release glucocorticoids, including cortisol. Increased sympathetic nervous system arousal increases heart rate and contractility, causes sweating to occur, blood flow to increase to the muscles, the adrenal medulla to release catecholamines (including epinephrine and norepinephrine), the GI tract to slow down, the liver to release glucose and the pancreas to release insulin. Changes in parasympathetic activity to the eyes and face cause the typical fearful face, (through III=oculomotor nerve and VII=facial nerve) and altered voice (through IX=glosspharyngeal nerve), increased heart rate and bronchodilation (through X=vagus nerve). Parasympathetic activity through the sacral division can lead to lower bowel evacuation.

The physiological result is mobilization of the body for *fight/flight:* increased heart rate and cardiac output makes the blood supply more ample; opening of the pharynx allows more air to enter the lungs and subsequently enter the bloodstream; blood is shifted from the skin and guts to the muscles where it is needed; reduction of blood to the skin and enhanced clotting minimize damage from a wound; and, finally, immunocompetence is enhanced.

It is presumed that inappropriate and frequent elicitation of this response also causes some of the symptoms associated with psychologically tense or upsetting situations: pain in tense muscles, headache, gastrointestinal upset, and sleeplessness. The archetypal fight/flight response is rarely seen in humans. Humans have unique patterns of physiologic response to threatening stimuli depending on their past experiences; medication, drug use, and other life-style habits; receptor sensitivity and architecture; and appraisal of the situation and other cognitive patterns. Furthermore, the same physiologic response is not routinely elicited in the same individual by the same stimulus. The complexities of these processes have intrigued many researchers. Theories explaining the differences will be discussed in the next chapter.

THE BEHAVIORAL DIMENSION

Behavioral symptoms associated with anxiety may be classified into acute and chronic responses. In animals there is first the recognition of threat, perhaps associated with behavioral signs of fear, followed by four basic responses to threat: withdrawal, immobility, aggressive defense, and submission (Marks, 1987). The behavioral signs of fear include a fearful facial expression, trembling, sweating, pale face, hyperventilating, increased muscle tension, and staring. The most overt and acute fear response—the fearful face characterized by raised and drawn-together eyebrows, a hard stare quality, and mouth corners drawn back—is universally recognized as fear.

Withdrawal, which may occur as flight, escape, or avoidance, is often associated with a fearful facial expression. Another response to threat is to become immobile. Immobility is classified as attentiveness, in which the animal remains inert while carefully observing its environment—a phenomenon suggested by the phrase "freeze in your tracks," or as tonic immobility, in which a previously active animal exhibits prolonged freezing and decreased responsiveness. An example of tonic immobility is the opossum "playing dead." Attentive immobility is associated with the animal being able to identify better the nature of the threat. Predators are less likely to attack an animal exhibiting tonic immobility. Aggressive defense is usually associated with displays of threat and has obvious survival value. Animals also may attempt to deflect an attack; for instance, a parent killdeer may lead a predator away from a nest through conspicuous behavior, sometimes by simulating being wounded. Finally, animals may be directly submissive. Signs of submission seem to reduce aggression and to be understood even across species. For instance, diverting one's eyes from an attacking animal may reduce the intensity of the attack.

Some of the acute behavioral symptoms of anxiety seen in humans may be related to these four basic responses to threat; they are further elaborated by the patient's experience, cognition, physiology, pathophysiology, and coping responses. For instance, during anxiety episodes some patients feel that their coordination is impaired, that they might faint and that they can't move their feet. All of these symptoms may represent immobility.

One curious yet often overlooked set of behaviors occuring during anxiety episodes, particularly those considered to be panic attacks, are subtle compulsive safety or avoidance rituals. For instance, a patient who had experienced panic attacks in high places would touch a stair tread a specific number of times at each floor when climbing stairs. A businessman who reported panic attacks but denied any avoidance revealed upon further questioning that he never scheduled morning business meetings for fear of being overanxious at those times. A manager at a machine shop would never close the door of a room behind him because of anxiety experienced in closed places.

Over time, the relationship of behavior to anxiety becomes complicated. One theory of agoraphobia postulates that panic attacks, often the first symptom of anxiety, lead to avoidance and that avoidance leads to a disability in a variety of domains. The behavior associated with anxiety frequently becomes independent of the anxiety itself. Furthermore, behavior engaged in for the purpose of controlling anxiety sometimes exacerbates the anxiety. For example, some patients

TABLE 1.5

Acute Behavioral Symptoms

Acute recognition of threat	*Immobility*
Fearful facial expression	Inhibition of movement
Sweating	Tonic immobility
Trembling	Impaired coordination
Pale or flushed face	Postural collapse
Withdrawal	Hypervigilance
Flight	*Submission*
Avoidance	Averted gaze
Aggressive Defense	*Other*
Anger	Hyperventilating
Irritability	Disoriented

drink excessive amounts of coffee when they feel anxious, yet the caffeine in coffee produces anxiety and even panic. One of our patients became panic-stricken on freeways. When he experienced a panic attack on the highway he immediately exited and returned to his office. Soon, he began to feel that the panic attacks were disrupting his ability to keep his business going, and he began to worry that he would not be able to support his family. This worry was associated with even more frequent panic attacks.

The most serious complications of anxiety disorders are often associated with the patient's attempts to cope with anxiety. Patients may become severely avoidant or depressed, abuse drugs or alcohol, or become helplessly dependent on their family, friends, and the medical system. The avoidance, when manifested as agoraphobia, may be one of the most disabling of all psychiatric problems. The following case illustrates the impairment of one of our patients:

Debra is a 31-year-old white female, never married, who lives with her mother. She reported that her first panic attack occurred two years earlier when her mother had begun to have fainting spells. She was reporting two panic attacks per week. The typical attack was characterized by palpitations, faintness, dizziness, depression, and hot and cold flashes. In her weekly diary she reported that she had left home on only seven occasions, each time accompanied and with extreme feelings of anxiety. On one trip to the store she wrote, "Very uncomfortable. Shopping in store. Unable to wait through check-out stand. I went and sat in car while my Mom paid for the items." She said she could not do such things as take an escalator, obtain a credit application, or choose a sweater in the store. Her problems made it impossible for her to work or date. She had become severely depressed with frequent thoughts of suicide.

Thus, chronic symptoms such as avoidance, which result from efforts to cope with anxiety, are often more disabling than the anxiety itself and need to become the focus of treatment.

T W O

········

Theories of
Anxiety

·········

The origins and meaning of anxiety and fear have preoccupied many of the great experimental and clinical theorists of the 20th century. Freud was concerned with the problem of anxiety throughout his career and revised his theory at least four times. Much of the history of learning theory has been devoted to understanding and treating simple fears and anxiety. Extensive work by neuroscientists has been devoted to characterizing the biological nature of anxiety. Interest in anxiety is keener today than ever before, and the resulting investigations have enhanced our efforts to treat most anxiety disorders. Yet, despite effective treatment, the nature of anxiety remains elusive. No one theory accounts for all the behavioral, biological, psychological, and physiological aspects of anxiety. Among the impediments to developing an integrated theory of anxiety is its multifaceted nature. Anxiety and fear can be observed and/or experienced in a number of dimensions—subjective, cognitive, behavioral, physiologic—and these dimensions largely determine how "the problem" is defined. In addition, the field is in transition.

Five years ago we largely endorsed a learning-theory view of anxiety; that is, we assumed that most anxiety disorders were learned. But recent biologic and pharmacologic studies provide a much richer and more complex view of the origins of anxiety. There is evidence that genes, development, cognition, behavior, learning, physiology, and biochemistry interact to some extent in all patients with anxiety disorders. The patient's family, culture, work, and social environment are also important. The septo-hippocampus, thalamus, locus coeruleus, and their afferents and efferents, and various neurotransmitters are clearly involved with anxiety. We believe the informed clinician needs to be aware of recent findings in these areas.

We will discuss three major perspectives on anxiety: psycho-dynamic, learning, and biological. In doing so, we outline the major publications, events, or research efforts in each of these perspectives. Because of the influence of psychodynamic theory on developmental studies, we include these two in the same section. The theories we discuss apply, for the most part, to all the anxiety disorders discussed in this book. In chapters on the different anxiety disorders we will discuss theories specific to them.

PSYCHODYNAMIC THEORIES

Contemporary psychodynamic theories of anxiety began with Freud. His first major discussion of anxiety was published in 1894 and his last in 1926, but his writings before and after these also address major issues of anxiety. New insight, observations, experience, and discussions led Freud to reformulate and elaborate his views. In his final model, and the one still followed by most psychoanalysts, Freud argued that the generation of anxiety occurs unconsciously, outside of the individual's awareness. Anxiety "as a signal" was viewed as the response of the ego to the threat of a traumatic situation. The dangers signaling anxiety involve fantasized situations regarding separation from, or loss of, a loved object or a loss of its love. These are perceived as real threats by the child, who sometimes finds himself helpless in the face of them. In adults, any aspect of mental life associated with these dangers triggers anxiety. Psychological defenses act to reduce anxiety, often by regulating or inhibiting the wishes related to the fantasized dangers.

Freud's model assumes that anxiety may be generated by unconscious ideas, thoughts, or fantasies, the content of which frequently relates to childhood events. The unconscious determinants of anxiety are revealed by the psychodynamic process.

For instance, in pursuing the cause of Katherina's panic attack (Freud & Breuer, 1966, pp. 165ff) described in chapter 1, Freud asks her: "When you have an attack do you think of something? And always the same thing? Or do you see something in front of you?"

She replies: "Yes. I always see an awful face that looks at me in a dreadful way, so that I'm frightened."

Freud asks if she recognizes the face and, after pursuing several possibilities, continues: "If you don't know, I'll tell you how I think you got your attacks. At that time, two years ago, you must have seen or heard something that very much embarrassed you and that you'd much rather not have seen."

Katherina: "Heavens, yes! That was when I caught my uncle with the girl, with Franziska, my cousin."

Further analysis, however, revealed that she was disgusted not so much by the sight of these two people as by the memory that sight stirred up in her. The memory was of her uncle who had made sexual advances towards her. Freud asks her if she can remember whose head she sees.

Katherina says: "Yes, I know now. The head is my uncle's head—I recognize it now—but not from that time. Later, my uncle gave way to a senseless rage against me, I always ran away from him, and always felt terrified that he would catch me some time unawares. The face I always see now is his face when he was in a rage."

Thus, the panic attacks involved images related to both immediate and past events in Katherina's life. (This case was originally published in 1895. He added a footnote in 1924 stating that Katherina was in fact his landlady's daughter, and the uncle was the girl's own father; see Freud & Breuer, 1966.)

Silber (1984) presents another example of how the relationship between historic events and current anxiety episodes is conceptualized within the psychoanalytic framework. In the middle phase of her 10-year analysis, the patient experienced intense anxiety attacks. The first attack while the patient was in analysis occurred when the analyst was on a brief vacation. The patient was riding on a bus and became aware of a feeling of anxiety. She was afraid that she would have a heart attack and soon became so panicky that she had to leave the bus. When she next saw her analyst she recalled that during the anxiety attack, she thought of her analyst and wondered about his age. She reported that the number of the street the bus was approaching corresponded to the age at which her father had died and that her father had had his heart attack near the hour that corresponded to the time her anxiety attack on the bus occurred. Silber says, "Her fear that she was going to have a heart attack was linked with her angry wish that the analyst would die for leaving her. Behind that wish lurked her unrecognized anger toward her father for his sudden death. The fear of having a heart attack represented a punishment" (p. 499).

Most psychoanalysts view inhibitions, symptoms, and anxiety as being inherently connected. Inhibitions restrict instinctual expression in order to avoid the anxiety occasioned by the associated unconscious dangers. For instance, Freud notes that writing block (the inhibition of writing) might occur because the fingers become too strongly eroticized or the act of writing is associated with the forbidden act. The symptom is a sign of, and a substitute for, instinctual satisfaction or conflict. This notion is further illustrated by the case of Little Hans, whose oedipal wishes and attendant castration anxiety were transformed and directed toward fears of being bitten by a horse (Freud, 1909).

Freud discusses the epigenetic unfolding of danger situations that generate anxiety:

1. *Birth Anxiety.* Freud believed that the act of birth involves the first experience of anxiety and thus is the source and prototype of the affect of anxiety.
2. *Separation anxiety*, a fear of the loss of the object of primary care and attachment. The next major anxiety occurs when the infant experiences separation from its mother. Freud writes: "In consequence of the infant's misunderstanding of the facts, the situation of missing its mother is not a danger situation but a traumatic one. . . . The first determinant of anxiety, which the ego itself introduces, is loss of perception of the object (which is equated with loss of the object itself)" (Freud, 1926, p. 96).
3. *Anxiety over loss of the loved object.* The child comes to realize that temporary separation from the mother does not indicate loss of the mother. However, a fear of loss of love from the object becomes a new and much more enduring danger and determinant of anxiety.
4. *Castration anxiety* and fear of other bodily punishment or hurt. Freud argued that fear of castration is a major cause of anxiety, particularly in animal phobias. He writes, referring to Little Hans, that he "gave up his aggressiveness towards his father from fear of being castrated" (Freud, 1909, p. 34). Freud's analysis of Little Hans and Wolf Man helped changed his view of anxiety. Of agoraphobia Freud notes: "The anxiety felt in agoraphobia . . . seems to be its fear of sexual temptation, a fear which, after all, must be connected in its origins with the fear of castration" (Freud, 1909, p. 35).
5. *Fear of the superego or of conscience.* In his final view, Freud noted that the affect associated with anxiety receives its energy from and is created by a transformation of excessive stimulation by the central nervous system (CNS), often derived from instincts, particularly the sexual instinct.

While Freud's writing on anxiety emphasizes the importance of the sexual instinct, other analytic theorists have noted that aggressive impulses are also important in generating anxiety (Deutsch, 1929; Flescher, 1955; Klein, 1952; Zetzel, 1955). For instance, Deutsch (1929) presented four cases of agoraphobia where defense against aggressive impulses towards parents or parental figures resulted in panic attacks. In one such case, a patient in analysis with Deutsch remembered having an anxiety attack on the street after her mother told her to apologize to a woman from whose garden she had stolen some fruit. Deutsch wrote that the patient "obeyed with fury in her heart, but she failed to carry out her mother's injunction because on the way she was seized with palpitation and trembling. She realized herself that it was a question of suppressed rage against both women" (Deutsch, 1929, pp. 60–61). Other psychoanalytic writers have emphasized the importance of interpersonal relationships, the patient's current experience (Sullivan, 1953), "narcissistic catastrophes" like fear of humiliation and fear of loss of self-esteem (Freud, A., 1946), and problems of self-identity (Kohut, 1971) in generating anxiety.

In summary, the psychoanalytic model of anxiety assumes that anxiety is a signal of the unconscious fantasies of imagined dangerous situations that are provoked by instinctual wishes or by perceptions of external situations (Michels et al., 1985). The specific fantasies that trigger anxiety are determined by a developmental progression that is influenced both by maturation and by learning. The avoidance of anxiety is a major factor shaping much normal and neurotic behavior. Of more clinical than theoretical interest, Freud writes, "One can hardly ever master a phobia if one waits till the patient lets the analysis influence him to give it up. . . . One succeeds only when one can induce them through the influence of the analysis . . . to go about alone and struggle with the anxiety while they make the attempt" (Freud, 1924, p. 399).

Implications for Treatment

Psychodynamic theory continues to influence the psychological treatment of anxiety. In particular, psychodynamic theory has revealed the intricate relationship among thoughts, feelings, images, and behavior. Among the important observations derived from psychodynamic theory are the following: (1) anxiety is a universal emotion; (2) people can appear anxious and be unaware of it; (3) people can feel anxious and not understand what causes it; (4) emotions besides anxiety, urges, thoughts, feelings, images, and fantasies can all generate anxiety; (5) the occurrence of anxiety during therapy often signals important information about the patient.

Many assumptions derived from psychoanalytic theory remain unproven, however, and may even be therapeutically counterproductive. The psychoanalytic theory of anxiety prescribes a treatment designed to produce insight into those unconscious processes that are believed to generate the symptoms, on the assumption that such insight can bring about improvement in the patient's condition. To quote Michels, Frances, and Shear (1985), "The psychoanalytic exploration of symptomatic anxiety . . . involves identifying the danger, the wish, the pattern of defense used in constructing the symptom, and the developmental history of each of these" (p. 608). Yet such insight may be of little benefit to the patient who is not helped in other ways to overcome symptoms of anxiety.

This is illustrated in a case presented recently by Wallerstein (1986) of a "phobic woman." Wallerstein cites it as one of eight cases with a "clear-cut very good treatment outcome" from a study of 42 patients in psychoanalysis. In the beginning of treatment the patient was unable to go to the movies or to a restaurant, to ride elevators, or visit friends. In other words, she was severely agoraphobic. The patient was in analysis for four years and nine months (1,012 hours). The analyst's goals were to "conduct a thorough analysis." By the end of treatment, the patient came to believe that the cause of her symptoms related to sexual feelings toward her father and aggressive strivings in general. She apparently felt that she both understood such feelings and could control them. Wallerstein reports, "By the end of analysis, the patient had made substantial major changes in remission of symptoms and in enhanced scope and style of life" (p. 276). Yet, at termination the patient was still unable to ride in automatic elevators or to drive alone on the freeway. She felt least constrained in Topeka where the analysis occurred, but a good deal more constrained elsewhere. She also said, "The minute the sun goes down there's more anxiety; all the awful sexual things that I was always taught can happen to you when you walk around the streets in the dark" (p. 276). She was still apprehensive when alone and required the presence of others to accomplish many tasks outside of her home.

One concept of psychoanalysis that has impeded the development of more effective treatments is that of symptom substitution. Symptom substitution posits that the elimination of one symptom will usually result in another, unless the underlying conflicts are resolved. Extensive empirical studies of symptom-focused treatments have proven that this is not the case.

DEVELOPMENTAL THEORIES

Many patients with anxiety disorders have a history of problems with separation, dating from their earliest memories. In two landmark books, John Bowlby (1969a, 1969b) reintroduced the importance of instinctual drives in determining anxiety. Bowlby attempts to integrate modern ethological concepts with data from child observation and with psychoanalytic and systems theory to explore the nature of

the infant's attachment to its mother and processes involved in separation as well as its effects. Bowlby considers attachment to be a
primary instinct. According to Bowlby, the characteristics of an instinct are as follows: (1) it follows a recognizably similar and predictable pattern in almost all members of a species; (2) it is not a simple
response to a single stimulus but a behavior sequence that usually
runs a predictable course; (3) it helps preserve or continue the species; (4) it manifests itself even when all the ordinary opportunities
for learning it are absent. Instincts are manifest as behavioral systems, which include innate behaviors and the "control" mechanisms
integrating and adapting them with the environment. Anxiety is an
innately programmed component of the response to separation
(nonattachment).

Two important aspects of behavioral systems are what activates
them and what deactivates them. Behavioral systems may be activated by a variety of both external and internal events or stimuli.
Behavioral systems are also subject to ontogenetic development. A
classic example of ontogeny is the "imprinting" that causes newly
hatched ducklings to follow the object they perceive after birth. But
the "imprinting" characteristic of behavioral systems disappears or
is suppressed soon after birth in the course of development, through
presumed, as yet unidentified, changes in the central nervous system.

Bowlby has argued that attachment occurs not because of an infant's needs or drives but as a result of the activation of certain
behavioral systems. Factors activating attachment include the condition of the child (tired, hungry, sick, in pain, or cold), the where-
abouts and behavior of the mother, and other environmental conditions, such as the occurrence of alarming events or rebuffs from
others. In the child from about 9 to 18 months, five patterns of behavior—sucking, clinging, following, crying, and smiling—all function
to maintain the child's proximity to his or her mother. Attachment
behavior begins to diminish both in its intensity and frequency after
about 18 months. Bowlby speculates that the change is due both to
alterations in the behavioral system mediating attachment behavior,
such as neuronal growth, and/or the emergence of other behaviors
like curiosity and exploratory activities that compete with or deter
attachment behavior. The change in attachment behavior is also affected by the consequences of the exploratory behavior. If the young
patas monkey, for instance, encounters alarming events during initial exploration, it clings to the mother more frequently and intensely
than otherwise. Also, forced or early separation or separation associated with punishment seem to increase the intensity of clinging.

Bowlby argues that attachment behavior begins to wane in the
human at about age 3 but continues to be important throughout life.

Regarding the affective component of attachment, Bowlby writes: "No form of behaviour is accompanied by stronger feeling than is attachment behavior. The figures towards whom it is directed are loved and their advent is greeted with joy" (Bowlby, 1969, p. 209).

So long as a child is in the unchallenged presence or within easy reach of a principal attachment figure, he or she feels secure. Threat of loss creates anxiety, and actual loss causes sorrow; both, moreover, are likely to arouse anger. Bowlby considers anxiety to be one component of fear. Fear is defined behaviorally as withdrawal, avoidance, and escape or clinging to an object of attachment. Fearful behavior is triggered by danger cues, while threats to the infant's basic safety result in anxiety. In one of his more provocative formulations, Bowlby argues that agoraphobia (which he calls "pseudophobia") is the feared absence of the attachment figure. Agoraphobia is thus a separation anxiety disturbance rather than a phobia and, according to Bowlby, is always associated with diffuse personality disturbance. On the other hand, neurotic anxiety—or separation anxiety—results from insecure bonding to the attachment figures, brought about by real life experiences of unavailable or unresponsive caregivers.

While agoraphobic patients do not show signs of "diffuse personality disturbance," there is evidence that they represent a more severe disturbance than generalized anxiety disorder; there is also evidence that separation from parents during childhood may predispose towards the development of a mixed anxiety/depression in adults. The clinician should obtain a careful history of separations, implied or actual, and parental caregiving patterns in anxiety-disorder patients. Reviewing such periods with a patient can help establish a better therapeutic alliance, help the patient understand his or her problem, and even indicate treatment directions.

Child Development Studies

From child development studies it has become obvious that there is a predictable parade of normal fears that emerge, plateau, and decline from infancy through adolescence, but that these fears are modified by environmental, familial, and genetic factors. A number of researchers (Ainsworth & Bell, 1970; Emde, 1981, 1985; Kagan et al., 1978; Lewis & Brooks, 1974; Marks, 1987; Spitz, 1950; Sroufe, 1979) have provided a comprehensive description of the development, course, and content of these infantile and childhood fears. Before they are 6 months old, human infants show little fear; fear of heights is apparent in many infants by six months. By 9 to 10 months fear of strangers has become apparent in most infants. Infants are less fearful when held by their mothers than when in their crib, and infants are less fearful in their crib or seat than when held by a stranger. Infants are most likely to cry at their caretaker's departure from 8 to 24 months, peaking at 9 to 13 months (Kagan et al., 1978). Identical twins display more similarity in manifestations of stranger fear than do fraternal twins (Plomin & Rowe, 1979). Girls show earlier, more intense reactions to strangers than do boys.

Children also exhibit a variety of fears. Fears of animals, darkness, storms, thunder, and strange events are particularly common. The most frequent fears at ages 2 and 4 are of animals; the most frequent fears at ages 4 to 6 are of darkness and imaginary creatures (Macfarlane et al., 1954). Fear of school appears when children start school. From ages 6 to 12 children most commonly fear mysterious events, animals, and bodily injuries. Older schoolgoers worry about social relations, shyness, and injury. Adolescents of ages 15 to 18 are most anxious about death and, perhaps, nuclear war.

One developmental theory posits that panic attacks in adults are a variant of separation anxiety in school phobic children (Gittelman & Klein, 1986). The evidence for this comes from studies which have found that a history of separation anxiety in childhood is consistently more frequent in patients with agoraphobia than other mental disorders (Berg et al., 1974; Klein et al., 1983), that imipramine blocks panic attacks in adults and reduces separation anxiety in school-phobic children (Gittelman-Klein & Klein, 1971, 1980), and that separation anxiety is more common in children whose parents had a history of both depression and agoraphobia or panic than in those whose parents had pure depression (Weissman et al., 1984.) Yet problems of differentiating between "nature and nurture" are apparent in such studies: Do the parents have trouble separating from their children thereby teaching them to be phobic, and, if so, are both the problems of the parents and the children partly genetic?

The most convincing evidence linking separation anxiety in children with agoraphobia in adults would be a prospective longitudinal study. Unfortunately, studies specifically linking separation anxiety and adult anxiety disorders have not been undertaken. Long-term follow-ups of school-phobic children suggest increased problems in later life, but the studies are handicapped by a lack of standardized initial assessment, failure to analyze the type and age of onset of the phobia, and other methodological weaknesses (Waldron, 1976; Achenbach, 1986). After reviewing the child development literature, Achenbach (1986) concludes that there is little hard evidence for predictive or causal relations between specific anxiety phenomena at specific developmental periods and later problems of any sort, anxiety or otherwise. Nevertheless, several longitudinal studies have reported that temperaments are stable from one decade to another in adults. Costa and McCrae (in press) have found, for instance, that men and women show little variation in scores on certain "personality" measures from one decade to another. Anxious temperament, for instance, apparent at age 30 is still likely to be present at age 50.

It is our view that the implications of these development studies are as follows: (1) simple fears and phobias and probably social phobia rise and fall in the course of development and bear little relationship to other anxiety disorders; (2) certain anxious traits, at least in adults, are stable from one decade to another; (3) problems with attachment and separation are linked genetically, developmentally, and causally with generalized anxiety, panic disorder, and agoraphobia in adults. The latter relationship is of particular importance for therapy. Patients who have generalized anxiety disorder, panic disorder, or agoraphobia when compared to patients presenting with other anxiety disorders will form rapid, intense bonds with caregivers that must be considered in therapeutic transactions. Such patients are very sensitive to implied or actual separations in the course of therapy, and termination can be difficult.

LEARNING THEORIES

Learning theories of anxiety and fear have undergone considerable transformation. For most of this century, learning theories of anxiety focused mostly on how simple phobias and fears are acquired. More recently, however, as simple models of classical conditioning have proven inadequate to explain even simple fears and phobias, and driven by the pragmatic tradition of behavior therapy to develop more effective treatments, learning theorists now embrace interactive models that attempt to explain the multifaceted nature of anxiety disorders.

Respondent Conditioning Theory

While Freud was completing his *Introductory Lectures on Psycho-Analysis*, Watson and Morgan (1917) were developing a radically different view of anxiety and fear. Influenced by Pavlov's theory of classical conditioning (Pavlov, 1927), Watson and Morgan argued that anxiety was a conditioned response. Unconditional stimuli (UCS) can produce unconditional responses (UCR); for instance, the sight of a fearful object (UCS) produces a change in autonomic activity (UCR). If a conditioned stimulus (CS) is frequently paired with an UCS, eventually the CS comes to elicit anxiety as a conditioned response (CR). Respondent conditioning theory postulates, for instance, that the occurrence of a panic attack (UCR), perhaps originally provoked by external stimuli (UCS), becomes conditioned to other stimuli (CS). The conditioned stimuli might become quite different from the original (CS) through the process of stimulus generalization, in which new stimuli with properties like the original (CS) can elicit the (CR). Watson and Rayner (1920) attempted to prove the theory with an 11-month-old child, Albert. The conditioning paradigm was as follows:

> Just as the right hand touched the rat (CS) the bar was again struck (UCS–loud sound). Again the infant jumped violently, fell forward and began to whimper (UCR). (Watson & Rayner, 1970, p. 4)

One week following this second (CS–UCS) pairing, Albert displayed defensive behavior (withdrawal of his hand from the rat) when presented only with the rat. Additional pairings of the loud sound and the rat increased Albert's response. Furthermore, Albert exhibited stimulus generalization; he began to cry and avoid certain other stimuli with characteristics similar to the rat (e.g., rabbit, dog, fur coat, cotton).

However, three subsequent researchers have tried, unsuccessfuly, to replicate the Watson and Raynor "little Albert" experiment (English, 1929; Valentine, 1930; Bregman, 1934), and there is little doubt now that the simple conditioning model is inadequate to explain the acquisition of simple fears (Mineka, 1986). In addition to these failed replications, a second problem casting doubt on strict conditioning theory is that traumatic events (aversive UCS) are rarely identified through careful clinical interviews. A third problem is that many traumatic events do not seem to produce fears. For instance, Englishmen failed to develop conditioned responses to air raid signals during World War II—unconditioned stimuli (air raid signals) paired with terrifying consequences (Nazi air raids).

If simple conditioning doesn't account for fears, how are they acquired? Mowrer (1939) and Dollard and Miller (1950) developed the so-called *two-factor* theory, which posits the following sequence:

1. A fear is acquired via respondent conditioning as described above.
2. The organism is motivated to reduce fear; the cues associated with fear cause the organism to try to reduce the fear. Fear functions as a drive.
3. Behaviors that reduce the fear are reinforcing.

This model has considerable clinical relevance because it suggests (in number 3 above) that avoidance helps to maintain the fear, but it does not account for much recent data (Delprato & McGlynn, 1984). For instance, fear continues even after avoidance responses have stopped (Riccio & Silvestri, 1973), and some fears even diminish under some avoidance conditions (Kamin, Brimer, & Black, 1963). Such problems led Rachman (1977) to develop the so called *three-systems* view of fear. Rachman posits three types of learning that can lead to fears: respondent conditioning, modeling and information, and instructions. There is little doubt that fears can be acquired through modeling (i.e., that fears can be acquired by watching others). One retrospective study of phobic patients found that phobics were significantly more likely than nonphobic controls to have had mothers with phobias and "neurotic" conditions (Solyom et al., 1974). Grings and Dawson (1976) have shown that instructions can be used to produce fear. Eysenck (1976, 1979) also contributed a number of important ideas as to how simple fears can be acquired. He argued that in humans, social events can function as the unconditioned aversive stimuli. Frustration-arousing circumstances such as withdrawal of positive reinforcement and conflictual situations, Eysenck said, might serve as the most common (UCS) for people. The developmental situations that Freud associated with fear could also represent such unconditioned aversive stimuli. Eysenck also noted that another sacred feature of Pavlovian conditioning—that the conditioned stimulus must precede the UCS—may not apply in the acquisition of human fears.

Rachman and Eysenck and their colleagues at the Maudsley Hospital in London not only elaborated the respondent conditioning theory into a viable model for clinical anxiety but also began to develop a number of treatment approaches. Flooding, implosion therapy, and modeling were derived from this theoretical model and the clinical and research experience it stimulated.

In South Africa, Wolpe began to study how neuroses can be produced and eliminated in cats (Wolpe, 1958). Building on experiments by Masserman (1943), he found that cats subjected to shock showed a variety of symptoms, including a resistance to being placed in the experimental cage in which the neuroses had been induced. The cats also showed signs of anxiety when placed in the cage and refused to eat in the cage even after three days of starvation. Since the neuroses seemed to inhibit the feeding, Wolpe wondered if feeding might inhibit the anxiety; in other words, if the reactions might be 'reciprocally inhibiting.' By forcing the cats to eat in the place where they were shocked, he found that once eating had been established, the neurotic reactions diminished. He then tried feeding the cats in a room like the one in which the neuroses developed to determine whether the anxiety would diminish and generalize to the original

fear-provoking stimulus. Wolpe designed four rooms, each one progressively more like the room where the neuroses developed. Beginning with the room most unlike the one where the shocks occurred,
cats were given several opportunities to eat until all signs of anxiety
decreased. The cats were then placed in the next room. In this fashion, the experimentally induced neuroses were extinguished. Wolpe
saw the implication for human neuroses: if individuals could be exposed to a hierarchy of anxiety-provoking situations while inhibitory
responses were also occurring, the anxiety would diminish. He assumed that responses of the parasympathetic portion of the autonomic nervous system are likely to be antagonistic to anxiety, which
he saw as a mainly sympathetic response. Therefore, activation of
parasympathetic activity in humans exposed to fearful settings
should reduce anxiety and fear. Conversely, Wolpe believed that activation of sympathetic activity would keep fears from being extinguished. In fact it had been shown, and was known, that clas-
sically conditioned fears in the laboratory do extinguish in a
moderate number of trials (Annau & Kamin, 1961) independent of
parasympathetic or sympathetic activation.

Nevertheless, Wolpe proceeded to design a treatment program,
called systematic desensitization, based on his theoretical notions.
Although his assumptions were erroneous, his technique revolution-
ized the treatment of neuroses with behavior therapy. With systematic desensitization, clients create a hierarchy of items from least to
most fearful. The items are imagined as the client relaxes deeply,
using progressive muscle relaxation (Jacobsen, 1929), the technique
Wolpe chose to antagonize sympathetic activity. With systematic desensitization, the client proceeds up the hierarchy as the anxiety for
an item becomes insignificant.

Wolpe's early studies and many since have shown that systematic
desensitization is effective in reducing fear attached to simple phobic
situations. An appropriate question, then, was to determine how this
process might work. Efforts to answer that question yielded important information regarding the nature of fear and anxiety. Lang and
Lazovik (1963) should be credited with creating an experimental paradigm that opened the floodgates to research in this area. The paradigm required subjects to interact with the feared object or situation
at the end of treatment. In their first study, the ability to touch a
harmless snake upon completion of treatment was used as a criterion
measure of success. Using this paradigm, it was eventually demonstrated that deep muscle relaxation or pairing of relaxation with
phobic scenes was not critical to the success of systematic desensitization. Furthermore, subjects did as well when their tasks were
arbitrarily chosen from the hierarchy as when they were ordered.

Most researchers concluded that "exposure" to the feared object was the critical factor in success and that systematic desensitization is "merely" a way to help people expose themselves to the feared situation (Emmelkamp, 1982).

But what is exposure and why does it seem to work? Marks defines exposure as the "continued exposure to the stimulus that evokes anxiety until discomfort subsides" (Marks 1987, p. 457). He notes that it resembles the way that repeated presentations of the relevant stimuli habituate and extinguish normal innate and acquired fears. In later chapters, we will discuss the technique and effectiveness of exposure in detail. The processes responsible for the effectiveness of exposure, however, remain unclear. It has been shown that neither low nor high arousal nor the use of a hierarchical approach to feared situations are critical to improvement. Further, neither modeling nor reward have been shown to be necessary for improvement. Exposure produces increases in subjective anxiety, pulse rate, blood pressure, plasma cortisol, norepinephrine, epinephrine, insulin, and growth hormone, but the mechanism for these effects and their importance for reducing anxiety are not known. One recent study (Kelly et al., 1987) has produced an interesting clue: the therapeutic effects of exposure can be blocked with the simultaneous administration of naloxone. The central nervous system effects of naloxone are quite sweeping; it blocks endorphin activity and affects many neuroendocrine activities so that it is not possible to make inferences from this study about specific central nervous system activities involved with exposure. However, the study does demonstrate that such trials—which focus on the biochemical effects associated with learning—may help to elucidate the mechanisms of exposure in humans.

Cognitive Theories

A recent trend in behavior therapy has been to attribute anxiety disorders to cognitive events. Cognitive formulations share, more or less, three basic assumptions (Bolles & Fanselow, 1980; Carr, 1979):

1. Expectancies of harm mediate anxiety responses
2. Expectancies of harm are learned
3. The magnitude of anxiety covaries with the subjective likelihood of harm

Individuals learn to anticipate danger/harm in the presence of certain cues. The anticipation or expectation of danger produces anxiety responses or anxiety states (Bolles & Fanselow, 1980). The model looks like this:

CUE——EXPECTATION OF HARM——ANXIETY

Cognitive theorists believe that conditioning requires awareness of the relationship between the cue and anxiety. The expectancy of harm may be learned through respondent conditioning, observational learning, and information. Finally, some cognitive theorists believe that the magnitude of anxiety covaries with the subjective likelihood of harm. Put differently, the greater the likelihood of harm estimated by the individual, the more intense the anxiety.

Beck and Emery (1985) have elaborated this model in some detail. For them, the process of developing anxiety begins with the patient's primary appraisal of the situation. Primary appraisal is a complex process affected by the patient's initial impressions, vital interests, and cognitive set. If the primary appraisal of a situation establishes it as dangerous, successive reappraisals are made by the patient in an attempt to assess further the threat to vital interests. Concomitantly, "secondary appraisal" aims to assess the availability and effectiveness of the individual's resources for coping with the threatening situation. The development of fear is related both to the appraised threat and perceived coping capabilities and resources. For instance, a threatening situation might produce no fear if a "safe" person is present but intense fear if that person is absent. The estimate of danger is also affected by the patient's previous success in coping with a situation. Increased self-confidence to cope directly with a threat reduces the threat.

However, there are many problems with the cognitive model. The basic model is difficult to evaluate empirically, and the few studies that have attempted to study its basic assumptions have not confirmed them. For instance, anxiety episodes are usually preceded by physical sensations and not cognitions as Beck posits (Hibbert, 1985; Zucker et al., submitted). The limitations of the clinical application of cognitive models will be pursued later. The cognitive psychophysiologic models of panic attacks, emotion, and anxiety discussed below are also relevant to cognitive theories of anxiety.

Social Learning and Social Cognitive Theory

The most comprehensive contemporary model of human motivation, thought, and action, called social cognitive theory, has been developed by Bandura (1986). Social cognitive theory advances an interactional model of causation in which environmental events, personal factors, and behavior all influence one another. As opposed to psychodynamic theory, social cognitive theory argues that people are not driven by inner forces; unlike radical behaviorism, it argues against a passive conception of humans shaped and controlled by external stimuli. Social cognitive theory incorporates the human capabilities of symbolizing, forethought, vicarious learning, self-regulation, and self-reflecting.

Bandura (1986) holds that no explanation is sufficient to explain the development of anxiety and fears. Rather, he suggests that experience creates expectations that regulate action. In the case of simple fears, the development occurs as follows: an aversive experience—either personal or vicarious—instills the belief that one is unable to control the unpleasant outcome associated with the aversive event. Threats that cue the aversive experience produce arousal and various defensive maneuvers. However, various coping mechanisms, including the development of strategies to avoid the aversive experience, may help a person avert the unpleasant outcomes, and the fear disappears. Once a person becomes adept at self-protective behavior, he is likely to carry out the behavior in potentially threatening situations, even before becoming frightened. Protective strategies are activated under conditions of predicted rather than actual threats. Once established, defensive behavior is difficult to eliminate because it perpetuates the individual's estimation that he is unable to cope with the fearful situation.

Bandura has argued that a person's self-efficacy—a belief in one's competence or ability—is a major mediator of fear reduction. Increases in self-efficacy are highly correlated with increased ability to engage in previously feared acts. In phobics asked to rate self-efficacy concerning the phobic task, self-efficacy is low before treatment and rises after subjects improve with exposure treatment. Therefore, the therapeutic task is to increase self-efficacy. Performance, however, is only one factor that influences self-efficacy. Instructions from important figures in a person's life, vicarious experiences, and physiologic changes are also important (Bandura, 1977, 1982).

The primacy of self-efficacy as the mediator of fear reduction is hotly contested by Kirsch (1985), who argues that expectancy is more important than efficacy, and by Marks (1987), who emphasizes the importance of actual performance in the feared situation over other factors. The issue is not settled, but it is obvious that self-efficacy is an important factor to measure in anxious patients. In later chapters, we provide references to various self-efficacy instruments which help guide therapy.

Implications for Treatment

The most effective treatments for anxiety disorders have evolved from the learning theories we have discussed above. In general, behavior therapists have developed interventions based on theory and, perhaps even more importantly, have refined and expanded interventions to account for inconsistencies between theory and practice or simply to make interventions more effective and efficient. This is most clearly the case in the history of exposure therapy, which was shown to be the effective component of systematic desensitization and other therapies. An understanding of the mechanisms of exposure will require an integration of learning theory and neurobiology.

PSYCHOPHYSIOLOGIC MODELS

The psychophysiologic models assume that psychological and physiologic components of anxiety are interactive. In some ways the cognitive models discussed previously could be considered interactive in that peripheral signs of anxiety contribute to cognitions. However, the psychophysiologic model places greater emphasis on physiology than does the pure cognitive model. For instance, Clark et al. (1985) postulate that internal sensations of anxiety lead to apprehension and fearfulness, which then causes hyperventilation; the hyperventilation exacerbates existing symptoms and may cause additional ones, further increasing apprehension and fearfulness. This vicious cycle may then lead to a panic attack. Most psychophysiologic models assume that panic is not qualitatively distinct from other forms of anxiety. We have undertaken some studies that validate some of the assumptions of the psychophysiologic model.

We have found that patients with panic attacks given false feedback of increased heart rate show an abrupt heart-rate increase, whereas controls given the same feedback show no increase (Ehlers et al., 1987). The panic patients seem sensitive to the feedback and response, with heart-rate increases probably suggesting increased alarm. The role of cognitions in producing physiological change is even more dramatically demonstrated in a study where we showed that expectancy of panic attacks during hyperventilation can cause panic attacks (Margraf et al., submitted). This study will be discussed in more detail in chapter 7.

Clinically, and theoretically, we think that a combination of cognitive, physiologic, and social learning theory is useful in describing panic. This model is illustrated in Figure 2.1. The outer circle represents the traditional psychophysiologic model in which physical sensations, thoughts, or images perceived as threatening lead to a feeling of anxiety and perhaps even physical sensations of anxiety. The interpretation of these symptoms as catastrophic may tend to amplify the physical sensations and anxiety and to increase hypervigilance

COGNITIVE MODEL OF PANIC

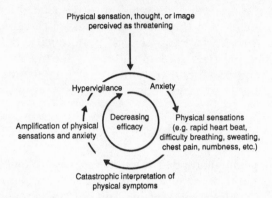

Figure 2.1 **Cognitive Model of Panic**

This illustration represents the cognitive-psychophysiologic model of panic attacks and anxiety. Threatening events or internal sensations lead to a feeling of anxiety and physical symptoms. Catastrophic interpretations regarding the physical sensations lead to increased apprehension and attentiveness to physiologic cues (hypervigilance) resulting in their amplification. The patient may hyperventilate or experience increased sympathetic activity, all of which lead to increased feelings of anxiety and physiologic symptoms. The process may accelerate into a full-blown panic attack. The inner circle indicates that the patient's self-efficacy or confidence to cope with these sensations is another factor determining the progression and intensity of symptoms. Failure to cope decreases self-efficacy and predisposes to increased fearfulness associated with threatening situations or stimuli.

and arousal, which further exacerbates the anxiety. The vicious spiral may result in the development of panic. However, this process is also associated with decreasing efficacy, represented by the inner circle. The decreasing efficacy results in a feeling of more vulnerability and increased anxious cognitions.

The psychophysiologic model is useful clinically, but many of its core assumptions need to be tested and elaborated. There are many facts that seem to contradict it. For instance, beta-blockers, which block many of the peripheral sensations of anxiety, are not effective in blocking panic. The biologic evidence discussed below suggests that some patients have a core vulnerability—are anxious cognitions a reflection of this process or do they cause it? Furthermore, how the patient behaves in the face of anxious sensations may be more important than what he thinks. Subtle behaviors that help to attenuate or avoid anxiety may increase cognitions rather than vice-versa. Nevertheless, as described in subsequent chapters the cognitive psychophysiologic model is useful as a framework for treatment of some aspects of anxiety and panic.

NEUROPHYSIOLOGIC MODELS

Because anxiety involves emotion, memory, arousal, attention, drive states, cognition, behavior, and other aspects of the central nervous system, a complete understanding of the neurophysiology of anxiety will need to involve many CNS systems. We have glimpses of some of the systems involved with anxiety, but an integrated model will require new neuroscientific methods capable of observing the actual functioning of the central nervous system under various conditions. In this section we first describe some of the basic neuroanatomical structures involved with anxiety, then turn to a discussion of the various neurotransmitters that have been implicated in anxiety.

Neuroanatomy

Many studies have identified neuroanatomical structures and systems involved with anxiety and fear, yet the details of which particular structures correspond to which aspect of fear and anxiety remain obscure. It appears that deep structures of the brain are more involved with the emotional aspects of fear and anxiety than the cerebral cortex. Evidence for this comes from a variety of studies where electrical stimulation of deep structures of the brain has been shown to elicit emotions, or ablation of these structures is associated with alterations in emotion. Among the important deep structures are (1) the limbic system, (2) the thalamus, (3) the locus coeruleus and the reticular activating system, (4) the median raphe and other midbrain nuclei, and (5) connections among these systems.

The Limbic System

The limbic system is a complex of nuclei and tracts which includes the hypothalamus, septum, hippocampus, amygdala, and cingulum. It is so named because it borders (Latin: *limbus*) the brain stem. An extensive array of pathways interconnect the various components (Issacson, 1974). The limbic system is concerned with integrating emotional and motivational behavior, particularly motor coordination in emotional responses (Watson et al., 1986). The limbic system, through the hypothalamus, is also critically important in autonomic function. The hypothalamus is the final common pathway in control of the pituitary gland.

Thalamus

Evidence suggesting that the thalamus plays a role in anxiety and fear comes from relatively few studies in which thalamic nuclei have been stimulated in conscious people. Stimulation of the medial thalamus or dorsolateral thalamic nucleus evokes feelings typical of anxiety (Delgado, 1969).

Locus Coeruleus

The locus coeruleus (LC) has been implicated as a particularly important neuroanatomical site related to anxiety (Redmond et al., 1976; Redmond, 1977). Noradrenergic activity is concentrated in the LC, which receives innervation from pain pathways in the spinal cord and cranial nerve nuclei. Pathways from the LC affect many of the physiological responses to pain and fear, and other pathways to and from the cerebral cortex provide feedback loops that might incorporate "cognitive" factors, like appraisal of the meaning of a stimulus. The LC serves as a relay center for a "warning" or "alarm." The warning or alarm may vary from normal attention to a novel stimulus to terror or panic depending on the extent of activation of the LC system. In the awake monkey there is a rapid "habituation" of LC activity to novel non-noxious stimuli as well as a consistent association of spontaneous LC activity with the level of "vigilance" and arousal. Fear-associated stimuli consistently produce activation.

Stimulation of the locus coeruleus in monkeys produces behaviors similar to anxiety. For instance, low intensity stimulation of the LC causes head and body turning, eye scanning, chewing, tongue movement, grasping and clutching, scratching, biting fingers or nails, pulling hair or skin, hand wringing, yawning, and spasmodic total body jerking (Redmond et al., 1976). Redmond (1979) has shown that increasing LC activation can move an animal from a stage of fearlessness to one of terror. He arrays minimum to maximum LC function as shown in Table 2.1. Behaviorally, the LC appears to have an inhibitory function throughout the entire range of its activity, which could be considered an "alarm" or "warning" function for the subject. While few would ascribe all anxiety functions to the LC, it is clearly an important component of the neurophysiology of anxiety.

TABLE 2.1

Effects of locus coeruleus lesions

LC Function		Mood
Maximum	Terror	
	Panic	
	Fear	
	Anxiety	Dysphoric
	Dread	
	Alarm	
	Vigilance	
	Wariness	
	Caution	
	Prudence	Euthymic
	Watchfulness	
	Attentiveness	
	Inattentiveness	
	Distractibility	
	Impulsivity	
	Carelessness	
	Recklessness	Anhedonic
Minimum	Fearlessness	

SOURCE: Adapted from "Current Concepts II: New Evidence for a Locus Coeruleus–Norepinephrine Connection with Anxiety" by D. E. Redmond, Jr., and Y. H. Yuang, 1979, *Life Science, 25,* 2149–2162.

Neurotransmitters

Thus far we have discussed the gross brain structures and nuclei possibly involved with anxiety and fear. More important than the brain structures, however, are the neurotransmitter systems that control brain function. Neurotransmitter systems are distributed only partially in the classical anatomic pathways. Neurotransmitters are the chemical "messengers" that control transmission between nerves. In general, they are released at the end of a nerve into the synaptic cleft, the space between the end of one nerve and the beginning of another. These neurotransmitters diffuse across the synaptic cleft to the postsynaptic neuron, where they activate specific sites on the cell membrane called receptors. Attachment to the receptor causes the postsynaptic neuron to alter its standing electrical charge, which in turn may cause it to discharge.

In addition, the central nervous system has other ways to control neuronal activity. Some cells secrete "hormones" directly into the bloodstream as a result of stimulation. These systems have been called neuromodulators, neuroregulators, or neurohormones; their exact nature is still being defined. Already, over 40 neurotransmitters and neurohormones have been isolated from the CNS. However, two neurotransmitter systems, the noradrenergic and serotinergic, seem particularly important to anxiety, and each has strong proponents arguing for its central role in anxiety disorders.

The Noradrenergic System

The noradrenergic system has received the most attention as the primary system involved with anxiety disorders (Charney et al., 1986; Breier et al., 1986). The noradrenergic system involves norepinephine, a catecholamine, as its neurotransmitter. Although there are many catecholamines, the term usually applies to dopamine and its two metabolic products, norepinephrine and epinephrine. While both norepinephrine and epinephrine play a critical role in controlling autonomic system activity outside of the CNS, of the two, only norepinephrine has an important function in the CNS (Watson et al., 1986). Norepinephrine is concentrated in the brainstem, particularly in the LC. Norepinephrine cells project down the spinal cord to the cerebellum and a wide variety of structures, including the cortex, limbic system, and hypothalamus. The brain noradrenergic system has been shown to be involved in the mediation of numerous brain functions, including learning and memory, sleep, blood pressure, consummatory behaviors, and probably anxiety or fear (Watson et al., 1986). Noradrenergic neurons are highly responsive to sensory input, and a global function of the system may be to enhance the effects of sensory information at a variety of brain sites.

The evidence that norepinephrine dysfunction is related to anxiety comes from a variety of sources. Neurotransmitters and drugs with anxiogenic or anxiolytic properties have important actions on noradrenergic neuronal activity, while drugs with anxiogenic effects, such as yohimbine, increase LC activity, cause anxiety in normals, and increasing anxiety in anxious subjects (Charney et al., 1983; Redmond, 1986). Other drugs produce antipanic effects by altering the regulatory effects of noradrenergic function rather than by simply increasing or decreasing noradrenergic activity (Charney et al., 1985.) Although it is assumed that some dysfunction in the noradrenergic system is responsible in part for anxiety, the nature of this dysfunction is not clear. It is possible that patients prone to anxiety disorders have too few noradrenergic receptors, that their system is too sensitive to input (it tends to overshoot), and that their receptors are subsensitive. Neurotransmitter systems are dynamic and it may be that environmental events, like a traumatic experience or separation, are necessary for the noradrenergic system to become disequilibrated.

Serotonergic System

Recently, the serotonergic system has also been implicated in anxiety (Gershon & Eison, 1987). Serotonergic neurons are distributed within the midbrain and pons. The evidence for the role of serotonin is partly anatomical, partly experimental, and partly clinical. Anatomically the serotonergic system has extensive connections with the limbic system, which is important in modulating emotions (Watson et al., 1986). Experimentally, the serotonergic system seems to be involved in behavioral inhibition. The supression of behavioral inhibition following punishment is a phenomenon that seems to be affected by drugs with antianxiety properties. Most important, new pharmacologic agents that increase serotonin activity seem to have strong antianxiety effects.

GABA-Benzodiazepine System

Thus far we have described two possible neurotransmitter systems that might be involved with anxiety. Two discoveries have paved the way for yet another neurophysiologic theory of anxiety. In the mid-1970s two groups (Haefely et al., 1975; Costa et al., 1975) established a close connection between the therapeutic action of anxiolytic drugs and their capacity to facilitate transmission in gamma-aminobutryic acid (GABA) synapses. It has been estimated that 40 percent of synapses in the brain are GABAergic, making GABA the most ubiquitous neurotransmitter. At about the same time, it was discovered that there are high-affinity binding sites for benzodiazepines that are effective anxiolytic drugs (Braestrup & Squires, 1977; Mohler & Okada, 1977). (We will refer to these high-affinity binding sites as BZ receptors.) It was soon shown that these BZ receptors have an important role in modulating GABAergic synaptic function (Costa, Guidotti, & Toffano, 1978). Therefore, the theory posits that GABAergic synaptic function is important for anxiety modulation.

The information on neurotransmitters and their role in anxiety is dazzling in its rapid growth but puzzling in its implications. Three major transmitters affecting most of the brain seem involved: noradrenergic, serotonergic, and GABA. Interactions among these and other neurotransmitters may be critical to the phenomenon of anxiety. It is unlikely that any one "lesion" in any neuroanatomical or neurotransmitter system accounts for all anxiety disorders.

Behavioral Inhibitory System—Gray's Model

Gray (1982a, 1982b) has attempted to link pharmacologic, behavioral, neuroanatomic, and neurophysiologic systems into a unified theory of anxiety. His basic theory is derived from extensive review of the effects in animals of drugs that reduce human anxiety. He has particularly emphasized data from the many hundreds of studies that have been conducted on benzodiazepines, barbiturates, and alcohol in species ranging from goldfish to humans. The antianxiety drugs counteract the behavioral effects of three classes of stimuli: those associated with punishment, those associated with the omission of expected reward, and those associated with novelty. Such stimuli produce three classes of behavior: behavioral inhibition, increased arousal, or increased attention. For instance, a rat conditioned to expect a shock when a red light is flashed (stimulus of punishment), will exhibit freezing (behavioral inhibition), increase in heart rate and other physiological functions (increment in arousal), and scanning (increased attention). Gray (1982) believes that these inputs are affected by a system that he labels the "behavioural inhibition system," one of three neurophysiologic systems involved with emotions. The other two systems are the behavioral activation system, said to control active approach and avoidance behavior in response to signals of reward (Fowles, 1980), and the fight/flight system described in chapter 1. The behavioral inhibition system (BIS) regulates extinction and passive avoidance in response to signals of punishment. Increase in activity of the BIS leads to behavioral inhibition, and increased arousal and attention. However, antianxiety drugs impair the function of the behavioral inhibition system. Gray's model is diagrammed in Figure 2.2.

For Gray, anxiety is related to activity in the behavioral inhibitory system, or more technically, anxiety "consists of a central state elicited by threats of punishment, frustration or failure, and by novelty or uncertainty" (Gray, 1985, p. 6–7). Having defined anxiety in this way, Gray then attempts to locate the neuroanatomy of the BIS by reviewing a variety of investigations. Important neuroanatomical structures include the hippocampal formation, the Papez circuit, and the septal area. Gray then goes one step further—and this is perhaps the most striking part of his model—to examine the purpose of the

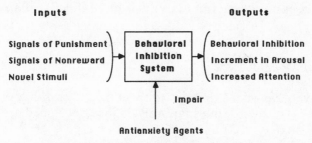

Figure 2.2 Behavioral Inhibition System

The Behavioral Inhibition System (BIS) is represented by the box. Signals of punishment and nonreward and novel stimuli increase BIS activity which increase behavioral inhibition, arousal and attention. Antianxiety agents reduce activity in the BIS.

From "Issues in the Neuropsychology of Anxiety," by Jeffrey A. Gray, 1985, A. Hussain Tuma & Jack Maser (Eds.), *Anxiety and Anxiety Disorders*, page 6, Figure 1. Hillsdale, NJ: Lawrence Erlbaum Associates, Inc.

BIS system. His answer is simple: the general task of the BIS system is to compare, quite generally, actual with expected stimuli. The system functions in two modes. If actual stimuli are successfully matched with expected stimuli, it functions in a "checking" mode and does not override other CNS functions. However, if there is a discordance between actual and expected stimuli or if the predicted stimulus is aversive, the BIS takes control over behavior and functions in a "control" mode. In the control mode, the BIS inhibits any motor program in the course of execution and records a "mismatch"—that is, a particular motor activity is tagged for further review. In the future, the "tagged" motor activity is executed with greater caution, and during its execution the environment is carefully watched for unexpected events. For instance, when a "tagged" motor event occurs, a rat exploring an unfamiliar environment might pause carefully, scan the environment, and be prepared for escape.

Gray's theory has been attacked on a variety of grounds. He has been accused of focusing on the wrong hormones (Bohus, 1982). He also has been accused of oversimplifying drug effects and ignoring data contradictory to his theories (Iverson, 1982; Lader, 1985). Yet, Gray's theory is of important heuristic value and has generated some interesting clinical predictions. He argues, for instance, that toughening up by repeated exposure to a feared situation should be enhanced by drugs that increase noradrenergic activity. Limited evidence supports this prediction. Exposure combined with imipramine (a drug that increases noradrenergic activity) is more effective than exposure alone.

MOLECULAR MODELS

Kandel, who has spent decades unraveling the working of the nervous system in the marine snail Aplysia, has developed a molecular model of anxiety (Kandel, 1983). Kandel argues that behavioral changes in Aplysia can be used as a model for anxiety in higher life forms. Mechanisms underlying anxiety are likely to be general throughout phylogeny. Even the lowly snail must learn to avoid predators, to search out food that is nutritious, and avoid food that is poisonous. It is unlikely that such information can be preprogrammed in the animal's nervous system. Instead, animals learn predictive relationships between related events. Some psychologists believe that common associative mechanisms of learning exist in all species capable of learning and that these common mechanisms are designed to recognize and store information about predictive relationships in the environment (e.g., Dickinson, 1980). Kandel cautions us that "I do not, even in my most optimistic moments, believe that the mechanisms for anxiety in simple animals are likely to be identical to those in humans" (Kandel, 1983, p. 1282.) Yet some of the phenomena are remarkably similar. As with humans, a fear response can be conditioned. Although Aplysia is a herbivore, eating only seaweed, its chemosensitivity readily detects the presence of shrimp, so that shrimp juice can be used as conditioned stimulus. The unconditioned stimulus can be head shock. The effect of conditioning is measured by the strength of escape locomotion. After several trials in which the CS is followed by head shock (UCS), Aplysia develops heightened arousal in the presence of the CS. This model is similar to anticipatory anxiety. However, Aplysia also shows evidence of chronic anxiety, defined by Kandel as a state in which anxieties serve as a motivational condition in which some responses are enhanced while others are suppressed.

Walters et al. (1981) showed that anxiety enhances defensive responses and inhibits adaptive responses. And here the story becomes interesting, because, having developed an invertebrate model for anticipatory and chronic anxiety, it becomes possible to examine the basic biological mechanisms for this anxiety. In this model, the events follow roughly the following sequence: First, serotonin released by the facilitating neurons acts on a serotonin receptor in the membrane of the presynaptic terminals of the sensory neuron. The receptor then activates a serotonin-sensitive adenylate cyclase that increases cyclic AMP within the terminals. The cyclic AMP activates an enzyme which adds a phosphoryl molecule to certain amino acids in the protein. The addition of the phosphoryl molecule changes the electrical charge of a protein, which controls the potassium channel in the nerve membrane. The change in the electrical charge of the protein changes the three-dimensional shape and function of the protein. The end effect of this process is that more calcium flows into the terminals and more neurotransmitter is released. Even more extraordinary, this "chronic anxiety" has been shown to lead to morphological changes in varicosities (expansions of the presynaptic terminal that act as storage sites for transmitters). These brilliant observations and experiments have profound implications for human anxiety. They demonstrate that learning can lead to morphological changes in the nervous system. Given this observation, any theories or models of anxiety attempting to dichotimize or even distinguish between learning and biological mechanisms are inappropriate: learning is a biological phenomenon.

CONCLUSIONS

What is the best theory of anxiety? We conclude that while there is no best single theory of anxiety, all the theories discussed have something to offer the therapist. Anxiety is best viewed from the biopsychosocial perspective, which posits that various systems interact in complicated ways to determine the final presentation of anxiety for a particular individual.

Figure 2.3 shows the major components involved in anxiety disorders. Past experience, genetic endowment, and development all influence the onset, maintenance and exacerbation of anxiety disorders. Perception of both internal and external events and the cognitive appraisal of these events, with the resulting changes in cognition and efficacy, interact to affect arousal. Memory also plays an important role in cognitive appraisal. Much of the modulation of feeling, physiology, and biochemistry associated with anxiety disorders occurs in the pons, limbic system, thalamus, and associated structures. The hatched areas indicate high concentrations of noradrenaline and serotonin, two transmitters thought to be important in regulating arousal, feelings, and biochemical, physiologic, and behavioral aspects of anxiety. Not drawn, because of their wide dispersal throughout the CNS but important in anxiety, are the BZ-GABA complex and dopamine. The locus coeruleus is particularly important for arousal and anxiety. The hypothalamus and pituitary are responsible for the peripheral neurohormonal aspects of anxiety. We have drawn this system unidirectionally, but anxiety disorders are interactive. For instance, with agoraphobia, behavior (avoidance) may reduce the

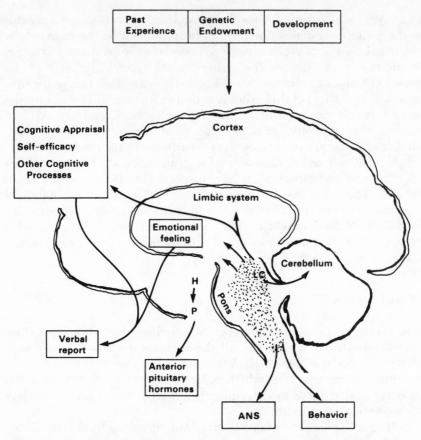

Figure 2.3 **Major Components of Anxiety Disorders**

Figure 2.3 represents an overview of central nervous system structures, systems, and other factors involved with anxiety. Noradrenergic and serotonergic neurotransmitters are concentrated in the pons, as indicated by the dots. Not indicated, but also important, are the widely distributed benzodiazepine receptors, and the GABA and dopamine neurotransmitters. Activity in the locus coeruleus (LC) seems to modulate fearfulness. Ascending pathways from structures in the pons connect to a wide variety of other brain structures, including the limbic system. The hypothalamus (H) influences the secretion of hormones from the anterior pituitary (P), which in turn influence peripheral structures. Anxiety, fear, and panic are manifest in peripheral autonomic nervous system (ANS) activity and actual behavior.

feeling of fear. The occurrence of feelings associated with fear and changes in autonomic function may result in cognitive appraisal of threat that leads to heightened arousal.

In subsequent chapters, we will highlight theories that apply to the specific anxiety disorders.

THREE
· · · · · · · ·

Anxiety
Syndromes and
Disorders

· · · · · · · · · ·

In the first chapter we reviewed the major subjective, cognitive, physiologic, and behavioral aspects of anxiety. Can certain syndromes or types of anxiety be identified by constellations of these symptoms, precipitating events, and course? This is a surprisingly controversial question and is related to the issue of how to diagnose anxiety. Our own position is that a number of different types of anxiety syndromes may be identified in clinical practice. These syndromes should not necessarily be considered disorders, a term we reserve for syndromes meeting the criteria established by the American Psychiatric Association's *Diagnostic and Statistical Manual of Mental Disorders* (American Psychiatric Association, *DSM-III-R*, 1987). The common syndromes are:

1. *Fear.* Fear or acute anxiety occurs in response to a definable real or imagined stimulus. These can sometimes be diagnosed as simple phobias.
2. *Generalized anxiety* (sometimes called trait or chronic anxiety), characterized by increased levels of arousal present most of the time. Such patients experience constant jitteriness, worry, and other symptoms, which may sometimes be diagnosed as generalized anxiety disorder.
3. *Episodic, intense anxiety attacks* characterized by rapid onset and multiple symptoms (panic attacks). Such attacks can be spontaneous—having no identifiable cause—or situational, that is, occurring in predictable situations. Such patients may some-

times be diagnosed as having panic disorder (uncomplicated) or panic disorder with agoraphobia.

4. *Anticipatory anxiety* related to internal or external actual or imagined threatening events. Most of us experience small levels of anticipatory anxiety fairly frequently.

5. *Mild episodic anxiety.* Mild episodic anxiety occurs for reasons that are difficult for the patient to identify. Such anxiety is a common phenomenon in therapy. We include so-called death or existential anxiety in this category.

6. *Mild anxiety and mild depression,* sometimes called distress. This is probably the most common anxiety disorder. Patients with mild anxiety and depression and concomitant medical problems are the most frequent users of sedative medications.

7. *Anxiety related to specific social, family, or work situations.* In such patients the anxiety is usually bearable and is seen as secondary to the primary problem. Such patients sometimes meet the criteria for social phobia.

8. *Anxiety following traumatic events.* Such patients may meet the DSM-III-R criteria for post-traumatic stress syndrome.

All of these types of anxiety exist on a normal distribution of intensity, frequency, and symptomology. However, these syndromes, when severe, often meet the criteria for DSM-III-R anxiety disorders.

The major *anxiety symptoms* requiring attention in patients who seek treatment include: (1) acute fear, anxiety, and distress (the focus of chapter 5), (2) the subjective, cognitive, physiologic and behavioral aspects of chronic arousal (the focus of chapter 6); (2) panic attacks (the focus of chapter 7); and (3) avoidance (the focus of chapter 8). Anticipatory, social, and simple fears also need to be treated as appropriate.

A CONTINUUM OF ANXIETY OR SEPARATE DISORDERS?

A continuing controversy exists as to whether or not anxiety syndromes or disorders are distinct or continuous. This is an important theoretical question, related to the possibility of separate etiologies for different disorders rather than a single cause for all anxiety problems that constitute one disorder. Psychodynamic theory assumes that anxiety disorders share common etiologies comprised of unconscious conflicts arising from early childhood experience. Traditionally, psychoanalysts have classified distress and generalized and panic anxiety together. Redmond (1977) also argues for a single disorder, but a biologic rather than psychoanalytic one. He arrays anxiety disorders on a continuum related to the extent of locus coeruleus activation. On the other hand, on the basis of different pharmacologic responses, Klein (1964) has long argued that panic disorder is distinctly different from other types of anxiety.

Our own view is that the following groups of disorders can be identified and that they may have different etiologies: (1) acute fears and phobias, (2) social phobia, (3) post-traumatic stress, (4) chronic or generalized anxiety, panic disorder with and without agoraphobia, and agoraphobia without panic disorder. These four conditions grouped under (4) share important phenomenologic features, as illustrated in Figure 3.1. In this figure we have created a schematic representation of the "severity" of these four types of anxiety for normals,

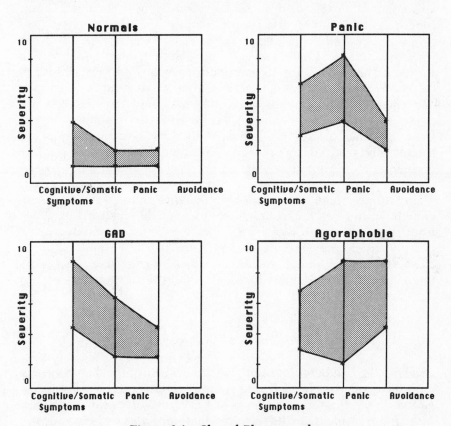

Figure 3.1. **Shared Phenomenology**

In this hypothetical description of anxiety disorder patients about 75 percent of patients with the diagnosis indicated on the top of the box would fall into the shaded areas. The severity of the dimension represents intensity and frequency, where 0 is no problem and 10 is extreme severity.

patients with generalized anxiety disorder, panic disorder without agoraphobia, and panic disorder with agoraphobia. We have arbitrarily lumped the cognitive and somatic symptoms of generalized anxiety together and combined frequency and intensity to create the severity rating.

As can be seen in this figure, normal subjects experience generalized anxiety, occasional and not very intense panic attacks, and some avoidance. Generalized anxiety disorder is characterized by severe cognitive, somatic, and behavioral symptoms of generalized anxiety, but these patients may also experience panic attacks and avoidance. Panic disorder without agoraphobia is characterized by the presence of panic attacks, but generalized anxiety symptoms are also apparent. Panic disorder with agoraphobia is the most severe condition and includes all of the pathology of the other disorders. We believe that the clinical evidence suggests, in fact, that panic disorder without avoidance is a less severe condition than panic disorder with agoraphobia. Post-traumatic stress disorder appears very similar to these other anxiety disorders, except that it has a different history and generally occurs in individuals who may not be predisposed otherwise to anxiety disorders. It is easiest to separate simple phobias from the other disorders. In most individuals, simple phobias are discrete and confined to the feared situation. Social phobia is more problematic. It is not clear whether social phobia is a separate disorder or related to the generalized panic attack–avoidance disorders. The extreme rituals and obsessive thoughts characteristic of individuals with obsessive–compulsive disorder distinguish this group from other anxiety sufferers. Yet, obsessive–compulsive patients frequently experience extreme anxiety; they probably have panic attacks and are prone to avoidance as well. Furthermore, obsessive thoughts and subtle rituals frequently occur with the other anxiety disorders.

THE DIAGNOSIS OF ANXIETY DISORDERS

Drawing the line between normal anxiety, syndromes of anxiety, and clinical anxiety is difficult and somewhat arbitrary. We have suggested that at least four groups of anxiety syndromes can be defined. Although treatment should focus on the symptoms, we believe that it is important to make clinical diagnoses, and we recommend that therapists use the DSM-III-R diagnostic system recently released (APA, 1987). DSM-III-R is a necessary evil. It is necessary because it often determines reimbursement, helps with clinical formulation and treatment, and facilitates communication of scientific and clinical information. The drawbacks of DSM-III-R are that it forces clinicians to classify patients into categories that only partially fit their complex problems; it makes assumptions not shared by many therapists (for instance, that mental health problems should be considered medical problems), and it gives undue emphasis to psychiatry over other mental health disciplines since psychiatrists were the ones who mainly developed and implemented the system. There is no doubt that the classification of anxiety disorders in DSM-III has been a major factor in stimulating the flowering of anxiety disorder research that has occurred in the past five years.

HISTORY

Descriptions of fear and anxiety states occur in the earliest literature. *Phobia* is a Latin word meaning terror or dread; it derives from the Greek, οβχος. The syndrome of recurrent panic attacks was recognized as a separate disorder as far back as 1871 when Da Costa described the "irritable heart" and later in 1894 when Freud first applied the name *anxiety neurosis* to the syndrome, separating it from the category of neurasthenia. Westphal (1878) had also described the syndrome of agoraphobia. The classification of anxiety disorders, however, is largely a 20th century phenomenon. Before this century, diagnostic nomenclature principally focused on problems considered to be organic. The 1869 American Medico-Psychological Association diagnostic system included only simple, epileptic, paralytic, senile and organic dementia, idiocy, cretinism, and ill-defined forms. The next major change in the U.S. occurred in 1917 when the American Psychiatric Association developed a 22-item nosology based on etiology. By then psychoanalytic theory had introduced the concept of neurosis, in which anxious symptoms were attributed to unconscious conflicts. Thus "psychoneurosis" was introduced as a diagnostic category. Disorders subsumed under this heading included hysteria (of which anxiety hysteria was a variant), psychasthenia or compulsive states, neurasthenia, hypochondriasis, reactive depression, anxiety state, and mixed psychoneurosis. With some variations in category and nomenclature, psychoneuroses continued to include and define clinical anxiety disorders through the American Psychiatric Association's Diagnostic and Statistical Manuals, I and II (APA, 1952, 1968). In 1980, however, the diagnostic system was radically changed to classify disorders based on shared descriptive features when the etiology is unknown, rather than on presumed etiology. The term "neurosis" was replaced by "disorder." Disorders are clinically significant behavioral or psychological syndromes or patterns associ-

Table 3.1

**DSM-III Classification
of Anxiety Disorders**

Phobic disorders
    Agoraphobia with panic attacks
    Agoraphobia without panic attacks
    Social phobia
    Simple phobia
Anxiety states
    Panic disorder
    Generalized anxiety disorder
    Obsessive-compulsive disorder
Post-traumatic stress disorder
    Acute
    Chronic or delayed
Atypical anxiety disorder

ated with distress, disability, and dysfunction. Those disorders having anxiety and/or avoidance as the predominant symptom (APA, 1980) were classified as anxiety disorders as listed in Table 3.1.

DSM-III-R

DSM-III-R is offered as an interim diagnostic system to be replaced by DSM-IV in 1992, at which time DSM-IV is meant to be published with the International Classification of Diseases-10, which will be published by the World Health Organization. Consistent with DSM-III, DSM-III-R defines a mental disorder as a "clinically significant behavioral or psychological syndrome or pattern that occurs in a person and that is associated with present distress (a painful symptom), or disability (impairment in one or more areas of functioning), or with a significantly increased risk of suffering death, pain, disability, or an important loss of freedom" (p. xxii). Of note, "There is no assumption that each mental disorder is a discrete entity with sharp boundaries (discontinuity) between it and other mental disorders, or between it and no mental disorder" (p. xxii). This is an important statement, and particularly relevant to anxiety disorders. A patient often meets the criteria for generalized anxiety disorder, panic disorder, and agoraphobia simultaneously, or, over time, exhibits changing symptomology that at one time may seem most consistent with one diagnosis and at another time with an alternative one. Furthermore, many "normals" have panic attacks that fail to

TABLE 3.2

DSM-III-R Anxiety Disorders

Panic disorder
  with agoraphobia (300.21)
  without agoraphobia (300.01)
Agoraphobia without history of panic dis-
  order (300.22)
Social phobia (300.23)
Simple phobia (300.29)
Obsessive compulsive disorder (300.30)
Post-traumatic stress disorder (300.89)
Generalized anxiety disorder (300.02)
Anxiety disorder not otherwise specified
  (300.00)

meet DSM-III-R criteria only in frequency and intensity. And perhaps, most important, the rigid hierarchical system of DSM-III, in
which one anxiety diagnosis precluded another, is loosened. The
DSM-III-R (APA, 1987) anxiety disorder classifications may be seen in
Table 3.2. Two structured interviews are available to help with diagnosis—the Anxiety Disorders Interview Schedule (Di Nardo et al.,
1983 and 1985) and the Structured Clinical Interview for Diagnosis
(Spitzer, Williams, & Gibbon, 1987).

We now turn to a consideration of the specific anxiety disorders
listed in DSM-III-R.

PANIC DISORDER

The essential feature of panic disorder is the occurrence of recurrent
panic attacks. The panic attacks are manifested by the sudden onset
of intense apprehension, fear, or terror, and are often associated with
feelings of impending doom. The most common symptoms experienced during an attack are listed below in the criteria presented in
Table 3.3. Attacks usually last minutes; occasionally they will last for
an hour or more. The individual often develops varying degrees of
nervousness and apprehension between attacks. The initial attacks
are unexpected or spontaneous, although over time, they may become associated with specific situations, persons or places. Table 3.3
provides the DSM-III-R criteria for panic disorder.

The disorder is considered *panic disorder with agoraphobia* (300.21)
if it meets the criteria for panic disorder and includes fear of being in
places or situations from which escape might be difficult or embar-

TABLE 3.3

Panic Disorder Diagnostic Criteria

A. At some time during the disturbance one or more panic attacks were unexpected.
B. Either four attacks (defined in criterion C) have occurred within a four-week period, or one or more attacks have been followed by a period of at least a month of persistent fear of having another attack.
C. At least four of the following symptoms developed during at least one of the attacks:
  (1) shortness of breath (dyspnea) or smothering sensations
  (2) dizziness, unsteady feelings, or faintness
  (3) palpitations or accelerated heart rate
  (4) trembling or shaking
  (5) sweating
  (6) choking
  (7) nausea or abdominal distress
  (8) depersonalization or derealization
  (9) numbness or tingling sensations (paresthesias)
  (10) flushes (hot flashes) or chills
  (11) chest pain or discomfort
  (12) fear of dying
  (13) fear of going crazy or doing something uncontrolled
D. During at least some of the attacks, at least four of the C symptoms developed suddenly and increased in intensity within ten minutes.
E. Not due to an organic factor.

SOURCE: Reprinted with permission from the *Diagnostic and Statistical Manual of Mental Disorders, Third Edition, Revised.* Copyright 1987 American Psychiatric Association.

rassing or in which help might not be available in the event of a panic attack. "As a result of this fear, the person either restricts travel or needs a companion when away from home, or else endures agoraphobic situations despite intense anxiety" (APA, 1987, p. 239).

DSM-III-R asks the rater to specify the current severity or agoraphobic avoidance as mild (some avoidance but relatively normal lifestyle), moderate (avoidance results in constricted life-style), severe (avoidance results in being nearly or completely housebound or unable to leave the house unaccompanied), in partial remission (no current avoidance, but some agoraphobic avoidance during the past six months), or in full remission (no current agoraphobic avoidance and none during the past six months.) Because there are reliable ways to quantify avoidance (discussed below), we do not endorse this aspect of DSM-III-R.

DSM-III-R also asks the rater to specify the severity of panic at-tacks as mild (during the past month, either all attacks have had fewer than four symptoms or there has been no more than one panic attack), moderate (during the past month panic attacks have been intermediate between "mild" and "severe"), severe (during the past month, there have been at least eight panic attacks), in partial remis-sion (the condition has been intermediate between "in full remis-sion" and "mild"), or in full remission (during the past six months, there have been no panic or limited symptom attacks.) This is a rather peculiar method to specify the current severity of panic at-tacks, and there are better ways to assess panic attack frequency and intensity (see chapter 7).

The disorder is considered *panic disorder without agoraphobia* (300.01) if the patient meets the criteria for panic disorder but does not have agoraphobia as defined above.

If patients meet the criteria for agoraphobic avoidance but do not have a history consistent with panic disorder they meet the criteria for *agoraphobia without history of panic disorder* (300.22). In field studies of DSM-III-R, patients who met this criteria often exhibited so-called "limited symptom attacks," that is, attacks with a single or a small number of symptoms. These limited symptom attacks may be functionally equivalent to full-blown panic attacks in the sense that the person may fear their recurrence and manifest avoidance much as a patient with panic disorder with agoraphobia avoids situations where the occurrence of panic attacks is anticipated. In any event, this disorder is quite rare, and of more theoretical than clinical sig-nificance, since treatment proceeds similarly to that of panic disor-der with agoraphobia (chapters 8 and 9).

SOCIAL PHOBIA

The essential feature of social phobia is a persistent, irrational fear of, and compelling desire to avoid one or more situations in which the individual may be exposed to scrutiny by others. The person fears that in such situations he may behave in a manner that will be humil-iating or embarrassing. Marked anticipatory anxiety occurs if the individual is confronted with the necessity of entering into such a situation, and he or she therefore attempts to avoid it. The distur-bance is a significant source of distress and is recognized by the individual as excessive or unreasonable. Examples of social phobias are fears of speaking or performing in public, using public lavatories, eating in public, and writing in the presence of others.

SIMPLE PHOBIA

Simple phobia is characterized by a persistent, irrational fear of and compelling desire to avoid an object or situation other than being alone or in public places away from home (like agoraphobia), or of humiliation or embarrassment in certain social situations (like social phobia). This disturbance is a significant source of distress. The criteria for simple phobia are that (1) the patient has a persistent fear of a circumscribed stimulus (object or situation) other than fear of having a panic attack (as in panic disorder), or fear of humiliation or embarrassment in certain social situations (as in social phobia); (2) during some phase of the disturbance, exposure to the specific phobic stimulus (or stimuli) almost invariably provokes an immediate anxiety response; (3) the object or situation is avoided, or endured with intense anxiety; (4) the fear or the avoiding behavior significantly interferes with the person's normal routine or with usual social activities or relationships with others or there is marked distress about having the fear; (5) the person recognizes that his/her fear is excessive or unreasonable; (6) the phobic stimulus is unrelated to the content of the obsessions of obsessive compulsive disorder or the trauma of post-traumatic stress disorder.

OBSESSIVE COMPULSIVE DISORDER

The essential feature of this disorder is recurrent obsessions or compulsions sufficiently severe to cause marked distress, to be time-consuming, or to interfere significantly with the person's normal routine, occupational functioning, or usual social activities or relationships with others (APA, 1987, p. 245). Obsessive compulsive disorder was classified under the anxiety disorders and with the anxiety states with the rationale that even though the predominant symptoms are obsessions or compulsions rather than anxiety itself, anxiety is almost invariably experienced if the individual attempts to resist the obsessions or compulsions. In addition, most patients with the disorder also experience considerable anxiety apart from the obsessions and compulsions. Obsessions and compulsions secondary to panic and agoraphobia are often readily amenable to treatment; obsessions and compulsions characteristic of obsessive compulsive disorder are far more refractory to change. The phenomenology, course, and treatment of obsessive compulsive disorder differs substantially from the other anxiety disorders.

Although we will not discuss the treatment of obsessive compulsive disorder, it is important to differentiate between patients meeting this diagnostic criteria and other anxiety disorders. For instance we have found that about 3 to 5 percent of patients who wish to participate in our anxiety disorder studies meet the DSM-III-R criteria for obsessive compulsive disorder. By DSM-III-R definition, obsessions are "persistent ideas, thoughts, impulses, or images that are experienced, at least initially, as intrusive and senseless. . . . The person attempts to ignore or suppress such thoughts or impulses or to neutralize them with some thought or action" (APA, 1987, p. 245). Compulsions are repetitive, purposeful and intentional behaviors that are performed according to certain rules, or in a stereotyped fashion (APA, 1987). The behavior is not an end in itself, but is designed to produce or prevent some future event or situation. However, either the activity is not connected in a realistic way with what it is designed to produce or prevent, or it may be clearly excessive. The act is performed with a sense of subjective compulsion coupled with a desire to resist the compulsion (at least initially). The individual generally recognizes the senselessness of the behavior and does not derive pleasure from carrying out the activity, although it provides a release of tension (APA, 1987).

POST-TRAUMATIC STRESS DISORDER

The essential feature of this disorder "is the development of characteristic symptoms following a psychologically distressing event that is outside the range of usual human experience" (APA, 1987, p. 247). The characteristic symptoms involve reexperiencing the traumatic event; numbing of responsiveness to, or reduced involvement with, the external world; and a variety of autonomic, dysphoric, or cognitive symptoms. Symptoms of depression and anxiety are common, (APA, 1987).

The most common traumatic stressors involve serious threat to one's life, physical well-being, significant others, or property. The trauma may be directly experienced or observed, occur alone, or with others. The specific criteria, condensed from DSM-III-R (APA, 1987) can be seen in Table 3.4.

GENERALIZED ANXIETY DISORDER

The essential feature is generalized, persistent anxiety or worry about two or more life circumstances of at least six month's duration. Although the specific manifestations of the anxiety vary from individual to individual, generally there are signs of motor tension, auto-

TABLE 3.4

Post-Traumatic Stress Disorder

A. The person has been exposed to a traumatic situation
B. The traumatic event is persistently reexperienced in at least one of these ways:
   (1) recurrent and intrusive recollections
   (2) recurrent and distressing dreams of the event
   (3) sudden acting or feeling as if the traumatic event were recurring
   (4) intense psychological distress at exposure to events that resemble the traumatic event
C. Persistent avoidance of stimuli associated with the trauma, or general numbing of responsiveness as indicated by at least three of the following:
   (1) efforts to avoid thoughts, or feelings associated with the trauma
   (2) efforts to avoid activities or situations that arouse recollections of the trauma
   (3) inability to recall an important aspect of the trauma
   (4) marked diminished interest in significant activities
   (5) feeling of detachment or estrangement from others
   (6) restricted range of affect
   (7) sense of foreshortened future
D. Persistent symptoms of increased arousal (not present before the trauma), as indicated by at least two of the following:
   (1) difficulty falling or staying asleep
   (2) irritability or outbursts of anger
   (3) difficulty concentrating
   (4) hypervigilance
   (5) exaggerated startle response
   (6) physiologic reactivity upon exposure to events that symbolize or resemble an aspect of the trauma
E. Duration of the disturbance (symptoms in B,C, and D) for at least one month

---

SOURCE: Reprinted with permission from the *Diagnostic and Statistical Manual of Mental Disorders, Third Edition, Revised.* Copyright 1987 American Psychiatric Association.

nomic hyperactivity, apprehensive expectation, and vigilance and scanning (APA, 1987). The specific criteria are as shown in Table 3.5.

OTHER DSM-III-R ANXIETY DIAGNOSES

There are several other DSM-III-R categories relevant to anxiety. When the individual appears to have an anxiety disorder that does not meet the criteria for any of the above anxiety disorders it may be

TABLE 3.5

Generalized Anxiety Disorder Diagnostic Criteria

A. Unrealistic or excessive anxiety and worry about two or more life circumstances
B. If another disorder is present, the focus of the anxiety and worry is unrelated to it (e.g., embarrassment in public in social phobia)
C. The disturbance does not occur only during the course of mood disorder or a psychotic disorder
D. At least 6 of the following 18 symptoms are often present when anxious
   Motor Tension
   (1) trembling, twitching, or feeling shaky
   (2) muscle tension, aches, or soreness
   (3) restlessness
   (4) easy fatigability
   Autonomic hyperactivity
   (5) Shortness of breath or smothering sensations
   (6) palpitations or accelerated heart rate
   (7) sweating, or cold clammy hands
   (8) dry mouth
   (9) dizziness or lightheadedness
   (10) nausea, diarrhea, or other abdominal distress
   (11) flushes (hot flashes) or chills
   (12) frequent urination
   (13) trouble swallowing or "lump in throat"
   Vigilance and scanning
   (14) feeling keyed up or on edge
   (15) exaggerated startle response
   (16) difficulty concentrating or "mind going blank" because of anxiety
   (17) trouble falling or staying asleep
   (18) irritability
E. Not due to an organic disorder

SOURCE: Reprinted with permission from the *Diagnostic and Statistical Manual of Mental Disorders, Third Edition, Revised.* Copyright 1987 American Psychiatric Association.

considered an *anxiety disorder not otherwise specified.* If the individual does not have a mental disorder but does have symptoms such as nervousness, worry, and jitteriness, she or he may meet the criteria for *adjustment disorder with anxious mood.* To meet the criteria for this disorder, the reaction must be to an identifiable psychosocial stressor(s) that occurs within three months of the onset of the reaction. Furthermore, the reaction must be "maladaptive" in that the patient experiences impairment in social or occupational functioning and/or symptoms that are in excess of a normal and expectable reaction to the stressor.

ANXIETY STATES, TENSION, AND STRESS

In clinical practice there are many patients who seek relief from anxiety but do not meet any of the above diagnoses. We know that over 80 million prescriptions for antianxiety agents are written each year in the U.S., and that 10–15 percent of the American population takes an antianxiety agent each year. How many of these patients meet the diagnostic criteria for any of the anxiety disorders? While we are unable to answer this question, we do know that most people taking antianxiety agents complain of symptoms of stress/tension or of life change/crisis and experience concomitant medical symptoms (Uhlenhuth et al., 1983). These patients can be classified in DSM-III-R as a *phase of life* or *life circumstance problem*, but this only seems to state the obvious. Our Flowchart for Clinical Diagnosis, which appears below, is designed to assist the clinician to make the appropriate DSM-III-R diagnosis and direct treatment towards the many patients who may not fit neatly into these categories.

OTHER DIAGNOSTIC SYSTEMS

The Europeans have taken a slightly different approach to the classification of anxiety disorders. The main European classification system is the International Classification of Diseases (ICD). ICD is not a true nomenclature in that it has a limited number of categories that are not systematically ordered. ICD does not use operational rules but describes the classification for purposes of making the diagnosis. The classification of anxiety in ICD-9 can be seen in Table 3.6. Anxiety states are defined in ICD-9 as "various combinations of physical and medical manifestations of anxiety, not attributable to real danger and occurring either in attacks or as a persisting state." The anxiety is usually diffuse and may extend to panic. Other neurotic features such as obsessional or hysterical symptoms may be present but do not dominate the clinical picture" (Jablensky, 1985, p. 755). Presumably, there will be some reconciliation between ICD-10 and DSM-IV when they are published in the future.

FLOWCHART FOR CLINICAL DIAGNOSIS

Figure 3.2 presents a flowchart for evaluating patients. We have developed the flowchart to help the clinician arrive at the best clinical

TABLE 3.6

The Classification of Anxiety in ICD-9

300 Neurotic Disorders
    300.0 Anxiety States
        300.00 Anxiety state, unspecified
        300.01 Panic Disorder
        300.02 Generalized anxiety disorder
        300.09 Other
    300.2 Phobic disorders
        300.20 Phobia, unspecified
        300.21 Agoraphobia with panic attacks
        300.22 Agoraphobia without panic attacks
        300.23 Social phobia
        300.29 Other isolated or simple phobias
    300.3 Obsessive-compulsive disorders
308 Acute reaction to stress
    308.0 Predominant disturbance of emotions
    308.1 Predominant disturbance of consciousness
    308.2 Predominant psychomotor disturbance
    308.3 Other acute reactions to stress
    308.4 Mixed disorders as reaction to stress
    308.9 Unspecified acute reaction to stress
309 Adjustment reaction
    309.2 With predominant disturbance of other emotions
        309.24 Adjustment reaction with anxious mood

focus or DSM-III-R diagnosis, if appropriate. The decision points are indicated by the shaded gray ovals. The response to each of the 10 questions leads to a different clinical diagnosis and a different treatment focus. Once these questions are answered, the disorder is classified as one of the anxiety disorders and/or some other psychiatric problem. We favor making a primary diagnosis that reflects the dominant clinical problem and secondary diagnoses as needed to indicate other problems. Although many of the shaded ovals include only DSM-III-R diagnoses, a good number of patients will come close to meeting the strict criteria but not do so entirely. The clinical focus still should be on the major clinical problem associated with the DSM-III-R diagnosis. For instance, a patient may come close to meeting the DSM-III-R criteria for panic disorder but may have too few panic attack episodes to qualify for that diagnosis. The focus of treatment should still be on the panic attacks if they are disabling.

The Flowchart for Clinical Diagnosis begins with the emotion of anxiety, although the presenting complaint of the patient may be panic attacks, avoidance, obsessions, compulsions, or other symptoms or behaviors. There are ten questions the clinician needs to

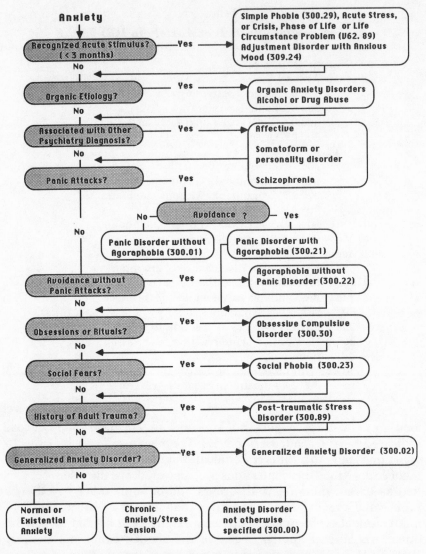

Figure 3.2. Flowchart for Clinical Diagnosis

answer to arrive at the right diagnosis. Those ten questions are indicated by the shaded ovals in the flow chart.

Question 1. *Is the anxiety acute (less than 3 months) and caused by a recognizable stimulus?*

If there is a recognized stimulus for the anxiety and an acute response (arbitrarily considered to be a response occurring within three months) the patient is usually experiencing an acute stress reaction, life crisis, or, in DSM-III-R terminology, a *phase of life* or *life circumstance problem*. Some patients with recent onset of panic attacks may see a psychotherapist early in the course of their disorder, but this is rare, as most consult a medical specialist first. Also, occasionally, patients with a simple phobia may seek therapy when their symptoms have been exacerbated by exposure to the frightening situation or situations.

Acute stresses, crises, and other such problems of living are common presenting problems to psychotherapists. Having an acute problem does not preclude having a chronic anxiety disorder, so inquiry should continue once the nature of the acute problem is determined. In the following case, Julie is an example of a person with acute tension and anxiety symptoms caused by conflict at work.

Julie, a 50-year-old married, mid-level manager in a large retail firm presented with complaints of nervousness, headaches, and trouble sleeping, which began when she was asked to transfer out of state because her position was being terminated. She refused to transfer. She was initially threatened with being laid off but was then offered another position in the same plant. However, the new position provided lower pay and less autonomy. She accepted the local job but soon developed the presenting symptoms. She decided she was under stress and took a leave of absence. Answers to all the subsequent questions in the flowchart were negative. She was diagnosed as having a life circumstance problem and therapy was directed at helping her to examine the impact of this job change on her life.

Question 2. *Is there an organic etiology for the anxiety?*

A variety of medical problems may cause symptoms indistinguishable from anxiety. Anxiety-like symptoms caused by medical problems are classified as organic anxiety syndromes. Table 3.7 lists symptoms of anxiety that might indicate the associated medical problem. Characteristics of the medical symptoms that may be used to differentiate them from the anxiety symptoms are also listed in the table, but a physical examination and laboratory tests are often necessary to rule out the medical diagnosis. In theory, if the anxiety-like symptoms are caused by the medical problem, then they should resolve when the medical problem is adequately treated.

The following case is an example of a patient whose panic attacks were caused by a medical problem (Carlson, 1986).

A 49-year-old postmenopausal woman had suffered from generalized anxiety for approximately 30 years. Her symptoms consisted of anxiety with inability to relax, trembling, sweating, apprehensiveness, worry, insomnia, and occasional depression. She had no history of panic attacks. In the course of psychotherapy her symptoms suddenly increased in intensity and frequency. There were no apparent precipitating stresses, conflicts, or medication withdrawals. She claimed that the symptoms felt worse than before, that the anxiety was constant, and that she developed panic attacks once or twice daily. Suddenly, she developed severe chest pain, and was diagnosed as having two spontaneous rib fractures. Further she was found to have marked osteoporosis (loss of bone density). Her serum calcium level was 7.2 mg/dL (normal 8.5 to 10.5 mg/dL). On correction of her hypocalcemia and the addition of estrogens, her mental and physical status improved. She had no

TABLE 3.7

Differential Diagnosis: Symptoms of Anxiety and of Medical Disorders

Acute Anxiety Symptom	Possible Medical Condition	Characteristic of Medical Symptom
Shortness of breath, smothering sensations	Congestive heart failure	Rapid, shallow breathing, worse on lying down
	Pneumonia, pleuritis	Fever, cough
	Asthma	Wheezing on expiration, cough
	Chronic obstructive pulmonary disease	Chronic cough history of smoking, yellow sputum
Dizziness, unsteady feelings, or faintness	Orthostatic hypotension, anemia	Worse upon standing up
	Benign positional vertigo	Triggered by rotation of head, jogging, stopping
Palpitations or accelerated heart rate	Paroxysmal atrial or supraventricular tachycardia	Sudden onset of rapid heart rate; rate > 120 bpm
	Mitral-valve prolapse	Systolic click or late systolic murmur
	Ventricular ectopic beats	Feeling of the heart flopping or turning over
	Tumors of the adrenal medula	Episodes of hypertension with tachycardia developing rapidly
	Thyrotoxicosis, hyperthyroidism	Fine tremor, excessive sweating, heat intolerance
	Hypoglycemia	Symptoms 2–4 hours after a meal
Sweating, flushes, or chills	Menopause	Female sex, appropriate age
Nausea or abdominal distress	Innumerable	

(continued)

TABLE 3.7 (*Continued*)

Acute Anxiety Symptom	Possible Medical Condition	Characteristic of Medical Symptom
Depersonalization or derealization	Temporal lobe epilepsy	Perceptual distortions, hallucinations
Numbness or tingling	Hyperventilation	Rapid, shallow breathing
Chest pain or discomfort	Angina pectoris	Precipitated by physical exercise, emotions, sex, or heavy meals
	Myocardial infarction	Severe pressing, constricting chest pain and pain radiating into left arm
	Costal chondritis	Tender spots in costochondral junctions
	Pleuritis, pneumonia	Fever

further panic attacks or exacerbation of her anxiety, although she continued to have the level of anxiety that preceded the panic attacks.

The clues to the organic nature of this patient's anxiety were the sudden appearance of the panic attacks and the exacerbation of the anxiety. However, the therapist was apparently not compelled to seek a medical explanation for these changes until the patient developed rib fractures.

More often than not, however, the medical problem accompanies the anxiety. Medical conditions associated with anxiety/panic include cardiovascular problems like mitral valve prolapse, cardiac arrhythmias, and angina pectoris; endocrine problems like hyper- and hypothyroidism, hyper- and hypoparathyroidism, pheochromocytoma, idiopathic postprandial hypoglycemia; neurological problems like vestibular abnormalities, and seizures; and respiratory problems like asthma and hyperventilation. These medical problems are discussed in chapter 12. We recommend that clinicians err on the side of caution and recommend that their patients receive a medical work-up for suspicious symptoms. Keep in mind that anxiety disorder patients often overuse the medical system and caution must be taken to make the appropriate diagnosis while avoiding or minimizing unnecessary tests. Chapter 12 presents a detailed discussion of the medical conditions that may cause anxiety-like symptoms and/or often accompany anxiety. The medical screening form we use can be found in Appendix 1.

Medication and Drugs. Many medications and drugs may also cause, exacerbate, or maintain symptoms of acute anxiety. The common ones include aspirin, anticholinergic drugs, steroids, sympathomimetics, cocaine, amphetamines, and hallucinogens. Alcohol, caffeine, and nicotine can cause anxiety and, paradoxically, are used to relieve anxiety symptoms. We have found that about 25 percent of our patients abuse alcohol. Frequently such patients report that the alcohol makes them feel much less anxious immediately, but that as the alcohol wears off, their anxiety increases. Nicotine may have a biphasic effect in which initial arousal is followed by tension/relaxation. Thus, high levels of nicotine may cause sufficient arousal to make patients feel very anxious. Caffeine also increases arousal and at high enough levels, or in sensitive individuals, may cause anxiety even though many people take it to relax. Illicit drugs may also be used to relieve anxiety; although in our experience, they are more commonly a cause of anxiety. About 15 percent of our patients report that their anxiety attacks started after they had begun to use cocaine, amphetamines, or marijuana (less common).

Withdrawal from any of the sedative-hypnotic drugs, from alcohol, and from narcotics is commonly associated with anxiety. It has been hypothesized that one reason that anxious patients abuse drugs and alcohol is to compensate for the withdrawal effects that occur when the drug or alcohol levels decrease. A careful drug and alcohol history is necessary for all patients. Such a history and other clinical information may lead to a formal DSM-III-R diagnosis of alcohol or substance abuse.

Because patients with medical diseases may present with anxiety and panic, and many panic patients have coexisting medical diseases that interact with the anxiety, it is important to have most patients undergo a complete history and physical. We feel that the basic examination should include a hematocrit, hemoglobin and CBC, serum electrolytes, cholesterol, urinalysis, and resting ECG. Other tests might be indicated if the history and physical or basic examination indicates other problems.

Question 3. *Is the anxiety secondary to some other psychiatric disorder?*

After organic etiologies have been evaluated, it is then appropriate to determine if the patient has some other psychiatric disorder besides anxiety. Affective disorders (depression and/or mania), substance abuse, somatoform and character disorders are often associated with anxiety symptoms and may need to be the focus of treatment. Depersonalization and schizophrenia are less common problems.

Depression. The relationship between depression and agoraphobia, panic disorder, and generalized anxiety disorder is complicated. First, the methods used to assess depression contain items that are also used to assess anxiety. For instance, the Hamilton Depression Inventory, (Hamilton, 1960) the standard clinical interview for rating depression, uses items that also require ratings of cognitive and somatic symptoms of anxiety. Second, apart from problems of measurement, depression is often associated with anxiety disorders. In Uhde et al.'s (1985) sample of patients with panic attacks, 50 percent had some incidence of depression during their lifetime. Although the symptoms were quite severe, only 24 percent had depressive episodes lasting longer than the 2 weeks duration required by DSM-III-R for major depression. Sanderson, Rapee, & Barlow (1987) studied additional diagnoses among anxiety disorder and affective disorders cases. Major affective disorders and dysthymic disorders (combined) occurred in 17 percent of agoraphobics, 4 percent of social phobics, and 5 percent of panic disorder patients. Of patients who received a diagnosis of major affective disorder, 8 percent received a secondary diagnosis of some type of anxiety disorder.

These studies indicate that anxiety and depression are frequently associated and that depression needs to be evaluated in anxiety disorder patients. The clinician should bear in mind the following two points when evaluating depression in anxiety disorder patients: First, in order to plan appropriate treatment it is important to determine whether the patient meets the DSM-III-R or clinical diagnosis for an affective disorder. Second, because most anxiety disorder patients are depressed, it is important to quantify the extent of their depression and monitor its course during treatment. Major depressive disorders are the most common type of affective disorders in patients with anxiety symptoms. Depressed patients report dysphoric mood or loss of interest or pleasure in all or almost all usual activities and pastimes. Four or more of the following symptoms are usually present on most days: poor appetite or significant weight loss; insomnia or hypersomnia; psychomotor agitation or retardation; loss of interest or pleasure in usual activities, or decrease in sexual drive; loss of energy or fatigue; feelings of worthlessness, self-reproach, or guilt; complaints or evidence of diminished ability to think or concentrate; recurrent thoughts of suicide.

Somatoform Disorders. As anxiety is defined by somatic and cognitive symptoms, it is sometimes difficult to distinguish between patients with DSM-III-R somatoform disorders and anxiety. The two types of somatoform disorders most likely to present with panic-like symptoms are somatization disorder and hypochondriasis. Somatization disorder is distinguished from the anxiety disorders by its course, number of symptoms, and phenomenology. The main feature of somatization disorder is a history of physical symptoms of several years' duration, beginning before the age of 30. To meet the DSM-III-R criteria, patients must complain of at least 12 symptoms in four different body systems, to have sought medical evaluation and treatment of these symptoms without a medical explanation being uncovered. At any one time, these patients usually have at least one or two symptoms that dominate the clinical picture and are present night and day.

Hypochondriasis is more difficult to diagnose and in our experience, is rare in the absence of a major affective disturbance. The predominant disturbance is an unrealistic interpretation of physical signs or sensations as abnormal, leading to preoccupation with the fear, or belief, of having a serious disease. Thorough physical evaluation does not support the diagnosis of any physical disorder that can account for the physical signs or sensations and the unrealistic fear or belief of having a disease persists despite medical reassurance and causes impairment in social or occupational functioning.

Many panic disorder patients meet these criteria. Patients with anxiety disorders readily report somatic symptoms. For instance, during a CO_2 inhalation, anxiety disorder patients and normals were asked to rate the intensity of a long list of symptoms, some of which, like increased twitching, are not caused by the procedure. Panic patients reported many more symptoms than normals and indicated experiencing intense symptoms that were unrelated to the induced physiologic changes (Margraf et al., submitted). However, compared to patients with somatoform disorders, most panic patients have symptom-free episodes and times when they are not bothered by somatic symptoms. Pilowsky (1967) has developed an instrument that addresses patients' perceptions of their illness. The instrument has been shown to be effective in identifying patients with hypochondriasis. However, the final differentiation between anxiety disorders and hypochondriasis is a clinical one.

Personality Disorders. The relationship of anxiety, particularly chronic anxiety, to personality disorders has preoccupied many researchers. One tradition holds that the absence of an ability to experience anxiety is typical of the antisocial personality. The characteristics of some disorders like the paranoid personality disorder include symptoms of sustained arousal, hypervigilance, and inability to relax. In an attempt to determine the frequency of personality disorders in patients with anxiety disorders, Mavissakalian and Hamann (1986) gave a personality questionnaire to 60 agoraphobic patients. Twenty-seven percent of the sample met a personality disorder diagnosis, with avoidant and dependent personalities the most common. We have found that about 25 percent of our patients meet a DSM-III-R, Axis II personality disorder diagnosis, with avoidant and dependent traits also most common. These two studies would suggest that personality disorders occur infrequently in anxious patients.

Although patients who meet the DSM-III-R criteria for anxiety disorders rarely have personality disorders, patients with some types of personality disorders often experience symptoms of anxiety and panic. A recent study found that 50–60 percent of patients with multiple personality reported having panic attacks (Putnam et al., 1986). Most multiple personality patients have a history of childhood physical and sexual abuse. Panic attacks are, in fact, common among patients who report childhood physical and sexual abuse. Most patients with borderline personality disturbances also have panic attacks. In clinical cases dominated by personality disturbances and anxiety, the focus of treatment needs to be on the personality disorder.

In our clinical experience, the most difficult patients to work with, and those who are often our treatment failures, meet DSM-III-R criteria for one of three types of personality disorder: borderline personality disorder, antisocial personality, and histrionic personality. The treatment approach for anxiety that we favor involves a sustained effort and commitment that is often difficult for patients with personality disorders to achieve. Even so, rather than exclude patients who appear to meet a criterion for a personality disorder on the initial interview, we use this information as a warning to proceed carefully with therapy, watching for signs of noncompliance, drug and alcohol abuse, and poor cooperation.

Drug and Alcohol Abuse. Drug and alcohol abuse must be identified and treated as primary problems in patients with anxiety disorders. We first treat alcohol or drug problems, or refer patients to specialists in this area, before addressing the issue of anxiety. The inability of a patient to stop using drugs or alcohol does not preclude treatment with antianxiety agents, particularly if the patient appears to be using alcohol to reduce social anxiety, but he or she must be able to demonstrate the ability to control the use of these substances. We rarely prescribe benzodiazepines to patients who have not been able to stop other drugs and alcohol if asked to do so. The issues that need to be considered before prescribing some classes of antianxiety drugs in patients with drug and alcohol abuse are discussed in later chapters.

Other Psychiatric Problems may occasionally present with symptoms of anxiety, although the differential diagnosis is usually not difficult. Of course, anxiety and panic attacks are common in many psychiatric disorders and may be the focus of treatment. For instance, anxiety is a major problem for most schizophrenic patients.

Question 4. *Does the patient have panic attacks, and, if so, how frequent are they?*

Once organic and associated psychiatric diagnoses have been evaluated, the next step is to determine whether panic attacks are present. The criteria for panic attacks were given previously under "panic disorder." Keep in mind that many patients who do not meet the strict DSM-III-R criteria for panic disorder have experienced distressing panic attacks and can be classified on clinical grounds as having panic disorder. If the patient also presents avoidance he meets the criteria for panic disorder with agoraphobia, described earlier. We next take up the question of assessing avoidance.

Question 5. *How Avoidant Is the Patient?*

Assessing the presence and extent of avoidance is somewhat problematic, particularly for patients who must work or take transportation despite dread of doing so. They may appear to have little restriction, when in fact they live with frequent dread. Four self-report instruments are available to assess avoidance: the Mobility Inventory (Chambless et al., 1985), the Phobic Avoidance Inventory (Telch, 1985), (see Appendix 2), the Stanford Agoraphobia Severity Scale (Telch, 1985), and the Fear Inventory (Marks & Mathews, 1979). Of these, the latter two are easiest to use.

The Stanford Agoraphobia Severity Scale asks patients to report the extent of anxiety they have when undertaking each of 10 tasks. The tasks include shopping alone, being alone at home for two days, and using public transportation. Patients circle one of five numbers for each task, where 0 designates "can do without anxiety" and 4 indicates "cannot do under any circumstances." We define agoraphobia as being present when patients report a rating of 2 (can do with severe anxiety) on two or more tasks.

The Mobility Inventory asks patients to rate their degree of avoidance in a variety of situations (e.g., theaters, supermarkets, restaurants) when accompanied and when alone. The Phobic Avoidance Inventory asks patients about their ability to carry out a more general activity, alone or with someone else. The 16 activities include "being alone," "riding an elevator," "being in a large coffee shop." Each activity has from 5 to 10 stages of difficulty. For instance, the stages for the activity "going up to high places" ranges from 1, "walk up to the second floor and look over the railing at the ground for 1 minute" to 10, "walk up to the 12th floor and look over the railing at the ground for 1 minute." Although the Fear Inventory asks patients to rate the extent of their fear relative to 12 items, the extent of their fear is also related to avoidance. Any of these four instruments, together with the clinical interview, is helpful in determining the extent of the patient's avoidance. (See Appendixes 1 and 2.)

Question 6. *Does the patient engage in avoidance without having panic attacks?*

If the patient does not suffer from panic attacks, the clinician must still determine how much, if any, avoidance is present. Patients with infrequent or symptom-limited panic attacks may meet the criteria for agoraphobia without panic disorder.

Question 7. *Does the patient have obsessions and compulsions?*

The next step is to determine whether the patient has obsessions and compulsions and, if so, if they meet the criteria for obsessive–compulsive disorder. A rare patient will have panic and/or avoidance and also meet the criteria for obsessive–compulsive disorder. However, many patients will report that they have obsessive thoughts and engage in subtle rituals only during panic attacks. Such patients should not be classified as having an obsessive–compulsive disorder.

Question 8. *Does the patient have social fears?*

Many patients with panic attacks fear that they will do something embarrassing in public situations. However patients with social phobia avoid public scrutiny, and the fear is not that they will have a panic attack in public places but that they will be viewed negatively or be the object of negative attention.

Question 9. *Is there a history of trauma as an adult?*

About 50 percent of patients with agoraphobia and panic disorder report that their problem followed a traumatic or stressful experience. Although helping patients cope with this trauma may be an important part of treatment, the trauma itself is not a dominant part of their symptomatology. The major factor motivating them to seek treatment is fear of recurrent panic attacks and among the agoraphobics, avoidance. This distinguishes these patients from those with post-traumatic stress disorder (PTSD), who remain preoccupied with the traumatic episode. In such cases, therapy must focus on helping patients cope with and integrate into their experience the traumatic event or events. PTSD is very rare occurring in less than 0.1% of the general population (Helzer, Robins, & McEvoy, 1987).

Question 10. *Does the patient have generalized anxiety disorder?*

As we note in chapter 6, it is unusual to encounter generalized anxiety disorder in patients without the presence of another anxiety disorder or other psychiatric disturbance. From a clinical standpoint, the treatment of symptoms of generalized anxiety disorder is the same whether or not the symptoms suggest a GAD diagnosis or are considered to represent a part of some other anxiety disorder, like panic disorder.

Many patients will not meet the criteria for any of the preceding diagnoses yet have apparent symptoms of anxiety. These patients can be classified as an adjustment disorder with anxious mood, an atypical anxiety disorder, or if a DSM-III-R diagnosis is not needed or appropriate, as having chronic anxiety/stress tension. Finally, we have added a category in the flowchart for normal or existential anxiety. This category applies to patients who are high functioning, able to cope with their anxiety, and who enter therapy for the primary purpose of trying to understand themselves.

SUMMARY

By following the systematic flowchart presented here, the clinician can reliably arrive at a clinical diagnosis. The chapters in the rest of the book are partly organized by the clinical diagnoses determined from the flowchart. After a general discussion of how we approach the patient, we discuss the treatment of patients who present with acute stress, crisis, phase of life, or life-circumstance problem (chapter 5), generalized anxiety symptoms and generalized anxiety disorder (chapter 6), panic attacks and panic disorder (chapter 7), panic attacks and panic disorder with agoraphobia and agoraphobia without panic disorder (chapter 8), social phobia (chapter 9), and simple phobia (chapter 10).

FOUR

. . . .

Approaching the Anxious Patient: An Overview of Symptom-Focused Treatment

. . . .

Our approach to therapy with patients presenting anxiety disorders is symptom-focused. By this we mean that we begin by intervening in ways designed to reduce the intensity and frequency of the patient's presenting symptoms. Once symptom relief has been achieved, we may change the format and address additional issues. As many therapists are ambivalent about or opposed to symptom-focused treatment we would like to begin this chapter by briefly attempting to persuade the reader of our point of view, if he or she does not already share it.

BEGINNING THERAPY WITH THE ANXIOUS PATIENT: FOCUS ON ENHANCING DAY-TO-DAY FUNCTIONING

One dimension on which different approaches to psychotherapy may be distinguished is the degree of specificity of treatment goals. In general, psychodynamic approaches proceed with somewhat diffuse or general goals, while behavioral, cognitive, and pharmacological treatments are more specific in their foci. Specific and nonspecific therapies, which have often seen themselves in competition with one another—witness the sometimes acrimonious exchanges between behaviorally oriented clinicians and their dynamic counterparts—have dissimilar goals. Each approach offers something different to the patient. To oversimplify a bit, psychodynamic therapy primarily offers insight, self-awareness, and general growth and development, while behavioral and other forms of brief, symptom-focused treatment concentrate on helping the patient achieve palpable relief from certain specific complaints. There is some overlapping among the different approaches to be sure: psychodynamic therapists are not uninterested in symptom relief, and behavior therapists are not averse to promoting insight and personal growth. Their emphases, however, differ.

As these approaches to psychotherapy differ in the degree of specificity of their goals, patients also differ along this dimension. Patients at present consult therapists for an endless variety of reasons ranging from such complaints as insomnia and inability to quit smoking, to sexual problems, difficulties resolving marital and family conflict, depression, difficulties achieving intimacy, grief over the loss of a loved one, and existential concerns regarding the lack of purpose and meaning in life. The degree of specificity in the presenting complaint largely determines what the patient expects from treatment. Most insomniacs who apply for therapy simply want to sleep better; they are unlikely to engage in treatment offering growth, development, and enhanced self-understanding. On the other hand, individuals who seek treatment because they are unhappily ambivalent regarding intimacy, or lack purpose and meaning in life, are more likely to embrace a treatment geared toward enhanced self-awareness and to reject efforts to reframe the goals of treatment in highly specific behavioral terms, such as disclosing a particular number of personal facts to a member of the opposite sex or engaging in more frequent charitable activities.

As Bordin (1979) has pointed out, the therapeutic alliance (Greenson, 1965, 1967; Weiner, 1975; Zetzel, 1958) consists not only of the degree of emotional connectedness between therapist and patient and their mutual involvement in the procedures of treatment; it is also a function of the degree of agreement between therapist and patient regarding the therapeutic goals. Part of creating a workable collaborative therapeutic alliance is the ability to design a treatment that appears to address the patient's immediate concerns. Whatever the therapist's skill level, and regardless of the presence of important personal qualities such as the ability to communicate warmth, empathy, and understanding, therapy is unlikely to be successful if there is a mismatch between patient and therapist goals.

For the present discussion, the key issue is, What do patients presenting with anxiety disorders seem to want from therapy? Several authorities on psychodynamic treatment have noted that patients with phobic and other anxiety-related complaints are not receptive to such therapy, or that they do not respond well once engaged in psychodynamic psychotherapy. For example, Arieti (1978) noted that even when anxious patients become involved in psychodynamic treatment, results are disappointing. He noted that success with such patients requires that psychotherapy be supplemented by "gradual exposure of the patient to the dreaded situation, in the beginning while he is accompanied by the therapist" (p. 200). Several therapists identified with brief dynamic psychotherapy routinely exclude patients with severe phobic or obsessional symptoms (Malan, 1976; Strupp & Binder, 1984). In a discussion regarding the prospects of engaging anxious patients in psychodynamic psychotherapy, Wolberg (1967) noted that the "average patient with an anxiety reaction is so upset by his symptoms that relief from suffering constitutes his prime motivation. Because he feels helpless and frightened, he is apt to demand an authoritative, directive relationship in which he is protected and through which he obtains immediate symptomatic relief" (p. 949).

Our experience of patients with well-defined anxiety disorders is congruent with the above comments: such patients enter treatment seeking symptomatic relief. Consider, for example, the agoraphobic patient. In the most severe cases, all facets of the person's day-to-day life are compromised: work is problematic and often impossible because of the difficulty traveling far from, or even leaving, home; personal and family relationships are distorted by the demands imposed upon intimates to organize their lives to protect the agoraphobic from exposure to anxiety; mundane, everyday tasks such as grocery shopping are either delegated to others, or are undertaken only after careful planning to minimize "unsafe" features of the situation such as lines or traffic; and socializing and other recreational activities are severely curtailed or entirely avoided. Depression is common. While one can always cite cases in which the symptoms appear to be used interpersonally in a hostile or controlling way, many of these patients experience tremendous guilt over the burden they present to others. Their most pressing initial concerns involve the ability to perform day-to-day tasks: they would like to be able to grocery-shop independently, or travel more freely, or shop in a department store, or attend a movie, or return to work. And it is here that treatment must begin. Depending upon the therapist's theoretical persuasion, a number of related issues may appear ripe for intervention. However, patients are generally so focused upon their symptoms, and in many cases upon the limitations they experience in their everyday life, that therapy which does not appear geared toward relieving their immediate suffering lacks face validity and results in premature termination. Moreover, the means to help panic disorder and other anxious patients achieve substantial symptom reduction are readily available.

While most anxious patients applying for treatment seek symptomatic relief, some have a different agenda. For example, some patients come in for treatment announcing a problem with anxiety of one sort or another, but on further examination, the impact of the symptom on their everyday life and on the lives of those in their social network proves trivial. Often what they want to deal with is another problem such as a difficulty in establishing close relationships or ambivalence about a particular partner, but they seem to need to formulate a more disabling problem in order to justify the need for psychotherapy to themselves or to others. Some, who may have a well-defined anxiety disorder, enter treatment with an a priori bias against behavioral or symptom-focused treatment as "superficial" and seek a therapy that is focused on the promotion of insight and self-understanding. But for the vast majority of patients presenting with anxiety disorders, symptom relief is the most salient *initial* goal. This is also the case for most of those patients who present as being highly depressed as well as anxious. In most such cases, treatment geared toward reducing symptoms of anxiety also reduces depression. As treatment progresses, the goals sometimes change, and patients may choose to focus on additional issues. Such changes in goals, however, usually occur *after* attenuation of the presenting symptoms has been achieved.

Objections to symptom-focused treatment have frequently centered on the theme of symptom substitution. Proponents of this position argue that focusing on the presenting complaint without sufficient attention to underlying problems is likely to lead to superficial rather than lasting changes; relapse or outbreaks of fresh symptoms are likely to follow. While there have been occasional reports suggesting symptom substitution or recurrence (e.g., Blanchard & Hersen, 1976; Crisp, 1966; Lazarus, 1971; Montgomery & Crowder, 1972), as an argument against the use of behavioral and other symptom-focused measures, this position has a number of flaws. First, there are a considerable number of reports indicating generalized beneficial effects of symptom-focused approaches to treatment (see Bandura, 1969).

Second, even if one assumes that behavioral symptoms have their roots in unconscious conflict, they may become functionally autonomous (Freud, 1936; Sluzki, 1981), and be maintained by a variety of other factors. Stated differently, the processes that "cause" a problem and those that maintain the problem are likely to be distinct. As the etiological factors may no longer be significant at the time of treatment, symptoms may be relieved without fresh outbreaks. Third, when new problems do emerge after treatment, it is difficult to label them as new symptoms or symptom substitutes with any assurance. As we will discuss later, problems that may have been present all along may simply become more prominent once the problem occupying center stage has been removed. They may now be more amenable to treatment. And as Kazdin (1984) has noted, such problems may have emerged anyway, with or without treatment.

Finally, the argument in favor of symptom substitution fails to account for the reciprocal relationships among behavior, environmental feedback, and more enduring global attitudes. The relationship is assumed to be linear and one-way as though changes in attitudes affect behavior without the reverse being true. As Marmor (1980) pointed out, such a conceptualization incorrectly views personality as a closed system. An alternative conceptualization would assume that if an anxious patient who exhibits phobic avoidance can be helped initially to confront those situations that provoke anxiety, his sense of helplessness will be attenuated. In addition, as he begins to behave in a less helpless fashion, others in his relationship network are likely to come to treat him as though he is more competent, which will, in turn, enhance his self-perception.

Many traditionally trained dynamic therapists view symptom-focused treatment as counterproductive; such intervention is often viewed as an *impediment* to the more important goal of understanding and resolving underlying issues. We shall not here belabor the point made earlier that many anxious patients have goals for therapy that are far more circumscribed than those of their therapists and are simply not candidates for longer term insight-oriented therapy. Equally important however, is the generally unacknowledged point that symptom attenuation often *enhances* the patient's ability to explore productively issues usually taken up in a psychodynamic format. As we have noted, the level of impairment among many patients suffering from such anxiety disorders as panic disorder, agoraphobia, generalized anxiety disorder, and others renders the patient unable to focus on issues and concerns that he or she experiences at another level of abstraction. However, once the severity of the symptoms has subsided, the nature of the patient's concerns shifts and other issues frequently come into sharper focus.

Thus our approach to treatment begins by attempting to help the patient achieve symptom relief. Depending on the particular diagnosis, therapy will begin with a combination of education, cognitive therapy, exposure therapy if behavioral avoidance is an issue, and, in many cases, medication to control panic and facilitate exposure, as well as other measures. Detailed accounts of procedures will follow in succeeding chapters. For now, it is important to note that we make few assumptions at the outset of treatment regarding what may be necessary for a successful outcome beyond a commitment to work intensively to ameliorate the presenting symptoms. The course of treatment, at least in the earliest stages, is determined by the patient's responses to such intervention.

Sometimes initial therapeutic measures directed toward symptom relief fail. The group of patients in question are often referred to as "nonresponders." For example, among agoraphobics, the rate of nonresponders has been estimated at about 30 percent of those who accept treatment (Barlow, O'Brien, & Last, 1984). Therapists have few guidelines regarding how to respond to such patients or how to think about the next step. It is to these cases that we will now turn our attention. What we shall offer is a series of questions for the therapist to consider. The answers to these questions dictate the appropriate therapeutic response.

Question 1. *Has the patient carried out the tasks prescribed by the therapist?*

In most of the cases where intervention aimed at symptom relief fails, the patient does not carry out the therapeutic tasks, or homework assignments. There may be several reasons for this.

One hypothesis to consider is that the therapist has failed to instill hope within the patient that the tasks and procedures of treatment will result in a positive outcome. Obviously, patients are unlikely to engage in procedures, some of which may occasion considerable discomfort, if they are not persuaded that they have something important to gain. Thus, the therapist must be willing to persuade the patient that the prescribed measures will bring results. Depending upon the patient, this may require the therapist to be in the role of the "expert," whose experience and knowledge regarding the problem may be relied upon. In cases where patients are failing to carry out therapeutic tasks, we ask them to rate their belief verbally that the prescribed measures will bring results. The patients' responses inform us about the need to engage in further efforts to persuade them of the efficacy of the procedures, or indicate that we must look in another direction.

In some cases, the task goals may be unclear to the patient. Sometimes a patient has somewhat magical expectations that a particular task is going to "solve the problem" quickly and becomes discouraged when the expectations are not met. For example, in the case of exposure therapy for agoraphobia, which we will discuss in chapter 8, patients must understand that the tasks involved are designed to help them "cope with anxiety," rather than eliminate it. Those who understand the function of exposure in terms of anxiety reduction rather than coping enhancement are likely to lose faith in the procedures if their level of anxiety is not reduced as quickly as anticipated.

The failure to use medication properly can sometimes interfere with task completion. The correlation between anxiety and depression is high, and in some cases, depression may be sufficiently severe to interfere with the patient's capacity to engage in a task-oriented therapy. Even where depression is not the issue, it is important to remember that patients have very different levels of tolerance for anxiety symptoms. For some patients, a performance-based treatment requiring them to experience the full force of their anxiety is simply too uncomfortable. This is particularly an issue when in vivo exposure therapy is a major focus of treatment. We use medication in cases where, in order to facilitate exposure, it is necessary to "take the edge" off some of the symptoms. Just as many psychiatrists never receive training in the administration of exposure therapy and so confine their treatment of anxious patients to pharmacotherapy, many psychologists and social workers trained to conduct exposure therapy are negatively disposed toward the use of medication and do not seek a medical consultation for patients who are failing to carry out therapeutic tasks because the symptoms are too distressing. Further, even when it is employed, medication is often improperly or inadequately applied. That is, the dosage is often too small to reduce the symptoms or it is so great that the anxious symptoms temporarily disappear, and the patient fails to learn to cope more effectively with them should they arise. Guidelines regarding the adequate administration of medication are discussed extensively in succeeding chapters.

Another hypothesis to consider when patients fail to complete therapeutic tasks is that there may be secondary gain issues amplifying ambivalence about symptom reduction. Marital or family issues are a frequent source of such ambivalence. Additional, and less frequently encountered, sources of secondary gain include the possibility that the patient is on disability of one sort or another that would have to be relinquished, or is involved in litigation that would be adversely affected if the symptoms diminished.

Question 2. *Has there been a misdiagnosis?*

In those cases where the patient has engaged in treatment and carried out the therapeutic tasks without benefit, the therapist should consider the possibility that there is an error in diagnosis. As we noted in chapter 3, anxiety symptoms are sometimes secondary to a personality disorder. Patients with severe characterological disturbances, such as borderline personality disorders, may carry out the tasks of therapy with minimal or no improvement in their symptoms. Patients with such disturbances may also fail to carry out the therapeutic tasks. Symptom-focused treatment of anxiety disorders is of only minimal benefit to many patients with such personality disorders.

Question 3. *Is the therapist proceeding with incomplete information?*

Occasionally patients will fail to respond to symptom-focused treatment when the therapist lacks critical information in treatment planning. For example, alcohol abuse is often a factor, particularly in cases of panic disorder with agoraphobia and social phobia. In some cases the extent of the substance abuse is not disclosed to the therapist in the initial evaluation. When this occurs, the patient will either fail to carry out the tasks as prescribed or will carry them out while inebriated and derive little benefit. Patients with substance abuse problems should be referred for appropriate treatment before focusing therapy on an anxiety disorder.

PATIENT RESPONSES TO SUCCESSFUL ATTEMPTS TO ACHIEVE SYMPTOM RELIEF

Our reading of the research literature together with our experience in treating individuals presenting with phobic and other anxiety disorders has led us to advocate an approach to therapy that begins with specific measures designed to facilitate symptom relief. However, we do not regard focused behavioral, cognitive, and pharmacologic intervention as incompatible with other treatment measures that might be indicated at a later time. For some, symptomatic relief marks the end of treatment, while for others it signals entry into other forms of psychotherapy. Predicting a patient's response to successful symptomatic treatment is difficult at the inception of therapy. In general, we have observed the following patterns: (1) the patient decides to leave treatment although we believe there are additional issues that might be fruitfully addressed in continuing therapy; (2) symptom relief results in improvement in a number of areas of the person's life and both we and the patient concur that termination is appropriate; (3) decreases in symptomatology have less than pervasive effects upon the person's overall functioning, but we mutually agree on the appropriateness of ending treatment; and (4) additional issues achieve greater prominence and the focus of therapy shifts as the patient elects to continue treatment to address these issues. We will consider these outcomes in a bit more detail.

In the first of these outcomes, the patient decides to leave treatment once his initial symptoms have subsided, though we believe other problems merit additional therapy. In most such cases, while the patient's day-to-day functioning improves, global patterns of dependency or helplessness are only minimally affected, and interpersonal relationships remain static. The person continues to relate to others as a symptomatic individual.

Often, however, such patients leave treatment with considerably more insight than when they arrived. As many writers before us have pointed out, insight not only precedes changes in behavior, it may also may be produced by such changes. We have found that many patients who make limited behavioral changes and then elect to stop treatment may take with them an increased awareness about their motives and often experience their symptomatic patterns as voluntary rather than involuntary.

For example, one elderly agoraphobic patient, Mrs. H., with a 40-year history of avoidances of various kinds, made considerable progress in her ability to travel freely and comfortably over a 6-month period. After years of being housebound, she was able to visit her children and grandchildren who lived nearby, take a course at a local college, attend church, and shop in department stores, all without a companion. At one point, she and the therapist agreed that the next task was for her to drive to a nearby city by herself to visit a relative. Like most other activities involving travel, this was something that she had always done with her husband. At this point, progress stopped. For several weeks, she would arrive for her sessions not having done the task, offering a variety of explanations involving inconvenience, but it quickly became clear that there were other issues involved.

When her reluctance to take the next step was explored, it became evident that this particular task had considerable symbolic significance for her: to be able to travel to the specified city unaccompanied signified autonomy and a shift from being a symptomatic individual to a healthy one. Such a shift would change the nature of her relationship not only with her husband, but with her entire family and social network. Cognitive themes associated with her resistance were explored, and what emerged was the patient's recognition of how successfully she was able to "control" the behavior of others, particularly her husband, with her symptomatic behavior, and that at this point in her life she was unwilling to give up these secondary benefits. The therapist's offer to initiate marital therapy at this point was declined, and the patient elected to stop treatment. While in this case, the changes as a result of therapy were not as extensive as the therapist might have hoped, the patient was functioning with far less impairment and with a greater sense of responsibility for her own behavior. A follow-up nine months later revealed the patient functioning at approximately the same level as at the end of treatment and feeling pleased about her ability to lead a richer life. She had not sought further therapy.

Such cases are somewhat disappointing to the therapist; after all, our work is always more gratifying the more profoundly people's lives change as a result of their therapy. However, from the patient's perspective, the goals of treatment had been met. Patients obviously differ in their ability, readiness, and willingness to make fundamental changes in their life. Anxious patients often suffer a level of impairment that is extremely debilitating, and the therapist should be prepared and willing to help them alleviate that suffering, or to refer them to someone else who is equipped to do so. Put differently, one cannot effectively treat anxious patients by imposing upon them the expectation of broad-based, fundamental changes in their character and ways of relating to others. The therapist ought to be prepared to help patients make those changes that they are ready and willing to make.

The second pattern of response to symptom relief is one in which changes in the target symptom are accompanied by positive changes in a number of other areas, and both we and the patient agree that further treatment is not warranted. Not surprisingly, many anxious patients suffer from concomitant depression, low self-esteem, and a variety of interpersonal difficulties. Symptom remittance frequently occasions changes in all of these areas.

Family therapists, using the family as the unit of analysis, have borrowed a number of concepts from systems theory (e.g., von Bertalanffy, 1950, 1967) and cybernetics (e.g., Wiener, 1948) in order to better comprehend the nature of relationships among intimates. Among these concepts is that of wholeness, which states that in any system, changes in one part or aspect necessarily occasion changes in other parts, and in the system as a whole (cf. Watzlawick, Beavin, & Jackson, 1967). Put differently, one cannot affect one part of a system without affecting all the other parts. While this concept has been invoked to point out that changes in one family member's behavior will inevitably lead to changes in the others (e.g., Jackson, 1957; Minuchin, 1974; Haley, 1963, 1980), the same principle applies at the level of the individual: changes in one part of the system (e.g., behavior) are likely to affect self-perception, affect, and ways of processing information, as well as transactional patterns. It is not surprising therefore that changes in an aspect of the person as important as symptomatic behavior frequently bring significant positive changes in the person's overall functioning. Indeed, a recent long-term follow-up study of agoraphobics who underwent short-term exposure in vivo combined with panic management revealed that along with highly significant changes in avoidance, patients demonstrated considerably less depression and reduced somatic complaints (Hand, Angenendt, Fischer, & Wilke, 1986).

In the third response to symptom relief that we have encountered, the effects on the person's general level of functioning are less pervasive. This occurs most frequently in cases of simple phobias, such as spider or injection phobias, or cases of relatively uncomplicated and limited social phobias, where the impact of the problem itself upon the patient's functioning is limited. In such cases, the relationship between the presenting complaint and such issues as self-esteem, levels of depression, and interpersonal relating are very limited, and symptomatic relief will have little impact on these areas. Psychotherapists are consulted for a broad range of problems; some are more complicated than others. If the anxiety disorders were arranged on a continuum from the least to the most complicated, such phobias as those mentioned above would occupy the least complicated end. As such, they respond best to simple, focused intervention (see chapters 9 and 10). We have treated many patients with such problems who have consulted therapists who either have engaged them in insight-oriented psychotherapy, in which the symptom is not directly addressed, or who have attempted to engage them in such treatment. In most of these cases, the patient left therapy with the symptom unchanged and with a cynical view of our field.

The fourth outcome we have observed is one in which changes in symptomatic behavior bring into sharper focus additional psychological issues, and the patient elects to stay in treatment to address them. Such problems may be intrapersonal, or transactional (e.g., marital). As we mentioned earlier, patient responses to symptom attenuation or removal are difficult to predict. For some, general positive changes render the continuation of treatment unnecessary. But for others, additional issues are brought into bolder relief.

One patient, for example, Mrs. K, 41 years old, came to us with a four-year history of panic attacks without behavioral avoidance. She was married and had one child. At the time of the initial consultation, symptoms of panic, which included palpitations, sweatiness, chest pain, dizziness, nausea, and fears of death and insanity were a daily occurrence. Despite numerous reassurances from her family physician and other professionals that her symptoms were not indicative of life-threatening illness, she continued to be fearful of impending death during panic episodes and was seen frequently at local emergency rooms.

Mrs. K had consulted two psychologists prior to being seen at our clinic, and each had attempted to engage her in insight-oriented psychotherapy. In each case, she experienced treatment as "irrelevant," and "off the track." She complained that neither therapist was willing to discuss her symptoms with her, and that each insisted on focusing on issues regarding her family history, difficulties with assertion, and feelings about her marriage. In each case, therapy was terminated within six weeks.

She described her parents as very supportive and loving, but when she talked about her interaction with them it was clear that they were extremely demanding, with a very rigid sense of right and wrong. The family had clear and definite rules regarding virtually all areas of behavior—what church to attend and how often, what kind of car one should and shouldn't drive, what kind of furniture one should have in one's house, when was a proper time to go to bed, how a dinner table was to be set, what color the napkins should be, and so on. Virtually all behavior was evaluated in terms of its "rightness" or "wrongness"; individual preferences were discouraged. Mrs. K was the clear favorite among the three siblings in her family. Her parents, who were both deceased by the time we first saw her, were moderately wealthy and were more generous with her than her siblings. Her father was prone to seek out her advice on business matters after she became an adult, while in subtle ways impugning the competence and "level-headedness" of his other children. Not surprisingly, her status as the favored child had been achieved through careful and rigid adherence to all the various rules promulgated by the family.

Mrs. K was somewhat envious of her siblings, who had been "rebellious" as children but seemed to her to have developed a sense of adventure and to enjoy life considerably more than she. She was outwardly compliant with the wishes of her family—she had married the "right person," went to a church of which her family approved, had her house decorated in the correct fashion, belonged to social organizations they approved of—but went through life with a sense of alienation and detachment. Not surprisingly, her compliant stance was manifested in her marriage. Her husband, a corporate executive, travelled approximately six months per year and tended to work late during the time he was at home. While she indicated that she sometimes felt "overwhelmed" with the responsibility that this arrangement placed upon her, it was not an issue in their marriage; it had never occurred to her that she might give voice to her misgivings.

From our perspective, while Mrs. K's previous therapists may have identified a set of issues that were relevant and important, their inability or unwillingness to address her presenting problems doomed the treatment. Mrs. K was completely preoccupied with her symptoms, wanted relief, and felt frustrated that the therapists she had seen, while she experienced them as caring, were not addressing her concerns. When it became apparent that treatment would not be helpful in diminishing the frequency of panic episodes, she dismissed the relevance of the issues identified by the therapists and left treatment in search of symptomatic relief.

The course of therapy with Mrs. K illustrates some of the advantages of a symptom-focused approach to treatment. Therapy began with a combination of information, cognitive therapy, and medication, combined with several other brief measures (see chapter 7) designed to alleviate her panic. A psychiatrist from our team was responsible for managing her medication, while a psychologist saw her for psychotherapy. Within four months the frequency of panic attacks decreased dramatically; over the last two of these months she experienced only two. Moreover, the degree of anticipatory anxiety had subsided to a point where she no longer feared the onset of panic. At this point she asked to continue in treatment to address some of the issues alluded to above. She noted that for the past four years she had been "totally preoccupied" with her symptoms of panic. During that time she had turned 40, and now, with the symptoms of panic under control, she wanted to reevaluate her way of approaching interpersonal relationships. At this point, the focus of therapy changed to a more dynamic, insight-oriented format, in which the focus of exploration was Mrs. K's compliant stance, and the various rewards and consequences involved. Considerable time was spent addressing her compliance as it manifested itself in the transference, including her overenthusiasm for the therapist's interpretations and her beliefs that she would be abandoned and the therapy relationship terminated if she failed to please the therapist and meet the expectations she imagined he had for her.

Treatment continued for a total of 28 months, during which time Mrs. K initiated a considerable number of changes, beyond acquiring the ability to cope effectively with panic attacks. In the area of her marriage, she became considerably more assertive, persuading her husband to travel considerably less and spend more time with her and their child. Her compliance and lack of assertiveness had been accompanied by distancing and detachment, and she reported feeling considerably closer to her husband by the end of treatment. She reported similar changes in the social domain, altering her style of relating with various friends. She also had been been very active as an officer in various social organizations—a task she found "tedious"—and decided to drop out of them. In general, Mrs. K was able to use the therapy to become more conscious of her own preferences and to make choices regarding her activities and social relationships on that basis. During the course of treatment, Mrs. K became considerably more assertive, and reported losing the general sense of

bemused detachment that formerly had characterized her relationships and activities and were a direct outgrowth of her compliant
posture.

In our estimation, our willingness and ability to provide effective
symptom-focused treatment at the outset enabled us to reach a point
later on where Mrs. K became available for more dynamically
focused treatment. The achievement of symptom relief enhanced
Mrs. K's beliefs in the efficacy of treatment, helping her to take the
risks involved in confronting a set of issues that may have been more
difficult to address than the initial symptoms of panic.

THERAPIST BEHAVIOR

Broadly speaking, our approach to the treatment of patients presenting with anxiety disorders involves an intensive effort at the beginning of treatment toward effecting a reduction in the presenting
symptoms, followed, if necessary, by additional therapeutic intervention directed toward any additional problems that may have become
prominent. We consider ourselves eclectic rather than predomi-
nantly behavioral, psychodynamic, cognitive, or pharmacologic in
our approach to treatment. What informs our intervention at any
point during the therapy are the particular goals we are working
with. When treating patients who elect to stay in treatment beyond
the point of symptom reduction, there are often shifts in therapist
behavior depending upon the particular problems being addressed.
For example, when working with the agoraphobic patient, the early
phases of treatment will involve formulating performance-based
tasks designed to help the patient confront situations they have been
avoiding; cognitive therapy aimed at changing catastrophic thinking
patterns; instructions for controlled breathing; and other approaches
(see chapter 8). If, after becoming more mobile the patient elects to
continue in treatment to address issues such as those presented above
by Mrs. K, the need for various instructions, monitoring of exposure
tasks, and attention to catastrophic thinking patterns will have considerably diminished. At this point, the emphasis may shift to interpretation and examination of interpersonal issues. However, we
wish to point out that it is a shift of emphasis we are describing
rather than a complete about-face. We feel free even in the earliest
stage of treatment, when the goals are most focused on symptom
management and relief, to employ interpretation and to focus on the
patient's way of interacting interpersonally with the therapist,
should that be relevant to treatment. Similarly, during later stages of
treatment, when psychodynamic issues are being addressed, we may

spend five or ten minutes during each session on instruction or refor-
mulation of any tasks the patient may still be engaging in. With that
said, it is possible to articulate, in general terms, some of the characteristics of our approach to treatment.

1. *An active, directive stance.* Symptom-focused therapies of all
   kinds require that the therapist be willing to be active and directive. When working with anxiety patients, the therapist must be
   willing to assign a variety of self-monitoring tasks, engage in
   problem solving, deliver instructions designed to enhance the
   ability to cope with anxiety, instruct the patient regarding appropriate tasks that constitute intermediate steps toward meeting the ultimate goals of treatment, point out cognitive distortions that may be problem-maintaining, and other such
   behaviors.
2. *Warmth, empathy, and understanding.* Little needs to be said
   here. We regard this as a necessary, though not sufficient, condition for a productive therapeutic relationship.
3. *Sensitivity to, and willingness to deal with interpersonal issues as
   they manifest themselves in treatment.* One unfortunate by-prod-
   uct of therapists affiliating with one "school" or another is the
   tendency to become somewhat one-dimensional. Those with a
   behavioral or cognitive-behavioral orientation are likely to be
   strong in the application of certain techniques but somewhat
   lacking in sensitivity to interpersonal dynamics, while those
   with a psychodynamic orientation tend to be highly sensitive to
   transference and other interpersonal issues and weak, by design,
   in the application of certain useful therapeutic approaches. We
   feel it is important at all stages of treatment, including the initial ones, that the therapist be alert to—and willing to take up—
   interpersonal issues as they emerge in treatment. For example,
   one particular agoraphobic patient of ours dealt with the demands of others in an outwardly compliant way, but when uncomfortable or unhappy with such demands found ways to sabo-
   tage them passively. The way this emerged in the therapy was
   that when the patient felt the therapist did not understand the
   severity of her problem and was "pushing" too hard for her to
   complete certain tasks on her own, she would agree to carry out
   the tasks and then "not find the time." The therapist's ability to
   understand this pattern in terms of the patient's general way of
   relating to the demands of others and to discuss it in a straightforward way with her, rather than "problem solving" at that
   point with the goal of finding ways for her to organize her time
   differently, allowed the therapy to move forward. We agree with

Wachtel's (1977) position on this issue: One can learn a great deal about how patients relate to others in the course of being directive, and discussing the patient's responses to the directives can be extremely fruitful. It is not necessary to maintain a position of neutrality in order to generate such material.

4. *Generating positive expectancies.* As we will note in several of the succeeding chapters, many of the therapeutic procedures that are most helpful for reducing anxiety symptoms require a considerable commitment from the patient and willingness to engage in activities that often evoke fear. Patients will be unwilling to undertake such actions if the therapist is unable to generate expectations that the discomfort involved will ultimately bring benefit.

5. *Pragmatism and flexibility.* While we have described a way to conceptualize treatment with the anxiety-disordered patient, we find that we often have to deviate from our plan. Though our model of treatment suggests, for example, intensively addressing the presenting complaint at the outset of therapy, this is not possible or desirable in all cases. Patients may present with crises in midstream that require the therapist to shift the focus of attention. We regard the availability of a plan—that is, a structure for treatment—that guides the therapist and the patient as necessary for a good outcome with anxiety patients. However, one cannot allow the treatment structure to become an albatross that prevents the therapist from responding to the patient's current situation.

Issues in Multidisciplinary Treatment

The approach we advocate for the treatment of anxiety disorders requires a multidisciplinary team. The necessity of providing medication, as well as evaluating the possibility of medical problems, makes the psychiatrist an indispensable part of treatment. However, it is impractical for psychiatrists to provide all aspects of therapy. In our clinic, psychologists and psychiatrists share responsibility for treatment.

It is important that the members of such a team be mindful of several issues. Some of these have been pointed out earlier (Chiles, Carlin, & Beitman, 1984). First, the patient must have an adequate explanation for the necessity of treatment by two therapists. For example, when treating agoraphobics, we emphasize that medication can provide some relief from symptoms of panic but that, by itself, medication is usually insufficient for changing avoidance patterns.

We note that exposure therapy, attention to thinking patterns, and certain other measures are necessary ingredients of the treatment and that a psychologist from our staff will provide such treatment. Second, the patient must be made aware that the contract for confidentiality is among the three involved parties; that is, the therapists will be in contact with one another and will be discussing issues relevant to the patient's treatment. Third, it is important that the areas of responsibility of both therapists be clearly spelled out. To return to the example of the agoraphobic patient, we make clear to the patient that the psychiatrist is responsible for monitoring the patient's medication, and the psychologist is responsible for all other aspects of treatment. Thus, if there is a problem regarding side effects or other concerns related to the medication, these are to be taken up with the psychiatrist. Of course, any questions related to the patient's medical condition, such as whether a given symptom may be indicative of a medical problem, should also be referred to the psychiatrist. All other issues should be addressed to the psychologist treating the patient. Clarity regarding the lines of responsibility are important for both the patient and therapists. The patient knows where to address particular questions and issues, and the therapists are less likely to overlap and give the patient conflicting advice.

Finally, the therapists must be mindful not to be drawn into a coalition, whether subtle or open, with the patient against one of the other therapists. While splitting is not unusually common among anxiety disorder patients, relatively few of whom display personality disorders (see chapter 3), it certainly can occur. Thus, if a patient brings up a problem or complaint regarding Therapist A, Therapist B, to whom the patient has addressed the problem should encourage the patient to discuss the issue with Therapist A.

ASSESSMENT

Quantification of patient problems is no small task. Surveys show that even behavior therapists, whose commitment to measurement is well established, find assessment difficult in clinical practice (Wade, Baker, & Hartmann, 1979) due to constraints of time and expense, lack of cooperation from patients, and unavailability or lack of feasibility of appropriate assessment methods. Despite the difficulties involved, we recommend that the clinician working with the anxious patient perform an assessment no less than once every three to four months. There are several reasons for this. First, assessment can help direct therapy. Sometimes gains are smaller than they appear to the therapist, and assessment will serve as a cue to alter procedures. At other times, positive changes may not be reflected in patients' global reports, and assessment instruments will inform both the therapist and the patient of discrepancies between actual changes and reported estimations. Second, there is an increasing demand for accountability from third party payers, peers, funding agencies, and even patients to substantiate treatment gains. Third, assessment facilitates comparison of the effectiveness of treatments; without such scrutiny, we will have considerable difficulty developing more effective therapy.

Table 4.1 lists the instruments used for screening and initial quantification of anxiety symptoms. Those reproduced in Appendix 1 are indicated with an asterisk. Alternatives are indicated with a double asterisk.

The assessment battery should include one measure from each of the above domains. That is, in addition to the clinical interview, there should be one measure assessing general anxiety, and additional instruments measuring fear and avoidance, depression, somatization, the frequency of panic attacks, and an assessment of disability. In subsequent chapters, we discuss instruments that can be used to assess aspects of specific anxiety disorders in more detail.

SUMMARY

We have outlined in general terms the characteristics and assumptions of our approach to treating the patient presenting with an anx-

TABLE 4.1

Basic Anxiety Assessment Battery

Component	Instrument
Diagnosis	Clinical Interview
	Brief Medical History*
General Anxiety Level	Trait Anxiety Inventory (Spielberger, 1983)**
Fear and Avoidance	Fear Inventory (Marks & Mathews, 1979)*
Depression	One of these:
	Zung (1965)
	Beck (Beck et al., 1961)
	Hamilton (1960)
Somatization	Somatization Scale (Pilowsky, 1967)*
Panic attacks	Stanford Panic Attack Frequency Form*
Disability	Modified Disability Scale (Sheehan, 1983)*

iety disorder. The treatment model we propose begins with the simplest, most direct interventions available to achieve symptomatic relief. The therapy is organized around the patient's progress. As a set of goals is achieved, treatment is either terminated, or the therapeutic emphasis shifts to another area. We have delineated some common responses to such treatment, and a set of questions for the therapist confronted with a patient who is unresponsive to symptom-focused measures. In addition to its cost-effectiveness, we believe that our approach is flexible and responsive both to patients' willingness to engage in treatment and to the often shifting nature of their paramount concerns.

While some patients elect to stay in treatment beyond the point where their presenting symptoms have been reduced or have remitted, it is beyond the scope of our current effort to describe the long-term treatment of the anxious patient. We will concentrate instead in the succeeding chapters on describing in detail the major anxiety disorders, their assessment, and how to intervene effectively to bring about symptomatic relief.

FIVE

. . . .

Acute Anxiety/Tension Disorders

. . . .

Acute anxiety, fear, and tension are common problems. We all experience these emotions when threatened or upset. Sometimes we can identify the cause of the distress and consider it fear. At other times, we are not aware of what is causing the problem. When anxiety, fear, and tension become uncomfortable or unbearable and a person seeks medical, psychological, or pharmacologic relief to reduce the distress, we consider it to be clinical anxiety. For such people presenting for treatment, it is appropriate to use the flowchart for clinical diagnosis (Figure 3.1).

In this chapter we consider the patient who presents with *acute* anxiety or crisis and wants relief. The presenting symptoms may be associated with a troubled marriage, disturbed interpersonal relationships, difficulty at work, or a myriad of other problems. Although short-term pharmacotherapy may be needed, the focus of therapy is to resolve the precipitating difficulty. Resolution of the precipitating problem usually results in significant reduction in anxiety. In contrast, patients with the kinds of anxiety disorder discussed in the following three chapters, have more intense, sustained, and long-lasting symptoms of anxiety. They may also have problematic marriages, or difficulties with other family and interpersonal relationships, or with sex, work, or self-image, but the anxiety seems to persist independent of the vicissitudes of these stressors, which are often easier to deal with once the patient has symptomatic relief.

The main symptomology of patients with acute anxiety was reviewed in the first chapter. The patient feels anxious, tense, nervous; he is preoccupied and worried and ruminates about some, perhaps, indefinable problem; he may appear worried, with a furrowed brow or tense muscles; he may sweat excessively and have trouble sleeping and concentrating. In many cases, the symptomology of acute anxiety disorders differs from chronic problems (such as generalized anxiety disorder) only in length and in having an apparent cause. It is usually not possible to determine when an acute problem will become chronic, but most acute anxiety and tension disorders resolve within six months. These patients do not have frequent panic attacks, avoidance, obsessive rituals, or social fears, and the anxiety is not due to organic problems or trauma. The remainder of this chapter will focus on the treatment of acute crises.

Patients presenting with acute anxiety/tension can be diagnosed under DSM-III-R criteria as having an adjustment disorder with anxious mood, if they appear to have a reaction to an identifiable psychosocial stressor(s) that occurs within three months of the onset of the stressors, psychosocial impairment, and predominant symptoms such as nervousness, worry, and jitteriness. Impairment and symptoms must be in excess of a "normal and expectable reaction to the stressor(s)" (APA, 1987, p. 330) a qualification that is difficult to make. Patients can be diagnosed under DSM-III-R as having a phase of life problem or other life circumstance problem if they are not impaired in social or occupational functioning or do not have symptoms that appear in excess of a normal and expectable reaction to the stressor.

There are three therapeutic approaches to resolving symptoms associated with acute anxiety/tension: crisis management, brief psychotherapy, and pharmacotherapy. Crisis management is a short-term process designed to help people resolve acute problems or return to their normal level of functioning through the use of personal, social, and environmental resources. The goal is to restore equilibrium, and the assumption is that the person has adequate methods and resources for coping, with some outside support. Crisis management is appropriate for individuals who have suddenly lost their ability to deal with with a life situation. Short-term or brief psychotherapy is also focused on removing specific symptoms through support, insight, and the acquisition of new skills and coping methods. Pharmacotherapy should be used only if the patient is severely impaired by the symptoms and only for a brief period.

CRISIS MANAGEMENT

The main goals of crisis management are (1) symptom reduction, (2) prevention of immediate adverse consequences of the crisis, and (3) prevention of long-term adverse consequences of the crisis.

The origin of crises fall into two broad categories: situational and transitional states (Hoff, 1984). Situational crises originate from (1) material or environmental problems (such as a fire or natural disaster), (2) personal or physical problems such as diagnosis of a fatal illness or a heart attack, or (3) interpersonal or social problems (i.e., separation from or death of a loved one). Transitional crises originate from (1) life-cycle or normal transitions related to human development, and (2) a shift in social status. From another perspective, Hansell (1976) notes that crises develop when any of the "basic attachments" are at risk of being lost and an individual's normal coping responses are not adequate to ensure their continuance. Hansell defines these seven "basic attachments":

1. Food, oxygen, and other physical supplies necessary to life
2. A strong sense of self-identity
3. At least one other person in a close, mutually supportive relationship
4. At least one group that accepts us as a member
5. One or more roles in which we feel self-respect and which we can perform with dignity
6. Financial and material security
7. A comprehensive system of meaning or a set of values

The Course of a Crisis

The course of the crisis is related in part to its origins. Catastrophic events like being raped, learning of a terminal illness, or losing a child may lead to the post-traumatic stress syndrome, characterized by recurrent and intrusive distressing recollections of the event, avoidance of stimuli associated with the trauma, or a general numbing of responsiveness. The course of less severe stressors—and even a seemingly minor stress may affect some people with the same consequences as a catastrophic event—can be conceptualized as following four stages as described by Caplan (1964).

Stage One

A traumatic event causes an initial rise in anxiety and associated phenomena. The individual attempts to cope with the traumatic event. If successful, the anxiety is lessened and a crisis is averted. For instance, a 42-year old man, John, suffers a heart attack. Following a brief hospitalization, and three weeks after the original heart attack, he is healthy enough to undergo a treadmill exercise test. His physician advises him that he has suffered an "uncomplicated heart attack" and that he may return to work when he wants to. However, his physician has found that John is hypertensive and has a high serum cholesterol level. Furthermore, he smokes. He has begun to experience anginal pain. He is told that he will need to take medication to reduce his blood pressure, alter his eating patterns to reduce his serum cholesterol level, and stop smoking. Although John is very upset at having had a heart attack and at the need to take medication (perhaps for the rest of his life), he is relieved that he can return to work and that he will be able to resume his former activities. He begins to take the medication as prescribed, adopts a low-fat, low-salt diet, and returns to work.

Stage Two

The individual's usual coping mechanisms fail, and the event causing the initial rise in anxiety and tension continues. The continued stress and the failure to cope lead to greater stress. Let's assume that rather than taking his medication and altering his life-style, John continues to smoke, feeling it to be the only way to reduce his anxiety. His blood pressure remains elevated, and he continues to have a very high serum cholesterol level. Furthermore, he fails to return to work.

Stage Three

Anxiety and tension continue to increase. The increased anxiety and tension and the consequences of the traumatic event place increasing demands on the individual's coping resources. At this point, the individual may "rally" internal, family, and social resources to resolve the impending crisis. John could alter his life-style, take his medication, and return to work. After some acute discomfort, these acts might help John by making him feel better, reducing his risk of a subsequent heart attack and improving his financial situation.

Stage Four

This is the state of active crisis, which results when internal strength and social support fail or are lacking; the person's problem remains unresolved, and anxiety and tension become unbearable. People cannot tolerate a crisis state for long. There are several possible outcomes:

Return to Precrisis State. Overcome with anxiety and tension, John decides to change his life-style. He enlists the support of his wife to help him stop smoking. He contacts his boss and arranges for an immediate return to work. He returns to his physician for reanalysis of his risk factor and health status and follows his physician's recommendations. All of these acts eventually help him feel much better.

Personal Growth. John examines his values and behavior. He realizes that he is being self-destructive. He realizes that he lacks self-esteem and that he is waiting for someone to save him, miraculously. He also realizes that he is not satisfied in his work. He enters psychotherapy in an attempt to understand these issues, or he acts on the insight that he has developed from the crisis. In the short run, he returns to work for financial reasons but sets about redefining his job and expectations to create a more satisfying work and life experience.

Chronic Problems Develop. John begins to drink excessively to reduce his anxiety. His depression worsens. He experiences another heart attack.

Caplan's description of the hypothetical course for crisis intervention is helpful in determining the goals of therapy. The minimal goal of crisis intervention is to help an individual return to his precrisis state. At the same time, the crisis might be used to help the individual learn to become a more effective problem-solver and to become stronger in other ways as well. The therapist should be alert to signs and symptoms indicating possible negative or destructive outcomes.

STEPS IN CRISIS MANAGEMENT

The usual approach to crisis management follows these steps (Hoff, 1984):

1. psychosocial assessment of the individual or family in crisis
2. development of a plan with the person or family in crisis
3. implementation of the plan, drawing on personal, family, and social resources
4. follow-up of the plan

Step One: Assessment

The purpose of crisis assessment is to determine the extent of risk to self or others, to understand the origins of the crisis and how the individual has been coping with the crisis, and to assess the individual's biopsychosocial resources available to help resolve the crisis.

Is the patient suicidal? The therapist must assess the patient's suicidal risk. Although prediction of suicide is by no means an exact science, many studies have identified risk factors for suicide. In general, feelings of hopelessness and helplessness are associated with greater suicide risk. Older depressed males, particularly those with concurrent illness, are at high risk for successful completion of suicide. The suicide plan is an important risk factor. Risk of suicide is increased if the individual intends to use a relatively lethal method, has the means available, has specific plans and/or has taken steps in preparation for suicide (such as writing or changing a will, collecting pills, buying a gun, writing a suicide note, and setting a time and place for suicide). Agitation combined with depression increases the suicide risk. Alcoholics, homosexuals, substance abusers, and individuals with chronic terminal illnesses are all at high risk for suicide. Previous suicides, or suicides by family or friends are also risk factors. But any person in crisis should be considered at risk for suicide. In considering how to manage the suicide risk, the therapist must assess the patient's biopsychosocial resources, coping patterns, and history. Suicidal patients in crisis may need to be hospitalized.

Is the patient a danger to others? It is difficult but necessary to determine if the person in crisis is a danger to others. The risk factors for a person being dangerous to others include a current homicidal threat and plans, a history of homicidal threats, a history of assault, possession of lethal weapons or plans to obtain them, use and abuse of alcohol and drugs, conflicts in significant social relationships, threats of suicide following homicide, and uncontrollable, intense anger.

Is the patient able to make appropriate decisions and exert adequate self-care? People will often make rash decisions in crises that may have very adverse long-term consequences. For instance, faced with divorce, they may agree to inadequate financial and property settlements. The crisis may be so overwhelming that the individual may be unable to exert adequate self-care.

The assessment of the patient should also involve a careful history of the presenting situation or problem, the patient's employment, living situation, financial status, medical problems, medication use, habits, intimate relationships, coping mechanisms, and any other factors that would be helpful in planning crisis management.

Step Two: Developing an Intervention Plan

The crisis plan should be (1) developed with the person in crisis, (2) problem-oriented, (3) appropriate to the person's functional level and dependency needs, (4) consistent with a person's culture and life-

TABLE 5.1

Crisis Intervention Techniques

Exploring resources
Facilitating patient decision making
Suggesting new resources
Listening, accepting patient's feelings
Involving patient in the plan
Facilitating patient's decision making
Involvement of significant others
Reinforcing coping mechanisms
Active encouragement
Expression of empathy
Conveying realistic hope
Specific and concrete plan
Follow-up plan

style, (5) inclusive of a significant other(s) and a social network, (6) realistic, time-limited, and concrete, (7) dynamic and negotiable, and (8) include follow-up. Some experts in crisis management even develop a formal service contract between the patient and therapist. The general intervention techniques (Hoff, 1984) are listed in Table 5.1.

The specifics of the intervention plan depend on a variety of factors elicited and evaluated during the assessment. Also crises stemming from violence by others require a special approach with attention to moral, social-psychological, legal and medical issues (e.g., see chapter 8 in Hoff, 1984).

PREVENTION OF LONG-TERM EFFECTS OF STRESS

An important component of crisis management is to set the stage for the prevention of the long-term effects of acute stress or crisis. Factors that seem to determine the long-term impact of the stressful event include the nature of the stressor (length, intensity, and quality); the patient's past experience, that is, how he or she has previously managed stressful life events; the patient's perception of the event; the physiological reactions that occur; and the person's ability to cope with psychological and physiological reactions to the stress and subsequent illness behavior. Dohrenwend and Dohrenwend (1981) have identified six processes or models (summarized in Table 5.2) that indicate how stressful life events might lead to adverse health changes.

The first four mechanisms of stress listed in the table affect many individuals in crisis.

Victimization. Some stressful life events causing adverse health consequences may override any person's coping capabilities. For instance, extreme situations, such as combat, incarceration in a concentration camp, or psychological torture, and some severe stresses such as the unexpected death of a loved one, rape or violence—all situations over which an individual has little or no control—may directly cause adverse health changes, set in motion biological processes with pathophysiological consequences, or force changes in health habits that increase risk for morbidity and mortality.

Stress-strain. The psychophysiologic effects of stressors may produce adverse health effects. For instance, acute stressors cause the release of free fatty acids, among other physiologic effects. Repeated release of free fatty acids might increase cholesterol levels and increase the likelihood of atherosclerosis. Amelioration of the psychophysiologic symptoms should reduce the likelihood of adverse effects from the stress.

Vulnerability assumes that certain people are vulnerable to the effects of stress. Past history of vulnerability to stress suggests continuation of the same vulnerability to stress, other factors being similar. We have seen patients with panic disorder, for instance, who experience recurrence of panic symptoms only when they feel stressed. In these people stress always seems to produce recurrence of the panic symptoms. Effective and early coping with stress minimizes adverse consequences.

TABLE 5.2

Mechanisms of Stress Leading to Adverse Health Consequences

1. *Victimization.* Intense acute or chronic stress, uncontrollable by the individual, has direct adverse health effects.
2. *Stress-strain.* Psychophysiologic "strain" leads to adverse health effects.
3. *Vulnerability.* Preexisting personal dispositions and personal habits determine the effects of stress on the individual.
4. *Additive burden.* Social situations and personal dispositions have independent effects.
5. *Chronic burden.* Acute transitory stresses have no effect on health. Rather, social and personal dispositions are entirely responsible for adverse health effects.
6. *Event proneness.* Symptoms of adverse health predispose individuals to stressful life events, which lead to health consequences.

Additive burden assumes that social situations and personal dispositions make independent contributions to the effects of stress in an individual.

Factors Contributing to Stress and Illness

Most stress researchers endorse a "biopsychosocial model," in which biological, psychological, and social factors interact to precipitate, maintain, and exacerbate, as well as ameliorate illness. For a particular patient, it is important to identify the specific biological, psychological, and social factors contributing to his or her stress and illness. For instance, consider the case of Marshall B.

Marshall came to the clinic with acute anxiety and panic following an episode in which his wife of five years left him (after an argument over finances) and didn't return home for three days. Marshall remained in frequent contact with his wife during the brief separation, during which she went to live with her mother. He claimed that now, a month later, they had successfully resolved their financial disagreements and were getting along "better than ever." He had, however, begun to experience constant anxiety accompanied by occasional panic attacks. He also developed headaches that his internist diagnosed as being secondary to tension but also found that Marshall was hypertensive (155/100) and recommended a repeat measurement in a month and stress management in the meantime.

Marshall's blood pressure in our office was 150/90. The clinical interview revealed that Marshall had resolved the financial differences with his wife by deciding not to discuss the matter with her; still, he felt irritated by her and was now spending more time worrying about money. He was terrified that his wife would want a divorce if he made more demands on her. He was also unhappy in his job although he was resigned to it. He had an uncle who was hypertensive and his father had died of coronary heart disease at the age of 62. Because of the family history of hypertension and the blood pressure increase during this crisis, we reviewed his customary diet and other factors that might predispose Marshall to hypertension. He consumed a high salt diet, drank 2–3 ounces of alcohol per night, and was about 25 pounds overweight. As for stress, he felt under continual pressure at work and rarely felt relaxed, even at home.

During the second session Marshall realized that he was angrier with his wife than he had been willing to admit originally. He worried that he would continue to resent what he perceived as his wife's excessive spending. We recommended that he consider couples therapy to help improve their communication and resolve differences.

Marshall and his wife met for five sessions, agreed on how to manage the family finances, and reaffirmed their mutual commitment. At
the end of therapy Marshall's blood pressure had dropped to around
140/90, still slightly elevated. He was now committed to losing
weight by changing his diet and to having his blood pressure monitored every six months or so.

BRIEF PSYCHOTHERAPY

While crisis intervention focuses on resolving the crisis, brief psychotherapy focuses on the removal of specific symptoms and the prevention of other problems. We define brief psychotherapy as involving
fewer than 10–20 sessions. Other characteristics of brief psychotherapy include limited therapeutic goals, therapeutic content focusing on here-and-now issues, directive therapy, rapid assessment, an
interpersonal relationship that is quickly established (Butcher &
Koss, 1978). Although many types of brief psychotherapies have been
developed, they may be grouped into three categories: psychodynamic, behavioral, and supportive.

Brief Psychodynamic Psychotherapy

As opposed to patients presenting with more chronic anxiety disorders, discussed in chapters 6–10, those presenting with acute anxiety
are sometimes ideal candidates for brief psychodynamic treatment.
In recent years, numerous accounts of this approach have been elaborated (e.g., Mann, 1984; Sifneos, 1972; Strupp & Binder, 1984). We
shall focus on Bellak's (1984) description of his methods to illustrate.
Bellak (1984), a New York psychoanalyst, has been the leader in the
development of the principles of what he calls intensive brief and
emergency psychotherapy (BEP). BEP focuses on the crucial features
of the presenting disorder but attempts to understand the patient's
presenting problem by establishing the connections among the patient's history, the precipitating situation, and related biological, familial, and social aspects.

The initial interview focuses on the chief complaint, secondary
complaints, life and family history, review, and planning. An important goal of the first interview is to create a therapeutic alliance. This
is achieved in part by helping the patient gain at least an intellectual
understanding of his problem, thus decreasing feelings of helplessness and giving the patient the feeling that his problem can be
understood. Bellak encourages the therapist to help provide some

feeling of hope, mixed with realistic limitations. Another important goal of the first session is to create the therapeutic contract. The therapist expresses the hope that the patient will be able to deal with the problems in five sessions, each lasting approximately 50 minutes but assures the patient that further sessions may be scheduled if necessary. The therapist also encourages the patient to provide feedback to the therapist.

The second session is used to explore the patient's dynamics. The third session is used to review what has been learned. The therapist refers to the impending separation and the fact that the patient may feel worse during the next few visits because of fears of separation and abandonment. The fourth session is dedicated to understanding more about the patient's problems. The fifth and final session are used to review the treatment. The therapist addresses issues of termination. A sixth follow-up session is scheduled. Bellak notes that this process is not helpful for very disturbed patients.

Behavior Therapy

Classifying behavior therapy by the length of the treatment (i.e., into brief and long-term) is not meaningful as most behavior therapy lasts less than a year and often less than 10 sessions. Thus, the principles and practice of the various behavioral approaches discussed in the next chapters could be considered appropriate to brief psychotherapy. However, some therapists have described brief behavioral therapy for patients who present to physicians with acute distress that is combined with medical problems and request immediate relief. These are the anxious patients most likely to be prescribed benzodiazepines, or are medical patients with two or more upsetting health problems (Uhlenhuth et al., 1978). Such patients usually have anxiety and somatic symptoms, together with depressed mood, irritability, and insomnia. The condition has been referred to as a minor affective disorder or as distress (Gath & Catalan, 1986).

While medication is often indicated on a short-term basis, use of benzodiazepines should be avoided when nonpharmacologic therapies are likely to be as effective. Gath and Catalan (1986) have developed a technique for use by general practice physicians with acutely anxious patients instead of medication. Their brief psychotherapy procedure begins with assessment similar to that discussed above for crisis intervention. The therapist provides explanations, reassurance, and help with problem solving. The problem-solving process involves these steps: identification of problems, clarification of goals, clarification of steps to achieve these goals, agreement on the "therapeutic" agenda and review of progress. Gath and Catalan (1986) found that this brief counseling by general practitioners was as effective as anxiolytic medication and as welcomed by patients, and that it did not increase demands on doctors' time.

Supportive Therapy

Although most therapists consider themselves to be practicing supportive psychotherapy at one time or another, there is little consensus about how to define it. Werman (1984) defines supportive psychotherapy as a "form of treatment whose principal concern and focus is to strengthen mental functions that are acutely or chronically inadequate to cope with the demands of the external world and of the patient's inner psychological world" (p. 5). The therapist "supports" the patient's ego functions. Another way to define supportive therapy is to examine the activities of the therapist. When giving "support," the therapist is directive, noninterpretive, reassuring, comforting, and informative.

As Werman points out, supportive psychotherapy has traditionally held second-class status, considered as appropriate only for those incapable of benefiting from psychoanalytically oriented treatment, or as a palliative until the patient is ready to enter such therapy. However, despite the assumption that supportive psychotherapy fails to alter deeper psychological structures, there is substantial evidence that short-term supportive therapy can make a major difference in a person's self-concept, at least as measured by factors like self-efficacy (Bandura, 1986).

PHARMACOTHERAPY

The first decision that often must be considered in treating the patient with acute anxiety is whether to recommend using a drug. Most acute anxiety and tension episodes are self-limiting as the person adapts and copes, or remissions occur naturally. Drugs should only be used if the symptoms are so severe as to interfere with everyday personal, social, or occupational activities or are subjectively intolerable. Antianxiety drugs, if prescribed, should be used for as short a time as possible as the length of exposure increases the likelihood of dependence.

Although many drugs are effective for reducing anxiety, benzodiazepines (BZs) remain the drugs of choice for acute anxiety and tension (Greenblatt & Shader, 1974, 1978; Greenblatt et al., 1983).

Many controlled studies have shown that BZs are superior to placebos in reducing acute anxious symptoms. Many other studies have compared one BZ to another and the differences between the drugs have been marginal. If the patient is experiencing intense, sustained anxiety, a BZ with a longer half-life, such as diazepam or chlordiazepoxide (Librium) might be appropriate. Shorter acting compounds such as lorazepam can be used to reduce situation-related intense anxiety. Allow 30–60 minutes for lorazepam to have an effect. The pharmacology of the BZs is discussed in detail in chapter 11; issues of long-term BZ use are discussed in the next chapter.

The precautions for BZ use in crises are the same as for long-term use. Avoid BZs when the patient has a history of drug or alcohol abuse. Keep doses modest to prevent psychological impairment. Limit the amount of drugs prescribed to that required to the interval between visits. Usual therapy in a crisis should be 2–6 weeks followed by a reevaluation of the need for a drug. Warn patients that sedation may occur, especially early in treatment and immediately after each drug dose, and that interactions with alcohol and other depressants are frequent, major, and hazardous.

There are not many desirable psychopharmacologic alternatives to BZs for reducing anxiety associated with crises. A new agent, buspirone, appears to be an effective antianxiety agent; its usefulness is still being evaluated. Short and intermediate half-life barbiturates and drugs such as glutethimide (Doriden), ethcholovynol (Placidyl), meprobamate (Miltown, Deprol, Equagesic, Equanil, Pathibamate, PMB 200, SK-Bamate), or methyprylon (Noludar) should not be used for acute anxiety. Antipsychotic medications are also not appropriate for treating acute anxiety in nonpsychotic individuals because of the risk of serious long-term side-effects. MAO inhibitors and tricyclics also have no role in an acute crisis unless the patient is suffering from depression requiring pharmacologic treatment. If so, the patient must be carefully evaluated for suicidal tendencies and given nonlethal quantities of medication.

SUMMARY

Acute anxiety and tension disorders are common problems presenting to psychotherapists and medical physicians. The symptoms usually resolve with time, but crisis intervention, brief psychotherapy and/or pharmacotherapy may be needed if the patient's day-to-day functioning is sufficiently impaired. In addition to helping to relieve the immediate symptoms, the clinician should try to help prevent any chronic problems that might result from the symptoms or crisis.

Benzodiazepines are effective for reducing acute anxiety, but they must be used cautiously because of their abuse potential and side effects. A new drug, buspirone, appears promising as an antianxiety agent and does not have the abuse potential of the benzodiazepines, nor does it enhance the effects of alcohol, impair motor performance, or cause sedation. Further studies regarding its risks and benefits need to be carried out. Many of the therapeutic strategies used to treat chronic anxiety, the subject of the next chapter, are also appropriate for treating acute anxiety and stress.

SIX

· · · · · · · · ·

Chronic Anxiety and Generalized Anxiety Disorder

· · · · · · · · · ·

Chronic anxiety is characterized by constant, pervasive feelings of anxiousness and worry. As discussed in the previous chapter, from a cognitive, physiologic, and behavioral standpoint, chronic anxiety may be conceptualized on a continuum with "normal" anxiety; it is distinguished from the anxiety most of us occasionally experience by its intensity and persistence. In extreme form, chronic anxiety may meet the DSM-III-R diagnostic criteria for generalized anxiety disorder. The boundary between generalized anxiety disorder and panic disorder is somewhat arbitrary. Generalized anxiety is often a feature of panic disorder, although some patients with panic disorder have all the symptoms of generalized anxiety; conversely, patients with generalized anxiety disorder are likely to have at least infrequent panic attacks, perhaps occurring with only one or two symptoms. Patients with chronic anxiety score high on "neuroticism" on standard personality inventories. The neuroticism factor includes anxious, depressive, and somatic symptoms, low self-esteem and low self-confidence, and irritability.

Among patients presenting with generalized anxiety disorder, "cognitive aspects" of anxiety may dominate the clinical picture. Patients report that they are frequently preoccupied, worried, or ruminative; their preoccupations often concern events that are highly improbable. For instance, a wealthy patient may worry that he will become a pauper; an excellent college student may worry that he will fail his classes. When the content of the ruminations involves anticipated problems whose occurrence is more probable, the experience is more accurately described as anticipatory anxiety. An example of the latter is the patient who worries about having a panic attack prior to entering a situation in which he previously experienced one.

Hibbert (1984) analyzed the subjective quality of the most important anxious thoughts for anxiety disorder patients with and without panic attacks. When compared with those who did not suffer panic attacks, patients who did found their thoughts more clearly articulated, instrusive, credible, and difficult to exclude. Most patients who had experienced panic attacks reported a physical feeling as the most frequent precipitant to episodes of anxiety, whereas patients in the generalized anxiety disorder group reported an anxious thought or a change in mood as the trigger. These data suggest that generalized anxiety disorder patients may be less likely than patients with panic attacks to systematically misconstrue their somatic experiences as dangerous. On the other hand, many studies show high levels of somatization in patients with anxiety disorders, although many of these studies have not specifically stated whether or not panic attacks were an important cofactor for greater somatization.

Patients with generalized anxiety disorder also have a number of motor and autonomic symptoms characteristic of autonomic hyperactivity. Symptoms of motor tension include trembling, twitching or feeling shaky, muscle tension, aches or soreness, restlessness, and easy fatigability. Symptoms of autonomic hyperactivity include shortness of breath or smothering sensations; palpitations or accelerated heart rate; sweating or cold, clammy hands; dry mouth, dizziness or lightheadedness; nausea; diarrhea or other abdominal distress; flushes or chills; frequent urination; trouble swallowing or a lump in the throat. Patients may also report vigilance and scanning, including feeling keyed up or on edge, exaggerated startle response, difficulty concentrating, mind going blank, trouble falling or staying asleep, and irritability. The following case illustrates the clinical picture of one patient with chronic anxiety who also presented with agoraphobia:

Irene is a 36-year-old white female, married with four children who began to have anxiety symptoms three and a half years ago after moving with her husband from San Francisco to an isolated region of Idaho. Several months after moving, she returned to San Francisco for a few weeks and then went back to Idaho. As soon as she arrived back in Idaho she had an "asthma attack" and was treated for it. She felt isolated and began to feel depressed. She was then seen by another physician, who prescribed diazepam (Valium) and suggested that her husband take her home to San Francisco, which he agreed to do. Upon returning home she became progressively more anxious and avoidant.

A short course of exposure with a behavior therapist lessened her avoidance, but she remained anxious and depressed. She was experiencing one or two panic attacks each week, characterized by shortness of breath, palpitations, sweating, dizziness, diarrhea, numbness, and flushes. She reported that the symptoms arose spontaneously. In retrospect, she decided that her asthma attack was actually a panic attack. Medical examination was normal. She reported feeling anxious 80–90 percent of the time even when she was not having panic attacks. She reported worrying continuously about her children, her health, and the health of her children. On a scale from 0 to 10, with "10" being the highest anxiety and "0" being none, she rated her anxiety a 10 most of the time. She met all the DSM-III-R symptoms for generalized anxiety disorder, including increased muscle tension, apprehensive expectation, multiple symptoms of autonomic hyperactivity and vigilance and scanning.

The interviewer was impressed with her extreme, obvious nervousness evidenced by shaking, vigilance, and scanning. She had no simple or social phobias and no obsessive thoughts or ruminations. At the time of the initial interview, she did not feel depressed and had none of the somatic DSM-III-R symptoms of depression. However, she met the criteria for a past depressive episode. While the GAD symptoms did not dominate the clinical picture, it appears on her history that Irene remained very anxious even when she was not avoidant or having panic attacks. Treatment would involve addressing her avoidance, panic attacks, and her symptoms of generalized anxiety.

The following example involving a patient presenting pure generalized anxiety disorder is more rarely encountered:

Ray is a 32-year-old rock musician. About five years before his evaluation at the clinic, he had begun to feel very anxious and nervous and found it difficult to sit still. He also found himself worrying constantly about his career, although he had more bookings than ever and had achieved financial independence. Although he had previously been a heavy cocaine user, he found that cocaine caused him to be intolerably nervous. Also, he found that marijuana and alcohol which used to calm him down no longer did so. He reported most DSM-III-R symptoms of motor tension, including trembling, twitching or feeling shaky, muscle tension and restlessness, and autonomic hyperactivity; he exhibited extreme vigilance and scanning during the interview. He was able, however, to sit in the chair for the entire interview. He often felt irritable and had more trouble dealing with frustration than before this episode began. He exhibited several features of hypomania including distractibility and increased sexuality but did not notice changes in his basic mood. The patient had been hospitalized at age 18 for "encephalitis," but noticed no change in his affect following this episode. He did not feel depressed and did not have other somatic symptoms. Treatment in this case was restricted in focus to Ray's chronic generalized anxiety symptoms.

The following case, characterized by a cluster of different symptoms some of which overlap with generalized anxiety, is more typical of those encountered in clinical practice:

Linda is a 32-year-old white female who complained of frequent anxiety and worry. She said that her main worries concerned her relationship with her parents and her boyfriend. He was planning to move to southern California and wanted her to accompany him, but she was reluctant to abandon her elderly parents who lived close to her. She said she felt anxious for about 60 percent of the time, even when she wasn't worried about her boyfriend and parents. In fact, she remembered feeling anxious even before she met her current boyfriend. Medical examination was normal. She drank occasionally and never used drugs. She met some of the DSM-III-R criteria for generalized anxiety disorder but not all of them. For instance, her worry seemed excessive and had lasted longer than six months, yet she described only four symptoms occurring during anxious episodes. The patient underwent relaxation training and experienced some symptomatic relief, but she desired, received, and eventually benefited from psychodynamic therapy focusing on the exploration of her conflicts with her parents and her difficulty separating from them, fear of closeness with her boyfriend, and sexual inhibition.

Physiologic Comparisons Between Anxious and Nonanxious Patients

Anxious and nonanxious subjects have been compared on a variety of physiologic measures. Most of these studies have grouped together subjects with generalized anxiety disorder, uncomplicated panic disorder, and panic disorder with agoraphobia. The findings show anxious patients with higher pulse rate and electromyographic activity than normal controls. Although the electromyographic activity recorded from the frontalis muscle is reliably higher in anxious patients than in controls, EMG activity from forearm, masseter, and other muscle sites does not appear to differ (Lader & Marks, 1971). Anxious patients show higher skin conductance rates at baseline than normals, but these levels habituate over time, attenuating the differences. Forearm blood flow is consistently increased in anxious patients. The amount of alpha activity in the EEG diminishes with increased anxiety, and there are differences in alpha frequency between anxious and normal individuals. There is no evidence of EEG abnormalities among anxious patients. Respiration is more rapid and shallow. Finally, although dry mouth is a common symptom of anxiety, there do not appear to be differences in salivation between anxious subjects and controls (Peck, 1966).

Physiologic Responses in Anxious Patients

The diagnostic criteria for anxiety include clinical features such as increased startle response, which suggests that anxious patients are more reactive to stimuli than nonanxious individuals. However, evidence of increased reactivity to acute stimuli among anxious patients is scant. Many researchers have demonstrated that anxious patients when compared with nonanxious controls achieve higher levels of arousal as measured by numerous physiologic variables, but if one considers baseline differences between the two groups, the net change is usually similar. The response of anxious patients to long-term or repeated stimuli may differ from normal subjects. Slower extinction of GSR and EMG in anxious patients compared to control subjects has been reported (Lader & Marks, 1971). However, in general, psychophysiologic studies attest to the uniqueness of the individual's physiological reactivity. Some will respond to a particular stimulus with increased heart rate and decreased blood pressure, while others will respond in the opposite fashion. Furthermore, different stimuli may produce different response patterns in the same individual, since response patterns are affected by learning and other factors. Thus, individual differences are sufficient to prevent generalizations regarding the physiological reactivity of anxious patients as a group.

Ambulatory Physiology

There has been some recent interest in ambulatory measures of anxious patients. Because of the difficulty of obtaining reliable ambulatory measures of skin conductance, most of the studies have focused on heart rate and have combined various types of anxiety disorders. Roth et al. (1976) did not find differences in ambulatory heart rate in anxious patients compared to controls. Consistent with this observation, Evans et al. (1986) found that average daily heart rate was not correlated with anxiety measures.

Biologic Measures

While fear and phobias produce marked changes in cortisol and catecholamines, such changes are not much greater than those induced by nondistressing experiences (Frankenhauser, 1978). However, urinary epinephrine and norepinephrine levels correlate with anxiety in normal men (Faucheux et al., 1983) and is raised in panic-anxiety patients (Nesse et al., 1984a). Nonanxious subjects show a faster return to baseline of autonomic responses to fears than do anxious subjects (Frankenhauser, 1978). The HYPAC (hypothalmic-pituitary-adrenal cortical) system is more activated if the task is uncontrollable and distressing rather than challenging yet controllable (Frankenhauser, 1983). However, at present, we lack a reliable peripheral biologic measure of anxiety.

Medical Issues

In reviewing the possible psychosocial factors leading to increased cardiovascular disease, Jenkins (1982) concluded that anxiety and neuroticism were risk factors for increased cardiovascular morbidity. It was assumed that this morbidity was caused in some way by the anxiety. Recent studies have helped clarify this issue. A "neurotic response" style, defined as being anxious, having somatic symptoms, and being preoccupied with bodily sensations, is associated with the report of angina but not with abnormalities in the ECG, treadmill, angiogram, or in death from cardiovascular disease (Costa et al., 1985). Furthermore, patients with a "neurotic response" style are high utilizers of the medical care system and are therefore more likely to have pathology identified. However, Costa (1988) has found that the neurotic response style is not a risk factor for any cause of death.

There is a large overlap between patients who score high on anxiety measures and those who score high on neuroticism. We can assume, therefore, that anxiety is not a risk factor per se, but that the habits patients engage in to reduce anxiety may confer risk. For example, anxiety is a risk factor for smoking relapse upon cessation, and excessive use of alcohol and overeating (leading to obesity, hypercholesterolemia, and other medical problems) often represent attempts to reduce anxiety. Furthermore, the medications used to treat anxiety may also confer some slight risk. Finally, although generalized anxiety may not be a risk factor for heart disease, panic disorder may be. The link between panic disorder and heart disease is discussed in the next chapter.

DIAGNOSIS

Therapists will find that many of their patients who met the DSM-II criteria for anxiety neurosis fall short of the new criteria for generalized anxiety disorder under DSM-III-R. Under the DSM-III-R system, patients must have unrealistic or excessive anxiety and worry more days than not for six months or longer, and have at least six symptoms selected from a group of four symptoms of motor tension, nine symptoms of autonomic hyperactivity, and five symptoms of vigilance and scanning when anxious. In our clinic, less than 25 percent of the patients meet the DSM-III-R criteria for GAD, whereas most met the old criteria for anxiety neurosis. From our experience, we recommend that patients not classifiable as GAD should often be treated as such, particularly if they have signs and symptoms of frequent anxiety, worry, and chronic arousal and if they do not fall into one of the other anxiety disorder diagnostic categories.

The reliability of a few of the new GAD criteria have been examined. It would seem unlikely that independent raters could concur about whether a patient's worry was excessive, but a study by Sanderson and Barlow (1985) found high agreement between two independent raters who listened to structured clinical interviews and rated the worry as excessive or not. The raters agreed 22/24 times that the episode they were listening to involved excessive worry. Evidence from the same study suggested that most GAD patients were preoccupied by concerns from at least two domains. The most common spheres of worry involved the family (11/14), money (8/14), work (7/14), and illness (2/14). The low rate of worry about illness is interesting given the somatic preoccupation of many patients presenting other types of anxiety disorders, but it fits with the results of the Hibbert study (1984) reported above. The mean amount of time spent being worried or anxious was reported at 68 percent for subjects in the study conducted by Sanderson and Barlow (1985).

In making a diagnosis, it is important to exclude possible medical problems, like hyperthyroidism, that might account for GAD symptoms. The common medical problems that need to be considered for exclusion are discussed in chapter 12.

Under DSM-III-R, patients can be diagnosed with both GAD and one or more other disorders, including other anxiety disorders. However, the diagnosis of GAD is not made if the anxiety occurs exclusively during the course of another Axis 1 problem. As anxiety and depression are closely associated, distinguishing between the two can pose a problem. In a community sample, 67 percent of subjects with a psychiatric disorder had features of both anxiety and depression that could not be differentiated (Tennant et al., 1981). It has also been difficult to differentiate between anxiety and depression in primary care populations (Cooper & Sylph, 1973). Brief depressive episodes have been found to occur in 44 percent of cases of anxiety states over a six year period (Noyes et al., 1980) and 60 over five to 12 years (Cloninger et al., 1981). Depression and anxiety scales have been shown to be highly correlated (Fleiss et al., 1972), and depression and anxiety factors are not easily distinguished in factor-analytic studies (Endicott et al., 1975; Spitzer et al., 1967). This observation has important clinical implications: it seems appropriate to consider patients with generalized anxiety disorder as having a mixed anxiety-depression (sometimes called a minor affective illness, Cooper & Sylph, 1973; or nonspecific distress, Dohrenwend & Dohrenwend, 1981), with treatment focusing on both the anxious and depressive features.

Generalized anxiety disorder correlates highly with other anxiety disorders. In Sanderson and Barlow's study (1986) 59 percent (13/22) of patients with GAD also had social phobia, 27 percent met the criteria for panic disorder, and 23 percent for simple phobia. Successful treatment of the social phobia or panic disorder is likely to facilitate reduction of GAD symptoms simultaneously.

Using the DSM-II diagnostic nomenclature, alcoholism was found among 15 percent of 500 anxiety neurotics, of whom only 10 percent had severe phobias (Woodruff et al., 1972). However, anxiety was unrelated to drinking among unreferred male social drinkers (Rohsenow, 1982; Schwarz et al., 1982).

PREVALENCE

Marks and Lader (1973) reported a mean of 3.4 percent prevalence of "chronic anxiety" for five different surveys in the U.S., U.K., and Sweden. Weissman et al., (1978) reported a prevalence of 4.3 percent in the US, and Angst and Dobbler-Mikola (1983), a mean of 8.4 percent for one year. The estimates for generalized anxiety disorder are lower within a sample where different types of anxiety disorders are reported. Weissman et al. (1978) reported a 2.5 percent point prevalence, Uhlenhuth et al. (1978) a 6.4 percent one-year prevalence and Angst and Dobbler-Mikola (1983) a 2.3 percent one-year prevalence. In the only study reporting both generalized anxiety disorder and panic disorder, GAD was six times more common than panic disorder (Weissman et al., 1978). Angst and Dobbler-Mikola (1983) reported that panic disorder and agoraphobia combined were about 25 percent more common than generalized anxiety disorder. It is our impression that many patients previously diagnosed with generalized anxiety disorder meet the criteria for panic disorder under DSM-III.

FAMILY STUDIES

Family and genetic studies have used varying diagnoses and methodologies. Until recently, anxiety disorders had been lumped together, making it difficult to determine genetic factors specific to generalized anxiety disorder. Overall, the prevalence of anxiety disorders among twins is 2–3 times greater than among nontwins (Marks, 1987). Twin studies also suggest a genetic predisposition to anxiety both as a symptom and as a syndrome (Fuller & Thompson, 1978). Noyes et al. (1987) have recently found that patients with generalized anxiety disorder are more likely to have relatives with the same problem and no more likely than controls to have relatives with panic disorder or other psychiatric diagnoses. This study both confirms the fact that genetics may be important in the transmission of anxiety disorders and suggests that GAD may have a different etiology than other anxiety disorders, including panic disorder.

COURSE

Little is known about the course of GAD. Thyer et al. (1985a) reported that the mean age of onset for GAD patients was 22.8 years. Noyes et al. (1980) have suggested that the onset is gradual. Studies indicating the stability of "neurotic traits" are also relevant here; in adults such traits seem stable from one decade to another. Given the chronic nature of the problem, helping patients learn to tolerate symptoms without abusing prescribed medications or other substances seems particularly important.

ETIOLOGY

The psychoanalytic view of anxiety, as discussed in chapter 2, is particularly relevant to patients who meet the DSM-II criteria for anxiety neurosis or score high on neuroticism inventories; it is less relevant for those patients who meet the new DSM-III-R criteria for generalized anxiety disorder. But even for patients with "anxiety neurosis," psychoanalytic explanations remain speculative and largely unprovable. Much has been written about this issue, which does not need to be discussed more here. Learning theories have also failed to provide a robust model explaining chronic anxiety. A theory specific to generalized anxiety disorder must account for the chronic and continuous nature of the dominant symptoms, which include hyperarousal/attention.

Biological accounts may shed the most light on etiology among this group of patients. Evidence of the moderate effectiveness of benzodiazepines in attenuating some of the physiologic symptoms of GAD suggests that the GABA-receptor benzodiazepine-binding site and anion channel complex are important in chronic anxiety. However, they may play a general role in the nervous system in which the symptoms of anxiety are only one of the many systems affected by the

GABA-BZ. The locus coeruleus and raphe may also play an important role in generating chronic anxiety. When the locus coeruleus is stimulated to a point sufficient to induce a panic attack, the animal remains hypervigilant for days afterward. This state seems similar to that of chronic anxiety. Evidence also suggests that both the serotonergic and noradrenergic systems play an important role in chronic anxiety.

Among the most interesting theories regarding etiology is that generalized anxiety disorder in humans is analogous to sensitization observed in animals. There are two basic processes involved in defensive learning: *habituation*, which is the response decrement that occurs on repeated presentation of a noxious stimulus, and *sensitization*, which is the increase in defense evoked by strong or noxious stimuli. Habituation is the process that allows an animal to eventually ignore repeated innocuous events, and sensitization is the process that leads it to attend to potentially dangerous ones. In chapter 2, we presented data from Kandel (1983), who has demonstrated morphological and functional changes in the marine snail *Aplysia* associated with sensitization. The analogues of these structures in humans remain unclear, but the potential to establish sensitization in cells brought about by learning is suggested by Kandel's studies. Perhaps generalized anxiety disorder represents chronic sensitization characterized by continuous over-attention to potentially noxious or dangerous stimuli. The brain structures discussed by Gray (1982) in conjunction with the behavioral avoidance system are likely to be involved, as well as nuclei in the pons.

What causes sensitization is not clear. We know that a variety of medications and drugs can cause anxiety and that their continued use can be associated with chronic anxious symptoms. Excessive caffeine use, for instance, looks and feels like chronic anxiety. The nervous system is wonderfully adaptable, resetting response levels in one system in response to input and output from other interacting systems. The system resetting involved in sensitization appears critical to the generation of chronic anxiety. The resetting is probably affected by genetic factors and may be stimulated by traumatic events, medications, drugs, and experience. If we are correct that sensitization plays an important role in generalized anxiety, then studies determining how sensitization in animals can be reversed might provide important clues regarding effective treatments in humans.

Although we have suggested a "biological" explanation for generalized anxiety, such an account does not rule out the possible role of psychological events in producing sensitization and other GAD symptoms. After all, learning was responsible for the changes seen in Kandel's snails.

ASSESSMENT

Because anxiety is manifest in subjective, cognitive, behavioral, and physiologic domains, which are interdependent in theory, assessment concerns itself with all four areas. Moreover, change in one domain is not necessarily associated with commensurate change in another. However, in many clinical as well as research settings, such multiple system assessment is not practical. We will here confine our discussion to those instruments which we believe to be potentially most useful to clinicians.

Self-report of Anxiety

Measuring the subjective components of anxiety has long fascinated and challenged psychologists. The measurement of any emotion involves a paradox. We attempt to measure anxiety in order to understand its nature better; yet how we choose to define and measure the phenomenon largely determines the nature of what we are trying to understand. This paradox has led to the many often irreconcilable theories of anxiety that have been developed.

Trait Anxiety Measures

Over the years, many trait anxiety instruments have been developed. In general these scales are highly correlated. We employ the Spielberger State-Trait Anxiety Inventory (Spielberger, 1983) because of its wide use, which permits comparison of our patients with other populations. It consists of 20 items describing anxiety that are scaled 0 to 4, resulting in a score range 0 to 80. In developing the STAI, Spielberger originally thought the same set of items could be used for both states and traits, with subjects answering "today" for the state scale and "usually" for the trait scale. However, he eventually decided to choose items for the A-trait if they correlated with the Manifest Anxiety Scale (Taylor, 1951), were stable over time, and were not much affected by situational stress. Items for the A-state were chosen if they seemed to change with situational stress. The STAI has undergone extensive evaluation. Spielberger claims that the STAI has been used to measure anxiety in more than 2,000 studies since it was published in 1970. In general, the assumptions of the STAI have been confirmed: the A-state is affected by situational factors, while the A-trait has shown stable properties (Spielberger, 1983).

Measures of chronic or trait anxiety are highly correlated with personality scales that tap some of the same dimensions. Eysenck and Eysenck (1969) developed the Eysenck Personality Inventory (EPI) which consists of two scales, extraversion and neuroticism. The EPI neuroticism scale consists of 24 items answered "yes" or "no." As psychotherapy outcome research moved to a tradition of specific and situational measurement, very general measures like the EPI fell out of favor. However, McCrae and Costa (1985) have recently created new interest in personality dimensions of anxiety. They began by analyzing personality scales widely used by personality researchers. From these they identified three groups of scales, which, following the example of Eysenck, they labeled neuroticism, extraversion, and openness to experience. They then generated a questionnaire, the NEO (after neuroticism, extraversion, and openness) Inventory designed to measure these three dimensions as well as some of the specific traits that constituted them.

Neuroticism on the NEO consists of these specific traits: anxiety, hostility, depression, self-consciousness, impulsiveness, and vulnerability. Using data from the National Institute of Aging's Longitudinal Cohort, Costa and McCrae (in press) have shown that neuroticism is stable over very long periods of time. While habits may change, traits do not. Furthermore, the measurement of neuroticism is helpful in resolving some of the apparent contradictions in anxiety research. For instance, it appears that neuroticism predisposes people to the self-report of cardiovascular symptoms (and is a risk factor for angiography), but that it is not associated with increased morbidity and mortality. Thus, neuroticism is associated with more self-reports of cardiovascular symptoms but not with more actual disease.

State Anxiety

A variety of symptom checklists have been developed to measure state anxiety. The Spielberger A-State Inventory has already been discussed. The Affect Adjective Check List, Today Form (Zuckerman, 1960) asks subjects how they feel right at the moment or how they felt at some immediately preceding point, rather than how they generally feel. A variation on the symptom checklist, is the SCL-90 (Derogatis et al., 1973), which asks subjects to rate the presence of symptoms from not at all (0) to extremely (4). These measures correlate highly with one another and there does not appear to be much advantage of one over the other. The Profile of Mood States (POMS; McNair, Lorr, & Droppelman, 1971) is also used to measure any of six moods, one of which is anxiety-tension.

The earliest, and still one of the most widely used clinical instrument for quantifying anxiety, is the Hamilton Anxiety Interview (see Appendix 2).

Assessment of Cognition

The ever-changing, abstract, complicated, and multidimensional nature of thinking makes the standardized assessment of cognition most difficult. Among the dimensions of cognition that have been subjected to measurement are frequency, intensity, predictability, controllability, intrusiveness, clarity, and content. Although instruments are available to help measure thoughts associated with panic, no standardized instruments exist to satisfactorily measure the cognitions associated with chronic anxiety. Perhaps the most important determination is the frequency and intensity of worry. At this stage of our knowledge, the easiest strategy is simply to ask patients questions like "How much of the time (percentage of the day) are you worried or do you worry?"

Clark and de Silva (1985) have made an attempt to develop a standardized instrument that measures anxious thoughts by taking the anxious statements most frequently reported in the Rachman and de Silva (1978) and eliminating those not frequently reported by control populations. This resulted in six thoughts or images (e.g., something is wrong with my health or may be in the future) rated on five parameters (frequency, sadness, worry, removal, disapproval). The resulting scale has acceptable test-retest reliability but its clinical utility is uncertain.

Another instrument for measuring anxious thoughts is the Cognitive-Somatic Questionnaire (Schwartz et al., 1978). The questionnaire consists of 14 items, half of which are considered to reflect anxious cognition (e.g., difficulty in concentrating; worrying too much) and half somatic items (e.g., perspiring, feeling jittery, tenseness in stomach). Not unexpectedly, a factor analysis found overlap between these scales suggesting that the cognitive and somatic scales share common factors (Crits-Christoph, 1986). The best cognitive items appear to reflect difficulty in concentration, worrying too much, having unimportant and anxiety-provoking thoughts and difficulty in making up one's mind.

Self-monitoring

Self-monitoring instruments can be very useful clinically. Beck and his colleagues (Beck & Emery, 1985) have developed a daily record of automatic thoughts (called the Daily Record of Dysfunctional Thoughts), which serves as both an assessment and intervention instrument. Subjects write down the situation and emotions associated with automatic thoughts, the extent of their belief in the automatic thought, the evidence for it, alternative views, and ways to reattribute and de-catastrophize the thought.

Physiologic and Biological Measures

A wide variety of physiologic and biological measures are available to measure anxiety. Galvanic skin response and conductance and cardiovascular function have been thoroughly studied because of the ease of their collection and their responsiveness to fear and anxiety. Unlike other sweat glands in most parts of the body, those in the palms of the hands and soles of the feet respond independent of the thermoregulatory system. As an individual sweats, the electrical conductivity changes. These changes can then be used as a measure of change in response to stimuli. Of the cardiovascular measures, heart rate is the easiest to obtain. Modern ambulatory microcomputers permit the continuous collection of heart rate in free living subjects for weeks at a time. The measurement of blood pressure requires relatively cumbersome and intrusive devices and has been less widely used. Two other interesting measurements are provided by the skin and forearm blood flow, both of which are sensitive to changes in sympathetic activity. However, the difficulty of measuring them has limited their usefulness in clinical practice.

Electromyography (EMG) is also widely used in physiologic studies. The EMG utilizes electrodes attached a standard distance apart to the skin overlying the muscles under study. The action potentials from the muscles are recorded by the electrodes, amplified, and then usually transformed into a more quantifiable measure. Respiration rate and related indices that vary with anxiety are also important measures. Modern devices measure respiration rate and depth with a net surrounding the chest fixed with transducers designed to detect changes. Finally, the electroencephalogram (EEG), which measures brain wave activity, completes the list of standard physiological assessment instruments used to measure anxiety.

Except in the case of biofeedback, collection of these measures is neither practical nor helpful in most clinical settings. Obviously, in the case of biofeedback, measurement of EMG, GSR, heart rate, and skin temperature in particular are critical for baseline assessment, determination of reactivity to psychological stressors, and feedback. There are no biological measures of clinical use to measure anxiety, although, of course, numerous clinical tests may be indicated to rule out medical causes when anxiety is a presenting complaint.

Summary of Assessment

The basic assessment package that we presented at the end of chapter 4 includes the instruments appropriate for assessing generalized anxiety. Anxious traits can be assessed with the Spielberger A-trait, the Taylor Manifest Anxiety Scale, or the SCL-90 anxiety scale. Anxious states can be assessed with the Spielberger A-state and the Hamilton Anxiety Interview. Items measuring anxious cognitions not specifically related to panic attacks or specific situations are included in these scales. Alternatively, the Cognitive-Somatic Anxiety Questionnaire can be used to measure cognitive anxiety (Schwartz et al., 1978). The cognitions associated with panic attacks can be assessed with the Stanford Panic Attack Inventory or by the Body Sensations Questionnaire and the Agoraphobic Cognitions Questionnaire (Chambless et al., 1984). The Hamilton Depression Inventory, and the Beck, the Zung, or the SCL-90 depression scales can be used to determine the extent of the patient's depression. Avoidance can be assessed with the Mobility Inventory (Chambless et al., 1985), the Fear Questionnaire (Marks & Mathews, 1979), or the Stanford Mobility Instrument. These instruments can also be used to monitor the patient's progress over time.

THE TREATMENT OF GENERALIZED ANXIETY DISORDER

Three general treatment approaches have been applied to the problems of chronic anxiety and generalized anxiety disorder. The oldest and still most widely used approach is to provide psychological support and reassurance to anxious patients in conjunction with attempts to help them understand the origins of their anxiety. More recently, interventions that attempt to reduce arousal directly have been applied to the problem. The third approach involves altering biological factors through psychopharmacologic interventions.

Our approach to generalized anxiety is determined by whether the anxiety symptoms are secondary to another Axis 1 disorder or are independent symptoms. Consistent with what many clinicians report using the new DSM-III-R GAD diagnosis, we find pure GAD to be a very rare disorder. Therefore, the first order of therapy is to focus on the primary Axis 1 disorder. If the patient has panic disorder and GAD, we treat the panic disorder first as described in the next chapters. Similarly, we treat major depressive, alcohol, or substance abuse disorders before GAD. Usually, resolution of the primary Axis 1 disorder alleviates many of the anxious symptoms. If the patient is suffering from a primary GAD yet able to function effectively and tolerate the symptoms, we usually introduce a relaxation reduction technique in the first few sessions. If the anxiety is incapacitating, we use medication. Most of our patients with GAD have chronic symptoms of anxiety exacerbated by some current life stressors. Treatment frequently centers on helping the patient to resolve such stressors. It is usually not realistic to alleviate the anxiety entirely. To avoid creating unrealistic expectations, we tell patients that the goal of treatment is to help them return to baseline levels of anxiety.

Our approach to the treatment of GAD incorporates five techniques:

1. Relaxation and related techniques aimed at decreasing hyperarousal/attention.
2. Cognitive behavior therapy
3. Skills training and coping
4. Alteration in life-style factors that may contribute to or alleviate anxiety
5. Psychopharmacology

Family and couples therapy, and in some cases psychodynamic therapy, may also be a part of treatment.

Relaxation and Related Techniques

A variety of techniques have been developed to reduce the symptoms of anxiety directly. Jacobson (1939), who popularized muscle relaxation through his progressive relaxation procedure, believed that peripheral muscle input directly affected the central nervous system and that when this input was reduced, tension "in the brain" would cease. This explanation has long since been discounted based on evidence from a variety of studies. For instance, subjects who have been given curare, a drug that blocks peripheral muscle activity, continue to report subjective anxiety. Another hypothesis, first introduced by Gellhorn (1965) and since popularized by Benson (1975) holds that relaxation affects autonomic balance, decreasing ergotropic (posterior hypothalamic) activity while increasing trophotropic (anterior hypothalamic) dominance. Trophotropic dominance is assumed to inhibit the sympathetic system. Benson suggests that relaxation is one of many procedures that elicit the "relaxation response." Others, such as autogenic training, hypnosis, some forms of meditation, and biofeedback share with relaxation training four properties: (1) the patient assumes a passive attitude or frame of mind—subjects are directly or implicitly encouraged to allow distracting thoughts or images to "pass"; (2) there is a decrease in muscle tonus; (3) a quiet environment is provided; and (4) a mental device is used (e.g., a word or sound repeated as a constant stimulus). Benson notes that hypnosis, autogenic training, relaxation and transcendental meditation have been shown to lower oxygen consumption, respiration, and heart rate while increasing alpha activity and skin resistance—all responses compatible with inhibited sympathetic activity.

Sherman and Plummer (1973) undertook an interesting study suggesting that the long-term benefits of relaxation may relate to cognitive rather than physiologic factors. In this study, follow-up data were obtained on 19 of 28 subjects previously trained in relaxation. These subjects reported that they continued to use relaxation to control anxiety and to cope with specific stressors but mostly as a means of helping them remain "aware of tension." In support of the importance of cognitive factors in producing the relaxation effects, Peveler and Johnston (1986) have shown that relaxation is associated with both decreased arousal and increased positive cognitions. Others have argued that relaxation decreases central nervous system arousal through the reticular activating system or even the locus coeruleus (Lader & Wing, 1966).

Relatively few studies have been undertaken to assess the effects of relaxation and relaxation-related techniques in clinically anxious populations. Taylor et al. (1982) compared the effects of relaxation, diazepam, placebo, or control with 23 panic disorder patients randomized into a crossover design. Anxiety was measured by a 3-day hourly diary, psychological tests, and assessment of heart rate and skin conductance level during baseline stress test and interview. Relaxation produced a significant reduction in state anxiety compared to the control or the placebo group. Relaxation was also associated with reduction in trait anxiety, mean hourly self-report of anxiety, and depression, but not with significant changes in physiologic measures. Raskin et al. (1973) gave EMG-based relaxation training for an average of 6 weeks to 10 outpatients with chronic anxiety. Therapist-rated anxiety symptoms were reduced and there was some evidence that patients could use the procedure to terminate episodes of anxiety, but only when lying down with their eyes closed.

Teaching Relaxation

The goals of relaxation training are (1) to teach the patient how to achieve a deep sense of relaxation and then (2) to teach the patient to generalize his relaxation to a variety of settings and situations. When employing relaxation, it is preferable to make a personalized tape for the patient. This allows the therapist to pace the instructions relative to the patient's behavior, to emphasize strategies that would be expected to be effective with that patient, and to avoid certain muscle areas that might be troublesome to the patient. Scripts for relaxation relaxation tapes have been published or are available (Ferguson et al., 1977; Schneider et al., 1980).

Having taught the technique to innumerable patients, we find it easier to simply give the patient a prepared tape. The tape we use consists of two sides. On the first side, the patient is guided through a long (30-minute) relaxation program. We encourage the patient to listen to the tape, which takes patients through most muscle groups, once or twice every day for the first week. A week or so later we ask the patient to relax in the office without using the tape while we observe how they do so. After the patient appears relaxed we gently lift his arm to determine if there is any muscle tension. It should be possible to lift the arm without encountering any resistance. We encourage patients to use the tape until they feel that they are able to achieve a very deep sense of relaxation. Patients need to determine exactly when, where, and how they will relax. Some patients like other family members to join them, while others prefer to practice relaxation only in privacy.

As part of the relaxation tape, we encourage patients to imagine a place where they feel extremely peaceful and relaxed. The imagery selected by patients is important and instructive. Occasionally patients will report that they are unable to imagine any such place. The absence of such soothing imagery usually suggests that the patient is either very resistant to the therapy or has led a psychologically impoverished life. Other patients prefer to repeat a religious word or phrase when they relax. For many patients this seems to invoke a more profound sense of relaxation than words like "relax" or "let go," customarily used in relaxation instructions.

After patients have learned to relax deeply we then teach generalization and speed, using the other side of the tape, which uses a shorter relaxation program. Patients are instructed to learn key phrases, images, and techniques to help them achieve a deep and rapid sense of relaxation. If successful, the patient should be able to demonstrate relaxation by simply squeezing his or her hand and letting go, or taking a deep breath and exhaling.

A number of procedures have been brought to bear to facilitate generalization of relaxation to anxiety-provoking situations (Suinn & Richardson, 1971; Suinn, 1984). Generalization usually involves helping the patient use relaxation at the onset of any somatic symptoms signalling anxiety and in a variety of real-life settings and situations associated with anxiety. Patients are often more successful in learning to generalize relaxation by first concentrating on less anxiety-provoking situations until they feel a sense of mastery over them. Diaries or patient logs are useful in helping patients identify such situations. The following case presents a discussion with Ray, an anxious and hypertensive patient, designed to help him generalize his anxiety management skills by becoming more aware of cues associated with anxiety:

> RAY: I was going to meet with John [a co-worker] at noon. I was already feeling uptight.
> THERAPIST: How were you feeling uptight?
> RAY: Well, my stomach was in knots. I felt like maybe I was getting a headache. I didn't feel like I could concentrate very well. I said to myself, "You're going to blow this meeting." Then I started to feel worse. My mouth got very dry. I started to sweat. I began to rummage through my desk trying to find a paper I needed for the meeting.

Ray's anxiety involves somatic, cognitive, and behavioral components. In the first stages of teaching generalization, it is often helpful for the therapist to replay the situation. Often the therapist can present the situation in slightly altered fashion to facilitate the patient's sense of accomplishment in using relaxation effectively. The therapist might replay the above described scene and symptoms as follows:

> THERAPIST: Now, I am going to recreate that scene, only I want you to practice relaxation to reduce the anxiety. Close your eyes. Imagine that you are in your office. You are going to meet with John at noon. You notice knots in your stomach and you start to get a headache. Now, relax, let go.

The therapist pauses as the patient relaxes. He observes the patient for behavioral indications of relaxation (reduction in muscle tension) and may lift the patient's arm to determine if it is free of tension. In the first phase of relaxation, we control the anxiety scene and relaxation. We may introduce part of the scene and ask the patient to relax and then return to the scene. Next, the patient learns to perceive early signs of anxiety, to relax before the anxiety has a chance to reach an uncontrollable level, and to assume more control regarding when and where the relaxation is initiated. Outside of the office, the patient first practices in situations that evoke only mild anxiety. As he gains mastery in those situations, he turns to more demanding ones.

In Ray's case, we instructed him to begin practicing relaxation at the first sign of anxious cues, well before the meeting began. For instance, he might learn that the first symptoms of anxiety on the day of the noon meeting began at 7:30 in the morning on his way to work when he was parked at a light and suddenly had a funny feeling in his chest. He would then practice relaxation.

Some patients prefer hypnosis or biofeedback to relaxation. These procedures are as effective as relaxation and using one or the other is mostly a matter of patient and therapist preference. In fact, relaxation techniques share many similarities with hypnotic induction including direct suggestions to relax, positive expectancy that obeying the instructions will lead to relaxation, actual relaxation training, and the use of imagination and suggestion.

Spiegel et al. (1982) report that severe anxiety interferes with hypnotizability, although this effect can be ameliorated with concomitant benzodiazepine use. He recommends that relaxation be achieved not by direct instructions but by physical metaphors or images. For instance, the subject is invited to imagine floating in a hot bath or a lake and may be told that each breath out will leave him feeling a bit more comfortable and that he will be able to breathe more deeply and easily. Spiegel encourages the patient to picture an imaginary screen in his mind's eye, a movie screen or a TV screen, and to visualize on that screen a pleasant scene, somewhere the patient enjoys being. After the patient has achieved the ability to produce a comforting scene and is able to achieve body relaxation, he is asked to imagine anxious images. The patient moves from anxious scenes back to comfort and floating—a process similar to desensitization. Other hypnotists primarily use direct suggestion, giving repeated instructions to patients that they will feel more comfortable and better able to master their own anxiety (Crasilneck & Hall, 1985). Patients who request hypnosis for anxiety reduction are most likely to benefit from it, particularly if they are good hypnotic subjects.

Biofeedback has also been used as a method to induce relaxation in anxious subjects. Stoyva (1979) describes a method for shaping low arousal. As increased arousal is a central feature of GAD, shaping low arousal is a critical goal; in theory, a patient could not have "low arousal" and be anxious at the same time. Stoyva's procedure consists of two phases: preparation and training. During preparation, the therapist creates a positive expectancy for biofeedback, obtains baseline data and a "stress profile." With the stress profile, the patient is given a mild stressor—for instance, subtraction of serial sevens, while the therapist observes in what physiological system the patient is most or too responsive. The training phase consists of four phases. First, the patient undertakes tension–relaxation exercises to learn to develop an awareness of muscle tension. The second step is to use EMG training, in which the patient learns how to increase and decrease the EMG level; the patient is expected to reach an average level of 2.0 microV. He develops an awareness of internal cues such as heaviness and warmth. The third step is learning to reduce frontalis EMG levels until he or she reaches an average level of 3.5 microV. If the patient has not achieved generalized relaxation with EMG feedback, he is then given instructions in hand temperature or GSR training. Finally, in step five, the patient attempts to maintain relaxation while visualizing stressful situations from everyday life. A home practice tape is provided.

Cognitive Approaches

Albert Ellis (1962), Arnold Lazarus (1971), Donald Meichenbaum (1979), and Beck and Emery (1985) have been the leaders in developing cognitive approaches to the treatment of anxiety. The cognitive approach to anxiety is based on theoretical assumptions presented earlier that anxiety is an emotional state related to threat. Clinical anxiety disorders are thought to result from the patient's way of processing information in situations construed to be threatening. The cognitive processes considered most important include the appraisal and assumptions regarding particular situations and the rules that are generated for the problematic situation. For instance, Beck and Emery (1985) report that patients with generalized anxiety disorder apply the following assumptions to a wide variety of situations:

Any strange situation should be regarded as dangerous.
My security and safety depend on anticipating and preparing myself at all times for any possible danger.

These assumptions translate into behaviors. For instance, a patient may decide, "When in doubt, keep my mouth shut." Violation of the rules results in a feeling of vulnerability. Unlike depressed patients, anxious patients have conditional rules. The anxious patient may say, for instance, "If I am in this situation, I might have anxiety," while the depressed patient has absolute and unconditional rules (e.g., "my problems doom me to inevitable failure"). The rules distinguishing anxiety disorder patients involve a sense of "core vulnerability." Strategies to change thoughts and assumptions that may be anxiety-maintaining are brought to bear to help reduce vulnerability and enhance coping.

The goals of cognitive therapy are (1) to help the patient become aware of what his thoughts are, (2) to examine them for cognitive distortions, and (3) to substitute more balanced or functional thoughts. The therapy begins with the patient learning to become more aware of his thought processes. The general rule is for the patient to engage in as much anxiety-provoking activity as possible during treatment. This procedure, while presented as a method to help the patient become more aware of his or her thoughts, has the added benefit of exposing the patient to anxiety-provoking situations. For instance, we may instruct a patient to enter previously avoided restaurants and stores while observing relevant thoughts. The patient is also encouraged to experience the feelings he is trying to shut off. Awareness is also facilitated by having patients keep records of anxiety-producing thoughts.

Once the patient has learned to identify faulty cognitive patterns, we attempt to teach him how to correct his distortions and how to "restructure his thinking." Following Beck and Emery (1985), the therapist and patient may discuss and reflect on one or more of the following questions: (1) What's the evidence? (2) What's another way of looking at the situation? and (3) So what if it happens? For instance, an assistant manager of a small business scheduled to make a presentation to his boss worries that "I will screw up this presentation. My boss won't be at all happy with the presentation. I may not get a raise I was promised." The therapist asks the patient what evidence he has for these thoughts. In fact, the patient has made many such presentations before, always successfully. He is well prepared for this one. In general, he has a history of worrying about the success of such presentations, but they usually go very well. On the other hand, the therapist may ask him to examine what is likely to happen if he does "screw up" and make a bad presentation. The patient realizes that others have made poor presentations without jeopardizing their jobs or salaries. He also acknowledges that he is well liked by his boss, that his section has been doing well, that he has made many good presentations, and that one poorly received presentation is unlikely to affect his supervisor's overall assessment of him.

All patients can discover examples in their lives where their thoughts cause anxiety and impede performance, and many benefit from generating alternative ways of appraising events. After five or six sessions, patients should be able to generate examples from their experience illustrating how they previously viewed a situation in a way that exacerbated anxiety and how they now view the situation without catastrophizing, overgeneralizing, or in other ways construing the situation to be worse that it was.

While patients are developing skills in reducing unpleasant feelings by correcting distorted cognitions, they may need symptomatic relief. The A-W-A-R-E strategy, designed by Beck and Emery (1985) to help patients accept anxiety, is useful in this regard. We explain that patients fear their feelings, and that their feelings will not harm them. The components of A-W-A-R-E as developed by Beck and Emery are:

A. Accept the anxiety.

W. Watch your anxiety. Rate the anxiety on a 0 to 10 scale and watch it change.

A. Act with the anxiety. Act as if you aren't anxious. Breathe normally and slowly.

R. Repeat the steps until it goes down to a comfortable level.

E. Expect the best.

Cognitive therapy is not a panacea for most patients and seems most effective when combined with relaxation and other coping skills, and in many cases exposure to feared situations. This latter observation is supported by a study by Ledwidge (1978) who found that Rational Emotive Therapy, a procedure to help people identify and challenge the rationality of undesirable thoughts, may make a person more reasonable, but that this did not not necessarily reduce generalized anxiety. We are unaware of any controlled studies on this point demonstrating the effectiveness of cognitive therapy with GAD patients. Yet, in our clinical experience, most patients derive some benefit from learning and using these techniques in conjunction with other procedures.

Skills Training and Coping

In addition to relaxation training and cognitive therapy, anxious patients often benefit from training in the use of other coping skills. Of the various skills training techniques that have been developed, assertion training is by the far the most effective. It is of great use with social phobia but may also help patients with generalized anxiety learn to cope with troublesome situations. With assertion training, patients are taught to directly address in a more effective and less helpless fashion the situation or, more typically, the person associated with their distress. It frequently involves teaching them to express feelings in an honest and straightforward manner. After patients have identified what they would like to say to whom, we model and role-play the situation. Often we suggest the kinds of things that the patient might say and play the role of the patient in the feared situation. We then reverse roles and have the patient practice the interaction. We provide feedback. When the patient feels comfortable with the role-played interaction we then encourage them to use the skills in the actual situation, cautioning them that such situations are rarely identical to the ones created in the office but offer some variations and challenges for them to work on. We agree on the situation they will try and then review it during the next session. Such review may also be useful in elaborating troublesome thoughts. Patients will usually downplay obviously successful interactions or attribute their success to some external factor. Thus, developing a proper cognitive appraisal of their performance is a part of the assertion training.

Often the cause of chronic anxiety is apparent and the appropriate intervention is not learning to reduce the physiologic impact of the anxiety but changing the situation responsible for the distress. By definition, the problem of GAD is that the worry is out of proportion to the reality of the situation. However, many people are responding to very real problems that require attention. That is, many anxious patients have a combination of both excessive worry and significant problems; the extent of worry may appear excessive, but the problems nevertheless demand attention. In such cases, the appropriate direction of treatment is to help the patient cope with or resolve those difficulties. If the problem is one of poor marital relationships, then marital therapy is probably indicated. If the problem is one of conflict at work, then the patient should be helped to address that issue. Marital therapy, assertion training, family therapy, and various skills training and coping techniques are often useful in helping patients cope with or resolve the situations triggering the anxiety.

Life-Style Changes

A variety of habits contribute to or may help reduce anxiety. It is probably unrealistic to expect patients presenting with GAD to adopt what amounts to a "heart-healthy" life-style (i.e., avoidance of smoking; exercising at aerobic levels 3–5 times per week for 20–30 minutes; eating a low-fat, low cholesterol diet, and maintaining a serum cholesterol below 200 mg/dl; blood pressure below 140 systolic and 90 diastolic; and weight no more than 10–20 pounds above ideal for height sex, and age). However, in some patients moderate life-style changes can make a difference in their level of anxiety. Patients with GAD who drink several cups of caffeinated coffee daily should certainly be encouraged to cut down to no more than one. Those who clearly work an excessive amount of hours should be encouraged to reduce their work load if possible and to build in time for recreation. Regular exercise is also useful in anxious patients. Many epidemiologic studies suggest that exercisers report feeling less anxious. GAD patients do not have the same problems in exercising that are experienced by patients with panic disorder, who may feel that they are going to have a panic attack, or by agoraphobic patients, who may dread spending time in open spaces or in group programs.

Relaxation and related techniques can reduce anxiety but patients often need direct encouragement to undertake changes in life-style habits that exacerbate the problems of anxiety.

Pharmacotherapy

The long-term pharmacologic treatment of chronic or generalized anxiety is one of the most controversial issues in medicine. The debate centers on the risk/benefit of such treatment. On one hand, some argue that effective agents should not be withheld from people who are suffering from anxiety disorders. Others argue that the agents are not, in fact, effective and that they carry considerable risk for long-term dependence, unknown side-effects, and life-threatening withdrawal. Let us examine these issues in more detail.

Are Benzodiazepines Effective for the Long-term Treatment of Chronic, Generalized Anxiety?

While there is general consensus that benzodiazepines are effective in the short run, given the importance of the question, it is surprising how limited our knowledge is regarding the long-term effectiveness of benzodiazepines. In 1980, after reviewing studies on benzodiazepine effects, the British Medical Association concluded that the tranquilizing effects of such drugs do not persist beyond three to four months. However, other experts have argued that benzodiazepines are effective beyond four months, particularly in patients with severe anxiety. Greenblatt et al. (1978) wrote, "Although the benzodiazepines do not cure their anxiety, the medications can restore some degree of functionality and render life bearable for a person who might otherwise be incapacitated" (p. 410). The difficulty in providing research evidence for the long-term effectiveness of benzodiazepines is illustrated in a report by Haskell et al. (1986), who studied 194 patients with a history of diazepam use. The patients on long-term diazepam were as symptomatic as patients presenting for anxiety treatment. Yet, 158 of the 194 had tried to stop at some time, and of these, 142 reported the reemergence of anxiety symptoms. This evidence could be interpreted as showing that the drugs were not effective (the continued high symptomatology of the patients); were effective (the emergence of symptoms after stopping the drug); and/or are associated with withdrawal (the emergence of symptoms after stopping the drug). The patients however believed they were deriving benefit from treatment. Overall, we are not impressed with the long-term effectiveness of benzodazepines in patients with chronic anxiety and rarely prescribe them beyond four to six months. However, there are instances when their long-term benefit seems clear, as illustrated in the following case.

Edward is a 44-year-old accountant with a lifetime history of anxiety and panic attacks. He had been in individual psychotherapy for four years without success. He had undergone an extensive course of relaxation therapy with no reduction in symptoms. In April 1985, at the time that he came to the anxiety clinic he was having 4–5 panic attacks/week, reported a state anxiety of 55 and a trait anxiety of 59, a Hamilton anxiety score of 24, and a Hamilton depression score of 32. He was seriously considering resigning from his firm because he dreaded meetings with clients and other professionals and was hardly able to stand the anxiety. He was drinking 1–2 oz. of alcohol per week; there were no medical causes for his anxiety. He had taken diazepam, 5–10 mg per week intermittently for the past three years with no apparent benefit. He met the DSM-III-R criteria for panic disorder and for uncomplicated and generalized anxiety disorder. Because of the panic attacks and an unwillingness to take imipramine, he was started on Alprazolam 0.5 mg BID. On this dose, he achieved immediate and almost complete relief of his symptoms. For the first time in his life, he said, he no longer dreaded going to work and no longer experienced anguish from hour to hour. We decided to continue the medication for four months and then try to discontinue its use, while instituting cognitive and relaxation interventions.

Coincident with his improvement, one of his senior partners in the accounting firm decided to retire and wanted to have the patient buy out his interest. Because of the reduced anxiety, the patient was now more confident to deal with clients and to try to obtain new business. He decided to buy the firm, a move that caused him some stress and demanded more intensive effort. This new business venture coincided with the end of the first six months on the medication and the patient did not want to stop the medication and possibly jeopardize both his ability to function effectively and his monetary investment. Over the six months, he had not increased his medication, was not using alcohol, did not have evidence of withdrawal symptoms, and remained improved. We agreed to continue the medication for another six months and then to try a drug-free period.

At the end of six months, now a year into therapy, the patient continued to use the medication as prescribed and maintained his improvement. We strongly encouraged him to try a drug-free period, reviewed the possible long-term risks associated with the drug, and reminded him of our initial agreement. Reluctantly, he gradually stopped the medication, and although he did not seem to have withdrawal symptoms, his anxiety and panic attacks had returned within three months and had begun to impair his work. The medication was resumed for another six month period.

Although this case is somewhat unusual in the dramatic relief obtained from the medication, the issues are typical for many patients: the medication was associated with improved functioning and alternative therapies seemed ineffective. However, the patient continues to rely on the medication in order to function effectively.

Dependence and Withdrawal

There is no doubt that regular treatment with benzodiazepines can lead to pharmacological dependence manifest primarily by withdrawal (Pertursson & Lader, 1984; Rickels et al., 1983; Rickels et al., 1986). In a few patients the withdrawal syndrome can be sufficiently severe to cause epileptic seizures, confusion, and psychotic symptoms (Owen & Tyrer, 1983; Noyes et al., 1986.). For most patients, withdrawal symptoms are more diffuse, including anxiety, panic, tremor, muscle twitching, perceptual disturbances, and depersonalization (Petursson & Lader, 1984; Owen & Tyrer, 1983; Busto et al., 1986). Minor withdrawal symptoms can occur if treatment is stopped after 4–6 weeks. Lennane (1986) claims that some patients—particularly those who have been dependent on other drugs—may develop dependence in five to 10 days. Such rapid development of dependence may seem impossible, but animal studies show that acute administration of benzodiazepines can lead to a rapid increase in brain benzodiazepine receptor density and the development of withdrawal symptoms within as few as seven days (Speth et al., 1979; Lukas & Griffiths, 1982).

After adjusting for a return of symptoms versus true withdrawal, Owen and Tyrer (1983) suggested that about 30 percent of unselected normal-dose users will experience withdrawal. Rickels et al. (1986) found evidence for physical dependence in 82 percent of 119 chronic low-dose benzodiazepine users. In a recent study, Busto et al. (1986) provided convincing evidence for the fact that benzodiazepine withdrawal occurs. Forty patients who had undergone chronic benzodiazepine treatment (mean treatment was 73 months; mean daily dose was equivalent to about 15 mg of diazepam) were randomized to either placebo or continued diazepam. There was a significant difference in symptoms reported between patients on placebos and diazepam, with the patients on placebos reporting symptoms such as increased sweating, difficulty concentrating, and sensory disturbances that were not typical of anxiety. Benzodiazepine withdrawal is a real and serious problem and sometimes life-threatening in chronic benzodiazepine users.

Risk Factors for Dependence and Withdrawal

In considering the risk factors for dependence, it is important to consider physical and psychological dependence. Of course, these two closely interact. With most pharmacologic agents, physical dependence is associated with increased dosage as tolerance develops.

However, physical dependence can develop with low doses and in patients who do not increase the dosage. It is likely that the best predictor of physical dependence is length of treatment. Any patient taking benzodiazepines longer than two months is likely to show some signs of withdrawal upon discontinuation. More severe withdrawal reactions have been associated with the abrupt withdrawal of the short-acting benzodiazepines, but it should be assumed that severe reactions can occur when stopping any of the benzodiazepines. The physical withdrawal can occur as early as 24 hours after stopping the BZs. Rebound insomnia and rebound anxiety during the day can occur with a decrease in dosage at any stage of treatment (Kales et al., 1978; Morgan & Oswald, 1982).

Previous drug or alcohol abuse is often cited as a risk factor for dependence on and increased use of benzodiazepines (Lennane, 1986; Haskell et al., 1986; Mellinger et al., 1984). In one study, higher doses were associated with more symptoms and disturbance, age (inversely), duration of use, weight, and having a VA disability (Haskell et al., 1986); higher doses were also associated with more withdrawal symptoms. Short half-life benzodiazepines produce a significantly more severe symptomatology than long half-life benzodiazepines during the first week of discontinuation (Rickels et al., 1986). There is also evidence that the severity of withdrawal might be partly dependent on nonpharmacologic variables such as premorbid psychopathology (Rickels et al., 1986). Patients without a psychiatric diagnosis and with normal Hamilton anxiety scores before discontinuation had no difficulty withdrawing.

The risk factors for psychological dependence and abuse, indicated by inappropriate use of the drug and/or refusal to stop the drug, have largely been developed from clinical experience. Past behavior of alcohol or drug abuse is an obvious risk factor for benzodiazepine dependence and abuse. Family history of alcohol or drug abuse is probably also a risk factor, and such patients must be carefully evaluated.

Long-Term Risks and Side Effects

There have been recent reports that subjects taking benzodiazepine medications regularly for years manifest signs of generalized intellectual impairment (Hendler et al., 1980; Bergman et al., 1980). Lader and Petursson (1984) have recently reported additional disturbing evidence regarding the side-effects of this class of medication. Twenty patients on diazepam, lorazepam, or clobazam for 2 to 20 years underwent computer axial tomography to examine brain structure.

The benzodiazepine users had ventricular/brain size ratios between controls and alcoholics. The meaning of this observation is not entirely clear, but it suggests the possibility that long-term benzodiazepine usage might be associated with alterations in brain structure characteristic of patients with cognitive impairment. Lucki and Rickels (1986) examined 54 subjects who had taken benzodiazepine medications regularly for approximately five years. These subjects were unimpaired on tests of choice reaction time, tapping rate, or digit span. However, the chronic benzodiazepine users had a reduced CFF (critical flicker fusion threshold) and continued to show evidence of short-term memory impairment following administration of the medication. These findings are disturbing and argue for extremely judicious use of these drugs over the long term. Plesiur-Strehlow et al. (1986) found no evidence of increased mortality in patients using benzodiazepines for many years, although there was evidence of increased mortality in patients with psychiatric diagnoses, particularly when the diagnosis involved alcohol and drug abuse. One recent article suggested that benzodiazepine users were more likely than nonusers to experience accidental injury requiring medical attention, but the study did not determine the reason for this association (Oster et al., 1987).

Risk/Benefit

After reviewing the risks and benefits of long-term benzodiazepine use, the issue remains cloudy. There is evidence that benzodiazepines provide benefit to very anxious patients, yet only 25 percent of patients with anxiety disorders are being treated with a BZ medication. On the other hand, the risk of dependence and withdrawal are substantial, and the long-term risks and side-effects are unknown.

It is frightening to consider the population at risk for benzodiazepine dependence. Ayd (1980) estimated that over 500 million individuals had taken benzodiazepines worldwide by 1980. Not surprisingly, several studies have suggested that 1–2 percent of the population is dependent on benzodiazepines (Fleischbacker et al., 1986).

When considering BZD use with chronically anxious patients, we recommend:

1. Chronically anxious patients in need of benzodiazepine therapy should be treated only for short periods of time (less than six months), with three to six month intervals between drug use.
2. The lowest doses possible should be used; longer acting agents are preferable to shorter acting ones.

3. The patient's status and diagnosis should be frequently evaluated and documented.
4. The patient's medication use should be carefully monitored.
5. Other forms of therapy should be applied concurrently with benzodiazepine use and during drug-free trials.
6. Patients should be carefully and slowly withdrawn from BZ medications under the guidelines below.

Withdrawal Guidelines

Withdrawing patients from benzodiazepines can usually be done safely. However, there is no way to relieve the withdrawal symptoms when they are present except by taking more medication. The mechanism for benzodiazepine dependence is unknown. It is generally assumed that withdrawal is related to changes in benzodiazepine receptor sensitivity or density and changes in endogenous substances that regulate these receptors; withdrawl appears to diminish with alteration in these receptors or with increased production of endogenous substances, a process that may require weeks or months. Some symptoms, such as rebound in sleep and in anxiety may occur within 24 hours of the last dose given, and the symptoms may persist for weeks or even months.

Lennane (1986) has reported that eight of 200 patients admitted primarily for detoxification from benzodiazepines had one or more seizures and that four had delirium, an incidence of 4 percent and 2 percent respectively. She notes that delirium differs from alcohol withdrawal delirium in that the patients do not appear toxic, are pale rather than flushed, and are normotensive. They tend to look blank rather than perplexed and may be paranoid.

There are two major issues to contend with regarding withdrawal: the psychological dependence and the physiologic withdrawal symptoms. The first principle for dealing with psychological dependence is to prevent physiological dependence by following the guidelines we have already discussed. Patients should be told that it will be necessary for them to stop the medication and then to use medication intermittently, if at all, thereafter. Patients should be given psychological support during the withdrawal period. As withdrawal tends to be more difficult and unpleasant with short-acting benzodiazepine agents, the patient may be switched to longer acting agents (usually diazepam), substituting an equivalent dose over three to four days. (For equivalent doses see Hyman, 1984, p. 259.) The medication should be reduced by 10–20 percent every 3–4 days. A more rapid withdrawal tends to be more uncomfortable for the patient, although it has been used with inpatients (Harrison et al., 1984). Few pharmacologic agents are useful in counteracting symptoms during this period. Other sedative/hypnotics may only confuse and prolong withdrawal if a long-acting agent is already being used. Clonidine, used to help narcotic withdrawal, has not been effective. Buspirone does not block BZD withdrawal (Lader & Olajide, 1987). If outpatient withdrawal is intolerable or is associated with dangerous symptoms, the patient should be referred for inpatient withdrawal.

Psychological methods for treating withdrawal symptoms have had limited success. Cormack and Sinnott (1983) sent letters to 50 patients who had used benzodiazepines for more than one year. Patients were offered a group treatment program. Forty-two patients were available for follow-up. Of these, 12 cut down on their own and 5 of 13 cut down in the group. Thus, rather minimal intervention resulted in about a third of patients (17/50) cutting down. Sanchez-Craig et al. (1986) used cognitive-behavioral treatment to help 20 patients cut down. Patients monitored drug use, set goals they were confident to achieve, prepared for symptoms, and developed cognitive-behavioral methods as substitutes for benzodiazepine use. Preliminary results suggested some benefit from the procedure.

Buspirone

Until recently there have been few medications as effective and safe as the benzodiazepines for reducing anxiety. However, a new drug, buspirone has been introduced which appears to have anxiolytic effects similar to the benzodiazepines without the abuse potential (Sussman, 1986; Feighner, 1987; Lader, 1987). Buspirone has the added advantage of not being sedating nor interfering with performance (Lader, 1987). Buspirone is a member of the azaspirodecandediones drug class. Although buspirone is the only agent now available, many others in this group are being tested. These agents do not bind to benzodiazepine sites nor block GABA reuptake. Such findings suggest considerable theoretical interest because the latter two effects are considered central to the anxiolytic effect of the benzodiazepines.

The most common side effects to buspirone are lethargy, drowsiness, and dizziness, but significantly fewer patients receiving buspirone experienced these side effects than do patients treated with alprazolam, lorazepam, or diazepam. Because buspirone can bind to central dopamine receptors, it has the potential to cause acute and chronic changes in dopamine-mediated neurological function, like tardive dyskinesia. While this effect is unlikely, the long-term sequelae will become more apparent as the drugs gain wider and longer use. We begin patients on 5 mg three times a day and increase by 5 mg every three to four days, up to a maximum dose of 60 mg per day.

Case Examples

The following cases illustrate our treatment approach to GAD. The first case represents the treatment of a patient with a major depressive episode and generalized anxiety disorder.

The patient, Jennifer F., was a 32-year-old recent law school graduate at the time that she was seen initially. She had worked as a nurse for five years prior to entering law school. She had a life-long weight problem, had recently gone on a very low calorie diet program and had lost 90 pounds. She still considered herself 50 pounds overweight. She had recently obtained her first position as an attorney, doing research for a corporate firm. While her salary was competitive with other recent law school graduates, she was promised a substantial raise upon passing the Bar. The patient lived alone, had an active social life, but had not dated for many years.

The patient presented to us, complaining of preoccupation with the possibility of "never passing the Bar Exam" though she had been an excellent student in all her academic endeavors. She also was concerned about her social relationships, particularly that she was unacceptable to men and that her lack of opportunities to date and attendant feelings of low self-esteem would "never go away." She reported being "panicky" about these issues, to a point where she felt unable to concentrate on the material she needed to be familiar with to pass the Bar Exam. She reported that her worry about these issues had been going on for the past year, but that over the past month, not only had her anxiety increased significantly but she had begun to lose her ability to function effectively at work and had suicidal ideas. She had numerous physiologic GAD symptoms, including muscle tension, dry mouth, shortness of breath, and dizziness, in addition to difficulty concentrating, sleeplessness, and irritability. She did not suffer panic attacks, and there was no evident behavioral avoidance. It was clear upon seeing the patient that she was also in the midst of a major depressive episode. In addition to depressed mood, suicidal ideas, sleep disturbance, difficulty functioning at work, and difficulty concentrating, the patient also suffered feelings of worthlessness. Furthermore, she was having difficulty controlling her intake of calories, which had been under control for the past few months. She reported some recurrence of episodes of binge eating.

Jennifer had a difficult family history. She described her father, also a lawyer, as extremely critical, distant, and contemptuous of her and her older sister. She reported that as an adolescent, he would frequently end arguments by saying "You're fat," as though this fact disqualified her from rendering opinions or having feelings worthy of consideration, and as though she was to be dismissed on all counts for this reason. She reported that her mother was a loving, "reasonable," person, who, however, never confronted the father, and, instead, attempted to accommodate to his irascibility.

Because of concern over the patient's suicidal ideas and difficulty in concentrating and functioning at work, depression was the initial focus of treatment. The patient did not have a plan for suicide and was willing to make a no-suicide contract, and cognitive therapy was begun. Instances of such thinking patterns as magnification, selective abstraction, and globality were pointed out, together with attempts to encourage the patient to engage in more pleasureable activities. In addition, the meaning attached to becoming a lawyer and passing the Bar Exam was explored. The patient readily agreed that becoming a lawyer was tied up with achieving equal status with her father, and that failure in the Bar Exam or as a professional, in general, were construed as evidence that she would always be in a position to be humiliated and, worse, that perhaps her father was justified in his contempt.

However, Jennifer was not initially responsive to treatment and began to become even more panicky that "things will never improve and I'll always feel this way." Accordingly, antidepressant medications were tried. The patient proved to be highly sensitive to a variety of medications including imipramine, desipramine, protriptyline, nortriptyline, and amitriptyline, complaining that each either caused increased fatigue or increased agitation. We continued with cognitive therapy during this period of about four months when numerous medications were tried, but the patient's depression and anxiety continued. Family therapy with a colleague of the primary therapist was also arranged. The patient reported that the first session "made a huge difference" in her outlook. While nothing was resolved, and she remained unsure whether she and her father could have an acceptable relationship, having her father hear her concerns seemed to lift a weight from her. She reported fears prior to the session that he would dismiss her, deny the validity of her complaints, or storm out of the session. She began to be somewhat more responsive to cognitive-behavioral intervention as well. Finally, a low dose of doxepin, very gradually raised to 250 mg daily, proved tolerable, and the patient's mood improved markedly. At this point, symptoms of both depression and anxiety diminished significantly. Her ability to function at work improved, she reported enhanced ability to study for the Bar, sleep improved, and physiologic symptoms of anxiety remitted. She no longer felt hopeless about the future.

It is difficult to ascribe the results to any one of the components of treatment. Clearly, pharmacotherapy, family therapy, and cognitive-behavioral treatment, all had some impact. However, although the symptoms of generalized anxiety remitted simultaneously with the symptoms of depression, the latter was the primary focus of treatment.

The second case represents the rather unusual presentation of primary GAD.

Mrs. Jones is a 59-year-old female who presented to the clinic with a chief complaint of "panic." Although she reported 10 symptoms consistent with panic attacks at one time or another, she denied having discrete episodes of anxiety. Rather she often felt a sense of "nausea, abdominal distress, and uneasiness." She said these symptoms were present most of the time. In fact, she said she always had these symptoms, although they were worse when she went into supermarkets or public eating establishments. Also, she often had two symptoms of motor tension (feeling shaky and muscle tension), four or five symptoms of autonomic hyperactivity, but no symptoms of vigilance and scanning. She denied feeling depressed and had no somatic symptoms of depression. Although she felt "anxious" in the situations mentioned above, she never avoided these situations and felt no better when accompaned. She did not meet the criteria for any other Axis 1 diagnosis and her medical and physical exam were normal.

The patient said that her anxiety had begun about one and a half years ago for no apparent reason. On careful examination, there were two important events occurring at this time: (1) her husband had begun to talk about retirement, and (2) her daughter had decided to separate from the patient's favorite son-in-law, and she feared losing contact with him. Although the patient denied ever having had a previous panic episode, she did experience symptoms of nausea and gastric upset at the time of her father's suicide. The symptoms had lasted for about one and a half years and then remitted. Finally, the patient had often felt "sick to her stomach" when she separated from her family as a child. The patient had been prescribed lorazepam 1 mg BID, which she only took intermittently, although the drug was very effective in relieving her anxiety.

The treatment plan involved: (1) teaching the patient relaxation cued to her anxious thoughts; (2) exploring the role of the present events in contributing to her anxiety and developing recommendations as appropriate.

The patient was seen for ten sessions. Offered a choice between relaxation tapes, biofeedback tapes, and hypnosis, the patient chose biofeedback because she "wanted to see a connection between what she was feeling and those squiggly lines." Hand temperature feedback proved most effective in helping her relax: she was able to raise her hand temperature by 10 degrees centigrade with two practice sessions and reported deep relaxation during the biofeedback. The biofeedback sessions included a review of the current episodes which the therapist felt were contributing to her anxiety. She came to realize that even if her daughter divorced, it was possible for her to continue to see her son-in-law. The fears generated by her husband's retirement included concern that they would not have enough money, and worry about how they would spend their time together. Three conjoint sessions were held to help resolve these issues. The husband was supportive of his wife's concerns, assured her that they had ample resources and would now have opportunity to spend more time together. She noticed a marked diminution in her anxiety.

After two months the lorazepam was discontinued. Four months, and ten sessions later, the patient was no longer reporting any clinical levels of anxiety.

To summarize, we offer the following premises regarding the treatment of generalized anxiety disorder:

1. The presence of GAD without additional Axis I disturbance is unusual; therefore the therapist should carefully assess for the presence of additional problems. Such disturbances may or may not involve anxiety, although many patients with GAD have symptoms of panic disorder.

2. When another disturbance is uncovered, consider GAD a secondary phenomenon and treat the other Axis I problem first.

3. As GAD involves primarily both cognitive (e.g., unrealistically apprehensive expectation) and physiological (e.g., motor tension) symptoms, when it is the primary focus of treatment, cognitive-behavioral and relaxation strategies should form the major focus of treatment.

4. In those cases where family or marital concerns are prominent, the therapist should consider including others in treatment as demonstrated in the cases described above. In such cases, the focus is less likely to be on marital or family therapy, per se, than on using frank discussions between family members as a way of altering anxiogenic thoughts.

5. Life-style factors contributing to anxiety should be modified; life-style factors reducing anxiety should be introduced.

S E V E N

· · · · · · · ·

Panic Disorder

· · · · · · · · · ·

The distinguishing feature of panic disorder is the presence of abrupt and frequently unexpected disturbances involving symptoms such as palpitations, sweating, tingling, chest pain, shortness of breath, dizziness, nausea, depersonalization, numbness, and hot flashes or chills. Patients frequently experience fears of dying, going crazy, or behaving in an out-of-control fashion concomitant with the physical symptoms. The term "panic" comes from Pan, the half-human, half-goat Greek god of the mountains and woodlands, whose unpredictable behavior was associated with mountain rumblings and unforeseen events. The following is a typical patient's description of a panic attack:

> One day I had a real mild panic attack just standing around talking to some other people. . . . I'll feel hot and the heat will come and go for up to like a half hour, and if it continues I'll start getting nauseated and the nausea will come and go. And then I get kind of shaking, and I can't concentrate on anything. My mind just keeps hopping and skipping all around . . . and, of course, I get worried that I'm going to vomit at an inappropriate time, and I might not be able to get away from people where they can't see it. . . . sometimes it stops fast . . . sometimes it goes away very slowly. It just ends up kind of fading away before I realize it.

The patient may appear outwardly calm while experiencing such disturbances. Despite the consistent patterning and striking phenomenology of panic attacks, patients are misdiagnosed or their suffering is discounted with surprising frequency. For instance, 40 percent or more of patients with normal coronary arteries found during angiography present evidence of panic attacks, yet such patients are rarely given this diagnosis (Beitman et al., 1987a, 1987b). Psychotherapists, too, may fail to obtain a careful history or may view some

137

of the symptoms, like the sense of impending doom—perhaps the most discomforting symptom to patients—as histrionic. Treatment of panic disorder, which we will discuss later in this chapter, must begin with a careful appreciation and understanding of the symptoms.

Panic attacks are usually associated with some avoidance (Sanderson & Barlow, 1986). If the avoidance is severe, the condition is called panic disorder with extensive phobic avoidance (agoraphobia). Sometimes the presence of avoidance is difficult to discern. For instance, an executive who had suffered panic attacks for about a year denied avoidance and appeared to be functioning normally, yet when questioned carefully, admitted that he would not drive across the Golden Gate Bridge for fear of having a panic attack. The same patient also avoided certain staff meetings if he thought an angry encounter might take place. Such encounters had been associated with panic attacks in the past.

Phenomenology

Table 7.1 lists the percentage incidence of specific symptoms recorded on self-report diaries for a cohort of 27 individuals who experienced a total of 175 panic attacks during the investigation (Margraf et al., 1987). As can be seen in the table, cardiovascular symptoms are most common. We have added a column that details the incidence of the same symptoms obtained by retrospective report. Interestingly, retrospective reports of such symptoms tend to be much higher (Margraf et al., 1987).

While cardiovascular symptoms occur most frequently, the most disturbing symptoms involve the feared consequences of a panic attack: fear of dying, going crazy, or losing control and doing something embarrassing. The symptom pattern for any given patient may change from one panic attack to another. Although DSM-III-R does not use "severity" as a criterion for diagnosis, patients seem more concerned by the severity of the attack than by the symptom pattern. We find that panic attacks rated by patients as having three symptoms are also usually rated as having a severity of 3 or greater (on a scale from 0 to 10, where "0" represents no panic and "10" a state of incapacitation). Interestingly, as many as 30 percent of "normals"— those who do not meet the criteria for an anxiety disorder and have not sought help for anxiety-related difficulties—experience occasional episodes of panic (Norton et al., 1985). However, normals rarely, if ever, experience spontaneous panic attacks with as many as four or more symptoms and a severity of 4 or greater on a 0–10 scale.

TABLE 7.1

Symptoms During Panic

	Measurement	
Symptoms	Concurrent[a]	Retrospective[b]
Palpitations	68%	100%
Dizziness/lightheadedness	47	89
Dyspnea	30	58
Nausea/Abdominal distress	29	69
Sweating	26	65
Chest pain/discomfort	25	65
Fear of going crazy/doing something uncontrolled	21	73
Tembling/shaking	21	81
Hot flashes/cold chills	17	73
Derealization/depersonalization	15	65
Faintness	10	69
Paresthesias	10	46
Choking	5	35
Fear of dying	3	31

Adapted from J. Margraf, C. B. Taylor, A. Ehlers, T. R. Walton, and W. S. Agras, "Panic Attacks in the Natural Environment," *The Journal of Nervous and Mental Disease*, 175(9):558–565, © by Williams & Wilkins, 1987.

[a]Concurrent represents the percentage of 175 panic attacks with this symptom.
[b]Retrospective represents the percentage of 27 individuals who reported having the symptom during a typical panic attack.

Depersonalization, a feeling of temporary estrangement, disembodiment, or being cut off or far away from immediate surroundings often accompanies panic attacks. With derealization, a related phenomenon, the world seems unreal or as though it is behind a screen or a veil. Patients describe these experiences with words and phrases like, "It was like I was outside my body, watching what was happening"; "I felt disconnected from the world." Depersonalization and derealization often occur during panic attacks. Some patients describe feeling that way most of the time. Depersonalization is a common phenomenon, occurring in up to 50 percent of normal men and women (Nemiah, 1975). It may also arise during periods of sensory isolation, illness, or extreme emotional upset or fatigue. Depersonalization frequently occurs with petit mal and temporal lobe seizures. It seems to occur in most dying patients and is sometimes associated in such patients with a feeling of great peacefulness or relief. In fact, some religions consider depersonalization episodes to be an important metaphysical experience. The context of the depersonalization experience seems critical as to whether it is interpreted as a horrifying or a peak experience. One wonders: Is depersonalization some evolutionary mechanism to "protect" the organism from intense pain and fear brought on by life-threatening experiences?

Most patients report that their first panic attack "came out of the blue." They then continue to experience spontaneous panic episodes, the frequency changing from one period of their life to another. Yet many therapists from both psychodynamic and behavioral orientations do not believe that panic attacks are truly spontaneous. Psychoanalysts, for example, have argued that spontaneous attacks are in fact related to unconscious processes. They suggest that panic attacks occur when the psychological defenses are overwhelmed and unable to ward off disturbing memories, feelings, or images, although the actual content of the unconscious material may only become apparent in the analytic situation.

Behavior therapists have contested the spontaneous nature of panic attacks on grounds that they represent a conditioned phenomenon in which a stimulus conditioned to elicit a panic attack may not be apparent. On the other hand, we are impressed that many patients *experience* their panic attacks as spontaneous. It is the spontaneous quality of the attack—its abruptness and the accompanying lack of preparedness—that is often most disturbing to patients. It causes them to view themselves and the world with considerable caution, and, at worst, it may lead to extensive behavioral avoidance.

Physiological Abnormalities

When compared with normals, patients who experience panic attacks, including patients with panic disorder, have been found to have elevated baseline heart rates, skin conductance, and forearm blood flow levels (Roth et al., 1986). In some studies, panic disorder patients have been found to have higher blood pressure, electromyogram levels, and respiration levels than controls, but the results of studies investigating these variables are inconsistent. Compared to controls, panic patients have shown differences in reactivity to, or recovery from, stimuli with diverse qualities of novelty, startlingness, intensity, or phobicity in some studies but not others (Roth et al., 1986). Differences between panic attack patients and normals on physiologic measures are subtle, and since panic attack patients cannot be easily identified with these methods, such measures are of little clinical use.

DIAGNOSIS

The diagnosis of panic disorder is usually not difficult. However, we have been surprised at how many of our patients have complained that physicians and previous therapists did not seem to recognize that they were having panic attacks. According to the DSM-III-R criteria the patient must have four symptoms from a list of 14. Some patients have fewer than four symptoms during their attacks and fewer attacks each week or month than required by DSM-III-R. These patients respond to therapy identically to those who meet the strict DSM-III-R criteria. Another criterion for panic attacks is that some of the attacks occur "out of the blue." Following the rules of the Clinical Flowchart (chapter 3), medical causes of panic attacks, like hypoglycemia (low blood sugar), hyperthyroidism, drug use and withdrawal must be ruled out (Raj & Sheehan, 1987).

Panic attacks occur with many other problems, although usually at a much lower frequency than in panic disorder. Barlow et al., (1985) found that most social and simple phobic patients and patients with generalized anxiety disorder and obsessive compulsive illness have panic attacks, although at a lower frequency than occurs in panic disorder. The focus of treatment in such patients should not be reducing the frequency of panic attacks. In the general population, panic attacks are also common, perhaps occurring in 30 percent of people in any given year, but these attacks are usually limited in the number of symptoms and severity. Panic attacks may also occur in the course of a major depressive episode. For instance, Breier et al., (1986) found that 70 percent of panic attack patients had a concomitant depression. In our experience about 50 percent of patients had a depression that preceded the onset of panic attacks.

Kaplan (1987) has described a syndrome of sexual avoidance and panic disorder. In her clinical work, about 25 percent of patients with sexual aversion and avoidance have panic attacks, although the clinical picture is one of atypical attacks, usually only occurring when the person is exposed to the feared sexual stimuli. Kaplan claims that these patients, otherwise poor responders to her behavioral-psychodynamic therapeutic approach, do well with antipanic drugs.

Rosenbaum (1987) has also discussed the importance of not overlooking "limited-symptom panic attacks," those characterized by only one or two symptoms, that may present like a medical problem. As one of four examples, he cites the case of a 36-year-old man who had noted the abrupt onset of "numbness and tingling" in his feet. These paresthesias progressed to involve both legs, the abdomen, and hands. Of note, the symptoms were intermittent and fluctuating in intensity. Extensive medical work-up failed to reveal an etiology of the problems. A careful history revealed that the symptoms began when he was going through a difficult period in his business, that he had a history of early school phobia, and that he had severe height and airplane phobia. Furthermore, he had become quite housebound, and his mother had a history of panic attacks. The author said that treatment with desipramine 75 mg/d. resulted in an early and marked decrease in his paresthesias.

PREVALENCE

With recent improvements in the reliability of psychiatric diagnoses brought about by specific criteria and structured diagnostic interviews it has been possible to obtain information on the prevalence of panic disorder. Table 7.2 presents the prevalence rates/100 of panic disorder based on three community studies. These data suggest that panic disorder is a fairly rare condition. As we will see in the next chapter, however, panic disorder with extensive phobic avoidance (agoraphobia) is common, with a six-month prevalence of 2–6 percent. Added together, panic attacks severe enough to meet the DSM-III-R criteria probably occur in 3–7 percent of the population.

GENETICS

Little is known about the specific genetic factors that might predispose the individual to panic disorder. Early studies suggested that familial presence of anxiety disorders predisposed patients to develop such conditions. More recently, it was found that anxiety and depression may be genetically linked. Environmental factors partially determine the type of psychiatric problem developed by a patient with a general susceptibility to anxiety or depression. In general, loss and bereavement seem to predispose to depression, while danger and separation may have a greater effect in determining anxiety (Torgersen, 1985; Finlay-Jones & Brown, 1981). Noyes et al. (1987) have found that panic disorder is *not* more common among patients with generalized anxiety disorder, suggesting, as mentioned earlier, that the two are separate disorders. Patients who have never asked their parents about family history of anxiety disorders are often surprised to learn that other members have had similar problems.

TABLE 7.2

**Six-Month Prevalence Rates/100
of Panic Disorder Based
on Community Surveys**

Community	Men	Women	Total
New Haven	0.3	0.9	0.6
Baltimore	0.8	1.2	1.0
St. Louis	0.7	1.0	0.9

SOURCE: Taken from Table 3 in "Six-Month Prevalence of Psychiatric Disorders in Three Communities" by Jerome K. Myers, et al., *Archives of General Psychiatry, 41,* 959. Copyright 1984, American Medical Association.

COURSE

As suggested by the epidemiologic data, panic disorder usually leads to avoidance within the first year of onset. However, some patients do not develop avoidance yet continue to experience panic attacks. Figure 7.1 shows the the age of onset for 800 patients with panic attacks requesting treatment in our clinic or to participate in studies.

Panic disorder usually begins with a spontaneous panic attack, though this pattern is not universal. For instance, Breier et al., (1986) found that 78 percent of their patients had had a spontaneous panic attack, that is, one which seemed to come out of the blue for no apparent reason, while 22 percent did not. Breier et al., (1986) reported that 65 percent (38) of their patients reported a stressful life event occurring within six months of the first panic attack. The most common stressful life event was separation (N = 11), followed by change in job (N = 8) and pregnancy (N = 7). Nonspontaneous attacks (N = 13) were precipitated by public speaking, stimulant drug use, family arguments, leaving home, exercising (while pregnant), being frightened by a stranger, or fear of fainting. Uhde et al. (1985) found that approximately 80 percent of patients with panic disorder reported one or more stressful life events within six months of their initial panic attacks. Ninety percent of our patients attribute the onset of their panic attacks to a recent stressful life event. The most common event is feared or actual separation from a loved one, followed by a medical illness, or use of stimulant drugs.

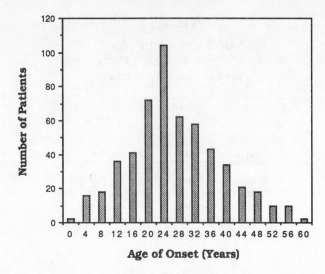

Figure 7.1. **Age of Onset of Panic Attacks**

This graph shows the approximate age of onset of panic attacks in 807 patients requesting treatment in the Stanford Anxiety Disorders Clinic. The numbers on the horizontal axis represent the midpoint of the range; thus the bar indicated by 4 includes patients whose panic attacks began between ages 2½ and 5½.

The course of panic attacks in patients with panic disorder is not certain. As discussed in the next chapter, most patients with panic attacks develop avoidance, usually within the first year following the first panic attack, and have periods of depression. Thyer et al. (1985b) found that 9 of 11 patients reported periods of remission from their anxiety symptoms. About 30 percent of patients on placebo report a marked reduction in panic attack frequency. Uhde, Boulenger, Roy-Byrne et al. (in press) found that many patients have short periods (weeks and months) without experiencing panic attacks, but that long remissions are rare. Clinically, few patients report sustained panic-free periods, although about 10 percent of patients with one panic attack for each of three weeks no longer has panic attacks when examined a month later. Taken together, these data suggest that panic attacks are part of a chronic disorder with short periods of remission.

The same factors involved in the onset of panic attacks seem to exacerbate them. Stressful life events, use of psychostimulants, medical illness and/or separation, may exacerbate the frequency and intensity of panic attacks. The complications of panic disorder seem to relate mostly to what the patient does to reduce the panic attack intensity and frequency. Alcoholism is common, for instance, in patients with panic disorder.

ETIOLOGY

The etiology of panic attacks and panic disorders is unknown. The available evidence suggests that panic attacks at least begin because of some central nervous system dysfunction. The nature of this dysfunction is also unknown, but evidence points to a central role of midbrain structures and of the noradrenergic and serotonergic neurotransmitter systems. Some of the neuroanatomy was presented in chapter 2. In this section, we will examine some of the methods used to identify this dysfunction in more detail. The central nervous system dysfunction model (sometimes inappropriately called the biological model) assume that panic attacks can be provoked by various biochemical and physiological mechanisms. Because of the importance of this issue, we will review the studies in some detail.

Provocation of Panic Attacks

Four general strategies have been used to provoke panic attacks: lactate infusions, CO_2 inhalation and hyperventilation, drug provocation, and behavioral provocation.

Lactate Infusions

Sodium lactate was among the first agents to be used in an attempt to provoke panic attacks. Based on the observation that some anxious patients have poor exercise tolerance and unusually high post-exercise blood lactate levels, Pitts and others wondered if lactate, a metabolic product of exercise might be associated with anxiety. They infused lactate into anxious patients, most of whom reported attacks. Figure 7.2 shows the change in heart rate levels during slow and fast saline and lactate, taken from one of our studies (Ehlers et al., 1986). Heart rates in the panic disorder patients exceeded a mean of 95 bpm during lactate compared to about 85 bpm in controls. At baseline, the panic patients had heart rates about 12 bpm higher than controls but the changes were similar for the two groups.

Many lactate studies have been reported since Pitts and McClure's (1967) early report. In reviewing lactate studies, Ehlers et al. (1986) found that, across 14 studies, the reported rates of lactate-induced panic in panic patients range from 26 percent (Lapierre et al., 1984)

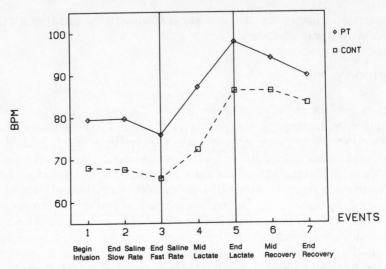

Figure 7.2 **Heart Rates for Patients (PT) and Controls (CONT)**
During Lactate Infusion

Mean heart rates during the one-minute epochs selected for statistical analysis are presented in beats per minute (bpm). Note that for 4 of 10 patients the end of lactate occurred before 20 minutes had elapsed.
SOURCE: "Lactate Infusions and Panic Attacks: Do Patients and Controls Respond Differently?" by A. Ehlers, J. Margraf, W. T. Roth, C. B. Taylor, R. J. Maddock, J. Sheik, and M. L. Kopell, 1986, *Psychiatry Research, 17,* p. 301.

to 100 percent (Rifkin et al., 1981), with a mean of 58 percent (158 of 271 subjects). This compares to panic rates of 0 percent to 30 percent found for normal control subjects undergoing lactate infusions, with a mean of 9 percent (7 of 76). Methodological problems may explain some part of these differences (e.g., the experimenters were not blind to whether a given participant was a panic patient or control subject). Nonetheless, the difference in panic attack frequency during lactate infusion between treatment and control subjects is still impressive. Several scientists, as discussed below, consider these lactate effects an important clue to the cause of panic disorder.

A recent study using the PET scan has provided additional information regarding the importance of lactate in producing panic (Reiman et al., 1984). The PET scan (PET stands for positive emission tomography) uses a radioactively labelled glucose infusion to determine the relative metabolic activity of various areas of the body. PET scan measurements were made during a panic-free period in normals and controls. Panic patients who showed subsequent sodium lactate vulnerability had blood flow asymmetry in the region of the parahip-pocampal gyrus. This abnormality was absent in all but one of the normal controls. The one normal patient with a flow asymmetry was found to have a panic attack during lactate infusion.

How lactate may cause panic attacks remains obscure. Among the hypotheses are that lactate causes changes in calcium metabolism (Pitts & McClure, 1967) or other peripheral metabolism effects (Shear, 1986), central neurophysiologic effects (Carr & Sheehan, 1984), or psychological effects (Clark, 1986) leading to increased re-port of panic. Neither lactate nor epinephrine levels of patients who showed panic responses were significantly elevated at the point of panic compared to controls measured at comparable time points (Liebowitz et al., 1985c).

Lactate infusions produce a metabolic alkalosis, whereas lactate production during exercise leads to metabolic acidosis. It has been shown that bicarbonate infusions may cause panic attacks, but Liebowitz et al. (1985c) demonstrated that there was no difference in blood pH between subjects who show lactate-induced panic and those who do not. Second, in a study of room air hyperventilation in panic patients, Gorman et al. (1984) found a low incidence of panic episodes despite the development of profound alkalosis. Carr and Sheehan (1984) note that lactate infusion and other maneuvers, like breathing CO_2 and hyperventilation, all produce a rise in the lac-tate/pyruvate ratio and a concomitant fall in chemoreceptor intra-neuronal pH. They speculate that the "primary lesion" susceptible to panic is in some minor ion channel in the chemoregulatory centers in the brainstem. Against this hypothesis is the fact that some panic patients panic when breathing room air, which would not affect chemoregulatory centers in the way they propose (Gorman et al., 1988).

Psychological mechanisms may also account for the lactate-in-duced panic attacks. Lactate infusion produces a number of pe-ripheral physiologic effects that patients may interpret as indicating the onset of a panic attack. Clark (1986) has suggested that the phe-nomenon of lactate-induced panic may be due to a "relatively endur-ing characteristic" (p. 465) among panic disorder patients to in-terpret certain bodily sensations catastrophically. Kelly et al. (1971) found that the presence of a reassuring physician seemed to block the occurrence of panic attacks in some patients. Furthermore behav-ioral techniques have been useful in reducing the development of panic during lactate infusions (Bonn et al., 1973; Guttmacher & Nelles, 1984). Also, Gorman et al. (1988) have shown that some panic patients continue to hyperventilate after a panic attack induced by room air.

We have recently completed a study that demonstrates the importance of expectation in physiological studies. One group of panic disorder patients was given the expectation that hyperventilation would result in panic; another group was given the expectation that hyperventilation would result in certain symptoms but not panic. Control patients without panic attacks were randomized to the same two expectations. Figure 7.3 shows the results. The panic disorder patients who had been given the expectation of panic experienced significantly greater increases in heart rate during hyperventilation than the other two groups, suggesting that expectation of panic may be a more important factor in producing panic than the physiological provocation used. Until lactate studies are carried out with careful attention to expectancy, its effects on producing panic will remain uncertain.

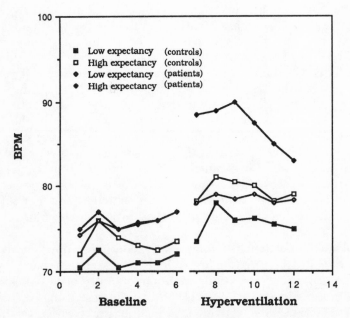

Figure 7.3 **Expectancy and Heart Rate Changes During Hyperventilation**

This figure represents the heart rates (BPM = beats per minute) during hyperventilation in four groups: patients and controls given the expectation that panic attacks might occur during the hyperventilation (high expectancy groups) or no expectation of panic attacks (low expectancy). There was a significant increase in heart rate in the patient group given the expectancy that panic attacks would occur.
SOURCE: A. Ehlers, J. Margraf, and W. T. Roth. Unpublished.

Breathing CO$_2$ and Hyperventilation

The observation that breathing CO$_2$ might cause panic was made serendipitously by Gorman et al. (1984). Since panic symptoms share many similarities with those of hyperventilation episodes, and panic patients have been observed to hyperventilate during panic episodes, Gorman et al. (1984) attempted to determine whether hyperventilation would induce panic in the laboratory. Five percent CO$_2$ was used to provide a control for increasing respiratory rate without causing the blood PH changes seen with room air hyperventilation. Surprisingly 7 of 12 patients experienced panic attacks with CO$_2$ while only 3 of 12 panicked on room air hyperventilation. In our laboratory we found that, compared with normals, panic attack patients report greater intensity of anxious symptoms during CO$_2$ inhalation (Ehlers et al., 1987). Woods et al. (1985) also found that panic patients had higher levels of anxiety while breathing CO$_2$ compared to normal subjects, an effect significantly attenuated by alprazolam.

Although Gorman et al. (1984) found little evidence that hyperventilation produces panic, clinical researchers report that hyperventilation can be used both to induce panic and to desensitize patients with panic atacks. Breathing CO$_2$ and hyperventilation may produce panic in ways similar to that of lactate infusion.

Psychological Methods

Several recent studies have used psychological manipulations to produce panic attacks. In one study, Margraf et al., (in press) provided real and false heart-rate feedback to patients with panic attacks. Patients led to believe that their heart rate was increasing reported more anxiety; one patient even reported a full-blown panic attack. Expectation also affects the occurrence of panic attacks during lactate infusions (see Figure 7.2).

Finally, exposure to a fearful situation can also be used to produce panic attacks. However, the rate of panic attacks during exposure conducted for purposes of evaluation is surprisingly low. In many of our studies we have subjects undergo a predetermined "test" walk that requires them to walk through an open parking lot into a busy department store and even requires them to try on a piece of clothing that they do not intend to buy. Although subjects report that performing many of these tasks causes extreme anxiety or terror, fewer than 5 percent report panic attacks during the test walk. This low rate may be due, in part, to the fact that they perceive a significant measure of control over the situation (e.g., they can stop the test walk at any point) and that they know a research assistant is waiting for them at a specific location.

Drug Provocation

Many patients date the onset of their panic disorder to the use of cocaine, amphetamine, or caffeine. All of these increase CNS noradrenergic activity. On the assumption that noradrenergic activity is central to the development of panic attacks, Charney, Heninger, and Breier (1984) gave yohimbine, a potent alpha-adrenergic receptor antagonist that increases noradrenergic function, to 39 drug-free patients with panic disorder and 20 healthy controls. Yohimbine produced significantly greater increases in patient-rated anxiety, nervousness, and somatic symptoms, and in panic attacks. Combining data from this study and observations from other studies that drugs with antipanic effects, such as morphine, benzodiazepines, tricylic antidepressants, and clonidine, reduce noradrenergic activity, the authors conclude that noradrenergic dysfunction is important in the generation of panic attacks. Although in need of further supporting evidence, and still imprecise as to the nature of the dysfunction, this hypothesis is the most attractive one available as to the cause of panic attacks. Assuming that the noradrenergic hypothesis is correct, as reviewed in chapter 2, the main neuroanatomic structures involved with panic disorder would include the locus coeruleus and other noradrenergic midbrain sites and their ascending pathways. Yet, again, abnormalities in other neurotransmitter systems cannot be ruled out.

The existence of a primary central nervous system lesion does not in any way minimize the importance of psychological mechanisms that might exacerbate, maintain, diminish, or control these same problems.

Although the issue is far from settled, we conclude (1) that psychological factors strongly influence the outcome of panic-attack provocation studies, yet (2) pharmacologic provocation discloses more panic attacks in patients subject to such attacks than in normals, and, therefore, (3) that there is some difference in biology between panic disorder patients and nonpanic disorder patients. Central noradrenergic dysfunction has been most strongly implicated as involved in this biologic difference—yet its exact nature remains uncertain. These provocative tests have no practical clinical use as yet.

ASSESSMENT

Subjective Experience

Assessment of the panic disorder patient's subjective experience begins with the clinical interview. This is the single best source of information regarding the internal experience of the patient presenting with panic disorder.

For both clinical and research purposes, it is important to have a quantitative estimate of the frequency and intensity of panic attacks. However, methods of establishing panic-attack intensity and frequency are somewhat problematic. Some patients may classify a sudden surge in anxious feelings or symptoms as "anxiety," while others may label it "panic." Although most patients appear to distinguish between intense anxiety and panic, there is little consistency in how they do so. For instance, during a lactate infusion, one patient said she was experiencing a major panic attack but only reported moderate levels of anxiety. Another patient reported intense anxiety without panic. Sheehan (1983) has proposed that panic attacks be classified into four categories: (1) major spontaneous attacks, those occurring out of the blue with three or more symptoms, (2) minor attacks that occur with one or two symptoms, (3) anticipatory attacks, which are essentially anticipatory anxiety, and (4) situational attacks. Our own experience in interviewing patients asked to record panic attacks by type, combined with analysis of their diaries, suggest that patients seem to have the most difficulty distinguishing anticipatory attacks from their usual anxiety. Overall, we have found that the most meaningful distinction patients are able to make is between spontaneous and situational panic attacks.

We use a panic attack diary (see Appendix 2) to complement the clinical interview and the self-report measures noted above. Patients are asked to rate the overall intensity of the attack, accompanying symptoms, and type of attack. In addition, they are asked to record where they were at the time of the attack, what they were doing, what their thoughts were during the attack, and when it began and ended.

As many panic disorder patients experience depression, in addition to the clinical interview, we recommend using the Beck (Beck et al., 1961) or Zung (Zung, 1965) depression inventories or the Hamilton Depression Interview (Hamilton, 1960).

Cognitive Assessment

"Fear of fear" (Goldstein & Chambless, 1978) has been described as the hallmark of panic disorders. As we noted earlier, panic disorder patients typically experience catastrophic thoughts along with the physical symptoms. A number of instruments have been developed to assess such fears. Notable among these are two developed by Chambless and her colleagues, the Agoraphobic Cognitions Questionnaire and the Body Sensations Questionnaire (Chambless et al., 1984). The former consists of 14 items comprising thoughts concerning negative consequences of experiencing anxiety (e.g., I am going to pass out). Patients are asked to rate the frequency of such thoughts while anxious using a 5-point scale, ranging from (1) thought never occurs to (5) thought always occurs. The Agoraphobic Cognitions Questionnaire has proven to be a reliable and valid measure of fear in patients with panic attacks (Chambless et al., 1984). The Body Sensations Questionnaire consists of 17 items concerning sensations associated with autonomic arousal (e.g., pressure in chest).

The Stanford Panic Appraisal Inventory has been developed by Telch and his colleagues at Stanford (see Appendix 2). The SPAI consists of 20 statements reflecting some common feelings and thoughts that people report during sudden attacks of panic or extreme anxiety. Subjects are asked to circle the number that best describes the degree to which they were troubled by certain feelings or thoughts during the past week. This instrument can be used to identify the presence of troublesome thoughts as well as to quantify the patient's level of subjective distress.

Telch et al. (submitted) have expanded the appraisal inventory to include three dimensions: (1) anticipated panic, which assesses the subject's perceived likelihood of experiencing panic in a variety of situations, (2) panic consequences, and (3) panic coping. "Anticipated panic" is the subject's perceived likelihood of experiencing panic in 10 situations; "panic consequences" asks subjects to rate the perceived consequences of panic on three subscales (physical concern, social concern, loss of control), and "panic coping" consists of 20 items asking subjects to rate their confidence in executing panic-coping behaviors (e.g., using distraction, controlled breathing, etc.). The test-retest reliability and internal consistency of all three scales is high. We have developed a somewhat different coping scale that measures the patient's belief in his or her ability to manage a panic attack effectively under a variety of conditions (see Appendix 2, the Panic Attack Self-Efficacy Scale). The scale provides the most meaningful information when the therapist helps the patient complete the form. In general, we have found that patients are able to engage in tasks where they report 70 percent or greater confidence. The form may be used as a guide to help determine the course of therapy.

Controllability, safety, and predictability are three dimensions of panic attacks that are also of importance. Rachman and Levitt (1985) have shown that unpredicted panic attacks contribute to increases in predicted fear and to decreases in predicted safety. Increases in confidence in any of these dimensions can reduce the intensity and frequency of panic attacks. In explorations as to the importance of these cognitive factors in precipitating subsequent panic attacks, we have developed another diary that asks subjects to make frequent ratings as to their sense of safety in a particular situation, i.e., how likely they think it is that a panic attack will occur, and how confident they are that they will be able to control it (see Appendix 2).

Finally, cognitive logs may be of some help in determining the content and situations of panic and anxiety relevant to a particular patient (Zucker et al., submitted).

Somatization

Because panic attacks, by definition, involve the experience of numerous physiologic symptoms, it is not surprising that panic disorder patients score high on questionnaires that assess somatization. Given false feedback about increases in their heart rate, panic patients will report greater cardiovascular awareness than controls and respond with even more accelerated heart rate increases (Margraf et al., in press). During CO_2 or lactate infusion, panic disorder patients will report more symptoms than controls, even endorsing symptoms that would not be caused by the test (Ehlers, Margraf, Roth et al., 1985). Thus, there is a predisposition both to monitor and respond to symptoms otherwise not felt or ignored by "normals." Somatization typically decreases along with reductions in anxiety (Noyes, Anderson, Clancy et al., 1984).

Various psychological instruments have been developed to measure somatization. The SCL-90 (Derogatis et al., 1973) contains a somatization scale. Pilowsky (1967) has developed a hypochondriasis scale that is effective in identifying patients with this condition.

Behavior

In animals, terror is associated with a number of behavioral responses, such as freezing, trembling, rigidity. Many patients report changes in their behavior during panic such as speech impairment, tightening of muscles, staring, and related behavior. Yet these responses are rarely observed in patients. *Physiological and biological assessment* are of interest theoretically but have no use in clinical practice as yet.

Disability

Panic attacks are accompanied by considerable impairment, even among those who report minimal or no avoidance. The panic attacks may undermine a patient's confidence in subtle ways. For example, patients may avoid job-related responsibilities because they anticipate the possibility of a panic attack, thus jeopardizing career advancement. In other cases, there may be subtle social avoidance, such as an unwillingness to invite people to the home. We therefore recommend the assessment of the patient's perception of disability. A disability scale, like that developed by Sheehan et al. (1984) for a multinational drug trial is appropriate for such assessment (see Appendix 1).

Medical Problems

All of the medical problems discussed in chapter 3 are particularly relevant to panic disorder. Therefore, the assessment procedure outlined in that chapter should be followed carefully in assessing and treating patients.

Recommendations

We recommend that every panic disorder patient be assessed at baseline and at least every six months thereafter. The basic assessment should include a measure of chronic anxiety (e.g., the Spielberger trait measure), depression (the Beck or Zung), panic attack frequency and intensity, avoidance, and disability (see Appendix 1). Other measures discussed above can be used to supplement assessment and guide treatment.

REVIEW OF TREATMENTS

The pharmacological treatment of panic attacks is now so effective that most patients can achieve significant decrements in the intensity and frequency of attacks, or in some cases outright remission. However, all pharmacological agents have disadvantages. Among the most important disadvantages for those agents used to control panic symptoms is the lack of data regarding long-term risks associated with their use. While the nonpharmacological treatment of panic attacks is still in its infancy, some techniques appear promising.

Behavioral Treatments

Imaginal Flooding

Imaginal flooding involves exposure to anxiety through the therapist's vivid description of a feared event or situation. For instance, after obtaining a clear picture of the patient's typical panic attack symptoms and fears, the therapist may guide a patient through a panic attack as follows:

> Therapist: Now, with your eyes closed, I want you to imagine that you are having a panic attack. Recall the last intense panic attack you had. Remember the situation. Where were you? Who were you with? What were you doing? What was the time of day, the temperature? How anxious were you? Now remember the first feeling that you had, like a wave of dread coming over you. Your heart starts to pound. You feel it pounding harder and harder. You feel it might burst. You look around worried that someone might notice how terrified you feel. You start to sweat. You feel dizzy and nauseous. You start to breathe rapidly and you can't catch your breath. Your throat is dry, too dry to speak. You feel like you may black out. Your chest is filled with pain and you think you will go crazy.

Many patients experience considerable anxiety with this therapeutic provocation, with the symptoms usually subsiding as soon as the therapist finishes the instructions. While imaginal flooding appears to be effective in reducing obsessive thoughts and has been employed in the treatment of phobic avoidance (see chapter 8), both Gelder, Bancroft, Gath et al. (1973) and Chambless, Foa, Groves, and Goldstein (1979) found it had no discernible impact on the frequency and intensity of panic attacks. Its limitations may be due to the fact that the symptoms experienced by the patient under these conditions do not approximate closely enough those panic symptoms experienced in the natural environment.

In Vivo Exposure

In vivo exposure, which was developed to help overcome phobic avoidance, also reduces panic attacks. This procedure involves the

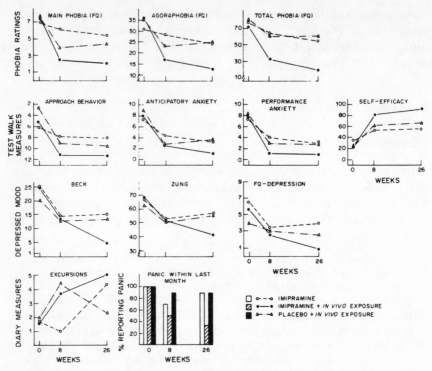

Figure 7.4 **Combined Pharmacological and Behavioral Treatment for Agoraphobia**

Thirty-seven agoraphobics were randomly assigned to imipramine with instructions not to engage in exposure for the first 8 weeks of the trial, to imipramine plus exposure, or placebo plus exposure. At 8 weeks, the group given imipramine plus exposure displayed more improvement than the other two groups. At 26 weeks, all groups had improved. The imipramine plus exposure group had significantly less fear, depression, and panic attacks than the other groups.

Source: "Combined Pharmacological and Behavioral Treatment for Agoraphobia" by M. J. Telch, W. S. Agras, C. B. Taylor, W. T. Roth, and C. C. Gallen, 1985, *Behavior Research and Therapy, 23*, p. 331.

patient in actual encounters with fear-evoking situations. Numerous techniques have been developed to help patients cope with panic attacks that may occur during exposure. For instance, we tell patients to allow the panic to "peak and pass" while carefully monitoring its course and suggest that the procedure is most effective when they experience some anxiety and panic. While the results are not entirely consistent, most studies investigating exposure have found a significant reduction in panic attacks. Data from one study illustrates this (see Figure 7.4). The results from Ghosh & Marks (1986) are even more dramatic. In this study, subjects were randomized to bibliotherapy, computer-assisted exposure, or exposure instructions delivered by a therapist. All treatments resulted in a marked reduction in panic attacks. None of these studies have differentiated the type of panic attacks reduced by exposure. It would be important to determine whether spontaneous panic attacks remit when situational panic attacks remit. It is also important for the therapist to assess carefully whether the panic disorder patient manifests avoidance. As mentioned earlier, panic disorder patients may engage in subtle avoidances that are revealed only upon careful examination. In most cases, the presence of behavioral avoidance argues for the use of in vivo exposure.

The effectiveness of in vivo exposure in reducing behavioral avoidance, has recently led to efforts to extend the procedure toward the specific treatment of panic attacks. Barlow (1986) reported considerable success in reducing the frequency of panic attacks accompanied by reductions in medication by incorporating a procedure involving exposure to those internal physiologic sensations associated with panic. For instance, in cases where elevated heart rate is the primary symptom, the therapist may have the patient run in place in the office or go rapidly up and down stairs. Rapid breathing may be used to bring on symptoms of hyperventilation. Barlow has combined this technique with the use of relaxation and cognitive therapy, which will be discussed in more detail below. In general, patients are taught to identify their thoughts at the onset of symptoms; to practice starting and stopping panic episodes; and to learn relaxation techniques to reduce symptoms. While this approach is a very recent one requiring considerably more study and refinement, it appears quite promising.

Paradoxical Intention

Paradoxical intention, symptom prescription, symptom scheduling, and "reverse psychology" are terms that apply to psychological interventions aimed at changing a behavior or attitude by prescribing or encouraging it (Jacob & Rapport, 1984). Alternatively, desirable behaviors may be increased paradoxically by forbidding the behavior. As applied to a student with test anxiety that escalated to panic episodes before a scheduled test, Malleson (1959) described the following effect:

He was made to sit up in bed and to try to feel his fear. He was asked to tell of the awful consequences that he felt would follow his failure—derison from his colleages in India, disappointment from his family—financial loss. Then he was to try to imagine these things happening; try to imagine the fingers of scorn pointed at him, his wife and mother in tears. At first as he followed the instructions, his sobbing increased. But soon his trembling ceased. As the effort needed to maintain a vivid imagining increased, the emotions he could summon began to ebb. Within half an hour he was calm. Before leaving I instructed him in repeating the exercise of experiencing his fears. Every time he felt a little wave of spontaneous alarm, he was not to push it aside but was to enhance it, to augment it, to try to experience it more profoundly and more vividly. If he did not spontaneously feel fear, every 20 or 30 minutes, he was to make a special effort to try and do so, however difficult and ludicrous it might seem. I arranged to see him twice a day over the next two days until his examination. He was an intelligent man, and an assiduous patient. He practiced the exercises methodically, and by the time of the examination he reported himself as almost totally unable to feel frightened. . . . He passed his examination without apparent difficulty. (p. 225)

Jacob and Rapport (1985) have described a treatment approach to panic attacks that relies on paradoxical techniques. Their treatment begins with a detailed behavioral analysis of the panic attack. Patients are then instructed to try to bring on a panic attack at home in the safety of their bedroom. If they are unable to bring on the panic attack by thoughts alone, they are then encouraged to use hyperventilation. This procedure usually results in a reduction in the incidence of panic; if not, the patients are taught relaxation and slow abdominal breathing exercises. After three to four sessions of home practice, the patient is then instructed to encounter situations in which they are likely to experience panic. In an attempt to preempt relapse problems, as patients improve they are cautioned that such remissions may be temporary and perhaps not even desirable. They are told that they should continue to have a few panic experiences and to practice coping with them.

A major problem with paradoxical instructions is patient compliance. Even when considerable care is taken to persuade the patient of the usefulness of the intervention, the instructions may be experienced as counterintuitive, leading to failure to carry them out.

Michelson, Mavissakalian, and Marchione (1985) randomized 39 patients with agoraphobia and panic attacks into one of three groups: paradoxical intention (PI), graduated exposure (GE), or progressive deep muscle relaxation training (RT). At posttreatment, only 50 percent of the PI, 45 percent of the GE, and 40 percent of the RT subjects reported experiencing spontaneous panic attacks. The three-month follow-up revealed that only 33 percent of the PI, 45 percent of the GE, and 50 percent of the RT subjects reported having spontaneous panic attacks, a nonsignificant difference among groups. Yet the study confirms that paradoxical intention, graduated exposure, and relaxation training can reduce panic attack frequency.

CO_2 Rebreathing

In an interesting and novel approach to incorporating the exposure paradigm with panic disorder patients, Griez and van den Hout (1983, 1984) used inhalations of 35 percent CO_2 as a way of repeatedly exposing patients to the physiologic sensations accompanying panic attacks. Inhalation is introduced gradually. Subjects first take small inhalations; after repeated exposure, as their anxiety reduces they eventually take several full depth inhalations. Griez and van den Hout (1984) evaluated the short-term effectiveness of this treatment using a crossover design in which two weeks of CO_2 inhalation therapy was compared with two weeks of the beta-blocking agent propranalol. Treatment effects were modest. However, better results have been obtained with a longer treatment regimen.

Hyperventilation

Clark has argued that panic attacks result from hyperventilation brought about by catastrophic misinterpretation of various bodily sensations. His therapy involves the following five stages:

1. Brief voluntary hyperventilation
2. Explanation and discussion of the way hyperventilation induces panic
3. Training in a pattern of slow, controlled breathing
4. Training in more appropriate cognitive responses to bodily sensations
5. Identification and modification of panic triggers

Clark has evaluated his technique in two uncontrolled studies. In the first (Clark et al., 1985) patients were selected who perceived a similarity between the effects of overbreathing and naturally occurring panic attacks. The data was analyzed by patients who reported that there were certain situations in which they consistently experienced anxiety (n = 11) and patients who were unable to identify any situations that were consistently associated with anxiety (n = 7). For the "situational" patients, panic attacks dropped from a mean of about 10/week at baseline to about 5 per week during treatment and to 2 or less at 6 and 24 month follow-ups. For the "nonsituational" patients, panic attacks dropped from about 5/week at baseline to about 3/week during treatment to less than 1/week at 6 and 24 month follow-ups. Salkovskis, Jones, and Clark (1986) repeated the procedure, this time with an unselected group of panic patients, and again demonstrated a substantial reduction in panic attack frequency. Effects appeared to be enhanced for those patients who perceived a similarity between the effects of overbreathing and episodes of panic.

Clark (1986) enumerated a number of other relatively benign sensations that might be misinterpreted catastrophically. These include perceiving palpitations as evidence of an impending heart attack, perceiving a minor episode of breathlessness as a harbinger of breathing cessation, and perceiving a shaky feeling or one's "mind going blank" as indicative of an impending loss of sanity. He has proposed a characteristic sequence of events that may begin with an internal (or external in some cases) stimulus that is perceived in a threatening way, followed by increased apprehension, which then increases the feared sensations, creating a vicious circle ending in a panic attack. A cornerstone of treatment, he suggests, would involve identifying those catastrophic interpretations, and replacing them with alternative constructions that could be tested through discussion and behavioral tasks. From this perspective, attributing panic symptoms to hyperventilation is one of several possible alternative reinterpretations that might be suggested.

Cognitive Approaches

There are many features common to both generalized anxiety disorder and panic disorder. Therefore, what was said about the cognitive approach to generalized anxiety disorder in the previous chapter applies equally to panic disorder. In addition to the hyperventilation procedures developed by Clark and his colleagues which incorporate cognitive reattribution, a number of other cognitive approaches such as self-statement modification (Meichenbaum, 1977) have been proposed for treating panic attacks (e.g., Emmelkamp & Mersch, 1982; Waddell, Barlow, & D'Brien, 1984). While there have been trials investigating the effectiveness of cognitive therapy for reducing symptoms of depression, there are few controlled investigations of the efficacy of this approach for reducing *panic attack intensity or frequency*.

Moreover, though cognitive techniques are frequently presented as powerful on their own, they are rarely employed without some form of behavioral intervention. For example, while Beck and Emery (1985) present a veritable encyclopedia of cognitive techniques, they acknowledge that "in vivo homework . . . is a crucial element in the treatment of anxiety" (p. 258). They devote one chapter of their book to such intervention. Because cognitive therapy is usually presented in conjunction with behavioral treatment, its relative contribution is difficult to evaluate. It seems likely that the in vivo exercises discussed by Beck and Emery (1985) are more powerful determinants of cognitive change than the cognitive interventions themselves. This is consistent with the argument of Bandura (1977), who conceptualizes change in terms of alterations in self-efficacy. He has argued that among the major sources of information influencing efficacy, expectations and performance-based experiences such as in vivo exposure will be more powerful than verbal persuasion techniques such as those highlighted by Beck and Emery (1985).

We have encountered a wide range of patient responses to cognitive intervention, such as self-statement modification particularly in the initial stages of treatment. While many patients are able to make use of logical challenges to their beliefs, others seem outright skeptical regarding the value of such procedures or seem to produce "coping thoughts" or other products of the specific intervention mechanically, without conviction and without benefit. Patient responses to such therapeutic tactics are an area requiring considerable research.

At this point it appears to us that when difficulty arises in the patient's ability to profit from cognitive intervention at the beginning of treatment, it is because the particular logical challenge conflicts with another belief the patient has about himself or his disorder at the level of "deep structure" (Guidano & Liotti, 1983). In these cases, that specific belief needs to be articulated, the issues giving rise to its development may need to be discussed in detail, and additional challenges may need to be devised. Further, it has often been our experience that initial logical challenges may be rejected or greeted coolly at first, only to be embraced later when performance-oriented "experiments" have been carried out.

Bibliotherapy

Many of our patients have read books about anxiety before coming to the clinic or wish to do so in the course of therapy. Ghosh and Marks (1986) have even reported that bibliotherapy works as effectively as therapist instruction for self-exposure, at least with agora-phobics. We have yet to see a patient benefit from bibliotherapy to the extent indicated by the Ghosh and Marks study. However, we have found such books useful to help patients gain an understanding of their problem and to feel less alone in struggling with their difficul-ties. Two books that provide a good discussion of panic are *The Anx-iety Disease* by Sheehan (1984) and *Panic: Facing Fears, Phobias and Anxiety* by Agras (1985); these books are not designed as self-help manuals.

There are some excellent self-help books. Weekes (1977), the "grandmother" of anxiety self-help approaches, has written about the subject for lay audiences for over 40 years. She claims that her self-help program, involving books, phonograph recordings, and cor-respondence, has a general sucess rate of 50 percent or better, de-pending on the age of the client. She is critical of "exposure" treat-ment alone and emphasizes the importance of patients learning to cope with internal symptoms of panic. Weekes teaches four basic coping strategies. First, patients practice *facing* the feared internal or external stimuli; in more conventional terms this translates into ex-posure. Second, patients learn to *accept* the reality of their panic attacks and of their anxiety but not to add to them. She differentiates between the panic fear and "second fear," or what the patient adds to the panic. She writes, "True acceptance means even welcoming pan-ic so you can practice coping with it, the way I have advised until it no longer frightens" (p. 27). Patients learn not to prevent panic at-tacks but to control their reactions to them. She is a persuasive writ-er. "I have watched many, many people, just as desperate as you and with no more courage than you think you have, come through panic to peace; so why shouldn't you?" (p. 28). Third, patients learn to *float*. The patient is instructed to "move forward with the panic" accepting all the feelings and sensations that are occurring. Finally, patients are told to *let time pass*, as the body can only sustain panic for a limited time.

Don't Panic, by Breton (1986), a clinical psychologist, provides a clear description of panic attacks and a rather conventional and sim-ple treatment approach. The book does not provide detailed instruc-tions on how to follow the author's three-step treatment process. On the other hand, *Your Phobia* by Zane and Milt (1984) is a detailed account of what amounts to self-directed exposure. A highly moti-vated patient might well benefit from this book. *Anxiety and Panic Attacks: Their Cause and Cure* is a well-written book by Handly in collaboration with Neff (1985); Handly is an individual who over-came anxiety and panic.

Pharmacologic Treatment of Panic Disorder

In 1964, Klein reported that patients with panic attacks seemed to respond to imipramine, while patients with generalized anxiety did not. This observation implied that there might be two types of anxiety syndromes of very different etiology. One, which has come to be called panic disorder, is characterized by panic attacks with or without avoidance; the other is generalized anxiety disorder. Subsequent studies have cast doubt on the validity of some of Klein's initial assumptions, but the fact remains that imipramine is an effective medication for reducing the frequency and intensity of panic attacks. In recent years, evidence has accumulated that at least two other agents, alprazolam and phenelzine, are also effective in the short run. Table 7.3 summarizes some of the recent studies. Since these studies combine patients with panic disorder with and without agoraphobia, we only focus here on the effects on panic attacks, anxiety, and depression.

As suggested by the data in the table, all three drugs have reduced panic attack frequency and intensity, as well as having favorable effects on general anxiety and depression. We will now look at these medications by drug group in more detail; the pharmacology of the three drugs is discussed in more detail in chapter 11.

Tricyclic Antidepressants

Imipramine has been demonstrated to be an effective antipanic agent. Six double-blind, placebo-controlled trials of imipramine have been conducted, with five of the six demonstrating clear superiority of imipramine over placebo (Ballenger, 1986). Clinical effects are usually observed after two to six weeks. Results from the four largest research trials suggest that more than 70 percent of patients experience moderate or marked improvement of phobic symptoms. It is to be noted, however, that most of the trials have also incorporated behavioral treatments, and the importance of imipramine independent of its effects in helping to promote exposure remains controversial.

The antipanic and antiphobic effect of other antidepressants have been studied less. Chlorimipramine has been shown to be effective in several open and placebo-controlled trials (Beaumont, 1977; Escobar & Landbloom, 1976; Karabanow, 1977). There is limited and generally anecdotal evidence suggesting that desipramine (Rifkin et al.,

TABLE 7.3
Pharmacologic Effects of Medication for Panic Attacks

Author	X̄ Dose (mg)	Weeks on Drug	Drug Effect On: PaFr	PaIn	Anx	Dep	Drop-Out Rate
Imipramine							
Zitrin et al., 1980	(up to 300)	26		+	+	+	29%
Sheehan et al., 1980	150	12		+	+	+	25%
Zitrin et al., 1983	(up to 300)	26	+	+	+	+	26%
Marks et al., 1983		26					
Mavissakalian et al., 1983	125	12	−/+	−/+	−/+	−/+	30%
Telch et al., 1985	179	26	+	+	+	+	14%
Charney et al., 1986	141	8	+				17%
Kahn et al., 1986	122	8		+	+	+	25%
Aronson, 1987	130	16	+				30%
Phenelzine							
Sheehan et al., 1980	45	12		+	+	+	25%
Buiges & Vallejo, 1987	55	24	+		+	+	12%
Alprazolam							
Sheehan et al., 1984	5	8	+		+	+	17%
Ballenger, 1986	6	8	+	+	+		
Dunner et al., 1986	(up to 10)	6	+		+		21%
Charney et al., 1986	3	8	+		+		20%
Liebowitz et al., 1987	4	12	+		+	−/+	

PaFr = panic attack frequency; PaIn = panic attack intensity; Anx = anxiety; Dep = depression.

1981), nortriptyline (Muskin & Fyer, 198ī), doxepin and amitriptyline are all effective (Lydiard & Ballenger, in press).

Monoamine Oxidase Inhibitors

Five placebo-controlled trials have demonstrated the effectiveness of phenelzine in improving panic disorder with or without agoraphobia (Mountjoy et al., 1977; Sheehan, Ballenger & Jacobson, 1980; Solyom, Hersetine, McClure et al., 1981; Tyrer, Candy, & Kelly, 1973). Tyrer et al. (1973) reported that 65–70 percent of patients improved and maintained this improvement for eight months. One other MAOI, iproniazid has also been shown to be effective (Lipsedge et al., 1973).

Benzodiazepines

It has long been assumed that benzodiazepines are of little benefit in reducing panic attack intensity and frequency. However, there is good evidence that alprazolam has significant antipanic properties. Preliminary results from a large, multicenter, double-blind, placebo-controlled trial of alprazolam confirm earlier studies suggesting that it is efficacious (Ballenger, 1985). In this study approximately 560 patients were treated with a flexible-dose schedule, resulting in a mean dose of 5.6 mg/day. The authors report significantly greater reductions in panic attack frequency, phobia severity, anxiety, work and social disability, and overall global ratings in the alprazolam group compared to the placebo group. Less than 5 percent of patients dropped out due to side effects. Such studies have renewed interest in other benzodiazepines for treating anxiety. Some evidence suggests that doses of diazepam greater than those traditionally used may have antipanic effects. One study has shown that clonazepam is also an effective antipanic agent (Spier et al., 1986).

Limitations of Medications

Although effective antipanic agents are available, none are without problems. As discussed in chapter 12, these medications produce uncomfortable, often intolerable, and sometimes lethal side effects. As seen in Table 7.3, drop-out rates exceeding 25 percent in these drug studies are the rule. Many of the medical problems accompanying panic disorder are relative or even absolute contraindications to the use of these drugs. Withdrawal from benzodiazepines can be problematic. However, perhaps most discouraging, relapse rates after drug discontinuation are very high. Zitrin et al., (1983) have observed that approximately 15–30 percent of patients who had experienced substantial improvement with 26 weeks of treatment with imipramine relapsed within the first two years after the drug was discontinued. Cohen et al., (1984) followed patients for two years after treatment with imipramine and placebo and observed that approximately one-third of each group contacted the therapist for further treatment. In Kelly et al.'s study (1970) of phenelzine about 30 percent relapsed. Preliminary reports on alprazolam suggest that the relapse rate is comparable. If drop-outs, patient intolerance, and relapse are combined, medication produces a benefit sustained after discontinuation in fewer than 50 percent of patients eligible for treatment. Such data make it important for therapists to combine psychological and behavioral treatment with any drug intervention.

Choosing a Drug

The main factors to consider in choosing a drug for treating panic are effectiveness, side effects and patient tolerance, contraindications, abuse potential, withdrawal, and cost. We will consider these factors only for the three drugs that have been extensively evaluated.

Effectiveness. The effectiveness of drugs for reducing the intensity and frequency of panic has been discussed above. Also a series of comparative drug trials have helped clarify the relative effectiveness of these medications. Imipramine and phenelzine appear to be equally effective (Sheehan et al., 1984). Of note, rather low doses of phenelzine were employed, which might have underestimated its potential. Comparative studies with alprazolam, imipramine, and phenelzine suggest that all three are equally effective. Alprazolam has the most rapid effect; the effects of imipramine and MAO inhibitors may not become apparent for several weeks to a month.

Side Effects and Patient Tolerance. Panic disorder patients are particularly sensitive to the side effects of imipramine. However, such unpleasant effects can usually be minimized or overcome. A low enough dose of imipramine can usually be found that provides initial benefit without causing intolerable side effects. We have started some patients on doses as low as 5 mg; over several months the doses usually have to be raised to 25–50 mg to have an effect. Also we have combined imipramine and alprazolam to minimize this effect (see below). Using a low-dose procedure, less than 10 percent of agoraphobic patients have an intolerable reaction to imipramine. Alprazolam is associated with drowsiness, which can compromise the patient's ability to perform tasks, such as driving, that require motor coordination or alertness. However, Ballenger (1986) reports that less than 5 percent of patients dropped out of a recent study due to alprazolam side effects. The most unacceptable part of MAOI use seems to be the many dietary and medication restrictions patients must follow. In this already somatic group of patients, many of whom are reluctant to take medications, such restrictions are particularly worrisome.

Contraindications. The contraindications of using imipramine, phenelzine, or alprazolam with panic disorder patients are the same as those for any population being considered for these agents. For instance, among the many concerns are that patients with prolonged QT intervals on the ECG should not be given imipramine, that benzodiazepines should be used cautiously in patients with a drug-abuse history, that suicidal patients should not be given enough pills to cause a lethal overdose, etc. The diagnosis of panic disorder should raise suspicions about other medical problems more common with this disorder (see chapter 12), of depression and suicidal tendencies, and of possible concomitant drug and alcohol abuse.

Abuse Potential. Imipramine and phenelzine have little abuse potential. The abuse potential of alprazolam is, as yet, unknown. We should assume that it will have the same abuse potential as other benzodiazepines. We have not had any patients in our clinic take more alprazolam than prescribed, but we have had patients reluctant to stop the medication.

Withdrawal. There are no major withdrawal problems with either imipramine or phenelzine. However, recent studies suggest that some patients have extreme difficulty withdrawing from alprazolam. This is a complicated withdrawal phenomenon in which the phenomenology can include actual withdrawal symptoms, return or even rebound of initial symptoms, or new symptoms. Assessment and management of withdrawal are discussed in the previous chapter and in chapter 11.

Treatment Recommendations

The guidelines presented below offer our psychopharmacologic treatment recommendations for panic disorder. Overall, our analysis of the effectiveness, side effects and intolerance, and other pharmacologic data leads us to choose imipramine as the drug of first choice for patients presenting with panic disorder. If patients are intolerant to imipramine, dislike the anticholinergic or other side effects, require more immediate relief, or receive no benefit, we then choose alprazolam, followed by another tricyclic or MAO inhibitor. We are reluctant to use alprazolam in patients who might become pregnant because of the difficulty of stopping it. In such patients we will turn to desipramine after imipramine or an MAOI. Clonazepam and other benzodiazepines and the azoazaspirodecanediones may also prove to be effective. We have not found beta-blockers to be nearly as effective as the agents listed above and, therefore, rarely use them.

Generally, we increase the dosage of the medication until the patient is not experiencing panic attacks with their customary level of activity. The reduction in anticipatory anxiety does not change at the same rate as panic attacks. Some patients who achieve relief from panic attacks are disappointed that their general anxiety does not diminish concomitantly; we inform patients that the persistence of anticipatory anxiety does not indicate they are still prone to panic attacks. Many patients experience a sense that panic attacks are "blocked" under medication. They report experiencing symptoms that in the past were indicative of an impending panic attack, but under medication the attack fails to develop. Thus, patients who expect complete symptom reduction are likely to be disappointed. Moreover, we do not advocate medicating patients to a point where they experience an absence of anxiety. We emphasize that some anxiety is normal. Because panic attacks may terminate spontaneously, and many patients seem to have fewer panic attacks after a medication trial, we stop medication after 6–12 months and encourage patients to remain drug-free for at least three months before reinstituting a drug trial. We also encourage patients not to resume medication unless they have experienced several panic attacks. In the last phases of medication treatment, we help patients develop strategies for dealing with panic attacks (see below).

PANIC ATTACK TREATMENT GUIDELINES

For Patients with Panic Attacks with and without Avoidance

Step 1. Imipramine Hydrochloride

Begin at 25–50 mg (or start with 5–10 if patient shows paradoxical reaction. If patient continues to have paradoxical reaction, consider adding alprazolam 0.25 to 1 mg for first month). Warn patients about possible paradoxical reactions.

Increase by 25–50 mg every 4–7 days until patient has intolerable side effects or experiences reduction in intensity and frequency of panic attacks to a tolerable level. Increase up to 300 mg.

Maintain patient for 6–12 months. Combine pharmacology with psychotherapy as appropriate. Prepare patient for possibility of recurrent panic attacks once medication is stopped.

If patient shows no response or has intolerable side effects, withdraw medication at a rate of 25–50 mg every 3–4 days and proceed to Step 2.

Step 2. Alprazolam, Phenelzine or Desipramine

a. Alprazolam.

Begin at 0.25–0.5 mg once or twice a day. First dose should be taken at night.

Increase by 0.25–0.5 mg once or twice a day every 4–7 days until patient has intolerable side effects or experiences reduction in intensity and frequency of panic attacks to a tolerable level. Increase up to 6 mg. (Doses above this are rarely effective for panic, although they may be helpful for depression.) If patient has reduction in panic attacks but remains depressed, consider increasing alprazolam to 6–8 mg or adding tricyclic antidepressant (even imipramine, which may have been beneficial for patient's depression but not other symptoms).

Maintain patient for 6–12 months, preferably 6 months. Combine pharmacology with psychotherapy as appropriate. If patient shows no response or has intolerable side effects, withdraw medication at a rate of 0.25 mg every 3–4 days, and proceed to Step 3. Encourage a 3-month drug-free period.

b. Phenelzine

Do not begin phenelzine until at least 2 weeks after tricyclics and/or alprazolam have been stopped. *Begin* with 15 mg once or twice a day.

Increase by 15 mg once a day every 4–7 days until patient has intolerable side effects or experiences reduction in intensity and frequency of panic attacks to a tolerable level. Increase up to 90 mg.

Maintain patient for 6–12 months. Combine pharmacology with psychotherapy as appropriate. If patient shows no reponse or has intolerable side effects, withdraw medication at rate of 15 mg every 3–4 days and proceed to use of alprazolam (if it has not been used) or to Step 3.

Step 3. Tricyclic, Alternate MAOI, Other Antidepressant

There is little outcome data to guide us beyond the first two steps. If the patient has not done well with imipramine, alprazolam, or an MAOI such as phenelzine, we will try another tricyclic (occasionally, for unknown reasons, a patient who has not responded to imipramine will respond to desipramine), another type of antidepressant (like trazodone, although at least one study has not shown it to be efficacious), or even another MAOI.

Step 4. After the first three steps, little is known about the relative efficacy of other agents. Long-acting benzodiazepines, like clonazepam or a beta-blocker, should be considered. Although not approved in this country, chlomipramine appears to be an effective antipanic agent.

Integrated Approach to the Treatment of Panic Disorder

Our approach to treating panic attacks in patients with panic disorder is pragmatic and symptom-focused. We use procedures that

TABLE 7.4

Integrated Treatment of Panic Attacks

Function	Intervention Component
Providing Information	Eduction by therapist
	Panic diaries
Decreasing the proba-bility of a panic attack	Relaxation
	Medication
	Diet and exercise changes
	Cognitive therapy
Increasing efficacy	Cognitive therapy
	Controlled breathing
	Exposure to symptoms

appear justified based on our clinical experience and the research literature. The goal of therapy is to reduce the intensity and frequency of panic attacks, often beginning with medication but ending therapy medication-free and with patients prepared to cope with possible recurrences. Table 7.4 presents an outline of the components of our approach.

Treatment involves three major functions. First, education is used to give the patient useful information regarding the phenomenon of panic. By useful information, we mean information designed to help correct any faulty assumptions that may be involved in maintaining the problem. For example, many panic disorder patients misconstrue their anxiety as evidence of physical illness, which then amplifies their hypervigilance regarding the physical manifestations of the problem. Information about the nature of panic disorder is offered to dispel such distortions and reduce their preoccupation and anticipatory anxiety. The use of panic attack diaries also serves an educational function, but here rather than helping the patient to learn more about panic in general, the focus is on their own idiosyncratic experience with the problem and any patterns associated with it that may have been obscured previously.

Second, our approach involves measures designed to decrease the incidence of panic attacks in the patient. Medication is one such intervention. The alteration of various life style habits serves also to reduce the probability of panic attacks. Third, we intervene in ways designed to enhance the patient's sense of efficacy in coping with panic when it occurs. These interventions involve controlled breathing, cognitive coping strategies, and exposure to sensations experienced during episodes of panic.

The outline in Table 7.5 presents an ideal progression, although the actual sequence differs from one patient to another depending on the

TABLE 7.5

Sequences of Interventions

Phase I Assessment, Education, and Symptom Reduction

Session 1	(Week 1)	History Taking. Assessment. Medical records requested. Medical tests ordered as needed (or patient referred to consultant.) Patient leaves with panic attack diary.
Session 2	(Week 2)	Additional history taking. Education regarding the nature of panic attacks. Panic attack diary reviewed. Patient and therapist discuss and agree on goals of therapy. Treatment plan devised. Medication prescribed as necessary.
Session 3	(Week 3)	Panic attack diary reviewed. Patient responses to education, medication reviewed. Importance of lowering general level of arousal is explained. Relaxation introduced, along with instructions to decrease caffeine intake, if appropriate, and to increase exercise.
Session 4	(Week 4)	Possible role of hyperventilation is presented and assessed. Controlled breathing introduced. Relaxation reviewed. Review necessity for medication changes.
Session 5	(Week 5)	Go over patient's record of thoughts during panic attacks and time when experiencing anticipatory anxiety, and review patient's beliefs regarding panic. Introduce coping self-statements.
Session 6	(Week 6)	Review use of coping self-statements.
Session 7	(Week 7)	Introduce in vivo exposure to symptoms of panic.
Sessions 8–16	(Weeks 8–26)	Revise and practice relaxation, controlled breathing, coping self-statements, and in vivo exposure to panic symptoms.

Phase II Stop medication

Sessions 17–22	(Weeks 26–31)	Reduce and stop medication. Prepare for relapse.

Phase III Maintenance

Sessions 31–36	(Weeks 31–41)	Relapse coping. Long-term maintenance.

171

patient's symptomatology, temperament, response style, comorbidity, family and social resources, and treatment response. Also, panic attacks without avoidance are rare, so that treating behavioral avoidance (discussed in chapter 8) is often a major part of the treatment program.

COMPONENTS OF TREATMENT

Education

As many researchers who have treated patients with panic disorder have noted, a major feature of the disorder, and one that appears to be involved in its maintenance, is the presence of catastrophic fears regarding the consequences of experiencing the symptoms themselves (e.g., Beck, 1976; Clark, 1986; Guidano & Liotti, 1983). These include fears related to physical well-being, social embarrassment, loss of control, and insanity. The purpose of education is to help the patient understand the nature of panic attacks and to offer an alternative to their catastrophic appraisal. There is considerable variety in the way patients respond to educational intervention. For some, it goes far toward dispelling their catastrophic fears; others are less responsive to purely informational intervention. Education is best regarded as the first of several steps toward changing the patient's view of panic.

As the purpose of such intervention is to provide reassurance and help dispel the patient's more catastrophic beliefs about panic, the therapist's credibility as a source of accurate information is an important issue. One way to establish credibility as a therapist with the panic disorder patient is to indicate familiarity with the range of symptoms such patients experience. In the initial interview, after we have asked the patient to catalogue his or her particular symptoms, we will ask about additional symptoms. Thus, if a patient notes experiencing palpitations, sweaty palms, and numbness in the hands, we will then ask whether he has ever experienced chest pain, difficulty breathing, feelings of unreality, and so on. After inquiring about the physical symptoms, we go on to ask about the perceived consequences of such sensations. Here again, if the patient emphasizes fears of dying, we will go on to ask about fears of self-embarrassment or impending insanity. Often patients will recognize one or more additional symptoms when they are mentioned. We also ask whether panic attacks are experienced as situational, spontaneous, or both. As a general rule we ask patients for considerable detail in describing their symptoms, and we are mindful of posing questions in a way that demonstrates our own knowledge about the problem.

The ability to establish familiarity and understanding of the problem is critically important in establishing a working alliance with the panic disorder patient. As we mentioned earlier, it is common for this group of patients to have been seen innumerable times in emergency rooms or other facilities before being seen by a mental health professional. They frequently report feeling that their problem has been poorly understood and are often wary of having the experience repeated. Often, they interpret their referral to a mental health professional as evidence that their symptoms are not seen as "real." While patients who present with panic disorder do not present unusual difficulties in their ability to form a collaborative relationship with the therapist, in the initial contact they are often skeptical until convinced that the therapist understands, is familiar with, and sympathetic about the problem they are presenting. Questions about the therapist's knowledge and empathy regarding panic disorder frequently constitute an initial "test." However, once the therapist has succeeded in demonstrating familiarity with and understanding of the problem, the working relationship generally proceeds smoothly.

Once we have obtained a detailed picture of the patient's cluster of symptoms, fears about the consequences of panic, and range of avoidance, we generally attempt to construct a model that in some way renders the patient's predicament more comprehensible and more under his or her control. We have found a variation of Clark's (1986) cognitive model of panic (see Figure 2.1) helpful in this regard. Most patients readily understand its implications. The model explicitly separates the physical sensations experienced during a panic attack from the catastrophic interpretations of the sensations characteristic of this population. In explaining the phenomenon, we emphasize that while the physiological experience of panic is very uncomfortable, the consequences are not nearly as drastic as those inferred by most patients.

The therapist's attitude toward the patient is another key variable affecting the latter's response to an informational intervention. While presenting an explanatory model is intended to correct misconceptions, it is important that the patient not feel diminished or criticized. We frequently tell patients that their way of construing their experience makes sense given their subjective sensations and the limited information that they have had available to them. For example, to patients who voice concern that they will behave in an uncharacteristic "out of control" or embarrassing fashion during a panic attack, we often note that it "makes sense" given that one's autonomic nervous system "feels out of control" that one might then begin to worry about "what's next," and become concerned that one's behavior will be affected. However, we point out that one's behavior is voluntary and governed by different systems within the body than, for example, one's heart rate or breathing, which are under the control of the largely involuntary autnomic nervous system.

The Use of Panic Attack Diaries

The patient is asked to log the severity of the attack on a 0–10 scale, the symptoms experienced, the time the episode began and ended, whether the attack was spontaneous or situational, where it took place, what activity was being engaged in, and what their thoughts were while the attack was going on. Such diaries serve several important functions. First, they serve as a source of information for the patient regarding his own pattern that often can demystify the experience. A significant number of patients with panic disorder label episodes as "spontaneous" or "out of the blue" when, in fact, they are associated with particular mood states, thoughts, or experiences.

In some cases, patients fail to make connections between panic attacks and events that are connected temporally and are palpably traumatic. For instance, we recently saw a patient who requested an evaluation following her first panic attack. She had been seen at a local emergency room following the episode and was told that her symptoms were due to anxiety. In taking a history and inquiring about the context in which the panic attack occurred, the patient noted that when she returned home from work on the Friday evening before the symptoms appeared, she had received a message on her answering machine from her gynecologist instructing her to call his office regarding the results of a Pap smear. His office was closed for the weekend, so that she was unable to reach him and was understandably quite anxious about the results of the exam. She suffered the panic attack during the weekend but failed to make the connection between her anxiety over the gynecological examination and the panic symptoms. As a result, when she experienced the attack she believed she was "going insane." While the relationships between panic episodes and other events are not always as dramatic as in this example, panic diaries frequently reveal patterns in which attacks previously labeled spontaneous are associated with interpersonal situations, moods, thoughts, physical sensations, or other circumstances that the patient had previously overlooked.

Second, patients frequently overestimate the duration of the attacks. It is not uncommon for them to report panic attacks lasting "for several days" when in fact the duration of the physical symptoms may have been 30 seconds to 5 minutes. Asking the patient to note when the physical symptoms actually began and ended aids the process of differentiating the symptoms themselves from the patient's thoughts and emotional reaction to them. Finally, the diaries help the therapist and patient track changes in the frequency and intensity of panic attacks that may occur during treatment.

Decreasing the Frequency of Panic Attacks: Changing Life-Style Habits

We make the point to patients that high levels of arousal can lead to "spikes" of panic. That is, we explain that if the patient's general level of arousal is sufficiently high, incremental additions are more likely to lead to surges that are experienced as panic attacks. One way that patients can take action to decrease the frequency of panic attacks is to lower their general level of arousal. There are several avenues for accomplishing this.

One area involves the modification of certain everyday habits. For example, several studies have demonstrated an association between levels of caffeine and the incidence of panic attacks. Thus, we suggest that patients eliminate or severely curtail their consumption of coffee and other caffeinated beverages. In addition, we have seen numerous cases of patients who experienced their first panic attack, as well as subsequent ones, while under the influence of marijuana or some other pharmacologic agent. We inform patients of this and encourage them to discontinue the use of any such drugs as well as the use of nicotine, which may also raise their level of arousal. We follow the procedure we have described in other publications to help patients stop smoking (Killen et al., 1984). We also encourage patients to become involved in daily exercise as an additional method of decreasing arousal; the method we recommend follows that which we have developed for sedentary populations (Juneau et al., 1987).

Finally, progressive muscle relaxation is introduced. It is important that the purpose of relaxation, its potential benefits, and its limitations are explained clearly to patients. The function of relaxation in the overall treatment program is to decrease day-to-day levels of physiologic arousal. Should a panic attack begin, we explain, relaxation is unlikely to be beneficial in reducing its severity. However, if practiced faithfully, it will reduce the patient's vulnerability to panic episodes. Issues in teaching and using relaxation are discussed in the previous chapter.

Several points are important in increasing patient compliance with such measures. First, we firmly make the point that they *will* make a difference in reducing the frequency of panic attacks. Second, we are clear regarding the limitations of these measures: they will not eliminate the problem. Clarity and specificity regarding the

usefulness and limitations of the measures enhances their face validity. Third, we make the point that while problems associated with
panic disorder can be overcome, patients will achieve the best results
only if they make changes designed to "stack the deck in their favor."
That is, there are no "miracle cures"; success is dependent on making
changes in several areas.

Controlled Breathing

Once we have performed a thorough assessment, presented information regarding the nature of panic, reviewed panic attack diaries,
prescribed habit and life-style changes and medication if indicated,
we begin to focus on intervention designed to enhance the patient's
ability to cope with panic attacks when they do occur. One such
measure involves teaching the patient controlled breathing.

A number of investigators have noted the similarity between the
physiological sensations associated with hyperventilation and those
involved with panic (e.g., Lum, 1976; Clark, 1986; Hibbert, 1984), and
have suggested that hyperventilation may play a significant role in
the etiology and maintenance of panic attacks. As we mentioned earlier, several investigators have reported obtaining reductions in panic attacks using a treatment protocol involving reattribution of panic
attacks to hyperventilation combined with training in respiratory
control (Clark, Salkovskis, & Chalkley, 1985; Salkovskis, Jones, &
Clark, 1986).

We have not been wholly successful in replicating these results
with our own clinic patients. More specifically, we have found that
while patients will concede that the symptoms of hyperventilation
induced in the office overlap with sensations they experience during
a panic attack, they often insist that there are important differences.
However, they frequently recognize that they hyperventilate during
panic episodes and that this may exacerbate their symptoms. Thus,
while we have not found respiratory control and reattribution of
physiological symptoms of panic to hyperventilation to be as powerful an intervention as is suggested by the studies cited above, we have
found it to be a useful coping technique in the context of a broad
treatment program for dealing with panic and avoidance.

When instructing patients to practice controlled breathing, we ask
them to put one hand on their chest, and the other on their stomach
and observe what happens when they breathe normally. They generally report that the hand on their chest moves noticeably, while the
one on their stomach moves hardly at all. We then instruct them to
breathe in such a way that the hand on their stomach moves out

when they inhale and in when they exhale. Once they can do this, we ask them to count to five between breaths. Patients are instructed to practice controlled breathing when anxious, and many report that it is helpful. In addition to reducing the intensity of some of the physical sensations involved with panic attacks, controlled breathing also seems to serve as a coping technique that reduces the patient's sense of helplessness when beset by panic episodes.

Enhancing Efficacy: Incorporating Cognitive Strategies in the Treatment of Panic Disorder

We begin the process of incorporating cognitive intervention by using the psychophysiologic model discussed above to educate patients (see Figure 2.1) regarding the role of thoughts in the maintenance of panic. In doing so, we emphasize that while we cannot entirely control the physical sensations associated with panic and anxiety, we can help patients change the catastrophic ideas they have formed about these experiences; this will help them to make progress in coping more effectively with anxiety. Thus we begin by highlighting to patients that their fear of the symptoms constitutes their most significant disability. Treatment success, we point out, should be measured not by the absolute number of panic attacks experienced, but rather by the patient's fear of them. A patient may experience panic sensations from time to time following treatment, but if their level of fear diminishes significantly and they feel confident of their ability to cope with such symptoms, they should consider the treatment successful.

Apart from educating patients regarding the role of cognitions in the maintenance of panic, we make use of several interventions designed specifically to change maladaptive thoughts.

Modifying Self-Statements

Self-statement modification is presented as a coping strategy, designed to increase the patient's ability to deal more effectively with fear-evoking situations. Developed by Meichenbaum (1974, 1977), self-statement modification involves changing one's covert speech (Luria, 1961; Vygotsky, 1962), or "self-talk." There are three steps involved in this intervention: (1) identifying one's negative or maladaptive self-talk; (2) developing more productive self-statements; and (3) practice in using the more adaptive self-statements in threatening situations.

We begin by asking patients to identify "what you say to yourself" in fear-evoking situations or when experiencing sensations associated with panic attacks. We find that, in many cases, patients are readily able to do so by imagining themselves in these circumstances. In other instances, catastrophic expectancies may not arise as self-statements and so may be less accessible. A useful technique with such patients is simply to ask, once they imagine themselves experiencing sensations characteristic of panic, "What did you think was going to happen?" Following this, we help them to develop more adaptive self-statements. Thus for example, the patient who says to himself "I must be having a heart attack" during a panic attack characterized by tachycardia will be instructed to substitute, "This is a symptom of anxiety not a heart attack"; the person who is afraid of "running my car into a ditch" while having a panic attack is instructed to substitute, "Rapid heart beat and sweating are physical symptoms—they don't affect my behavior"; the person who is afraid of fainting during a panic attack is asked to substitute, "I've had many panic attacks and I've never fainted."

The production of coping self-statements is an ongoing process. It often works well to have patients develop their own statements as treatment progresses. When a patient reports a frightening panic attack, we usually ask "What could you have said to yourself that might have reduced your fear?" Patients are asked to carry a list of coping statements with them to refer to at times when beset by symptoms of panic.

While self-statement modification has an important place in the treatment of panic disorder, the therapist working with the anxious patient should be aware of its limitations. Asking the patient to substitute positive for negative self-statements is sometimes experienced as comparable to the therapist's reassurance in effect—that is, it is somewhat comforting, but by itself it is often far from convincing. What we are asking the patient to do is to reassure himself in our absence.

The importance of acknowledging the initial skepticism of many patients about coping self-statements and other logical challenges cannot be overstated. We tell such patients that we do not expect them to believe their coping self-statements or other reminders of their illogical thinking at the outset, but we think it important that they try to use these techniques, particularly during any performance-oriented tasks that are assigned. Following through will often require the patient to temporarily treat hardened beliefs as "hypotheses to be investigated," rather than immutable truths. Becoming convinced about the validity of the self-statements and other cognitive changes, we emphasize, will take time and will grow out of performance-based tasks and discussions of the tasks with the therapist.

The evidence on the relative contribution of self-statement modification in the treatment of panic disorder as well as agoraphobia is currently equivocal (see chapter 8). Our reasons for employing it have less to do with its potential for changing catastrophic expectations or self-efficacy estimations in causal fashion than with its usefulness as a strategy to distract patients from preoccupation with their physical sensations, and to direct them toward a more objective and reasoned appraisal of the consequences of panic. Further, we view the use of "cognitive" techniques as inseparable from performance-oriented tasks. Cognitive change is seen as a process emerging over time, as the patient's beliefs are subjected to a series of disconfirmatory experiences discussed in detail with the therapist.

Paradox

An additional cognitive strategy, as we noted earlier, involves the use of paradoxical intention. Here the patient is instructed to attempt amplifying the most salient panic symptom rather than engaging in efforts to ward it off. The rationale usually employed in convincing patients to engage in such activity emphasizes that fear of panic initiates a cycle of anticipatory anxiety; when combined with heroic efforts to control and reduce panic the result is an increase in the overall level of arousal and in the incidence of panic (Ascher, 1980, 1981; Jacob & Rapport, 1984; Michelson & Ascher, 1984). While paradox has been viewed as an alternative to the strategy of developing coping self-statements (Mavissakalian et al., 1983a), more recently it has been combined with training in positive self-statements (Ascher, Schotte, & Grayson, 1986).

It is important to point out that the combination of paradox, which asks patients to "welcome the fear" (Mavissakalian et al., 1983a), with measures such as coping self-statements or relaxation to reduce the overall incidence of panic episodes can be confusing. The confusion can occur because one measure asks the patient to actively bring on or amplify the symptoms, while the others are aimed at reducing the incidence of symptoms or ameliorating their effects. Therefore, we do not usually present paradox to patients as a separate technique or coping strategy. However, the instructions we give on how to orient oneself to panic and respond when it occurs do incorporate certain paradoxical features. We emphasize that while patients must take measures to reduce the probability of panic episodes (e.g., the use of medication, relaxation, etc.), they can never be entirely sure that such methods will "guarantee" a life free of panic. Consequently, in addition to acting in ways designed to reduce the incidence of panic, they must be prepared to cope more effectively when it occurs; only when they feel a greater sense of confidence in their ability to handle panic episodes will they feel a significant measure of relief.

Thus, when patients feel a panic attack developing, we encourage them to "bring it on" as a way of creating an opportunity to use the techniques they've been taught for coping with anxiety. The rationale for accepting or welcoming the uncomfortable sensations experienced during episodes of panic relies less on the way such a change of attitude will interrupt the vicious panic-attack cycle *by itself* and more on the benefit to be derived from practicing strategies designed to enhance the individual's sense of efficacy.

A major part of our approach to the treatment of the panic disorder patient involves exposure to the sensations characteristically experienced during episodes of panic. This intervention incorporates the paradoxical feature of asking patients who generally take measures to avoid such sensations to actively court them. While it is not possible to bring on all of the sensations associated with panic at will, in many cases some of the main features can be reproduced deliberately. Our reasons for incorporating in vivo exposure to the major panic symptoms are twofold. First, the procedure allows the patient to experience the feared sensations under circumstances in which a variety of coping skills may be brought to bear. Second, patients are afforded a controlled opportunity to test their often catastrophic assumptions about the consequences of panic. In many cases, the symptoms can be experienced in the office with the therapist present to help the patient review the actual consequences and compare them with previously held assumptions.

The timing of this intervention is important in enhancing its effectiveness. It is the last major technique we introduce. Thus by the time we begin this phase of treatment, the patient should (1) have a clearer understanding of the nature of panic in general; (2) be knowledgeable about his or her idiosyncratic pattern, including characteristic antecedent events, thoughts, or mood states associated with the onset of panic; (3) have made relevant life-style changes, including cutting down on caffeine and other agents that might induce panic, increasing exercise if appropriate, and relaxation; (4) be on an appropriate dose of medication if indicated; and (5) be able to use cognitive coping strategies during a panic attack.

There are a number of methods we have used for replicating panic symptoms. For patients who report palpitations or sweating as the primary symptom, running in place or running up and down stairs will frequently bring on the feared sensations. For those who experience dizziness, turning rapidly in a swivel chair is often effective in creating panic-like symptoms. Patients who report difficulty catching their breath can sometimes create similar symptoms by hyperventilating. Many of the other commonly reported symptoms—such as faintness, hot and cold flashes, and chest pain—are secondary to the sensations mentioned above. For example, many patients who report faintness also report dizziness, and if the therapist can help the patient find a way to induce dizziness, faintness will usually accompany it. Some patients report primary symptoms that are unusual. One patient, for example, experienced a stiffness in the back of her neck as a major feature of panic episodes. She found that she could reproduce the symptom by lying prone on a hard floor. Another patient, whose primary complaint involved unsteadiness, found that she could induce the same sensations when she walked along the edge of a curb. Still another patient, who reported a "falling down" feeling as primary, was able to induce the symptom on an escalator.

The rationale for asking the patient to engage in activities that will bring on distressing sensations emphasizes coping enhancement rather than habituation. That is, we attempt to persuade the patient of the benefits of deliberate exposure to panic symptoms on the grounds that with the use of cognitive coping skills and strategies such as controlled breathing, they can gain enhanced mastery over the symptoms and decrease their sense of helplessness. While habituation to the symptoms may, in fact, serve an important function, we do not stress its role in the patient's symptomatic improvement. Panic disorder patients are already overly sensitized to their physiological responses. If one emphasizes the role of habituation, the patient is likely to increase further his or her physiological self-monitoring, which has a tendency to amplify the problem. Further, if habituation takes longer than the patient anticipated, he may lose faith in the procedure.

SUMMARY

Panic disorder is a disabling and serious problem. As we have described in this chapter, combinations of psychotherapeutic and psychopharmacologic interventions can reduce or stop panic attacks and minimize other disability in most patients. Newer psychological interventions, such as exposing patients to internal cues associated with panic attacks, are particularly promising. The development of such techniques is particularly important because many patients have difficulties with medication side effects, or withdrawal, and effective medications are relatively contraindicated among individuals who are liable to abuse them or in young women of childbearing age. Many of the therapeutic interventions discussed in this chapter are also useful in treating panic disorder with agoraphobia.

EIGHT

· · · · · · · ·

Agoraphobia

· · · · · · · · · ·

Agoraphobia, also referred to as panic disorder with agoraphobia, is the most common and among the most debilitating of the anxiety disorders among adults. Although the issue is far from settled, agoraphobia appears to be a more severe form of panic disorder. It is also the most frequently reported phobic disorder, comprising about 60 percent of the phobias treated by clinicians (Marks & Herst, 1970).

The term agoraphobia comes from the Greek *agora*, which refers to public places of assembly: thus, agoraphobia implies fear of public places. Agoraphobics typically complain of a variety of fears and avoidances including fear of going out alone, of going into stores, of being home alone, of driving alone, of being far from home, of crowded places such as movie theaters or stadiums, of wide open spaces, of eating in restaurants, of using public transportation, or of waiting in long lines. Actually, the avoidance is a secondary phenomenon because what agoraphobics most fear is the consequence of a panic attack: thus "fear of fear" (Goldstein & Chambless, 1978) constitutes the central feature of the disorder. Because agoraphobics have two main domains of psychopathology, panic attacks and avoidance, and neither panic disorder nor agoraphobia completely characterize the problem, a more appropriate nomenclature might be "panic disorder with avoidance," which would highlight both features.

Many patient accounts attest to the severe disability associated with the disorder. Clevenger (1890) described in the first person a patient who experienced a panic attack at age 22. The first symptoms included extreme nervous irritability, sleeplessness, and loss of appetite. Then:

> A sense of impending danger seemed to descend, spoiling every pleasure, thwarting every ambition. The dread of sudden death, which was at first marked, gradually subsided, giving way more to a feeling of

dread—not of dying suddenly—but of doing so under peculiar circumstances or away from home. I became morbidly sensitive about being brought into close contact with any large number of people. Finding myself in the midst of a large gathering would inspire a feeling of terror (which) . . . could be relieved in but one way—by getting away from the spot as soon as possible. Acting on this impulse I have left churches, theatres, even funerals, simply because of an utter inability to control myself to stay. For 10 years I have not been to church, to the theatre, to political gatherings or any form of popular meeting, except where I could remain in the background, with means of egress convenient. Even at my mother's funeral . . . I was utterly unable to bring myself to sit with the other members of the family in the front of the church. Not only has this unfortunate trait deprived me of an immense amount of pleasure and benefit, but it has also been a matter of considerable expense. . . . Time more than I can recall I have gone into restaurants or dining rooms, ordered a meal and left it untouched, impelled by my desire to escape the crowd. . . . I have . . . often . . . walked long distances—perhaps a mile—to avoid crossing some pasture or open square, even when it was a matter of moment to me to save all the time possible. . . . This malady . . . has throttled all ambition, and killed all personal pride, spoiled every pleasure. . . . over this the will seems to have no control. (Pp. 538–539)

The features of this case are typical of what occurs with most agoraphobics. The problem begins with a panic attack, usually a spontaneous one. The patients are caught off guard by the attack. Occasionally, the agoraphobia seems to begin with the so-called "symptom-limited attack," involving only one or two symptoms and, in our experience, frequently involving gastrointestinal upset. The threatened or actual loss of bowel function leads to a fear of possible humiliation.

The initial spontaneous episode is followed by continued attacks, although they frequently change in intensity and frequency. Some patients become extremely avoidant and experience fewer panic attacks, including fewer spontaneous ones. But most patients continue to have panic attacks, sometimes with increased levels of severity, and continue to experience dread both when they occur and when they are anticipated. The feared consequences of the panic attacks fall into two categories: fear of public humiliation, embarrassment, or loss of sanity, or threats to life and well-being. The fears are frequently alleviated by the presence of a trusted person. Thus, one frequently encounters patients who can venture far from home, shop, or use public transportation when with a partner, although they are unable to do so when alone.

The symptoms of the panic attacks are identical in agoraphobic patients and patients with panic disorder without agoraphobia. Curi-

TABLE 8.1

Main Phobias of 900 Agoraphobic Women

Phobias	Percent reporting fright or terror	Other Problems	Percent reporting the problem very often
Speaking to audiences	60	Exhaustion	42
		Tension	38
Underground trains	50	Obsessive thoughts	37
Trains	47	Loneliness	32
Crowds	28	Depression	29
Buses	38	Fears of fainting	31
Heights	36	Giddiness	26
Theaters	39	Panic	24
Hairdressers	31	Irritability	19
Street, open spaces	23	Headaches	22
Tunnels	36	Depersonalization	22
Elevators	30	Fears of dying	22
Dentist	28	Overchecking, tidiness	22
Parties	21	Palpitations	20
		Suicidal ideas	15
		Fears of disease	9

From *Fears, Phobias, and Rituals: Panic, Anxiety, and Their Disorders* by Isaac M. Marks. Copyright 1987 by Oxford University Press, Inc. Reproduced by permission.

ously, the type of symptoms change from one situation to another, do not follow a predictable order, and are difficult to explain on an anatomical basis. The most common symptoms, as reviewed in the past chapter, are cardiovascular: the most dreaded symptoms are the panic itself, fear of fainting or collapsing, losing control, or causing a public disturbance, going crazy or dying.

The fears characteristic of agoraphobics are remarkably similar from one patient to another. Table 8.1, shown above, summarizes the chief phobias and other problems of 900 agoraphobic women studied by Marks (1987).

Table 8.2 shows the percentage of 800 panic attack patients we have studied who rate the fears listed as causing extreme anxiety.

TABLE 8.2

Percent of 800 Panic Disorder Patients
Reporting Extreme Anxiety

	Females (610)	Males (234)
Shopping	11.9%	9.4%
Being alone	10.6	6.0
Driving alone	22.6	11.5
Walking alone	13.6	8.9
Crowded places	18.4	9.8
Crossing the street	7.9	5.2
Eating	18.5	8.1
Public transportation	23.7	12.8
Waiting in line	16.7	9.0
Overall	14.3	10.7

The various fears are highly correlated. However, there is some evidence that the fears might also be hierarchical; that is, having one fear indicates that one is likely to have those below it in the hierarchy. Johnston et al. (1984) and Margraf et al. (submitted) found, for instance, the following order for five fears:

Walking around nearest large shopping center
Walking away from home by yourself for 15 minutes
Going to a local shop
Talking to a neighbour in the street
Answering the door bell

Subjects reporting a higher fear also were very likely to have all the fears below it. The following fears were hierarchical (Johnston et al., 1984; Margraf et al., submitted):

Traveling by bus by yourself for 15 minutes
Traveling by train
Going into tunnels
Traveling in a car
Sitting in a hall

The agoraphobic dreads the unavoidable excursion or event. He or she may suffer for weeks in advance, carefully going over every possible calamitous outcome, planning methods of escape or rescue, and imagining or creating ways to avoid the situation.

Agoraphobic patients may also behave in seemingly contradictory ways. When necessary such patients can be quite calm and brave, suspending their otherwise constant fears. For instance, we were monitoring one patient with a heart-rate device when she saw a woman fall on the sidewalk. She immediately provided assistance, arranged for an ambulance, and waited until the patient was taken away. During this time, her heart rate was lower than during other periods of monitoring and substantially lower than when she reported feeling panicky.

Although agoraphobic patients do not differ from other anxiety disorder patients on most dimensions of psychopathology they seem to be more sensitive to internal bodily sensations. Thus, exercise, extreme hot or cold weather, hunger, or fatigue may generate concerns and may even be associated with increased avoidance. In one study, we provided "false heart-rate feedback" to agoraphobic patients. When told their heart rates were increasing even though their actual heart rate remained the same, they then demonstrated an increase in heart rate compared to normals. This sensitivity to bodily sensations obviously confounds the meaningfulness of most biological examinations meant to distinguish between agoraphobic and nonanxious patients, because, even at early stages, the very test may produce changes in body sensations that are then interpreted by the patient as indicating panic (Margraf et al., submitted).

Most agoraphobics are also quite depressed. In one of our studies (Telch et al., 1985), the mean level of depression at baseline was about 25 on the Beck Depression Inventory (Beck et al., 1961), and 65 on the Zung Self-Rating Depression Scale (Zung, 1965). In comparison, many depression outcome studies consider scores above 25 on the Beck and 50 on the Zung to indicate moderate to severe depression. Depressive episodes may precede, occur during, or follow agoraphobic episodes and yet be independent of the agoraphobia; more commonly the depression appears secondary to the agoraphobia. Most outcome studies have found an improvement in depression coinciding with improvement in agoraphobia.

Measures taken by the patient to reduce the incidence or severity of panic symptoms account for much of the secondary problems and disability. Long ago Westphal (1871) noted that alcohol allowed patients to pass through feared situations they would otherwise avoid. Although alcohol is an effective short-term anxiolytic, habitual use is associated with a biphasic response: initial intake may lessen fear but is soon followed by dysphoria (Logue et al., 1978; Stockwell et al., 1984).

Studies of the prevalence of alcoholism among agoraphobics are contradictory. Several studies have reported alcoholism rates of 10 to 20 percent in adult agoraphobic outpatients (Bibb & Chambless,

1986). Compared to nonalcoholic agoraphobic subjects, drinking ago-raphobics had more intense panic, depression, social phobia, fear of somatic symptoms, and catastrophic thoughts. Alcoholic agorapho-bics also reported more abusive upbringings. Breier et al., (1986) found that of 60 agoraphobics, alcoholism began before the agora-phobia in 14 percent and after it in only 4 percent. In our sample of 800 patients, only 1 percent reported a history of or current alcohol abuse on a questionnaire. A family history of alcoholism is more frequent among agoraphobics than among social and simple phobics (Munjack & Moss, 1981). Taken together, these studies suggest that agoraphobics have an increased risk of alcohol abuse. However, the rate does not appear to be substantially greater than that for the normal population.

Several studies have failed to find evidence for a strong linkage between personality disorders and agoraphobia. Mavissakalian and Hamann (1986) found that 27 percent of 60 agoraphobic patients exhibited evidence of some personality disorder with dependent, avoidant, and histrionic personalities or traits most common. We have found similar rates of personality disorder in our patient population.

Agoraphobics are also at risk of becoming dependent on a variety of medications. Because sedative/hypnotics are likely to be prescribed to these patients and these drugs carry a risk of abuse and depen-dence, it not unusual to see addicted patients. However, there is no evidence that agoraphobics are at risk independent of exposure to the medication.

The marriages of agoraphobic and nonagoraphobic women were very similar on most measures of attitude, behavior, marital interac-tion, and social interaction (Buglass et al., 1977). Not surprisingly, agoraphobic women had less active social contacts than non-agoraphobic women. Arrindell & Emmelkamp (1985a, 1986) found that the measures of marital adjustment in agoraphobic couples were similar to that of happily married controls.

Family systems theorists have suggested that psychiatric symp-toms may serve a stabilizing function in certain families (e.g., Bateson, 1961; Haley, 1963, 1980; Hoffman, 1971; Jackson, 1957; Jackson & Weakland, 1959; Minuchin, Rosman, & Baker, 1978). In one of the few clinical descriptions of agoraphobia in the family sys-tems literature, Fry (1962) used the term "compulsory" to charac-terize the marriages of the phobic patients he treated. He noted that the marriages appeared bereft of genuine commitment and seemed to be held together by the patient's helplessness and the necessity of the spouse's caretaking. Later, Hafner (1976, 1977, 1979; Milton & Hafner, 1979) introduced evidence that successful in vivo exposure therapy for agoraphobia had an adverse impact on marital satisfaction or spouse functioning. Bland and Hallam (1981) and Hudson (1974) reported an association between marital or family satisfaction and response to treatment. However, these studies contained numerous methodological problems, including the use of median splits on marital questionnaires to designate "good" and "poor" marriages, overreliance on self-report measures of marital satisfaction, and in some cases inadequate statistical procedures (Arnow, 1984). Other recent studies (e.g., Barlow, O'Brien, & Last, 1984; Himadi, et al., 1986) have failed to confirm deleterious treatment effects on marital interaction or spouse functioning and have not found an association between pretreatment levels of marital satisfaction and treatment outcome.

Disability is significant in agoraphobic patients. In a survey of 930 patients, Thorpe and Burns (1983) found that in male patients, the main effects were inability to work (42 percent), lack of social contacts (29 percent), "personal psychological effects" (11 percent), and marital disharmony (9 percent). In female patients the main effects were social restrictions (29 percent), "personal psychological effects" (23 percent), marital disharmony (14 percent), inability to work (14 percent), and travel restrictions (11 percent).

COURSE

We have already described the typical mode of onset: agoraphobia begins following a spontaneous panic attack. Figure 8.1 shows the distribution of the age of onset for 95 patients with agoraphobia with panic attacks, reported in a recent study (Thyer, Nesse, Cameron, & Curtis, 1985). The mean age of onset was 26 with a range of three to 51 years. However, some agoraphobic patients do not report spontaneous panic attacks. For instance, in Thyer et al.'s sample, 83 percent of patients reported spontaneous panic attacks, with 17 percent presenting as agoraphobic without panic attacks.

In an intensive clinical interview of 55 patients with panic attacks, Breier et al. (1986) found that 78 percent had a spontaneous first panic attack (that is, an attack that seemed to come out of the blue), and 22 percent had a nonspontaneous panic attack (an attack associated with some apparent precipitating event). They found that approximately three-fourths of the agoraphobia episodes were reported as beginning within the first year following the first panic attack. This early onset of avoidance following panic is in contrast to Thyer & Himle (1985), who reported nine years between the first panic attack and avoidance. In Breier's study none of the patients with avoidance reported being symptom-free after the onset of the disorder. Avoidance and disability began an average of 15 months after onset of the agoraphobia in members of a correspondence club called the Open Door (Marks & Herst, 1970).

There has been much speculation as to why avoidance develops following a panic attack. Agoraphobia begins earlier in cases with past separation anxiety as children (Breier et al., 1986). We have found some evidence (see Figure 8.2) that the frequency of panic attacks may relate to development of avoidance. The distribution suggests that there is a "threshold effect"—more than two or three panic attacks per week does not cause increased avoidance. How patients interpret their initial and subsequent panic attacks may make a difference in whether or not they become agoraphobic. Breier et al. (1986) reported that patients with a spontaneous first panic attack had a significantly more rapid onset of agoraphobia following that attack than did patients with a nonspontaneous first attack. Seventy-three percent of the patients had an inaccurate understanding of the first panic attack and felt it was potentially life-threatening. It seems more likely that the intensity and degree of unpleasantness of the attack may also be a critical factor in determining whether or not subjects will try to avoid situations and stimuli associated with it. The avoidance of situations may thus relate to the perceived probability that an attack will occur coupled with the individual's perceived efficacy in coping with the panic attack in that situation.

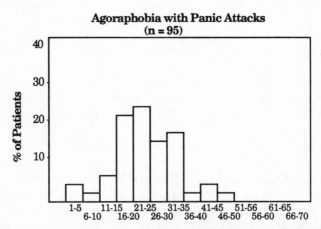

Figure 8.1. **Age of Onset for Agoraphobic Patients with Panic Attacks**

SOURCE: "Ages of Onset of DSM-III Anxiety Disorders" by B. A. Thyer, R. T. Parrish, G. C. Curtis, R. M. Neese, and O. C. Cameron, 1985, *Comprehensive Psychiatry, 26,* p. 117.

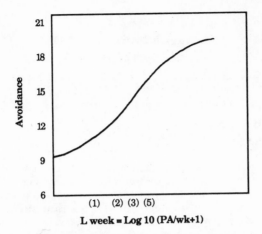

Figure 8.2. **Cubic Fit of Avoidance with Panic Attack Frequency**

This figure shows the plot of avoidance measured by the Stanford Phobic Avoidance Inventory (maximum score is 40) and the logarithmic number of panic attacks per week in 807 patients. The numbers in parentheses on the horizontal axis represent the actual number of panic attacks. There is an acceleration in avoidance associated with having 2 to 3 panic attacks per week.

Untreated agoraphobia appears to be a chronic condition characterized by few periods of remission. In Marks and Herst's (1970) sample of 900 agoraphobics, once phobias had developed 80 percent of patients were never again free of them.

PREVALENCE

With the recent improvements in the reliability of psychiatric diagnoses it has been possible to obtain information on the prevalence of agoraphobia. A few prevalence studies have differentiated agoraphobia from other anxiety disorders. Agras et al. (1969) found a point prevalence of 0.6 for agoraphobia. More recent studies have found higher rates. The six-month prevalence rates/100 of agoraphobia in the NIMH epidemiologic catchment area study can be seen in Table 8.3.

Available evidence suggests that agoraphobia is 2 to 4 times more prevalent in women than men.

FAMILY STUDIES

Most of the family studies relevant to agoraphobia have combined the anxiety disorders into one or two categories. Hence little is known

TABLE 8.3

Six-month Prevalence/100
of Agoraphobia

Community	Men	Women	Total
New Haven	1.1	4.2	2.8
Baltimore	3.4	7.8	5.8
St. Louis	0.9	4.3	2.7

SOURCE: Taken from Table 8 in "Six-Month Prevalence of Psychiatric Disorders in Three Communities" by Jerome K. Myers, et al., *Archives of General
Psychiatry, 41*, 963. Copyright 1984, American Medical Association.

about agoraphobia independent of panic disorder and generalized
anxiety disorder. Leckman et al. (1983) found that patients with depression plus panic disorder or generalized anxiety disorder had
twice the rate of depression among their first-degree relatives
(20/200) compared to the first-degree relatives of patients with depression plus agoraphobia, whose rates were 11.5/100. This study
suggested that panic disorder and GAD were strongly associated with
depression but agoraphobia less so (Harris et al., 1983; Torgerson,
1983).

ETIOLOGY

We have argued that agoraphobia is a more severe form of panic
disorder and shares a common, as yet unspecified, etiology. We agree
with Marks (1987) that despite the recent intense interest in and
enthusiasm for biological explanations of agoraphobia, the demon-
stration of various biological changes during anxious episodes have
not been shown to be specific to agoraphobia and may result from
rather than be the cause of anxiety. Even the role of learning in
producing avoidance remains somewhat clouded. It has been a long-
held and attractive hypothesis that the avoidance in agoraphobia is a
learned phenomenon.

The learning theory model posits that individuals learn to avoid
situations where they have experienced, or expect to experience, a
panic attack. For instance, a person experiencing a panic attack while
driving might begin to avoid driving. Eventually, even the anticipation of driving might cause anxiety. Yet there are problems with
conditioning theory. For instance, conditioning theory predicts that

patients would develop avoidance specific to the situations where panic attacks occur. One agoraphobia patient might then avoid a bank where he had a panic attack, driving where he had another, and eating where he had a third. Another patient would have a different pattern of avoidance depending on where his attacks occur. As we have seen, however, agoraphobics have a very common set of situations that they avoid; the similarities across agoraphobics are more striking than the differences.

If avoidance and panic attacks were entirely separate phenomena, then reduction in avoidance should not coincide with reduction in panic attacks. In fact, one might think that patients would have more panic attacks as they began to encounter their feared situations. The data on this issue are mixed. We have generally found that exposure is accompanied by a reduction in panic attacks but that correlations between reduction in exposure and reduction in panic attacks is low. We have also treated patients with medication who have experienced cessation of panic attacks yet remained avoidant. We suspect that the tendency to avoid is related neurophysiologically to the tendency to having panic attacks; however, learning may also play an important role in determining the form and strength of the avoidance.

DIAGNOSIS

Patients with severe behavioral avoidance are not difficult to identify. Work, family, and other obligations, however, force some patients to encounter feared situations that they would prefer to avoid; these encounters usually occasion extreme anxiety. Such patients may look more like patients with panic disorder without agoraphobia than agoraphobics. In all patients with panic attacks, a careful history of avoidance should be obtained. Whenever the clinical picture is dominated by avoidance, a diagnosis of agoraphobia should be entertained.

The differential diagnosis is also not difficult. Among the other disorders to be considered are obsessive-compulsive disorder, paranoid states of various kinds, alcoholism, and depression. Some agoraphobic patients may have obsessive thoughts related to panic, but the clinical picture of obsessive-compulsive disorder (which is dominated by obsessions and rituals) is clearly different from that of agoraphobia. The house-bound obsessive-compulsive does not leave home for fear of contamination, which is not the main concern of the agoraphobic patient. Paranoia is sometimes associated with isolation; we have seen one severely housebound agoraphobic who presented with paranoia apparently secondary to her isolation. Rarely, alcoholism and drug abuse can exacerbate, mask, or mimic agoraphobia. A major depressive episode, melancholic type (involutional melancholia), is often associated with increased phobias and somaticization and sometimes with avoidance and being housebound.

Finally, the clinician should not overlook the coexistence of agoraphobia or panic disorder in patients with a clinical picture dominated by other psychopathology. The following case illustrates the coexistence of agoraphobia and schizophrenia, residual type:

Katherine is a 38-year-old female who presented to our medical-psychiatric unit with symptoms of nausea and vomiting lasting for six months and a 6 kg weight loss. She had a history of schizophrenia, treated in the past with hospitalizations and psychotropic medications. However, for the preceding five years, perhaps because of a happy second marriage and compliance with thiothixine medication (10 mgm BID), her schizophrenia was in remission, though she continued to have auditory hallucinations and displayed blunted affect. The patient was reluctant to leave her room not because of the voices but for fear of a panic attack. Her attack consisted of the rapid onset of a number of symptoms (palpitations, nausea, vomiting, depersonalization, and fears of dying). These episodes had been dismissed in the past as being secondary to her schizophrenia; however, they appeared to be classic panic attacks. Furthermore, the patient had classic agoraphobic avoidance.

ASSESSMENT

Because of the complexity of agoraphobia, comprehensive multifaceted assessment is extremely important. The clinician must understand the patient's subjective experience, cognition, and behavior. Ideally, physiologic assessment should complement the subjective, cognitive, and behavioral domains, although physiologic assessment is not practical in most clinical settings. Fortunately, extensive treatment-outcome research on agoraphobia has generated a variety of methods for assessing agoraphobia.

The clinical interview is the most important source of information regarding the subjective experience of the agoraphobic patient. Self-report instruments used to measure anxiety are also important here. Most agoraphobic patients experience constant low levels of anxiety with occasional more intense sustained periods. This anxiety often remains even after the avoidance and panic attacks have been overcome. Therefore, periodic assessments of anxiety are appropriate using the Spielberger State-Trait instrument or the SCL-90 Anxiety Scale, which have been mentioned before.

A recent international conference on anxiety disorders sponsored by the National Institute of Mental Health (NIMH) has recommended that the Fear Questionnaire (Marks & Mathews, 1979) be used in all research studies on phobias (Barlow & Wolfe, 1981). This one-page instrument, which we have discussed before, provides four measures: (1) level of avoidance of the main fear, (2) a global phobia rating (0–8) of all phobic symptoms in general, (3) avoidance ratings of 15 items derived from factor analytic studies with clinical phobias, which can be divided into three types of phobia (agoraphobia, social phobia, and blood-injury phobias) or summated as a total phobia, and (4) an anxiety-depression scale of five items of the most common nonphobic symptoms. The scale has acceptable levels of reliability, sensitivity, and validity (Marks & Mathews, 1979).

The NIMH conference also recommended that the clients' ratings of phobic anxiety and avoidance items be developed into a hierarchy at the beginning of treatment and the hierarchy used to guide treatment. We use a phobic avoidance inventory that includes hierarchies in 16 domains such as walking away from home, riding an elevator, being in a large coffee shop (see Appendix 1). Gelder and Mathews and their colleagues (Gelder et al., 1973; Mathews et al., 1976; Mathews et al., 1977) have used 10- and 15-item hierarchies on which clients rate their subjective levels of anxiety for each item according to 0–10 scales. Fear and avoidance are, of course, closely related, so that many of the self-report measures of fear are also measuring behavior.

Cognition

"Fear of fear," or, put differently, catastrophic thoughts regarding the consequences of panic, dominate the life of the agoraphobic. The instruments for measuring cognitions discussed in the previous chapter are appropriate here. The intensity and frequency of panic attacks need to be measured. The Stanford Panic Attack Appraisal Instrument, and the Agoraphobic Cognitions Questionnaire (Chambless et al., 1984) are appropriate. Self-report cognitive diaries are also useful. Self-efficacy instruments, particularly when tied to specific behaviors are very helpful in determining patients' confidence that they will be able to undertake a particular task.

Behavior

Measuring avoidance is one of the more interesting aspects of assessing agoraphobia. Self-report instruments of behavior developed for research studies that are particularly useful to the clinician include the Mobility Inventory (Chambless et al., 1985), the Fear Questionnaire (Marks & Mathews, 1979), and the Stanford Phobic Avoidance Inventory (Telch, 1985). The Mobility Inventory is a 27-item inventory assessing self-reported avoidance. Patients are asked to rate separately the extent of avoidance when they are accompanied and when they are alone in a variety of situations. Subjects note whether they never avoid, rarely avoid, avoid about half the time, avoid most of the time, or always avoid the place or situation. For instance, subjects note their avoidance at theaters, elevators, riding buses, or walking on the street when accompanied or alone. The instrument has been shown to be reliable and to be sensitive to change. Available evidence suggests adequate concurrent and construct validity. We use a 10-item inventory that asks subjects to report their anxiety in ten situations. Each item is rated from "can do without anxiety" to "cannot do under any circumstances." The Fear Questionnaire is also an adequate measure of avoidance.

Behavioral avoidance tests have been widely used to measure outcome in research projects. These assessments involve having the subject walk along a predetermined course while noting confidence, anxiety, and thoughts. Physiology, time, or other factors can be monitored. However, such a procedure is rarely useful in clinical practice.

A major disadvantage of standardized walks is that only a single behavior is assessed. Many patients may not experience restrictions in that particular area. Furthermore, the generalizability of the task has not been demonstrated. Mathews, Gelder, and Johnston (1981) have developed an instrument that is clinically more useful. Prior to treatment, these investigators develop with the patient an individualized 15-item hierarchy of public situations. The patient tries more difficult items progressively until he is unwilling or unable to proceed.

A third approach is to have patients keep diaries of their activities. We use a simple self-monitoring form on which patients note what activities they do, their anxiety during the task, and whether they did it accompanied or alone. The self-monitoring forms can also be used as homework sheets, with the assignment written on the form for the patient to take home and review at the next session.

Physiology

The laboratory-based physiologic assessment of agoraphobia and the methodology for assessing panic attacks has been presented earlier. Ambulatory measures of panic attacks are of interest scientifically but have no use in clinical practice as yet.

Clinically Significant Improvement

Agoraphobia outcome research has focused on measures that can produce statistical significance. Yet, every clinician knows that a statistically significant effect may not represent a clinically important change in the patient. However, patients who have an agoraphobia score of less than 10 on the Fear Questionnaire can be considered clinically improved (Mavissakalian, 1986). Even stricter clinical improvement criteria might require that patients be assessed at six months, posttreatment and off medications.

It is also important to consider global levels of functioning in determining outcome. At the end of treatment and at follow-up, patients should report no more than mild impairment in work, social life/leisure, and family life/home responsibilities using the form provided in Appendix 1.

THE TREATMENT OF AGORAPHOBIA

Beginning in the 1960s a variety of behavioral treatments for agoraphobia were investigated including systematic desensitization (Gelder & Marks, 1966; Gelder, Marks, & Wolff, 1967), and imaginal flooding (Marks, Boulougouris, & Marset, 1971; Mathews et al., 1974), in addition to prolonged in vivo exposure (Hand, Lamontagne, & Marks, 1974; Teasdale et al., 1977). Of these, in vivo exposure is clearly superior. Systematic desensitization, developed by Wolpe (1958), involves having the patient construct a hierarchy of fear-inducing situations that are then recalled during deep muscle relaxation. The rationale for the procedure is that deep muscle relaxation is incompatible with anxiety and will inhibit anxious arousal in the feared situation. In imaginal flooding, the therapist describes in vivid detail a fear-evoking situation, thereby exposing the patient to increased anxiety. In vivo exposure, of course, involves actual contact with a situation feared by the patient.

In each of the behavioral procedures, the individual is exposed to fear-provoking situations; what distinguishes them is the mode of presentation. Systematic desensitization and imaginal exposure involve exposure in imagination, while in vivo exposure calls for direct contact with the fear-evoking situation. Studies that investigated the relative efficacy of the imaginal procedures have indicated an advantage for imaginal flooding over desensitization in some cases (Boulougouris, Marks, & Marset, 1971), and in others an equivalence between the two (Crowe et al., 1972; Mathews et al., 1974). However, when imaginal procedures were contrasted with in vivo exposure, a consistent advantage was demonstrated for the latter (Emmelkamp & Wessels, 1975; Mathews et al., 1976; Stern & Marks, 1973; Watson, Mullett, & Pillay, 1973).

Numerous parameters of in vivo exposure have been investigated. Group exposure appears to be as effective as individual treatment (Hafner & Marks, 1976); social cohesion seems to enhance the immediate effects of group exposure, but evidence supporting its ability to promote better long-term results is inconsistent (Hand et al., 1974; Teasdale et al., 1977); self-directed exposure, which is characterized by less intensive therapist involvement, has produced excellent results (Greist et al., 1980; McDonald et al., 1979), as has self-directed home-based spouse-assisted treatment (Jannoun et al., 1980; Mathews et al., 1976); additional studies have suggested that including spouses in treatment may provide some particular advantage among patients in problematic marriages (Barlow et al., 1984; Himadi et al., 1986), and that communication training between couples may enhance the effects of exposure therapy (Arnow et al., 1985).

Despite consistent demonstrations of the effectiveness of in vivo exposure for agoraphobia, it has important limitations. While many who undergo such treatment achieve significant decrements in symptomotalogy, others fail to make gains considered clinically significant. Barlow et al. (1984) have estimated that 30 percent of those who undergo in vivo exposure therapy for agoraphobia become treatment failures. In one long-term follow-up study (McPherson, Brougham, & McLaren, 1980) involving 56 agoraphobics who improved following treatment, 61 percent of whom underwent in vivo exposure therapy, only 18 percent reported themselves symptom-free four years later. One must also consider dropouts from treatment. Mavissakalian and Barlow (1981) have noted dropouts rates between 8 and 40 percent, with a median of 22 percent. Recent efforts to obtain better outcome results with agoraphobics have been geared toward enhancing exposure therapy by incorporating additional treatment strategies, particularly pharmacotherapy, but also cognitive therapy.

Among the first investigators to report on pharmacologic treatment of phobic disorders was Sargant (1960), who reported considerable improvement among patients with atypical depression and phobic anxiety with MAO inhibitors. Later, Klein and his colleagues reported a series of studies suggesting the effectiveness of imipramine in the treatment of panic disorder and agoraphobia (Klein & Fink, 1962; Klein, Zitrin, & Woerner, 1977; Zitrin, Klein, & Woerner, 1978). Though these early studies appear to have confounded the effects of the medication with the effects of instructions given to subjects on exposing themselves to feared situations (Telch, Tearnan, & Taylor, 1983), a well-controlled more recent study (Telch et al., 1985) suggested substantial benefit for combining imipramine and in vivo exposure therapy.

The results of combining cognitive therapy with in vivo exposure are more equivocal. The rationale for such treatment is based on clinical observation pointing to a cluster of cognitive themes common among agoraphobics, including fear of losing control or going insane, threats to physical health, fear of social humiliation, and inability to cope effectively with environmental danger (Beck, 1976; Beck & Emery, 1985; Coleman, 1981; Guidano & Liotti, 1983). Several studies have failed to demonstrate an effect for cognitive therapy in the treatment of agoraphobia either alone or in conjunction with in vivo exposure (Emmelkamp et al., 1985; Emmelkamp, Kuipers, & Eggeraat, 1978; Emmelkamp & Mersch, 1982; Williams & Rappoport, 1983). It remains uncertain whether future studies will establish evidence to justify the current enthusiasm for cognitive therapy. At the present time, we continue to incorporate cognitive interventions as adjuncts to exposure therapy.

One other possible adjunct to exposure therapy worthy of mention is marital therapy. We have already briefly reviewed the evidence regarding marital or spouse problems as impediments to symptomatic improvement among agoraphobics and have concluded that *in general*, such issues are not significant factors. Nevertheless, anecdotal reports regarding the importance of considering the marriage as a potential factor affecting outcome abound (e.g., Chambless & Goldstein, 1981; Emmelkamp, 1974; Hand et al., 1974; Lazarus, 1966; Wolpe, 1970), and we have found that *in a few cases*, marital problems or deterioration in spouse functioning can interfere with treatment or with the patient's ability to maintain treatment-related gains. Thus while including marital therapy as a standard part of treatment is unwarranted, the therapist should be alert to the possibility of marital or spouse difficulties during or following treatment. As a rule, even when the agoraphobic patient presents coexisting marital problems, we do not begin treatment with marital therapy unless, of course, the presenting complaint is couple problems and the couple presents themselves as the unit of treatment. More commonly, the agoraphobic patient presents him- or herself as the problem, and we may note in the initial assessment the presence of marital problems.

Our reason for eschewing marital therapy at the outset of treatment is the difficulty of predicting the direction in which such problems will change with changes in symptomatic behavior. Measures of marital satisfaction, for example, are poor predictors. Symptoms of agoraphobia may put an enormous strain upon a marriage, and improvement in the symptomatic partner often results in overall improvement in the marriage. On the other hand, a marriage rated satisfactory prior to treatment may falter once the symptoms have remitted, if the partner has difficulty accomodating to the changes associated with treatment. The only safe assumption is that if there is substantial change in the patient's level of symptomatology, there will be significant changes in the marital system. Hence, the most efficient and cost-effective posture for the therapist is to treat the agoraphobic symptoms, to be attentive to the effects of treatment on the marriage, and to be available to intervene if there is substantial deterioration.

Thus, effective symptom-focused treatment of agoraphobia involves exposure therapy, the use of medication in many cases, and cognitive restructuring. However, exposure is the cornerstone of treatment, the intervention around which other measures are organized in a facilitative, or secondary, role. Though there is wide consensus regarding the importance of exposure therapy in the treatment of avoidance behavior, there are relatively few accounts that deal with how to conduct such treatment and how to deal with the therapeutic issues that characteristically emerge during the process. The remainder of this chapter will be devoted to a discussion of these issues, together with comments regarding the integration of cognitive treatment and medication. We have also included the protocol for exposure therapy, which we use in our research studies (see Appendix 3).

Introducing Exposure Therapy

In the opening phases of treatment, it is critical that the therapist be mindful of the degree of fear with which most agoraphobics anticipate confronting the situations they have been avoiding. The therapist must be able to deliver a rationale that convinces the patient to complete the therapeutic tasks, despite considerable fear. Convincing the patient is not only a matter of choosing one's words carefully; one must be knowledgeable about the phenomenon of agoraphobia and about its treatment and be willing to communicate one's expertise. Unlike the traditional psychodynamic therapist who functions as a partner in a self-discovery process, the therapist carrying out exposure therapy functions as a consultant who is willing to direct and reassure the patient. The degree of discomfort patients experience while carrying out exposure therapy will only be tolerated if they believe such tasks will prove helpful in the end. Their belief in the usefulness of the tasks partially depends upon their estimation of the therapist's expertise and knowledge regarding the problem.

Differences between the initial interview with the agoraphobic patient and the uncomplicated panic disorder patient are minimal. Most agoraphobics avoid situations not because they fear them in themselves, but rather because they fear the consequences of panic symptoms in such situations. One must begin by inquiring about symptoms of panic, and demonstrating one's knowledge and one's empathy for the difficulties the patient experiences. After obtaining detailed information regarding symptoms, the patient's specific fears regarding the consequences of panic, and the extent of avoidance, we frequently refer to a variation of Clark's (1986) cognitive model of panic (see chapter 7) to help the patient distinguish between the physical symptoms associated with panic and the perceived consequences. For example, one agoraphobic patient, Michael H. who is a lawyer, had symptoms of tachycardia, sweaty palms, chest pain, and a "bloating" sensation during panic episodes. These episodes would occur in a variety of situations, among which was driving. His fear regarding driving consisted of a perceived inability to control the car in the event of a panic attack; he feared that he would "go off the deep end and crash the car." The cognitive model was used to advance the notion that while the symptoms described by the patient were certainly real and unpleasant, the interpretation that his judgment and ability to handle an automobile would be compromised was catastrophic and unwarranted.

Agoraphobic patients are, of course, notoriously unmoved by rational disputation of their catastrophic beliefs about the consequences of panic. It is important for the therapist to acknowledge this, since the rationale for exposure therapy begins with this acknowledgment. Because the therapist's reassurance is inadequate, exposure therapy is explicitly presented as a way of gathering information designed to "disconfirm" patients' worst fears regarding the consequences of panic, and as a way of enhancing their sense of efficacy to cope with a variety of situations while experiencing panic. In the case of Michael H., exposure therapy was presented as a way of providing evidence that, in fact, his judgment and ability to handle the car while feeling anxious or panicky were uncompromised. The following exchange took place:

Therapist: Now it's very easy for me to sit here and to say to you that I've worked with a hundred or so patients with symptoms of panic and agoraphobia and heard concerns from many patients that are very similar to those you raise but that, in fact, there is no connection between the physical discomfort you experience during a panic episode and your judgment or ability to handle the car. It's easy for me to sit in this chair and say that and probably very hard for you to believe it.

Patient: Well, I guess that's right.

Therapist: I understand that. There's no way you're going to be convinced of your ability to drive a car or function in other situations during a panic attack simply on my say-so. The only evidence that is going to convince you is evidence that you yourself can gather first-hand. So I think the best way to go about this is for you and me to come up with a set of tasks which gradually puts you in some of the situations you fear most. I'll help you with some strategies for coping with the symptoms you experience, and let's see whether as a result of those first-hand experiences some of your catastrophic notions about what you can and can't do during a panic attack don't change.

As is apparent from the above exchange, exposure therapy is presented as a way for the patient to learn to cope more effectively with symptoms of panic and anxiety and as a way of disconfirming catastrophic beliefs about such episodes. It is not presented as a way of eliminating the symptoms of anxiety. While the issue of how exposure therapy reduces fear remains open to question, we have found that it is counterproductive for patients to approach such treatment as though it were a passive desensitization process during which repeated exposures gradually reduce or eliminate anxiety. These patients are already overly keyed to their physiological sensations. If the treatment is understood as a way of eliminating such anxiety, the patient is likely to continue monitoring the extent of physical sensations in hypervigilant fashion, possibly amplifying them, and losing faith in the treatment approach if the sensations fail to diminish quickly enough. We attempt to direct patients away from preoccupation with their physiological sensations by explicitly asking them to focus upon their own performance during panic and on the changes in catastrophic beliefs accompanying such a focus.

The Use of Medication Concomitant With Exposure Therapy

Medication often plays a key role in the treatment of the agoraphobic patient. In the previous chapter we reviewed the effectiveness of pharmacological treatments for reducing the intensity and frequency of panic attacks. In general, these medications have similar effects in reducing panic attacks in agoraphobic patients. The treatment guidelines provided in that chapter can be followed in treating agoraphobic patients. However, while avoidance and panic attacks are closely linked, a reduction in the incidence of panic is rarely sufficient to facilitate significant changes in avoidance behavior. Rather, agoraphobic patients must be given instructions and help in exposing themselves to feared situations.

The usefulness of combined pharmacology and exposure is demonstrated in a study undertaken at Stanford with 37 agoraphobics

(Telch et al., 1985). Patients were given a placebo with exposure instructions, imipramine with exposure instructions, or imipramine alone without the element of exposure entering in. In the imipramine-alone group, subjects were told not to confront fear-evoking situations for the first eight weeks of the study. After the period during which the anti-exposure instructions were no longer in effect, the imipramine alone and placebo plus exposure groups did about equally as well. However, there was a significant superiority for the imipramine plus exposure group (see Figure 7.4).

There are several considerations in choosing a drug for the agoraphobic patient as opposed to the uncomplicated panic disorder patient. First, agoraphobic patients seem to be more sensitive than uncomplicated panic disorder patients to the unpleasant side effects of medications. About 20–25 percent of agoraphobic patients report imipramine intolerance even at low doses. The symptoms of this intolerance were described earlier, and the problem can usually be overcome by prescribing very low doses of imipramine or adding alprazolam. Second, patients should not be medicated to the point that they do not experience anxiety or panic attacks. We inform patients that the purpose of medication is to make the anxiety and discomfort they experience sufficiently tolerable for them to engage in exposure therapy.

Thus, the function of medication is to facilitate patients' encounters with previously avoided situations. We emphasize that some anxiety is normal and that exposure will not be effective unless they experience some degree of anxious symptoms. Overmedicated patients will tend to discount the usefulness of the exposure tasks and fail to develop increased self-confidence for coping with fear-evoking situations on their own. As patients accomplish more tasks, we often reduce the medication, although we try to ensure that patients will not experience incapacitating anxiety when practicing exposure. As with uncomplicated panic disorder patients, we have agoraphobics stop medications after 6–12 months to determine whether the symptoms have resolved. Third, although benzodiazepines affect learning in animals in ways that would seem to diminish the long-term effects of exposure, in clinical practice patients on alprazolam seem to do as well with exposure as those on imipramine, and we have not noticed any differences in long-term outcome.

Incorporating Cognitive Strategies in Exposure Therapy

Despite the uncertain empirical status of cognitive procedures in a program of exposure, we recommend their use. We view exposure itself as a cognitive procedure, which is successful to the extent that it changes patients' estimations of their ability to cope with previously avoided situations (i.e., that it alters perceived self-efficacy). While purely cognitive interventions may ultimately prove less powerful than exposure in changing self-efficacy estimations, we believe they make a contribution when combined with exposure procedures. We incorporate self-statement modification (see Chapter 7) and in addition, the following two strategies with particular application to agoraphobic patients.

Planning for the Worst

The agoraphobic patient is frequently immobilized by the anticipation of catastrophic results should panic or severe anxiety occur. In many cases, patients imagine themselves as helpless, without any effective coping strategy short of precipitously leaving the situation. While coping self-statements frequently function to reassure the patient regarding the low probability of their worst fears occurring (e.g., "Though I'm afraid I might faint during a panic attack, I never have in the past"), due to the catastrophic nature of their fears, even a remote possibility of a panic attack occurring can continue to trouble them and maintain avoidance. Put differently, while coping self-statements remind the patient that their worst fears are unlikely, patients still frequently think, "Yes, but if it happens even one time, the results will be catastrophic."

One cognitive intervention we have found useful is to help patients devise a detailed plan for coping with their worst fears without fleeing the problem situation. This can be particularly useful in situations where fears of embarrassment predominate. For example, one patient with a fear of fainting during a panic attack virtually avoided all public places. When questioned carefully regarding her worst fears should she faint in a public place, she indicated imagining herself being attended to by bystanders who would ask her why she fainted and feeling humiliated when she revealed that she had suffered a panic attack. Because one of the places she avoided and wanted to begin going back to was a shopping mall, a plan was devised for how she would field questions from bystanders or store employees once she "came to," if she had a panic attack in a department store. She was instructed to say that she had been suffering from a "middle ear infection" and became dizzy and fainted. With this plan, she was able to begin entering department stores, gradually increasing the length of time she stayed. It is not at all uncommon for patients to fear that bystanders will "find out" that they have a "psychiatric problem" and expose them to ridicule. Helping patients to develop coping strategies that "plan for the worst" by devising medical explanations for the problem will frequently facilitate their exposure to previously avoided situations.

We have also seen a number of patients who avoid driving because they fear being unable to control the automobile should they have a panic attack. We have had considerable success in helping such people begin driving again by having them start on well-traveled streets or on freeways with exits that are not widely spaced, developing a detailed plan for pulling off the road should a severe panic attack occur and waiting for it to pass before getting back on the road and going toward their destination. Such plans also include what they will tell a police officer or highway patrolman about why they were temporarily unable to continue. In such cases, we stress the importance of continuing on and reaching their predetermined destination once the symptoms of panic have subsided, rather than turning around and going home.

Modeling

Another strategy with particular applicability toward changing catastrophic fears of social embarrassment during panic attacks is modeling. This involves having the therapist perform the feared action with the patient watching. For example, one patient, a college student, had a fear that her anxiety and "shaking" during a panic attack would be obvious to strangers and that they would ridicule her. To help change her catastrophic fears she accompanied her therapist to the student union on her campus, and sat some distance away while the therapist began to simulate in exaggerated fashion a panic attack. There were 25–30 people in the room at the time. The therapist shook somewhat violently and said in a voice loud enough for people nearby to hear "Oh no, I'm having a panic attack." The patient watched from a short distance as two people came up to the therapist and asked whether he needed any help; the therapist said that he was having a panic attack that would soon pass, thanked them, and indicated that he wouldn't need any help. The other people present, perhaps noticing that the therapist declined help, paid him no further attention. The patient indicated surprise that the bystanders were either helpful or indifferent, and did not ridicule the therapist at all.

The Behavioral Component

Among the first tasks faced by the therapist in planning treatment with the agoraphobic patient is deciding how to instruct the patient to respond to symptoms of anxiety and panic during exposure. There are two approaches to this issue. The first, *graduated in vivo exposure*, involves instructing the patient to enter the fear-evoking situation and stay only until the anxiety becomes uncomfortable; at this point the patient is expected to return to his/her starting point. The second, *prolonged in vivo exposure*, involves staying in the fear-evoking situation until the anxiety "peaks and passes." Clinical experience favors the second approach.

Agoraphobics most frequently fear events (e.g., "losing control," public humiliation, heart attack), which have never taken place. In a sense, they are constantly projecting themselves into the future and ruminating on the consequences should their symptoms worsen. Their avoidance and "escape behavior," however, prevent them from actually experiencing the consequences of their symptoms worsening, as well as from experiencing the self-limiting nature of panic attacks.

Instructing patients to remain in fearsome circumstances until the anxiety subsides short-circuits their avoidance and escape maneuvers and puts them in direct contact with evidence disconfirming their worst fears and enhancing their sense of competence in coping with anxiety. Instructing patients to leave a situation when it becomes too uncomfortable preserves the principle of avoiding intense anxiety at all costs and implicitly maintains the myth that symptoms are likely to get out of control with dire consequences. Moreover, such instructions continue to encourage patients to allow their perceived internal state, rather than their performance goals, to guide their behavior.

Setting Goals

Once the patient has been instructed on how to respond to anxiety during exposure, behavioral targets must be chosen. We generally use a combination of sources to assess the extent of avoidance, including the Mobility Inventory (Chambless et al., 1985), the Fear Questionnaire (Marks & Mathews, 1979), and the clinical interview. A list of situations is generated, and the patient is asked to rank them in order of difficulty. It is at this point that we incorporate the principle of gradualism; the patient is encouraged to begin exposure in those situations that are perceived to be less anxiety provoking.

The first interview with one patient, for example, resulted in the following rank-ordered list of potential targets:

(1) Supermarkets
(2) Department stores

(3) Driving on freeways
(4) Restaurants
(5) Beauty shops (i.e., getting hair done)

The patient chose supermarkets as the first target for exposure, indicating that of all the situations she found problematic and wanted to address in treatment, this would evoke the least amount of anxiety. Her goal before going on to the next target was to be able to grocery shop by herself in a large and often crowded supermarket near her house; a major stumbling block was her fear of having a panic attack while waiting in line to pay for her groceries. Initially, she was instructed to simply enter the store (which she had not done unaccompanied for five years) at mid-morning when it was not crowded, browse for three minutes, and leave without buying anything. She was told to repeat this task twice a day over the following week. In the next step, she was again to go to the store at a time when it was not crowded, buy two items, and choose a line with only one person ahead of her. As she became more comfortable with this task, she was encouraged to enter longer and longer lines. The patient was seen weekly, minimal tasks were agreed upon for the week and the patient was instructed to complete them regardless of her anxiety level. That is, the patient was discouraged from having her level of anxiety determine whether or not an agreed-upon task was completed. If she had a panic attack, she was expected to complete whatever task was agreed upon. However, the patient was instructed to let her level of anxiety guide her in moving to the next task in the hierarchy.

Thus, our method of managing exposure therapy is graded in the sense that we encourage patients to move through a hierarchy of tasks at their own pace; however, once they have agreed to a specific task, we strongly encourage them to follow through with it regardless of the level of anxiety experienced. Typically, patients begin a task with considerable anxiety and repeat it to a point where it becomes tolerably comfortable before moving on to the next step.

In the case discussed above, the patient spent four weeks exposing herself to the supermarket daily, beginning by simply walking in and gradually moving toward longer and longer lines. By the middle of week three, she was able to perform the tasks at times during the day such as the late afternoon and early evening when the store was more crowded. At the end of this period, she felt comfortable buying as many groceries as she needed. She then turned her attention to coping with buying clothes in department stores, something she had not done unaccompanied for many years. The sequence of steps was similar, though by this time the patient's sense of efficacy in coping with symptoms of anxiety was enhanced, and she was less tentative at the outset. Her major difficulty in negotiating department stores involved going above the first floor. Thus, she was instructed to begin by spending brief periods of time browsing on the second floor, and when she became comfortable with that task, to try on one item of clothing. After increasing the number of items of clothing she was able to try on while on the second floor, she was able to begin working on becoming comfortable with the third floor in similar fashion; except by this time, she was able to skip the step of browsing and began by trying on one item of clothing.

We strongly encourage patients to practice exposure tasks daily. They are asked to keep a log of their daily activities. Patients frequently ask how much time we think they should devote to practice during the day. We generally suggest that they spend a minimum of one hour daily. In attempting to convince patients to practice every day, we often stress that the goal of treatment involves enhancing their ability to cope with anxiety. Coping with anxiety, we argue, is a skill and like any other skill requires a considerable amount of practice.

Agoraphobic patients frequently report variation in their symptomotology. They note "good" and "bad" days; their ability to function on good days is often considerably better than on bad days. For example, a patient may be able to go into a department store alone on a good day but might require the presence of a trusted companion on a bad day. While patients frequently have difficulty identifying factors separating good from bad days—often it is simply a "feeling that's hard to describe"—it is important that they not avoid practicing exposure tasks on bad days. Hence, we stress the importance of daily practice. In cases where patients seem to be avoiding practice on bad days, it is helpful to remind them that practice on such days is more effective than on good days since they are exposing themselves to more significant levels of anxiety.

When necessary, we encourage patients to incorporate response aids, that is, objects or people whose presence facilitates the performance of a given task with a tolerable level of anxiety. As the patient becomes more comfortable with the task, the response aid is faded out. For example, in the case discussed above, when the patient began to expose herself to driving on freeways, she found that her level of anxiety was intolerable. She was able to drive short distances, however, with her husband in the car. Thus, we began instructing her to drive very short distances on the freeway—she began repeating a distance of one exit which was one mile—with her husband in the car. Once she became more comfortable, she was instructed to fade her husband out. She continued driving further and further on the freeway by herself in increments of approximately one freeway exit for several weeks, until she reached a point where there was a six-mile distance between exits. At this point, she reintroduced her husband as a response aid for a period of one week, until she again felt less anxious and resumed driving on her own. By this time, the distance she was covering in her daily exposure was approximately 15 miles in each direction.

The question of whether, when, and how to incorporate partners in treatment is a complicated one that we will take up in more detail in the next section. For now, it is sufficient to note that while we find it useful in most cases to educate partners regarding the nature of agoraphobia, we do not involve them in exposure therapy in all cases; such decisions are made on a case-by-case basis.

In summary, we utilize several organizing principles in planning the behavioral component of exposure therapy with our patients. First, our instructions for how to respond to an episode of panic during exposure involve allowing it to "peak and pass" before leaving a given situation. Second, we encourage patients to set specific goals and rate them for difficulty, beginning with tasks they believe will induce the smallest amounts of anxiety. However, once a performance target is agreed upon, we encourage them to go through with it regardless of the level of anxiety they experience. We encourage repeated exposures to the same task until the patient becomes comfortable enough to move on to the next one. Third, we encourage the use of response aids at the beginning of a difficult task that are to be faded out as the patient repeats the task and becomes more comfortable with it. Fourth, we encourage daily practice for a period of at least one hour.

Preventing Rituals

Patients who are preoccupied with anticipatory anxiety or who may be in the throes of a panic attack often engage in subtle behaviors that amplify their symptoms. We have found it helpful to assist patients in becoming aware of such behaviors and work actively to change them. For example, among patients who demonstrate fear of operating an automobile, it is common to find that when they are approaching a part of the road or an intersection they find difficult, they will sit further up in their seats, straighten their backs, and grip the wheel more tightly. Other patients may find that when they are in a fear-evoking situation they clench their fists, or tighten their facial muscles, or grit their teeth. One patient, who avoided waiting in lines, found that when performing exposure tasks involving being in line, she would tap her feet incessantly and pull on her fingers. We point out to patients how such behaviors increase their levels of arousal and contribute to their symptoms of anxiety; we engage them in an effort to consciously change.

We generally wait until we have an exposure program under way and have incorporated cognitive interventions before asking patients to become aware of counterproductive behaviors. Patients vary in their ability to track them; many are able to identify the behaviors on their own, while others are unsuccessful. In the latter instances, the therapist may have to accompany the patient and observe him or her carefully to assist in the process of identification. The utility of this process lies not only in its ability to decrease arousal but in the implicit message it conveys that anxiety and panic are partially maintained by voluntary behaviors the patient can alter.

EXPOSURE THERAPY: MODES OF DELIVERY

Exposure therapy for agoraphobia may be conducted in several ways. Many patients appear to require assistance in initiating exposure to previously feared situations, and the question of who provides such assistance and when, is one that often has significant treatment ramifications. Some investigators have advocated a home-based approach (Mathews et al., 1977; 1981), in which partners assist the patient to plan and carry out exposure, with the therapist in the role of a supervising consultant. In other cases, therapist-assisted exposure may be carried out. This procedure involves the therapist actually accompanying the patient out of the office to situations that evoke fear. In still other cases, exposure may be carried out by the patient largely alone, on a self-directed basis. This method involves meeting with the therapist in the office for consultation and instruction. Finally, the procedures may be combined into group or individual formats. Each of these modes of delivery has certain strengths and weaknesses.

Therapist-Assisted Exposure Therapy

The presence of the therapist during exposure therapy may serve several functions. First, it affords an opportunity for in vivo assessment. Many patients have difficulty identifying automatic thoughts and images that may amplify panic episodes. Similarly, they are usually unaware of more subtle behaviors that increase their level of arousal during or prior to panic episodes, such as clenching their fists or tightening their facial muscles. Having the therapist accompany the patient in an anxiety-evoking situation and elicit the patient's thoughts or observe the patient's behavior often facilitates assessment of such factors.

Second, accompaniment by the therapist provides the opportunity to facilitate the patient's use of coping strategies. Particularly during the earliest stages of treatment, it is not unusual for patients to become overwhelmed with anxiety during exposure and fail to use coping strategies suggested in the therapist's office, such as controlled breathing or the use of positive self-statements. With the therapist present, there can be on-the-spot instruction in the use of anxiety management techniques, as well as feedback about how well such measures are working and how they might be modified.

Third, some patients are so beset with anticipatory anxiety that they have difficulty initiating exposure to fear-evoking situations on their own. Therapist accompaniment has been used to assure that exposure takes place. Among the distinguishing characteristics of agoraphobia is difficulty entering certain situations without a trusted, or "safe," companion. Such companions, who are often partners or family members, are frequently unsure about how to respond to the patient's helplessness in a way that promotes greater autonomy. There are also cases reported where the partner appears to have an interest in the patient's continuing dependence (Fry, 1962; Hafner, 1977; Milton & Hafner, 1979). Therapist-assisted exposure has been employed as a way of short-circuiting patterns between agoraphobics and their companions that unwittingly or deliberately maintain the patient's avoidance. Thus, a therapist working effectively with a patient who has difficulty entering stores may initially go into the store with the patient but, unlike the companion, will begin to gradually withdraw and encourage the patient to experiment with more autonomous behavior by waiting outside the store and urging the patient to spend longer and longer periods in the store alone.

Thus, the strengths of this approach lie in the opportunity provided to conduct a detailed and fine-grained assessment in anxiety evoking circumstances, insuring that strategies for coping with anxiety are used effectively and assuring that the patient initiates an exposure program. Initially, the therapist's presence can help to assure that the patient has a successful experience, challenging his or her beliefs about lack of efficacy in coping with anxiety. Furthermore, therapist-assisted exposure sensitizes the therapist to the difficulties faced by agoraphobics in overcoming their symptoms. Agoraphobics frequently appear asymptomatic outside of anxiety-evoking situations. The therapist treating agoraphobics who has only observed and interacted with them in the safety of the office is unlikely to appreciate the nature of agoraphobia and the difficulty faced by such patients in coping more effectively with their difficulties.

However, there are several problems in conducting therapist-assisted exposure. An obvious one is the expense. It is extremely time-consuming for a therapist to accompany patients to settings that evoke anxiety; in many cases, the cost will be prohibitive. Second, few therapists will have the necessary time to devote to one patient. Third, the therapist's availability as a resource during exposure increases the patient's sense of "safety," which in turn enhances the possibility that the patient will fail to achieve sufficient levels of anxiety during therapist-assisted exposure to bring about changes in efficacy estimations. Put differently, the patient may think: "I could do that because Dr. X was in the vicinity, and I knew that if I panicked, someone would take care of me, but I'm not at all certain I would risk performing that task entirely on my own." Fourth, many therapists do not want to assume the personal or professional liability for treating patients outside of the office setting.

Perhaps most important, therapist-assisted exposure may intensify the patient-therapist relationship in unanticipated ways. The therapist must be very sensitive to cues during exposure indicating that the procedure has taken on a meaning to the patient (or the therapist) extending above and beyond the application of the technique. For instance, one patient proceeding well with exposure was assigned the task of entering a grocery store by himself and purchasing an item. He returned with a bouquet of roses indicating his affection for the therapist. In another instance, in reviewing the progress of one patient during our weekly case conference, it seemed that the therapist was spending more time than necessary or appropriate with him. Discussion with the therapist made clear that she had developed sexual feelings toward the patient and very much enjoyed her time with him. In yet another instance, the patient always seemed to do the opposite of what she had agreed to. In reviewing the homework, it became apparent that the patient was responding to the therapist much as she had to her mother; out of fear of displeasing her mother she would agree to undertake tasks she found disagreeable, and a similar pattern emerged during the therapy. Much as she used to "punish" her mother for placing her in such a difficult situation, she was now failing to complete the therapeutic tasks and experiencing again a sense of gratification in "punishing" the therapist. An additional common transference issue involves overdependence. Agoraphobic patients frequently relate to others in a helpless, dependent way. Therapist-assisted exposure runs the risk of merely replicating other relationships in the agoraphobic's life in which the patient experiences himself or herself as helpless and incompetent vis-à-vis a better functioning, seemingly more powerful, other.

Exposure therapy developed within the behavioral tradition, where emphasis is on the performance of the task as a way of reducing fear, rather than on understanding the dynamics of the patient–

therapist relationship. From the standpoint of psychodynamic therapy, or even more integrative approaches to treatment (e.g., Wachtel, 1977), such issues as those discussed above provide a rich source of data that can help promote the patient's insight into unconscious motives and how they impact upon interpersonal relationships. However, our own treatment goals and those we have found most compelling to our patients involve enhancing day-to-day functioning at the outset of treatment, rather than promoting insight derived from consideration of the therapist–patient relationship. And yet it appears that by moving the therapy outside the confines of the office and allocating to the therapist such an overt and directive role in the patient's recovery, therapist-assisted exposure may predispose both patients and therapists to a variety of transference and countertransference issues for which they may be unprepared.

Accordingly, we attempt to steer a middle course. It is critical that therapists be sensitive to the presence of such issues. When they do emerge, their full implications must be discussed both in general and as they relate to the current treatment situation. On the other hand, we are mindful that the emergence of strong transference/countertransference issues at the beginning of treatment can interfere with the patient's efforts to enhance functioning and reduce fear. Thus, we offer the following suggestions designed to reduce the intensity of the therapist-patient relationship during therapist-assisted exposure therapy:

1. Such treatment should be brief and explicitly time-limited. The patient should have a clear idea before beginning approximately how many sessions will involve direct therapist assistance. We recommend that there be no more than six such sessions.
2. Therapist-assisted exposure must be accompanied by self-directed exposure (i.e., between sessions).
3. Wherever possible, therapist-assisted exposure should be conducted in groups.

Partner-Assisted Exposure Therapy

Partner-assisted therapy was designed to address some of the practical and logistical problems associated with therapist-assisted treatment (Mathews et al., 1981), including issues of cost-containment and the generalization of treatment effects. In addition, it has the added virtue of involving partners—who after all are already involved—in a way designed to promote autonomy rather than to maintain dependence. Regardless of how effective the therapy, if family members continue to behave in ways that fail to encourage autonomy, treatment progress—or further progress after treatment has ended is likely to be retarded. Thus, the home-based, partner-assisted approach to treatment involves the participation of a partner or another trusted companion in the role of facilitator.

In a manual designed for partners involved in this mode of treatment delivery (Mathews et al., 1981), instructions are given on assisting the agoraphobic in selecting behavioral targets, praise and encouragment of the patient's progress, going over the patient's practice diary, responding to a panic attack, accompanying the patient during practice, and fading oneself out. For example, the partner is instructed, "When you judge that your partner is ready to start a new practice item, take the initiative and make a *firm* suggestion about what he/she might do. Don't let your partner do the same thing *too* many times before you suggest moving on" (Mathews et al., 1981, p. 201, italics theirs). Thus the partner performs many of the tasks performed by a therapist. The role of the therapist in such an approach is as an educator and consultant to the couple.

It is an approach with several obvious strengths. First, of course, it costs considerably less than therapist-assisted treatment. Second, exposures are carried out in the patient's home environment, which removes the problem of the generalization of treatment effects from the office to the home and allows the patient to confront with supervision those real-life situations that he or she finds problematic. In addition, the partner, who may be behaving unwittingly in ways that amplify the symptoms, can now be involved in ways specifically designed to attenuate agoraphobic behavior.

However, there are several potential problems in involving partners in treatment this way. First, it amplifies the assymetry characteristic of many of the relationships between agoraphobics and their partners. The inability to travel alone and the necessity of involving and frequently inconveniencing partners causes many agoraphobics to feel overly indebted to their spouses. Difficulties with assertion among the agoraphobics and a sense of entitlement among the spouses is not uncommon. To accord the partner the role of cotherapist, with responsibility for insuring that the patient makes progress, institutionalizes an imbalance within the relationship and complicates the agoraphobic's effort to feel and behave more autonomously.

Second, the assumption on which this approach is based, that partners unwittingly encourage dependence, is not universally true. We have seen many marriages in this population where the spouse is very vocal about being inconvenienced and resentful feelings are engendered. In these marriages the partner often is already pushing the patient to become more independent, and a power struggle has ensued over the patient's symptoms, with the partner often complaining of being "manipulated" or "used." In such relationships, where the couple has been unable to resolve issues of power and control, the symptoms, whatever their etiology, become a battleground in the couple's ongoing struggle. When that is the case, it is obvious that the partner is unable to assume the role of helper or cotherapist effectively.

Self-Directed Exposure

In this mode of treatment, patients direct their own practice, without the in vivo participation of a therapist or partner. Meetings with the therapist take place in a professional setting, and the time is used to plan exposure targets, identify cognitive and behavioral patterns that maintain anxiety and avoidance, instruct the patient in the use of strategies for coping with anxiety, and deliver any support or advice necessary for helping the patient cope with interpersonal or other problems related to the therapeutic goals.

Like the partner-assisted approach to treatment, a major advantage of self-directed exposure is its cost-effectiveness and its more reasonable demands on professional time than therapist-assisted approaches. Additional strengths and weaknesses of this approach both stem from the amount of personal responsibility placed on the patient for initiating and carrying out treatment. On the positive side, with the weight of progress unambiguously on the shoulders of the patient, any gains are likely to be attributed to self-initiated efforts rather than to the presence of a therapist or partner. On the minus side, some patients do have difficulty initiating exposure on their own, while others may fail to use coping strategies effectively in an anxiety-evoking situation that were explained in the therapist's office. In addition, as we mentioned above, the therapist is often in a better position to assess relevant cognitions and other factors maintaining anxiety and panic if he or she has access to the patient in situations that evoke such symptoms.

Group Versus Individual Treatment

Any of the above modes of treatment—therapist-assisted, partner-assisted, or self-directed exposure may be incorporated into a group format. In the case of therapist-assisted treatment, we usually begin by taking a very avoidant group to a shopping center or busy commercial area and providing 12 hours of therapist-assisted exposure over three days. Gradually in the course of the three days, the therapist encourages the autonomy of group members in performing feared tasks. Toward the end of the period, he or she will remain at predesignated "checkpoints," where all patients are encouraged to congregate every hour to discuss their progress and share with other group members strategies that have helped them confront previously avoided situations.

While the in vivo group support can be extremely useful, the approach is limited by the variable rates of progress of the participating individuals; this makes it increasingly difficult as treatment progresses to find exposure targets that will provoke sufficient anxiety in all group members to be useful. Moreover, one also must start out with a group of individuals who are similar in their level of avoidance and encounter difficulty in similar situations. We have carried out therapist-assisted group exposure with groups of highly avoidant individuals over a period of one to two weeks (three–six sessions), followed by self-directed exposure in which patients meet weekly as a group to report on their progress and discuss problems that arose and strategies for coping with them. In the case of partner-assisted exposure, one can have couples meet together on a once weekly basis to discuss similar issues and strategies.

There are other advantages to the group format besides its lower cost. Exposure therapy evokes considerable discomfort. While patients acknowledge the gains related to exposure, many report that they have to "push" themselves, or "force" themselves, to get out and practice each day. The support of a group of other individuals coping with the same issues can be extremely effective in maintaining motivation at levels sufficient for progress to continue.

Physician-Based Exposure Treatment

Many studies have shown that exposure instructions combined with physician visits can facilitate exposure. One procedure used by psychiatrists in our group is to build self-directed exposure around the medication prescription. During the initial visit, patients complete a phobic avoidance inventory, which is then used to guide treatment. The physician creates the positive expectation that the medication will help the patient to reduce panic episodes but that conquering avoidance will require additional effort on the patient's part. During each visit, the patient and therapist set new goals based on the patient's confidence that he or she will be able to complete the agreed-upon tasks. Patients keep diaries detailing progress and the incidence of panic attacks. At each visit, the diary is reviewed, medication adjusted, and new goals set. Essentially the physician undertakes the combined function of prescribing medication and conducting the exposure therapy. Unfortunately, few psychiatrists are interested in or sufficiently trained to follow this procedure.

Recommendations for Clinical Practice

1. Wherever possible, self-directed exposure should be the preferred mode of treatment delivery.
2. Patients should be treated in groups. Obviously, in private practice this will not always be possible.
3. Therapist-assisted exposure, when employed, should be used for the following purposes: (1) to help the therapist make a thorough assessment (e.g., to identify subtle ritualistic behaviors the patient may be unaware of, to inquire about relevant fear-inducing cognitions, to acquire an overall sense of the level of fear and impairment); (2) to instruct patients on how to conduct the therapeutic tasks and how to use anxiety-management skills appropriately; and (3) to insure a successful experience at the beginning of treatment. When used for the latter purpose, it should be remembered that the goal is for the patient to be able to carry out his or her own program of self-directed exposure, with the therapist in a supportive and consultive role. Therapist-assisted treatment should be conceptualized as an initial phase designed to insure that exposure therapy begins on a successful note by giving patients "on the spot" instructions on how to use cognitive and other strategies for reducing anxiety effectively. Therefore, as we noted earlier, this phase should be time-limited (we suggest a maximum of six therapist-assisted sessions).
4. Partners may be involved in exposure therapy in two ways. We recommend that they be educated about the nature of agoraphobia. This may be done in group sessions or in conjoint sessions with the agoraphobic patient, depending on whether treatment is being carried out in a group or individual format. Partners may also function as response aids, if necessary, assuming both members of the couple are comfortable with this.
5. We do not recommend that partners serve as cotherapists or be responsible in any other way for insuring that self-directed exposure is carried out. That is the responsibility of the patient.

SPECIAL PROBLEMS ASSOCIATED WITH EXPOSURE THERAPY

In addition to issues associated with delivery, exposure therapy often poses a number of other unique problems requiring discussion.

The Patient Resistant to Carrying Out Exposure Tasks

Marks (1978) has noted that behavioral treatments occur within a "dual process framework." One process involves motivation. The patient must be sufficiently motivated to enter and complete treatment. Marks refers to the second process as execution. The patient must then carry out specific tasks necessary to bring about improvement or resolution of the presenting problem. For example, the patient involved in exposure therapy would need to directly confront fear-evoking situations, engage in the production of coping self-statements, learn to use other anxiety-reducing strategies such as controlled breathing, and so on. Our discussion so far has focused on the execution side of this process. However, agoraphobic patients by definition avoid situations that evoke anxiety; thus it is hardly surprising that the issue of under-motivation, or failure to execute prescribed tasks is one that surfaces frequently.

Patients fail to carry out prescribed tasks for a variety of reasons. The most common include: (1) insufficient information regarding the benefits of performing prescribed tasks; (2) low self-efficacy (Bandura, 1977), or put differently, low estimation on the patient's part that he or she can successfully carry out the task; (3) a perceived cost/benefit ratio in which the benefits are believed insufficient for the patient to tolerate the discomfort involved in exposure therapy; and (4) secondary gain issues perceived to reduce the benefits of improvement. It is also important to consider the phase of treatment when such resistance manifests itself. Patients who fail to complete tasks at the outset of treatment usually do so for different reasons than those who have been successful and then suddenly report "losing motivation."

Insufficient Information

Patients reluctant to engage in exposure therapy at the beginning of treatment may be unsure that the tasks will be beneficial. Patients are unlikely to place themselves in situations they find highly uncomfortable, if they are not persuaded that they have something important to gain. Because the discomfort is so palpable, it is important

that the therapist be willing to persuade the patient that the prescribed measures will bring results. In cases where patients are failing to carry out therapeutic tasks at the outset, we ask them to rate
their belief verbally as to whether the prescribed measures will bring
results. Their responses inform us about the need to engage in further
efforts to convince them of the efficacy of the procedures, or whether
we must look in another direction.

Interestingly, we encounter few patients who doubt the wisdom of
the procedures; exposure therapy appears to have considerable face
validity for agoraphobics. Nevertheless, we have treated a few who
were unsure about the value of this approach at the outset. In the vast
majority of such cases, the patient has been treated with exposure
procedures before coming to see us, without benefit. As a general
rule, among those who have been treated with exposure previously
and have doubts about embarking upon that course again, we find
that expectations regarding habituation to anxiety were not met.
Such patients frequently say: "I've tried that and I'm still anxious so
why should it be any different this time?" Three issues are important
to consider in such cases. First, it is important to assess whether the
patient has had an adequate trial of medication concomitant with
exposure. If not, medication can be used to reduce anxious symptoms
and permit exposure therapy to proceed.

Second, in our experience, it is frequently the case among this
group that exposure therapy has been conducted in a way where the
patient has not been encouraged to allow the anxiety to "peak and
pass." Such patients have often been given instructions to leave an
anxiety-evoking situation at the point where they become overly anxious, depriving them of the opportunity to experience a sense of mastery over the symptoms. With such patients we emphasize the differences in the way we conduct exposure and the benefits involved in
experiencing the self-limiting nature of panic attacks. Third, the habituation effects involved with exposure have often been overstated
to these patients in prior treatment. We have seen many cases of
therapists conducting exposure therapy who assume that anxiety
will disappear strictly as a result of a sufficient number of exposures.
They do not emphasize cognitive coping skills, controlled breathing,
or other measures to facilitate a sense of effectiveness when confronting anxiety. When treatment is presented in this fashion, patients
seem to wait for anxiety to "disappear," and when they continue to
experience symptoms of anxiety and panic, they lose faith in the
treatment.

As we mentioned earlier, the therapist working with the agoraphobic patient must often be willing to assume the role of an "expert,"
whose experience and knowledge regarding the problem may be re-

lied upon. While exposure therapy has a built-in logic that appeals to the agoraphobic, the therapist must be a credible source of information if the therapeutic tasks are to be carried out in earnest. In addition to being empathic, and indicating an understanding of the patient's predicament, the therapist must also be able to actively communicate his or her belief in the efficacy of the procedures.

Low Self-Efficacy

It is not surprising that some patients are reluctant to carry out exposure therapy for the same reasons that they avoid anxiety-evoking situations in their everyday life—that is, they have catastrophic fears regarding the consequences of experiencing anxiety and believe that their symptoms will become uncontrollable if they enter situations likely to provoke panic. Such patients usually believe the procedures make sense for others, but that in their case, the symptoms are so severe and their ability to manage them so inadequate that they fail to execute the therapeutic tasks. This is a problem that surfaces at the outset of treatment, and we generally incorporate therapist-assisted exposure with this group as a way of insuring an initially successful experience.

For example, one agoraphobic with an intense fear of freeway driving approached us to help her get over her fear. She had been seen previously by a behaviorally oriented therapist who accompanied her while driving on the freeway for a period of three months, two years prior to her consultation with us. She indicated that she had "dreaded" her visits and never experienced any reduction in her anxiety as a result of treatment. She indicated that she had tried verbal psychotherapy, also, without result and that while exposure therapy made the most sense to her, she feared that it would continue to be ineffective with her.

When the therapist from our clinic accompanied her the first time, she reported symptoms of sweatiness, tachycardia, tingling in her fingers, and a fear that she would lose control of the auto and cause an accident as soon as she got onto the entrance ramp to the freeway. She became quite upset at the onset of these symptoms, and immediately expressed skepticism that exposure would be helpful, saying "See, this is what happened the last time and it never got any better." The next exit on the freeway was a half mile away, and the therapist suggested she get off at that point. The therapist asked her to verbally rate her belief that she would drive off the road on a 0–10 scale and indicated that, as an "experiment," they would spend the next 45 minutes covering the same ground to see what effects there were on her beliefs about her inability to control the car while anxious. The therapist deliberately avoided asking her to rate her anxiety during this session, for two reasons. One, it was assumed that her constant monitoring of her physical symptoms was in part what maintained the anxiety; two, since she was expressing doubt that the procedure would "reduce anxiety," it was important not to put her in a position where she had to be wrong and the therapist right in order for her to appear to derive any benefit.

While the patient was driving over the same terrain repeatedly, the therapist took the opportunity to differentiate between anxiety and performance, noting that while the anxiety might be uncomfortable, it did not seem to affect her ability to drive. At various points over the next 45 minutes, during which the same area was covered a total of eight times, the patient was asked to rate her belief that she would drive off the road. By the end of the 45 minutes, the patient agreed that while she still felt anxious, she was less convinced that she would lose control of the car; she had begun by rating her belief at a 6 on a 10-point scale, and ended at 2. In addition, she conceded that while she still felt anxious, the symptoms were somewhat less severe at the end of the session than they had been at the beginning.

This case illustrates how we approach the patient whose low self-efficacy at the outset of treatment appears to be inhibiting the initiation of exposure therapy. The therapist was mindful of: (1) breaking the overall task, in this case freeway driving, into the smallest possible parts; (2) using the principle of repeated trials to demonstrate the potential of exposure therapy as a way of altering efficacy estimations; and (3) orienting patients toward evaluating their performance while being anxious rather than attending to possible changes in their level of anxiety.

High Cost/Benefit Ratio

As we noted previously, many patients experience a significant degree of discomfort carrying out exposure tasks. While we favor the use of medication in many cases to reduce the intensity of the symptoms, we conceptualize the goals of treatment in terms of enhancing the patient's ability to cope with anxiety. Thus, we do not medicate patients to a point where they are free of all symptoms. Moreover, even with high doses of medication most patients continue to experience some anxiety. While exposure therapy itself decreases anxiety, even after considerable gains have been made and patients report an increased ability to engage in activities they previously avoided, they often continue to report being troubled, albeit less so, by symptoms of anxiety. Some of these patients stop engaging in exposure tasks before they reach goals they have set for themselves.

It is frequently the case that such patients have made significant progress, are functioning with less impairment, and report that the quality of their life has improved. What appears to happen is that the perceived cost/benefit ratio changes in a way that lowers their motivation to continue engaging in uncomfortable, anxiety-provoking tasks.

For example, one patient of ours, a self-employed accountant, suffered severe panic attacks and agoraphobia, which at the point of consultation with us, had a major impact on his relationship with his wife and limited his ability to conduct his business. He represented a number of large corporations, which required that he attend meetings often a distance of 30–40 miles from his home. When he first applied for treatment, he had cancelled a number of such meetings for fear of experiencing debilitating panic on the way and felt that he was jeopardizing his relationship with these important clients. His wife had also begun to express irritation with his unwillingness to engage in any recreation outside of their suburban town. A member of their family owned a mountain cabin approximately an hour's drive from their home in which they used to spend weekends but which he now refused to go to because he was fearful of traveling that far even in her company. Similarly, he was fearful of going to the beach and of going to restaurants, movies, or plays that were not in their hometown.

After four months of treatment consisting of medication and exposure therapy combined with training in coping self-statements and controlled breathing, the patient was able to travel to business meetings, to go away for weekends, and out for evenings with his wife. He still experienced some anxiety but felt much better able to manage it and no longer felt that he was jeopardizing his business or his marriage. He continued to avoid certain situations, however; most notably, he avoided airplane travel and was unable to cross bridges by himself. Yet, at this point in treatment, he suddenly stopped engaging in the exposure tasks that had been so beneficial. He reported being unable to "motivate myself" to practice crossing bridges, which was the next step agreed upon. When his reluctance to engage further in practice was explored with the therapist, it became clear that the anxiety experienced when confronting previously avoided situations continued to be unpleasant. The symptoms were less distressing than they had been when he first applied for treatment—he rated his usual anxiety when confronting new situations at 2–3 as opposed to 7–8 on a 10-point scale at the beginning of treatment—but they were still at an uncomfortable level. He was no longer concerned about losing his ability to function in business, and his marital problems had largely been resolved; thus the impetus to engage in self-exposure, to devote a significant number of hours per week to expanding his radius had decreased. The patient had reached a point where the costs of engaging in exposure in terms of time spent and discomfort experienced outweighed the perceived remaining benefits.

This is a frequently encountered pattern. Patients whose symptoms of avoidance are successfully treated often continue to experience some anxiety in situations they previously avoided and, incrementally, more anxiety in those situations they have not yet managed to confront through treatment. The most important task for the therapist at this stage is to congratulate the patient on the progress already made and insure that they do not feel they have failed because they continue to experience anxiety, or do not feel "cured." The therapist must bear in mind that these patients often experience their symptoms as a kind of failure, and that even after considerable progress in reducing avoidance the persistence of symptoms of anxiety continues to be appraised as indicative of their inadequacy. When this stage of treatment is reached, we point out that the cost/benefit ratio appears to have changed and that, given the progress and the continued inconvenience and discomfort involved in continuing to engage in exposure, it is understandable that their motivation to continue has waned.

If there are no additional issues the patient wants to take up in treatment (see chapter 4), we generally encourage such patients to discontinue therapy for the time being and to return should they want to go further or encounter any new problems. Continuing exposure-based treatment at this point conveys a message that more needs to be or should be accomplished; this undermines the patient's feeling of accomplishment regarding the substantial gains that have been made. We are explicit regarding the limits of treatment for agoraphobia and panic; we explain that the current state-of-the-art is such that some continued anxiety is to be expected. The fact that they are not "cured" is presented as a comment on the limitations of currently available treatment, rather than as a comment about the patient.

Secondary Gain

Secondary gain refers to cases in which the patient's symptom provides some significant benefit. When present, secondary gain reduces the perceived benefits of engaging in treatment. We attempt to assess the presence of such issues at the outset of treatment. One question we ask is why the patient is seeking treatment at this particular time. The answer to this question will occasionally reveal that a patient has sought treatment at the behest of someone else—a spouse, a parent, or some other significant person in her network—and that he or she may be complying outwardly with the request to seek help but that there is a lack of urgency about resolving the problem. Issues of secondary gain are frequent in such cases. Another question we ask is whether the patient can anticipate in advance any negative consequences that might be involved with improvement in the presenting problem. We generally prepare patients for this question by noting that we have found that even eagerly anticipated changes can sometimes have their drawbacks. Most patients are unable to come up with any undesirable consequences. Occasionally, we have encountered patients who are involved with legal problems involving the symptom (e.g., pending disability claims); we usually instruct such patients to resolve the legal issues before returning to treatment.

However, most patients who are able to respond to this question express concerns regarding their marriage or other primary relationship. Patients will sometimes wonder whether their partner will remain with them should their symptoms abate. Others express doubts that their partners will be happier should they become more independent. At this point it is advisable to frankly discuss the extent of such fears and to assess the possibility that an alternative form of treatment be considered (e.g., marital therapy).

While some agoraphobics obviously do have disturbed marriages, the fact that they express concerns about the effects of successful treatment upon their relationship does not *necessarily* signal a distressed relationship that will interfere with treatment. The dependence and need for accompaniment of the agoraphobic introduces a measure of coercion into the relationship, which may cause the patient to question the partner's commitment. For some, the question arises, "Would my partner continue in the relationship if he didn't feel he had to?" That is, it is the perceived necessity of staying together which itself introduces doubts. While we have seen a number of therapists who appear to interpret the posing of this question as proof positive that the relationship would founder without the symptom to hold it together, we have found that more often than not this is not the case. Such doubts are not unusual, given the agoraphobic's predicament as one who behaves in a helpless fashion, and they frequently dissipate with reassurance from the partner.

Characteristics Affecting Patient Acceptance

Different therapies make different demands of patients. For example, pharmacotherapy, which requires little in the way of psychological-mindedness or verbal ability, nevertheless often demands of the patient a willingness to tolerate uncomfortable physical side effects. Insight-oriented psychodynamic psychotherapy requires a considerable number of attributes among which are verbal ability, a capacity to tolerate interpersonally oriented anxiety, psychological-mindedness, and patience. Exposure therapy, too, makes certain unique demands of patients. While it is generally considered a short-term treatment, the rate at which patients progress varies considerably. We have seen patients who derive spectacular benefit over several weeks, and others who, despite diligence in carrying out between-session tasks, progress far more slowly.

The issue of patient acceptance of exposure therapy is usually discussed as a function of the number of dropouts during relatively brief clinical trials; a dropout rate of, for example, 15 percent would be interpreted as evidence that the treatment is "acceptable" to 85 percent of those who originally seek it. However, even among those who are seen in clinic settings and may be seen for a considerably longer period of time than in the average clinical trial, acceptance of the treatment, that is, willingness to continue to engage in anxiety-provoking tasks, often remains a continuing issue affecting the ultimate outcome. A major limitation of exposure therapy is that it demands a willingness to invest a considerable amount of time and effort, an ability to tolerate significant doses of discomfort, and organizational ability. The patient's willingness and ability to expend the necessary efforts may vary during the course of treatment, profoundly affecting the degree to which the desired results are achieved.

The problem is perhaps best illustrated with a case that was highly successful. A patient, Carol S., a 35-year-old housewife with two children, consulted us for agoraphobia. She was able to function reasonably well within a one-mile radius of her house but was unable to travel beyond that. She was also unable to drive a car by herself over any distance and within the two months prior to her initial consultation with us, was finding it difficult to travel in a car even as a passenger. She reported somewhat atypical anxiety symptoms that included a "falling-down" feeling and a perception of impaired concentration, in addition to the more common symptoms of sweatiness, gastrointestinal distress, and a fear that she would "lose control" of her behavior while driving and drive the car off the road. She indicated "sensitivity" to medications, hence none was prescribed. During the initial evaluation when we discussed target behaviors to address, she indicated that her inability to drive was the most troublesome avoidance and the one she would most like to address. Initially, she began practicing daily driving on side streets with little traffic. After two weeks, she began driving on more busy thoroughfares. After six weeks of treatment, she felt able to drive locally by herself; she still experienced considerable anxiety but felt better able to cope with it. At this point, she began to attempt driving the freeways, beginning very slowly and traveling over and over again between two exits approximately a half mile apart, with considerable anxiety. Gradually, she increased the distance by only one exit every week or two. After about five months of treatment—which also included training in coping self-statements, controlled breathing, and relaxing certain muscle groups when confronted with anxiety while driving—the pace of her progress quickened. After eight months of treatment, she was able to drive approximately 45 miles alone with virtually no anxiety.

The gains made were obviously substantial. She reported little or no anxiety in other situations that formerly disturbed her, such as going up and down escalators or waiting in lines. However, what was most striking about Carol and her course of therapy was the diligence she displayed. Over the eight months of treatment, she practiced driving daily for one hour. It was rare for her to miss a day. Her husband was cooperative; while she generally drove during the day when the children were in school, on weekends he agreed to look after the children while she practiced driving.

The important point here is how much is required of the patient if exposure therapy is to be successful. Few of our patients have the time, organizational ability, and resourcefulness to carry out between-session tasks with the determination and consistency that Carol displayed. She remained undeterred despite enduring considerable anxiety every day for several months. Moreover, many patients are considerably more impaired than Carol and need a longer course of treatment before the symptoms will abate. Not all of the partners are as willing or as helpful as Carol's husband. As we mentioned earlier, many patients will stop practicing self-exposure once their most pressing concerns have been tolerably addressed, although initially they may have had aspirations to progress much further. Thus, one factor that appears to account for the limitations in the outcome associated with exposure therapy is the nature of the demands placed upon the patient.

There are no ready answers to this problem. It is important not to mislead patients about the difficulties they will face in undertaking treatment. Failure to acknowledge such difficulties and the length of time that might be necessary for adequate treatment creates a set of unrealistic expectations, which sets the patient up to experience a sense of failure that may itself result in premature termination. One measure that may be helpful, although we do not as yet have data to support it, is to organize long-term groups of agoraphobics who can meet weekly with a professional, plan self-exposure tasks, and discuss progress and setbacks with one another. It may be that group support, and accountability to other group members, will help patients to stay "on task" and follow through for a longer period of time than they might with an individual therapist.

Relapse Prevention

Most patients are able to resume a normal life with few panic attacks and reduced avoidance. However, the course of agoraphobia is such that it is likely they will experience an increase in the frequency and intensity of panic attacks at some time in the future. Patients must be prepared for this possibility. It is sometimes disconcerting to see how rapidly a patient may resume avoiding anxiety-provoking situations after only one or two panic attacks following months or even years of being essentially symptom-free. Without stretching too far the analogy between relapse prevention for agoraphobics and relapse prevention for substance-abusing patients there are some techniques developing in the relapse-prevention literature (e.g., Marlatt & Gordon, 1985) that are useful in working with agoraphobics.

First, patients should be told to expect a return or amplification of troublesome symptoms at some time in the future. They should be helped to construe such episodes as challenges and as opportunities to apply the techniques they have learned. Patients should *write* down what they will do when symptoms recur. The goal is not to avoid having panic attacks—they have little control over this—but to prevent spiralling into a cycle of increasing avoidance. Two very simple strategies appear most useful: patients are told they can always go back on medication and they can always come back to see us. We request a commitment from them to do so if they have a relapse. Some patients may be concerned that they are disappointing the therapist or feel embarrassed for some other reason to return after relapsing. We point out that returning to see the therapist is a sign of progress in their ability to cope with the problem if they are able to do so before their symptoms become too troublesome or overwhelming. Also, we schedule a check-up visit about six months after the end of therapy. While many patients do not find it necessary to come in at that point, having the appointment scheduled insures that they have a graceful way of returning should difficulties arise.

Several cases will illustrate how we handle the maintenance or relapse visit.

In the first case, José, a successful lawyer, had been having 10–20 panic attacks/week at the start of treatment. Two months before beginning treatment he began to avoid driving, exercise and dating—all situations associated with panic attacks. He was started on a low dose of imipramine, which was gradually raised to 150 mg/day, and participated in exposure therapy conducted by his psychiatrist. After two months, he was symptom-free and had returned to driving, exercise, and dating.

As the medication was reduced, however, he began to experience panic attacks and more avoidance, particularly associated with work situations. While José was being taught coping strategies for these work situations, it became apparent that he was very angry at his boss, who José felt had denied him a deserved promotion. Several sessions were spent discussing how he could be more assertive with his boss. As he dealt more effectively with his boss, his anger subsided and so did the panic attacks. The medication was discontinued, and he remained symptom-free for a month until he began to feel rejected by his girlfriend. Three more sessions focused on his relationship with his girlfriend. These issues also resolved, and the patient was scheduled for a maintenance visit six months later. However, several months before the scheduled visit, he called to say that he had again experienced panic attacks and wanted medication. He was given a prescription of sufficient quantity to last him until his therapist could see him, but then he canceled the appointment. Over the telephone the patient said that he was somehow able to control the panic by himself and that simply knowing the therapist was available and that he could obtain medication was helpful. A follow-up phone call was scheduled six months later, at which time the patient was symptom-free.

John presented a somewhat different situation. His panic attacks and rather minimal avoidance responded to a short-term course of imipramine. One year later he called to say that he wanted to stop smoking (he had smoked up to four packs daily for ten years), and had listed this as a potential high-risk situation for the return of his panic attacks and avoidance. He wanted his therapist to help him with the smoking cessation and to be available if the panic returned. He was able to stop smoking successfully (with the help of nicorette gum), and even though he again experienced panic attacks, he decided to "last them out" without using the medication that was available to him. John reported no further avoidance.

CONCLUSIONS

Although it is beyond the scope of this book to discuss treatment issues other than those arising in the course of attempting to bring about symptomatic relief, it is important to reiterate that in some cases, the focused treatment of agoraphobia just described is a preliminary to other forms of psychotherapy. As we noted in chapter 4, other issues may emerge following symptom attenuation. In some of these cases, the couple has difficulty adjusting to the agoraphobic's newfound ability to function autonomously, or long-smoldering conflicts become exacerbated as the necessity of remaining in the marriage is questioned by one or the other partner. In other cases, a successfully treated agoraphobic may become depressed and rueful about lost opportunities during the years spent preoccupied with panic and avoidance. In still others, issues related to dependence, such as separation from one's family of origin or the need to establish one's own identity, achieve prominence.

We developed a symptom-focused approach with agoraphobic patients because we have found that this is the type of treatment for which they are available; it is for us, a question of responsiveness to the patient. But concern with the patient's psychological well-being (as opposed to the status of their presenting symptoms) demands in

some cases an ability and willingness to shift one's focus of attention to issues other than agoraphobic symptoms as they arise. Although there is a tendency in psychiatry, psychology, and social work to specialize in one or another type of treatment, it is often in the best interests of the agoraphobic patient if a therapist involved with symptom-focused therapy is available to become involved in the next phase of treatment. Even if the ground rules or format of therapy need to be changed, an important therapeutic relationship involving significant risk taking on the patient's part has already been established and can provide a context in which changes in other domains can often be fruitfully negotiated.

NINE

· · · · · · · ·

Social Phobia

· · · · · · · · · ·

The distinguishing characteristic of social phobics is fear of scrutiny by others. In general, sufferers fear that such scrutiny will prove embarrassing, humiliating, will cause them to look foolish, or to be evaluated negatively. The fear of scrutiny may manifest itself in many ways. For example, we have seen patients who avoid speaking in public situations; in most such cases, they fear that their anxiety will become evident to others either through a tremor in their voice or through an inability to speak. Others may avoid eating in public places. For these patients, the fear may be that their hands will shake or that their throat will become tight and they will choke or be unable to swallow their food. Other patients avoid situations in which they feel they will blush or vomit. Another way that social phobia sometimes presents is avoidance of public bathrooms. The above manifestations of social phobia involve relatively circumscribed fears, but social phobia often presents as a more diffuse problem (see also Marks, 1987).

The fear of negative evaluation may cause an individual to avoid most forms of social contact. The following two cases are illustrative of the range of impairment seen in this population.

The patient, James K., a 35-year-old hospital technician, was referred for treatment of an aversion to urinating in public bathrooms. He was unable to articulate clearly his ideas about how others might be evaluating him or what they might be thinking, but he reported an awareness of "being watched" which caused him extreme discomfort.

The patient reported that while he was always concerned and uncomfortable in public bathrooms, it was not until he was a student in junior college that the problem began to affect his actions. At the time of consultation, he would procrastinate at work if he had to urinate, finally using a private stall when he became very uncomfortable. When using a stall, he reported concern that others would be aware of his problem or would think he was "strange" for not using the urinal. He would avoid public places where stalls were not available. When forced to urinate in a public setting, he would wait until no one was in the bathroom, but if he heard the door opening, signalling someone's entry, he became very anxious and would stop urinating immediately. He reported that he was able to use public showers and locker rooms in a local gymnasium after lifting weights without embarrassment or other difficulty. He was otherwise neither anxious nor depressed.

The patient had been married for three years, and then divorced. He had a number of close male friends and was actively dating. He reported a stable work history and no evidence of difficulties on the job.

In other cases, the effect of the disturbance upon the person's life is considerably more pervasive.

The patient, Mary M., a 29-year-old female, married with a three-year-old child, referred herself for treatment of "social anxiety," consisting of avoidance of all social situations involving "one on one" contact with another person other than her husband or daughter. She reported being socially isolated with no friendships. She occasionally interacted with a group of other mothers in her daughter's nursery school but was only able to do so if it was a group situation. She avoided one-to-one contact fearing that she would inevitably disappoint the other person, leading to embarrassment, rejection, and humiliation. She reported that when she was in a social situation, she was obsessively preoccupied with the perceived negative evaluations of those she was with. For example, when she took her daughter to the pediatrician, she became upset wondering whether the physician thought she was an "uptight, insecure, and incompetent mother." She wondered further whether the pediatrician would side with her "if anyone thought I was an unfit mother and tried to take my daughter away." She reported that when in such situations, she would become very conscious of tension in her facial muscles and would then look for signs in the other person's face that they noticed her anxiety, and became uncomfortable. She and her husband did not socialize with other couples, largely due to her anxiety about such encounters. She reported a fervent desire to have friends, and frequent depression and crying spells over the difficulties she was having.

Beck and Emery (1985) have noted that the threats perceived by sufferers of social anxiety often appear to have a greater likelihood of realization than the threats perceived by sufferers of other anxiety disorders. For example, while the agoraphobic's fear of losing control and driving his or her car off the road during a panic attack can be easily viewed as "irrational," the social phobic's fear of verbally stumbling during a talk or fear of being rejected as a suitor on a date might reasonably occur. Indeed these writers and others (e.g., Trower & Turland, 1984) have noted that often the anxiety experienced by the sufferer enhances the possibility of the feared reaction. The musician who is very anxious is certainly more likely to make mistakes;

the anxious individual who avoids eye contact and is unable to initiate conversation on a date is more likely to face rejection. Thus a vicious cycle often develops in which the anxiety is actually instrumental in potentiating the consequences most feared by the patient through interaction of the cognitive, physiological, and behavioral aspects of the problem.

Cognitive Aspects of Social Phobia

Social phobics appraise problematic situations as threatening and potentially catastrophic and assume an inability to meet the demands of the situation. In most cases the threat involves fear of negative evaluation, but the precise nature of the threat may take several different forms. These have been well-summarized by Buss (1980) and later by Trower and Turland (1984). They include most prominently embarrassment and shame. Embarrassment may be caused by a variety of different situations, including verbal inappropriateness, clumsiness or some other action that might be perceived as incompetence (e.g., inability to respond), and breaches of psychological privacy. The latter is particularly important, inasmuch as one of the factors often maintaining social anxiety and social phobia is awareness of one's anxiety and fear that others will become aware of it. Shame involves a perceived failure to perform up to a predetermined standard; the standard may be generated either internally or externally. Thus, failure to perform in an academic setting, failure to achieve a standard of sexual performance, or failure to perform adequately in front of an audience (e.g., musical performance anxiety) may all be anticipated as shame inducing.

Beck and Emery (1985) have made certain important observations on the phenomenon of shame as it applies to individuals who experience anxiety regarding evaluation. As they note, shame involves insult to one's public image. Strangers, who are perceived as representatives of a group, may more easily arouse feelings of shame than those with whom we are on intimate terms. However, the stranger or acquaintance must be seen as representative of a group whose approval is valued. Since shame is so closely tied to public scrutiny, concealment of the weakness, deficit, or objectionable behavior may come to be seen as the solution; one does not experience shame in private. The individual who experiences shame also feels helpless in the face of the group's disapproval. Such judgements are viewed as "absolute, finalistic, irrevocable."

One final observation made by Beck and Emery that may have important treatment implications is that one may feel shame whether the perceived disapproval is communicated or not; shame is tied to the perception of how others think, rather than what they specifically communicate. Thus, an individual might expose him- or herself to problematic situations regularly without diminution of anxiety, if he or she continued to believe that others' negative evaluations continued to be present. Moreover, one could draw such conclusions without clear feedback from others. Thus, exposure therapy in the absence of intervention aimed at altering perceptions about the evaluations of others or about their *importance* might be less effective than exposure combined with cognitive therapy addressing such concerns. This point may partly account for the observation made by Butler (1985) that 75 percent of a sample of social phobics seen in a clinical trial (Butler et al., 1984) were already entering situations that frightened them without any diminution of anxiety. Similar observations were reported by Liebowitz et al. (1985a). Beck's observation (Beck & Emery, 1985) that unlike anxiety, which usually ends when the individual exits the fear-evoking situation, the experience of shame continues beyond the individual's participation, fits with Liebowitz et al.'s (1985a) report that the anxiety of the social phobics they have seen "does not seem to attenuate during the course of a single social event or performance . . . [but rather] augment[s], as initial somatic discomfort becomes a further distraction and embarrassment to the already nervous individual" (p. 731).

After assessing a situation as threatening, the individual is then likely to make an estimation of his or her ability to cope effectively with it. According to Bandura's self-efficacy theory (1977), the tendency toward initiating coping behavior will vary with the strength of the individual's conviction that he or she can successfully execute the desired behavior. Those with low self-efficacy are likely to withdraw from fear-evoking situations. Trower and Turland (1984) have called attention to the fact that among those with low self-efficacy in the social interaction arena, some may actually lack the requisite skills to succeed, while others may have the necessary skills but fail to call upon them. They refer to cases where skills are lacking as primary social failure; presumably in such cases, even if the individual did not withdraw, social failure would result. Cases in which the individual possesses the skills but fails to use them are referred to as secondary social failure. Greenberg and Stravynski (1983) have suggested that the unskilled are more likely to fall under the diagnostic category of avoidant personality disorder, where avoidance of social situations is more pervasive; this group, they argue, would most likely benefit from social skills training, while the social phobics, whose avoidance is more circumscribed and who, they presume, have better developed social skills would be more likely to benefit from exposure.

The importance of cognitive factors in the etiology and maintenance of social phobia may in fact be greater than for many of the other anxiety disorders. Turner and Beidel (1985) subjected a group of 26 socially anxious individuals to a laboratory-based social encounter, assessing cognition and physiological reactivity. Most subjects fell into one of either of two groups. One group demonstrated negative thoughts and high physiological reactivity, while individuals in the other group were similarly high on negative thoughts but low on physiological reactivity. Thus, negative thoughts were present in virtually the entire sample, while physiological overresponsiveness was present in only some of the participants.

Two additional points regarding the cognitive organization of social phobics are in order. First, there are some indications that the social performance standards of those with increased levels of social anxiety are unrealistically high (Alden & Cappe, 1981; Alden & Safran, 1978). Thus, the discrepancy between actual performance and the desired standard may be more likely to be pronounced; this effect would be further amplified among those with low social skills (Trower & Turland, 1984). Second, Beck (Beck & Emery, 1985) has called attention to the extent to which those prone to social and "evaluative anxiety" tend toward global judgments regarding their behavior. Thus, "errors, missteps, inappropriate actions represent only a fraction of his overt behavior, but the damage is to the entire person" (p. 146).

Physiological Aspects of Social Anxiety

Evidence regarding physiological reactivity among the socially anxious is limited. Lang et al., (1983) found increased heart rate among speech phobics while giving a speech, but the study did not incorporate a nonfearful control group for comparison. Dimsdale and Moss (1980) reported two to threefold increases in plasma epinephrine levels among normals during public speaking.

In a study investigating differences between a group of socially anxious versus nonsocially anxious individuals, Beidel, Turner, and Dancu (1985) involved subjects in three tasks: a role play with a confederate of the opposite sex, a role play with a same-sex confederate, and an impromptu speech. Measures included systolic and diastolic blood pressure, and heart rate. Results indicated evidence of significantly greater physiological reactivity among the socially anxious group during the opposite-sex role play (for systolic blood pressure and heart rate), and the impromptu speech (heart rate). There was also evidence that the socially anxious group was slower to habituate than their nonsocially anxious counterparts. There were no differences in arousal on the same-sex role play, but socially anxious

TABLE 9.1

Somatic Symptom Check List

Item	Social phobia per cent	Agoraphobia per cent	P less than*
Blushing	51	21	.001
Twitching of muscles	37	21	(.07)
Weakness in limbs	41	77	.001
Difficulty breathing	30	60	.001
Dizziness/faintness	39	68	.01
Actual fainting episode	10	25	.05
Buzzing/ringing in ears	13	30	.05
Palpitations	79	77	
Tense muscles	64	67	
Dry throat/mouth	61	65	
Sinking feeling in stomach	63	54	
Feeling sick	40	40	
Trembling	75	75	
Sweating	74	68	
Lump in throat	33	33	
Needing to pass water	30	39	
Fullness in stomach	13	30	
Blurring of vision	21	33	
Flatulence	16	12	
Feeling hot/cold	57	61	
Pressure in head/headaches	46	44	
Needing to open bowels	24	12	
Pins and needles	10	12	

SOURCE: Reprinted with permission from "Social Phobia: A Comparative Clinical Study." P. L. Amies, M. G. Gelder, and P. M. Shaw, 1983, *British Journal of Psychiatry, 142,* pp. 174–179.

*If no value is shown, the difference is not significant.

participants nevertheless rated themselves as significantly more anxious than nonsocially anxious individuals, suggesting the possibility of heightened sensitivity to internal cues.

In a study comparing symptomotology among agoraphobics and social phobics, Amies, Gelder, and Shaw (1983) found some interesting differences in the incidence of somatic symptoms reported. As Table 9.1 indicates, while there is considerable overlap in reported symptoms, there were some significant differences reported. Interestingly, social phobics reported higher incidence of blushing and twitching of muscles, while agoraphobics reported significantly higher incidence of limb weakness, breathing difficulty, dizziness/faintness, buzzing/ringing in the ears, and actual episodes of fainting. Thus there is some limited evidence that social phobics report a higher incidence of symptoms that are visible to others.

However, it is also clear that there is considerable overlap in the somatic symptoms reported by both groups. For example there was little difference in the incidence of palpitations, tense muscles, trembling, sweating, etc. Social phobics appear to experience many of the same autonomic symptoms which are labelled panic attacks by agoraphobics. A major difference is that among social phobics, these symptoms are usually experienced in conjunction with a particular situation in which they feel under scrutiny, while agoraphobics with panic disorder are currently believed to experience at least some spontaneous panic attacks.

Behavioral Symptoms of Social Phobics

Amies et al. (1983) also presented data on situations provoking anxiety among social phobics and agoraphobics. As is evident from Table 9.2, social phobics are most concerned about, and presumably avoid, interpersonal situations in which one might be scrutinized by others. Thus, being introduced, meeting people in authority, and being watched while doing something are among the more difficult situations for this group, while agoraphobics fear circumstances including being alone, being in unfamiliar places, and open spaces. These differences are consistent with what we have noted already regarding the cognitive themes among these two populations: while there is some similarity in the physiological experience between the two groups, the situations which evoke anxiety suggest that the agoraphobics fear an "internal disaster" (Beck & Emery, 1985, p. 152), while social phobics fear embarrassment, or shame.

Although in one study, family history of alcoholism was reportedly more frequent among agoraphobics than among social phobics (Munjack & Moss, 1981), incidence of alcohol dependence itself was considerably higher among social phobics (20 percent) than among agoraphobics (7 percent) (Amies et al., 1983). Social phobias are reportedly quite common among alcoholic inpatients (Bowen et al., 1984; Mullaney & Trippett, 1979). In our experience, alcohol abuse is a significant problem among social phobics and must be carefully assessed before proceeding with treatment.

TABLE 9.2

Fear Survey Schedule

More severe when main complaint is agoraphobia:	*More severe when main complaint is social phobia:*
Being alone	Being introduced
Unfamiliar places	Meeting people in authority
Crossing streets	Using the telephone
Public transport	Visitors to home
Department stores	Being watched doing something
Crowds	Being teased
Open spaces	Eating at home with acquaintances
Small shops	Eating at home with family
. . . .	Writing in front of others
Mice, rats, bats	Speaking in public
Snakes	
Flying insects	
Deep water	
Aeroplanes	
Blood, wounds	

Not significantly different between the two groups:

Drinking at coffee bar

Eating in an informal restaurant

Eating in a formal restaurant

Enclosed spaces

. . . .

Spiders	
Worms	tended to be more
Crawling insects	severe in the
Injections	agoraphobic group
Doctors	

SOURCE: Reprinted with permission from "Social Phobia: A Comparative Clinical Study." P. L. Amies, M. G. Gelder, and P. M. Shaw, 1983, *British Journal of Psychiatry, 142,* pp. 174–179.

Diagnosis

The critical issue in diagnosing social phobia is to determine whether the patient's fear involves one or more situations in which the person will be exposed to scrutiny and fears embarrassment or humiliation. When anticipating the fearful situation, or when participating, the social phobic characteristically experiences physiological symptoms that may include tachycardia, tightness in the chest, sweatiness, shaking, and other symptoms of panic. Most patients avoid situations that provoke the anxiety, but as we noted earlier, some continue to enter such situations without remittance of the symptoms.

The major conditions to be aware of in the differential diagnosis of social phobia include the other anxiety disorders and avoidant personality disorder. In general, panic attacks associated with agoraphobia have been experienced as spontaneous at least some of the time, while with social phobics they are, by definition, associated with specific circumstances. However, these conditions can coexist and frequently do as in the following case:

Joanne A., a 30-year-old female, married with one child, was referred by a psychiatrist for treatment of "social anxiety." She began experiencing spontaneous panic attacks 15 months prior to the initial consultation; symptoms included blushing, tachycardia, sweating, difficulty catching her breath, disorientation, combined with fears of embarrassment should others notice her condition. The patient reported approximately one spontaneous panic attack daily, in addition to situational panic attacks particularly while conversing with others. She worked as a secretary and reported blushing several times daily in addition to the experience of full-blown panic attacks; the blushing was extremely distressing. She felt particularly humiliated at work because her immediate superior had noticed her blushing and would comment about it in a way that the patient experienced as demeaning. She had recently begun to avoid the grocery store, department stores, and a variety of social situations, including parties, and church functions. She reported that she had always been shy, and had difficulty meeting new people and entering new situations. As a young child, her mother had "forced" her to join organizations like the Brownies and the Girl Scouts.

While in the above case, the patient met the criteria for both panic disorder with agoraphobia, and social phobia, the clinical interview revealed that her major fear associated with spontaneous panic attacks was that they were accompanied by blushing, and that others would "know" of her anxiety. She felt that "if I wasn't fair skinned and didn't blush so easily I could tolerate the other symptoms." Thus, our primary diagnosis was social phobia. Fear of embarrassment is quite common among agoraphobics, but frequently such fear is associated with a fear of "losing control"; that is, the patient is afraid of losing control of his/her behavior and as a result, *subsequently* suffering embarrassment. In general among social phobics, the fear of embarrassment is associated with a feared decrement in performance or with others noticing their anxiety rather than a loss of control. Thus, a major issue to consider when attempting to differentiate panic disorder with agoraphobia and social phobia is the issue of whether the consequences feared by the patient involve an internal or external disaster.

The distinction between avoidant personality disorder and social phobia is somewhat less clear. According to the DSM-III-R, avoidant personality disorder may be characterized by "marked anxiety and avoidance of most social situations," but the recommendation is that in such cases a diagnosis of both social phobia and avoidant personality disorder be considered. The suggestion noted earlier that those manifesting more pervasive withdrawal be classified avoidant personality disorder and those whose fear is more circumscribed be designated social phobics (Greenberg & Stravynski, 1983) makes sense, but we are unaware of convincing evidence that the former respond better to social skills training. In general, our experience has been that effective treatment for both problems is similar, but that those with avoidant personality disorder have fewer strengths and consequently fewer successes in other areas of their life, and have less of a support network; given the current intervention options, they are more difficult to treat and require a longer period of therapy.

Another much rarer condition sometimes confused with social phobia is dysmorphophobia (Marks, 1987). Dysmorphophobia involves preoccupation with a physical defect not evident to others. The complaint may involve one or several body parts, or may involve a perception of offensive odors emanating for example, from one's breath, rectal area, or genitals. As a result of such preoccupation and fear of embarrassment, sufferers may avoid social contact. However, unlike social phobics, dysmorphophobics do not believe that their anxiety is irrational, or in any way contributory to their problem. As Marks indicated, among this group of patients the "fixity of the idea can amount to a delusion" (1987, p. 370).

The following case of dysmorphophobia involved preoccupation with a perceived bodily defect:

John A., a 56 year old, divorced man referred himself, noting that "I've been getting kind of depressed lately and I think I should talk with someone." The clinical interview revealed an obsession with the size and shape of his nose. At the age of 33, he underwent plastic surgery to fix his nose. As an adolescent, he felt his nose was too large. Though not completely satisfied with the result, he was not preoccupied with his appearance until the last several months. During this time, he became convinced that his nose looked strange, "tilted, and too small." He also became convinced that others noticed the same defect, and were surreptitiously ridiculing him by holding their noses, rubbing them, or otherwise touching their noses. He believed he was unable to see the supposed defect clearly in the mirror, and so he had recently rented a video cassette recorder and camera, taking videos of his nose at different angles; this experience convinced him that he was correct in his assessment. He had recently begun avoiding calling on clients (he worked as a salesman), and avoiding other public places, particularly restaurants, as he believed he was being ridiculed by the other patrons. He also reported recent difficulty sleeping and a loss of appetite. His manner and appearance were appropriate, and other than his preoccupation with his nose, there was no evidence of psychosis or other form of psychopathology.

Social phobics sometimes develop unusual fears about themselves in interpersonal situations that they do not reveal immediately. Often when they come to trust the therapist they will confide such fears; occasionally their preoccupations appear sufficiently bizarre to cause the therapist to consider the possibility of a thought disorder, as in the following case:

Michael F., a 21-year-old college student was referred by his physician for treatment of a public speaking phobia. When called upon to speak in class or at dormitory meetings, he would experience intense anxiety causing his voice to quaver. He experienced considerable anticipatory anxiety over these situations, and felt humiliated that others would know of his anxiety. He had begun to avoid small seminars in which he felt class participation would be required. Though verbally appropriate and attractive, he had done little dating, and had had no sexual experiences of any kind with women. He would also become sufficiently nervous over the prospect of asking a young woman for a date that in this situation too, he worried about his voice quavering and was avoiding such encounters. During the sixth week of treatment, he confided to the therapist that he believed that when he thinks about women, he emits an offensive odor that causes others who may be physically near him to leave. This idea had started when he was 17 and a senior in high school. His parents had gone out for the evening and he had masturbated in the family room. His parents however, came home unexpectedly early, within a minute or so of the time he had finished masturbating. Though he had managed to collect himself before they entered the family room, and there was no overt evidence they knew what he had done, he believed that in the act of masturbating he had given off an odor that they could detect. This idea had progressed to the point where he now believed that just thinking about an attractive woman caused him to give off such an odor. He was in the habit of sitting by himself in a corner of the library or cafeteria due to fears that others could smell when he was thinking about women.

The patient's questionable reality testing and other phenomenology raised the possibility that he might be schizophrenic. However, after discussing these issues with the therapist, and feeling somewhat reassured, he agreed to a consultation with a urologist who was quite understanding and also reassured him. He was greatly relieved by this reassurance, and stopped isolating himself in the school library and cafeteria. Social isolation is often a feature of social phobia, and in such cases, without the availability of corrective feedback, ideas such as the above can develop. The patient's ability to respond to reassurance and other corrective measures is obviously critical in ruling out dysmorphophobia or psychosis.

Prevalence

The six-month prevalence rate of social phobia in two urban populations was recently reported to range from 0.9 percent to 1.7 percent for men and 1.2 percent to 2.2 percent for women (Myers et al., 1984). However, these rates are inflated by cases in which social anxiety was part of another disorder (e.g., panic disorder with agoraphobia). Thus the prevalence of social phobia meeting DSM-III-R criteria in the general population is probably lower. In an earlier study focusing on first-year students at a British college, the rate of typical social phobias was reported to be between 3 percent and 10 percent (Bryant & Trower, 1974). Bryant and Trower (1974) also noted that their sample could be roughly divided into two groups, one of which had most difficulty with situations in which the interpersonal contact was of a public, casual nature, and the other reported greater difficulty with contact of a more personal or intimate nature.

Marks (1987) has noted that social phobia is the second most common phobic disorder he has encountered, comprising about 25 percent of the cases. Similar data has been reported in a Canadian clinic (Solyom, Ledwidge, & Solyom, 1986). Liebowitz et al., (1985a) reported that social phobia is the third most common anxiety disorder they encounter following panic disorder and agoraphobia. Our experience is similar to the above reports; social phobics are the third most numerous problem we see in our own anxiety disorders clinic after panic disorder with agoraphobia and panic disorder without avoidance, representing approximately 20 percent of the total cases.

The gender distribution of social phobia appears to be different than that of other phobic disorders. Amies et al., (1983) reported that 60 percent of the social phobics in their study were male, as against only 14 percent males among the agoraphobic sample. Shaw (1979) reported a similar male/female ratio among a sample of 30 social phobics she treated. While some reports suggest a slightly lower ratio of males to females (e.g., Marks, 1969; Nichols, 1974) available evidence suggests that males comprise about 40–60 percent of the social phobics applying for treatment.

Family Studies

Little is known about the families of patients presenting social phobia. We are unaware of any controlled investigations that might inform us regarding the relative contributions of genetic and acquired factors. One study that does suggest a genetic contribution (Torgerson, 1979) investigated the incidence of social fears among a sample of monozygotic and dizygotic twin pairs and found significantly more concordance among the monozygotic twins in such situations as being watched while working or eating with strangers.

Two studies have retrospectively investigated the perceived parental characteristics of social phobics. In one, Parker (1979) recontacted 123 patients assessed five to seven years earlier by Shaw (1976) and classified as either agoraphobic or social phobic. Eighty-one patients responded (40 agoraphobics and 41 social phobics). Each patient was asked to fill out the Parental Bonding Questionnaire (Parker, Tupling, & Brown, 1979), a 25-item instrument measuring parental care and overprotection. Results indicated that when compared with controls, the agoraphobics differed from controls only in rating their mothers as providing less care, while the social phobics rated both parents as lower on care and higher on overprotectiveness.

Onset and Course

The onset of social phobia appears typically between ages 15 and 20. Marks (1969) noted that among a sample he studied onset appeared to peak in the late teens. Amies et al., (1983) reported a mean onset of 19, as opposed to 24 among the agoraphobics. Nichols (1974) reported that two thirds of his sample developed the problem before age 25. Shaw (1976) reported that 60 percent of the social phobics in her sample had developed the problem by age 20 (as compared with 20 percent of agoraphobics), and 19 percent of the social phobics rated the onset as acute (as compared with 53 percent of the agoraphobics).

Available evidence suggests that the course of social phobia is chronic and unremitting (Liebowitz et al., 1985a). Its effects on the life of the sufferer vary from avoidance of only specific situations (e.g., public bathrooms, public speaking, etc.) to catastrophic disability. Liebowitz et al. (1985a) reported that among a sample of 11 social phobics meeting the DSM-III criteria for social phobia "two of 11 patients were unable to work, two dropped out of school, four had abused alcohol, one had abused tranquilizers, six were blocked from work advancement, and five avoided almost all social interaction outside their immediate family" (p. 730). In our experience, the most severe problems of social phobics stem from both the social avoidance and, in many cases, abuse of alcohol or other substances.

Etiology

The etiology of social phobia is unclear. Sheehan (1983) has argued that social phobia is one presentation of a biologically determined anxiety "disease." He notes that many of those who suffer panic attacks begin to avoid social situations before developing more extensive avoidance behavior. However, the absence of spontaneous panic attacks and phobias in nonsocial situations among many sufferers of social phobia suggest important differences in these disorders. Further evidence of differences among these groups is suggested by an investigation of the response to sodium lactate among agoraphobics and social phobics (Liebowitz et al., 1985c). Results indicated that four of nine agoraphobics panicked during the lactate infusion, while only one of 15 social phobics panicked, a statistically significant difference.

Several other hypotheses have been suggested. Nichols (1974) has noted the presence among social phobics of unusual sensitivity to criticism, disapproval, and scrutiny from others, low self-evaluation, rigid ideas regarding appropriate social behavior, a tendency to overestimate the extent to which visible symptoms of anxiety are evident to others, and a fear of being seen as ill or losing control. He argues that perception of loss of regard by others leads the individual to become hyper-aware of his or her anxiety in social situations, leading to increased sensitivity to physical cues and increasing concern that further lack of regard will ensue should such symptoms be noticed. According to Nichols, avoidance follows.

Others have suggested that social anxiety is generated through a process in which poor performance in social situations leads the individual to expect negative evaluation and rejection from others (Curran, 1977). Another hypothesis is that social anxiety and social phobias are mediated by faulty cognitions regarding performance demands and the consequences of negative evaluation, which then, in fact, interfere with effective performance (Beck & Emery, 1985). Trower and Turland (1984) have developed a complicated theory suggesting that while all social phobics will manifest low self-efficacy in social situations, some will actually have skill deficits and others will have the necessary skills but will have difficulty calling upon them due to perceived inability. One factor they cite in the development of low self-efficacy is the tendency in the social phobic toward setting unrealistically high standards and goals. They further suggest that some of the avoidant strategies employed by social phobics such as gaze aversion, facial inexpressiveness, and reduced talkativeness can engender rejecting responses from others.

Assessment

Interest in social phobia has lagged behind agoraphobia, panic disorder, and some of the other anxiety disorders; thus, there is a dearth of specialized assessment instruments. Two self-report scales that have been used frequently are the Social Avoidance and Distress Scale (SAD) and the Fear of Negative Evaluation Scale (FNE) both developed by Watson and Friend (1969). The SAD is a 28-item true-false scale, assessing social avoidance and anxiety in such situations. Some of the items include "Being introduced to people makes me tense and nervous" and "I often think up excuses in order to avoid social gatherings." The FNE is a 30-item true-false scale, assessing fear of negative evaluation defined in terms of "apprehension about others' evaluations, distress over their negative evaluations, avoidance of evaluative situations, and the expectation that others would evaluate oneself negatively" (p. 449). Among the items are "I rarely worry about seeming foolish to others" and "Sometimes I think I am too concerned with what other people think of me." Both scales have high indexes of reliability.

In addition, Watson and Friend presented evidence that those who scored high-anxious on the SAD showed less interest in participating in group activities and spoke less in an interpersonal situation. When compared with those scoring low on the FNE, high anxious FNE subjects showed a tendency toward avoiding disapproval and seeking approval. However, in a recent study (Turner, McCanna, & Beidel, 1987), the SAD and the FNE were given to a group of 206 patients receiving a primary DSM-III diagnosis of agoraphobia with panic attacks, agoraphobia without panic attacks, social phobia, simple phobia, panic disorder, generalized anxiety disorder, and obsessive-compulsive disorder, with results indicating that the scores of social phobics were not significantly different from any of the other groups other than simple phobics. Thus these measures appear to lack discriminant validity.

Recent evidence suggests that another questionnaire, the Willoughby Personality Schedule (WPS; Willoughby, 1932) reliably discriminates social phobics from other anxious patients and controls. The WPS, a 25-item inventory, employs a 5-point Likert scale with responses ranging from 0–4, with 0 indicating that the item in question never characterizes the individual's behavior. Scores range from 0–100, with higher scores denoting increasing interpersonal sensitivity. Several reports had indicated that the WPS is a reliable and valid measure of social anxiety (Thurstone & Thurstone, 1930; Turner, DiTomasso & Murray, 1980; Willoughby, 1932, 1934). In a study specifically investigating the construct validity of the WPS (Turner, Meles, & DiTomasso, 1983), 173 outpatients meeting the DSM-III criteria for simple phobia, sexual dysfunction, obsessive-compulsive disorder, agoraphobia, and social phobia were administered the questionnaire. A control group was also included. Results indicated that the WPS correctly identified social phobics from controls in 88 percent of the cases. When data from all diagnostic groups were examined, significant differences in the scores emerged among all groups except between controls and simple phobics, and agoraphobics and obsessive-compulsives. Social phobics had the highest scores.

Other self-rating scales that have been used to assess social anxiety and social phobia include the Fear Questionnaire (Marks & Mathews, 1979), which has a social phobia subscale, and the interpersonal sensitivity subscale of the Hopkins Symptoms Check List (SCL-90; Derogatis, Lipman, & Cove, 1973). One instrument designed specificially to assess cognitions that might be relevant to social anxiety is the Social Interaction Self-Statement Test (Glass et al., 1982), a 30-item inventory cataloging thoughts that an individual might have during a heterosocial encounter.

Another method of assessment that has been used with the socially anxious involves direct ratings of behavioral performance (e.g., Beidel et al., 1985; Bryant & Argyle, 1978; McEwan & Devins, 1983; Neftel et al., 1982).

For clinical purposes, we use the social phobia subscale from the Fear Questionnaire (Marks & Mathews, 1979) as a screen for social phobia. We also are careful to assess for the presence of alcohol abuse. However, the need for additional assessment instruments specifying avoidances, relevant cognitions, and physiological responses is evident.

THE TREATMENT OF SOCIAL PHOBIA

Broadly speaking, individuals encountered in clinical practice who fit the DSM-III-R criteria for social phobia appear to fall into two groups. One group suffers anxiety that is restricted to one or two specific situations, while the other group suffers more pervasive social anxiety and may have other anxiety disorders. Though this latter group is more difficult to treat and requires a considerably longer course of therapy, some of the same procedures used with more circumscribed social phobics are often indicated.

The treatment approaches that we use with social phobics include the following: pharmacotherapy, exposure therapy, cognitive restructuring, and social skills training. We shall discuss each of these interventions briefly before presenting case examples.

Pharmacotherapy

The evidence that medication is effective in the treatment of social phobia is limited. Two major classes of drugs have been investigated, the MAOIs and beta-blockers. Beta-blockers have been prescribed to block the peripheral manifestations of anxiety on the assumption that peripheral autonomic arousal increases social anxiety. Beta-blockers have been shown to reduce performance anxiety among such groups as musicians (e.g., Brantigan, Brantigan, & Joseph, 1982; James et al., 1977; James, Burgoyne, & Savage, 1983; Liden & Gottfries, 1974), and college students (Hartley et al., 1983; Krishnan, 1975). However, other studies of performance anxiety have failed to show an effect from beta-blockers (e.g., Gottschalk, Stone, & Gleser, 1974; Krope et al., 1982; Siltonen & Janne, 1976).

Two studies have evaluated the effects of beta-blockers in social phobics. In the first study (Falloon, Lloyd, & Harpin, 1981), the efficacy of four weeks of propranolol (160 to 320 mg/d) was compared with placebo among a group of 16 social phobics receiving social skills training. The addition of propranolol did not improve performance. In a recent uncontrolled investigation, five of 10 patients meeting the DSM-III criteria for social phobia were given atenolol 50 mg/d; if they had not improved dramatically in one week, the dosage was raised to 100 mg/d, given in a single dose and continued for an additional seven weeks. Five of these patients were considered markedly improved and four were judged moderately improved (Liebowitz et al., 1987).

Evidence for the usefulness of MAOIs is limited. Clinical studies in mixed phobic groups have suggested that MAOIs may be of benefit for social phobia (Liebowitz et al., 1985a). Furthermore, in patients with atypical depression, MAOIs seem to reduce interpersonal sensitivity, which is a measure of sensitivity to rejection, criticism and indifference on the part of others (Liebowitz et al., 1984; Nies et al., 1982). One recent uncontrolled study (Liebowitz et al., 1986b), which investigated the efficacy of phenelzine with 11 patients meeting the DSM-III criteria for social phobia, described seven as markedly improved, and four as moderately improved.

These studies did not justify the routine use of medications with social phobics. However, patients who have social phobia and generalized anxiety disorder, panic disorder, or agoraphobia may benefit from medication if appropriate for the latter conditions. Reduction in panic attacks and avoidance seems to help the social phobia as well.

Exposure Therapy

The few controlled investigations of the efficacy of exposure therapy for social phobia suggest that it can be extremely effective (e.g., Butler et al., 1984; Emmelkamp et al., 1985). We discussed our approach to exposure therapy with the agoraphobic in detail in chapter 8, and will confine the current discussion to those issues concerning the process of exposure that are unique to the patient presenting with social phobia.

In a thoughtful article, Butler (1985) articulated many of the difficulties encountered in applying exposure therapy to the social phobic patient, together with certain suggested solutions. One problem she noted was the difficulty in establishing a hierarchy of graduated and repeatable tasks when social fears predominate. For example, when treating an agoraphobic who is fearful of waiting in grocery lines one can easily construct a hierarchy where they initially wait in a line with one person ahead of them, followed by a line with two people ahead of them, etc. Among social phobics, coexisting problematic situations such as inviting an acquaintance to lunch, or talking to a coworker about an issue that is not work-related, do not lend themselves to hierarchical or gradual exposure plans. Butler suggested that therapists carrying out exposure attempt to structure practice in terms of the amount of time spent engaging in anxiety-provoking tasks. Thus rather than working his or her way up a hierarchy as we often have agoraphobics do, the social phobic may agree to spend a specific amount of time each day engaging in difficult activities; this approach is likely to involve him or her in a number of different tasks requiring different lengths of time. While the problems typically confronting social phobics do not lend themselves so obviously to hierarchical ordering, they sometimes can be ordered in terms of difficulty, if the therapist is willing to take the time to do so. For example, patients who are socially isolated can often list a number of people they would like to approach and roughly order them in terms of how "threatened" or "vulnerable" they believe they will feel in each person's presence.

A second problem in carrying out exposure with the social phobic involves the difficulty in prolonging exposure to anxious cues. Our agoraphobic patients are instructed to enter situations and wait for the anxiety to "peak and pass," but many of the situations that social phobics find difficult may involve contact that is too brief for such a strategy. However, as Butler noted, even brief participation in fear-evoking situtions may be sufficient to disconfirm catastrophic expectations, such as humiliation or rejection.

Butler also noted that pervasive fear of negative evaluation encountered among certain social phobics is frequently resistant to a course of exposure therapy alone, because of the importance of cognitions in maintaining such problems (see also Butler et al., 1984). Like Butler, we also incorporate cognitive restructuring procedures to help call attention to irrational, catastrophic, perfectionistic, and other thoughts that appear to be involved with the anxiety and avoidance. We shall discuss these in a bit more detail below.

While Butler's paper focused on problems conducting exposure therapy with social phobics, it is also true that in some cases the characteristics of their concerns lend themselves to unusual and often powerful interventions within an exposure-based approach. The catastrophic concerns preoccupying a number of social phobics involve public humiliation; they often expect strangers to respond to them in hostile and injurious ways. Sometimes, the actions that they believe will evoke ridicule or hostility in fact evoke expressions of concern, while at other times they are trivial and may be barely noticed. Unlike the agoraphobic who frequently worries about his own reaction (e.g., losing control, having a heart attack, etc.), the social phobic is often more concerned with the reactions of others. Having the social phobic enter a situation, perform the action they fear will evoke ridicule from others (e.g., shake while writing a check at the grocery stand), and observe carefully the reaction of others can often be a powerful exercise that effectively alters expectancies regarding the responses of others. In some instances we have incorporated a participant modeling procedure as a way of facilitating the disconfirmation of some of the catastrophic beliefs harbored by social phobics regarding the responses of others. This procedure involves the therapist in performing the feared action and having the social phobic observe the reactions of others. Such a technique can also be used with agoraphobics with public concerns (e.g., the responses of strangers to a panic attack or fainting spell), and was described in chapter 8.

Cognitive Restructuring

Though few studies have investigated the effectiveness of cognitive intervention with social phobics, preliminary studies suggest that it is valuable (Butler et al., 1984; Emmelkamp et al., 1985). The study conducted by Butler and colleagues employed an anxiety management intervention that involved rational self-talk among the coping procedures; this group achieved lower scores associated with treatment on cognitive measures of social anxiety than did another group receiving exposure only. Emmelkamp's study compared exposure, self-instructional training, and rational-emotive therapy in a group of 34 social phobics and found the interventions to be approximately equally effective in reducing anxiety; moreover, only the cognitive treatments were associated with significant decrements on the cognitive measure used in the study.

We incorporate cognitive restructuring in our approach to treatment with many social phobics. As a group, social phobics suffer from a number of cognitive errors. While it is true that the underlying theme of these errors involves sensitivity to the evaluation of others, they may take a variety of forms. The most common cognitive errors we have encountered among social phobics are the following: (1) overestimating the extent to which their behavior will be noticed by others, thus exposing them to scrutiny or evaluation; (2) overestimations about the likelihood of rejection, embarrassment, or humiliation in a particular situation; (3) unrealistic assessments about the character of others' responses to displays of anxiety; (4) attributional errors; and (5) overresponsiveness to actual rejection or lack of acceptance.

Overestimating the Extent of Others' Scrutiny

As others have noted (e.g., Trower & Turland, 1984), social phobics suffer from an excess of self-consciousness or self-focus (Buss, 1980; Carver, 1979; Fenigstein, 1979; Schlenker & Leary, 1982). Fenigstein (1979) has differentiated between private self-consciousness, which involves heightened awareness of one's thoughts and feelings, and public self-consciousness, which involves similar awareness of how one is viewed by others. Those in the latter group report a sense of being observed when with other people, an increased awareness of how others regard them, and they assign considerable importance to others' responses toward them (Fenigstein, 1979). Their attention is focused on their appearance and behavior to an extent that effectively turns them into observers. Social situations often trigger an assessment process (Schlenker & Leary, 1982) in which the individual monitors his effect on others in hypervigilant fashion much as the panic disorder patient monitors internal sensations hypervigilantly (Clark, 1986). One effect of this process is an overestimation as to the extent to which others are scrutinizing them. The social phobic often

erroneously assumes that others are monitoring his social performance as closely as he is. Thus if his voice trembles, or if he has a
tendency to blush, or shake while holding a glass, he assumes that the
attention of others is equally focused on such displays.

Overestimating the Likelihood of Rejection, Embarrassment, or Humiliation

Several studies have indicated the presence of perfectionistic social
standards among the socially anxious (Alden & Cappe, 1981; Alden &
Safran, 1978; Goldfried & Sobocinski, 1975). To put the same concept
slightly differently, what we have encountered among many social
phobics is an unrealistic appraisal of what is required of them in
social situations. For example, they may assume that in an initial
heterosocial encounter they will inevitably be rejected if they are not
"totally at ease," or if they fail to demonstrate a quick sense of
humor. As the hypothesized demands of social situations become
higher and more unreasonable, the social phobic's self-efficacy drops,
and the risk of perceived failure is increased, leading to overestimating the likelihood of rejection, embarrassment, or humiliation. The
social phobic's tendency to underestimate his skill in a social situation is often associated with unrealistic ideas regarding what is
required.

Catastrophic Expectations Regarding Others' Responses to Displays of Anxiety

In addition to unrealistic assessments regarding the likelihood of
rejection and the magnitude of the attention likely to be focused on
their actions, social phobics frequently expect others to respond to
their anxiety in harsh, judgmental, or shame-producing ways. One
common theme we have observed is that displays of anxiety will
cause others to evaluate the social phobic as "flawed," "strange," or
"weak." This theme is also frequently encountered in agoraphobics
who fear fainting during panic attacks; they assume that strangers
will respond to their plight with judgments, hostility, and contempt
rather than with concern.

Overresponsiveness to Rejection

The above cognitive errors involve catastrophic estimations regarding the likelihood, character, or magnitude of others' responses.
However, social phobia is not simply a problem involving anticipa-

tion of events that rarely or never occur; social phobics are highly sensitive to negative evaluation or rejection when it does occur. They tend to respond to such rejection as a comment about their general acceptability. While social phobics as a group may be characterized as having low self-esteem (Marks, 1987), in our experience it is this latter group—who are more preoccupied with and sensitive to lack of acceptance by others than they are to public humiliation, shame, or embarrassment—who suffer most severely on the dimension of self-esteem. Among these individuals, feelings of self-worth are sufficiently low and simultaneously so tied to acceptance by others that in each social encounter they experience themselves as "on trial," with the verdict determining, in global fashion, their worth.

Attributional Errors Leading to Self-Blame

It is not surprising that social phobics expect others to respond to their anxiety with contempt or blame, since they evaluate themselves in that fashion. As Trower and Turland (1984) noted in their review, early research in the area of attribution theory (Heider, 1958) indicated that individuals tend to view their own behavior as situationally determined, and the behavior of others as determined by personality (Jones & Nisbett, 1971). Somewhat later, evidence emerged that under most circumstances individuals ascribe success to effort, ability, and other internal factors but attribute failure to situational factors such as bad luck, task difficulty, etc. (Bradley, 1978). This is frequently referred to as "self-serving bias." However, there is a body of evidence suggesting that the socially anxious are prone to a reverse bias in which they attribute failure to personal flaws (Trower & Turland, 1984).

We have observed a similar phenomenon in the social phobics we have treated. Specifically, social phobics tend to assume that the anxiety or awkwardness they experience in social situations marks them as different, defective, and strange. Yet in many instances, the situations arousing anxiety for the social phobic arouse anxiety in many of us (e.g., public speaking, first dates, job interviews, etc.). The labels social phobics attach to themselves as a consequence of their anxiety, which are often global, absolute, and self-blaming, have the effect of increasing their arousal and levels of anxiety. In general, these labels reflect their lack of self-acceptance.

We draw on a variety of techniques to facilitate cognitive change in social phobics. These include self-statement modification, and the use of a "Daily Record of Dysfunctional Thoughts" (Beck et al., 1979; Beck & Emery, 1985). However, as we noted earlier some instances of social phobia involve relatively circumscribed complaints, while others involve more pervasive avoidance. Those who present with extreme avoidance across a wide variety of social situations usually manifest an oversensitivity to rejection, and the reverse attributional bias discussed above. These individuals are the most difficult to treat and usually require longer-term therapy, in which deeper cognitive structures relating to self-esteem and personal identity (Guidano & Liotti, 1983) become the focus of treatment.

Social Skills Training

We discuss social skills training as an intervention separate from exposure therapy, although as Emmelkamp (1982) suggested, some of its effects may be due to in vivo exposure experiences that are prescribed as part of skill enhancement. This approach assumes that social phobics lack the requisite skills to succeed in social situations and that their anxiety stems from such deficits. Studies evaluating the effectiveness of social skills training indicate that it is a useful approach to treatment with the socially dysfunctional (see Brady, 1984a, 1984b; Curran, 1977; Stravynski & Shahar, 1983, for reviews). Social skills enhancement interventions involve instruction (e.g., instructing a patient to make better eye contact or speak more loudly), modeling, role playing, feedback, social reinforcement (e.g., praise from the therapist when the patient's response approximates the behavioral goal), and homework assignments (e.g., greeting one person per day, asking someone out for a 30-minute coffee date, etc.) (Brady, 1984a). We incorporate such interventions selectively with social phobics when it appears that actual skill deficits are present. In general, we have been more impressed with the cognitive errors common among social phobics which, as we noted, distort the demands and risks involved in social encounters. Most of the social phobics we see appear to have adequate skills but have difficulty in deploying them or underestimate their own performance. Thus we favor a combination of exposure and cognitive restructuring. Nevertheless, we do encounter some social phobics who demonstrate social skills deficits and in such cases we incorporate the interventions listed above.

Case Examples

We will begin by presenting several examples of individuals presenting with relatively circumscribed social phobias before describing an example of a more diffuse case.

Janice R., a 33-year-old married nursing student with three children, presented with a fear of shaking in public. In general, she experienced a variety of anxious symptoms, including tachycardia, sweating, and hand tremors specifically in situations in which she felt she was being evaluated, but she found the hand tremor most distressing because it was most likely to be noticed by others. When trying to describe how she believed others would evaluate her were they to notice her anxiety she used words such as "awful," "weird," and "strange." She reported that for several years the problem had only moderate impact on her life; she did however avoid parties, coffee dates with friends, or other settings in which she might have to drink in front of others for fear that her hand shaking would be obvious. In the few cases where she forced herself to attend a social gathering (e.g., a party or a dinner invitation) she would "quickly down a glass of wine" before the evening began in order to calm herself. However, she was now about to enter her third year of nurses training in which she would begin participation in clinical practicums and was afraid that she would be unable to give injections or draw blood when she was being observed. She reported a stable and happy marriage and no other major difficulties. She had once before sought treatment, which had centered around relaxation; she reported this only slightly helpful.

In vivo exposure was chosen as the major intervention tactic in this case. The therapist noted that all of Janice's previous attempts to cope with the problem (e.g., relaxation, alcohol, avoidance of social gatherings) involved attempts to control the anxiety. The theory she had propounded was that if others noticed her anxiety, she would be subject to humiliating judgments. However, it was explained, her pattern of avoidance kept her from investigating whether in fact her theory was correct (i.e., whether others would evaluate her negatively if they observed her shaking). In this case, we were able to organize treatment around a hierarchy of situations; the patient noted that it would arouse the least amount of anxiety to drink a full glass of liquid in front of her family, followed by close friends, fellow students, and faculty. Instructions were given to place herself in these situations in turn, and to allow herself to experience anxiety and expose herself to scrutiny by having a full glass of liquid. If the hand shaking did not manifest itself, she was instructed to "pretend" to shake. The rationale given for pretending was that experiencing anxiety was not the most important element; rather, what was most important was that she expose herself to the scrutiny of others and observe their reactions. The patient was able to proceed through the hierarchy devised in a matter of eight weeks; weekly sessions were devoted to going over her experiences with her and discussing her impressions of how others had responded to her. Within the first two weeks, she reported considerably less anxiety in such situations. By the end of treatment she also reported a "change in my attitude," noting that she now realized that she had assumed others were far more concerned about her hand tremors than in fact they were. Six month and one year follow-ups revealed her to have discontinued her pattern of social avoidance and to be proceeding satisfactorily with nursing school.

Margaret J., a 60-year-old female, referred herself for treatment of what she described as a 35-year history of fear of public bathrooms. Her fear was complicated by a history of spastic colon, and she reported being virtually housebound on and off since her mid-20s depending upon her bowel symptoms. She had seen a number of therapists, and undergone psychodynamic treatment on three separate occasions, each time for periods between six months and three years with no result. She had also been tried on numerous medications without noticeable benefit. Most recently she had been misdiagnosed as agoraphobic, and was placed on alprazolam 0.25 mg qid, also with no benefit. She reported numerous spells of depression because of her symptoms and indicated considerable guilt over the effect of her problem upon her husband. The impetus to enter treatment at this point was that her husband had recently retired and wanted to spend more time with her in recreational activities including travel.

Treatment involved exposure in vivo, with some attention to cognitive restructuring. A female therapist in our clinic treated Mrs. J. and began by persuading her to bring in a tape of herself urinating and then playing it. This was followed by a tape of her defecating. In addition to serving as a first step in a hierarchy of situations designed to reduce her anxiety, it facilitated discussion of the thoughts Mrs. J. experienced while having the therapist listen to the tape. Thoughts such as "She must think this is disgusting" and "She must think I'm awful" were discussed. Mrs. J. agreed that since everyone is prone to make the same noises as she, that such thoughts were irrational and that she had considered this "a thousand times," but that discussing the thoughts openly with a therapist who had just listened to an audiotape of her in the bathroom had a significant impact.

Treatment proceeded with the therapist accompanying the patient to a public bathroom and, finally, to a point where the patient was able to relieve herself in a public bathroom when others were present. Her avoidance ceased, and she reported feeling unburdened of her fear and discomfort for the first time in over 30 years. A total of 11 weekly sessions were spent before the patient reported the ability to use public bathrooms freely. She elected to stay in treatment for several months beyond the point where her avoidance ceased, but the focus of treatment shifted to other concerns. These included difficulties she was having with her grown children and difficulties obtaining help from her siblings in caring for her 85-year-old mother, who was suffering Alzheimer's Disease and for whom she was primarily responsible.

Some cases of social phobia in which the avoidance is circumscribed and the patient has an unrealistic fear of public humiliation lend themselves to a participant modeling approach as in the following case.

Lucy M., a 56-year-old married female, referred herself for fear of having her hands shake in public, particularly when writing. She had been troubled by this problem for more than 20 years, but it had recently grown worse. For some years she coped with the problem by avoidance; she always paid for items such as groceries in cash and, in general, avoided using credit cards (which would necessitate signing her name) when she shopped alone. When she was with her husband, he would use his credit card or write any checks that were required. The problem bringing her to therapy was that her driver's license was due to expire in four months, necessitating a written test, and she was afraid she would be unable to complete it.

The first session was devoted exclusively to a history, but during the second session the therapist requested that the patient attempt to write her name in the presence of the therapist; she shook considerably and accomplished the task with great difficulty. When asked about her thoughts regarding the consequences of shaking in public, her responses were that she would be "mortified" if anyone knew that she was anxious; she assumed that anyone who watched her would consider her "weak," or "the nervous type" and might comment in a way that was humiliating or at the very least feel contempt for her.

While this was a problem that did not lend itself easily to a *graduated* in vivo exposure approach, an attempt was made. The patient agreed that her anxiety would decrease if writing in public did not involve someone actually waiting for her to sign a check, credit card, etc. Put differently, she reported less anxiety if she experienced more control in the situation. Consequently, tasks were devised in which writing was performed in public but without the demand of someone waiting for her to produce something like her signature. Thus, she was asked to wait in a grocery line and pay for her groceries in cash but to take out a list and pretend to write something on it while she was being checked out in line. Another task involved sitting at an outdoor coffee shop, writing a letter. Within three weeks, the patient reported being able to perform such tasks with minimal anxiety, and it was decided that she should attempt to write a check at a grocery store outside her neighborhood. However, at the next session the patient reported being "overwhelmed with anxiety" and unable to perform the task. Accordingly, it was agreed that rather than meet next time at the office, they would meet at a well-frequented grocery near the therapist's office. The therapist would perform the task, and the patient's task was to observe the responses of others.

After meeting at the prearranged location, the patient stood behind the therapist in line with a few groceries. The therapist had chosen a crowded line and when paying for the groceries took out a checkbook and pretended to have great difficulty writing the check, shaking in an obvious fashion. In order to insure that the patient have the experience of watching a stranger respond to someone's anxiety (i.e., that there be no doubt that the problem was attributed to anxiety) the therapist apologized for holding up the clerk, saying "I don't know why this kind of thing makes me so anxious." The grocery clerk, as if on cue, said "That's all right, just take your time," and began a conversation with a customer she knew who was further back in line. After struggling for three–four minutes to write the check, the therapist finally finished.

Later at the office, the therapist and patient discussed the incident, and the patient expressed considerable surprise at how kind the clerk was and how others on line did not appear to become angry at the delay. She agreed to proceed with the plan to expose herself to similar situations. She was instructed to "exaggerate" the anxiety, as the therapist did, if for some reason it failed to materialize. It was explained that the point of this was for her to further test her assumptions about the responses of strangers to displays of anxiety. The patient was able to perform the task, and after two weeks reported that she felt herself "over the problem." A six month follow-up revealed that she had taken her written driving test without difficulty and had no problem writing in public.

In the above case, the individual's avoidance pattern was instrumental in maintaining a catastrophic belief regarding how strangers might respond to demonstrations of anxiety. From our perspective, modeling followed by self-exposure helped to correct this key belief and resulted in behavioral change. However, in other cases, social phobics may already be putting themselves in anxiety-producing situations (i.e., they may already be practicing self-exposure) with little or no benefit reported. In such cases, small behavioral changes during therapeutically directed exposure may be sufficient to alter the character of the experience and change it from an anxiety-maintaining situation to one promoting change. The treatment of Joanne A., whom we presented briefly in the diagnosis section of this chapter, illustrates this point:

Joanne A., a 30-year-old secretary, married with one child, was referred by a social worker with whom she had been in treatment for one year for persistent "social anxiety." She described herself as having been shy all her life but had developed spontaneous panic attacks 15 months before our initial consultation, with blushing as one of the symptoms. She now found herself blushing several times a day, both during panic attacks and in a variety of interpersonal encounters, particularly at work. She had to work but had begun avoiding grocery and department store shopping as well as other public situations. Blushing was her major complaint; she felt she could tolerate the panic attacks, but she felt extremely embarrassed that her anxiety was evident to others. Since the blushing was at least partially associated with spontaneous panic attacks, we began measures addressing the latter including medication, controlled breathing, and self-statement modification in the hope that this would impact her blushing response. These measures proved successful in controlling spontaneous panic attacks, but blushing in interpersonal situations persisted and continued to cause the patient distress. As blushing was a daily occurrence, self-exposure was not having an effect. The patient indicated that what disturbed her about blushing was that people would see she was anxious.

It was therefore decided to attempt to bring about a change in that aspect of the experience. The therapist explained that measures to prevent blushing were ineffective, and that this was not likely to change. However, her distress and anxiety in interpersonal situations was not due to the blushing per se but rather to her feeling of being exposed, and a change in her verbal behavior might be helpful in correcting this. After considerable discussion regarding what kind of different verbal response she might be comfortable with when she felt herself blushing, it was finally decided that she would attempt to treat the incident humorously as a way of "regaining privacy." Her supervisor at work frequently commented about it when he noticed her blushing in a way that embarrassed her. Accordingly, she was instructed not to avoid this supervisor but, in fact, to seek him out, and when blushing did occur to say, "Uh-oh, menopause already," or "Oh no, not those hot flashes again," or to fan herself with her hand and say, "Whew, it's hot in here."

Interestingly, as frequently happens with interventions such as these which reduce the patient's sense of helplessness and restore a measure of control, Joanne reported no incidents of blushing over the next three weeks. After that, she reported making use of the intervention suggested on two occasions, but thereafter the frequency of blushing diminished considerably. Moreover, when it did occur, it no longer occasioned distress. She stopped avoiding the grocery store and such tasks, as well, without further intervention targeting those difficulties. The patient elected to stay in treatment for several more months to obtain help with marital issues and job-related stress, but blushing and behavioral avoidance were no longer the focus of treatment.

As we noted earlier, social phobia may be restricted to one or more isolated situations or it may be pervasive. The following case involved diffuse fear of social contact with severe consequences for the patient.

Linda J., a 33-year-old computer programmer, referred herself for treatment of social avoidance. She lived alone and was not dating, although she had experienced one brief heterosexual relationship in the past. She reported that she had a history of shyness and had been socially isolated since childhood. Currently, she had almost no social contacts; she neither dated nor had female friends. For the past 15 years, when she found herself in a social situation with anyone—either male or female—she experienced numerous autonomic symptoms including dry mouth, tachycardia, flushing, dizziness, and tension in her facial muscles. In addition, in such situations she reported, "My mind goes blank, I can't think, and I can't speak." Her family physician had prescribed 75 mg of imipramine to help control her anxious symptoms, but she reported no effect. When engaged in social interaction she reported constant preoccupation with the fear that the other person or persons would notice her anxiety. She did not have problems interacting with strangers; symptoms of anxiety were experienced only with those whom she regarded as "potential friends."

Linda was the youngest of three children. She described her mother as self-involved and highly critical of all her children but perhaps most critical of Linda, her only daughter. Her father was alcoholic, and he and her mother had divorced shortly after Linda's birth. She noted that as a child and an adolescent her mother discouraged her from having friends, refusing to allow her to invite people to their home, and forbidding her from socializing at the home of others. She noted that her family was "less well-off" than other families in her neighborhood, and that she was teased and suffered social rejection as a child. She expressed a fervent desire for both male and female companionship but avoided any social opportunity for fear that her anxious symptoms would appear and the encounter would prove humiliating.

Treatment began with attempts to promote self-exposure. Linda did not have trouble greeting people casually, and so the simplest task appeared to be making "coffee dates" with coworkers. However, she was unable to complete the initial tasks agreed upon. She arrived for her scheduled appointment following her failure to complete the first task assigned very upset and fearful that the therapist would "give up on me." She indicated that she very much wanted treatment for her problem but felt too terrified of an "anxiety attack" to complete the tasks. At this point, the therapist decided to increase her regimen of imipramine to 150 mg, with the goal of facilitating her self-exposure. In addition, therapy began to focus more directly on her cognitions regarding the requirements for friendship and dating. Since she anticipated less difficulty placing herself in social situations with potential female friends than with males, we began exploring her ideas regarding friendship. She generated the following list of traits that she believed were requirements for a friendship:

1. A sense of humor—ability to make people laugh.
2. Relaxed, easygoing manner. Ability to make people feel comfortable.
3. Educated, interesting background, and ability to tell stories and discuss world issues intelligently.
4. Fun to be with.
5. Quick-witted, glib.
6. Confidence in oneself.
7. Positive about things.

Not surprisingly, Linda felt anxious in most social encounters, feeling that she was unable to meet the above demands. Before reassigning exposure tasks, several sessions were spent going over her list and discussing how she arrived at it. Her tendency toward turning social encounters into a "performance" was pointed out, and the therapist suggested that since she had not had experience with friendships as an adult, she might be overestimating the demands. Her childhood experiences involving social rejection were discussed in some detail; the therapist pointed out that she seemed to be generalizing from those experiences what people expected of friends, although, in fact, adults want very different qualities than children do and usually respond very differently when their expectations are not met. Self-exposure tasks were framed as experiments designed to test her ideas regarding what people wanted of a friend.

After about two months, the patient began a program of limited self-exposure, discussing each task in detail with the therapist. In addition, her ideas regarding what was expected of her in such situations were continually scrutinized and discussed. Considerable time was also spent discussing issues related to self-esteem; Linda's sensitivity to rejection was clearly related to doubts about her self-worth. Part of the fear of rejection in social situations had to do with the extent to which she was searching for evidence regarding her own worth in such encounters.

In addition, when necessary, social skills training interventions, such as role playing, were employed to help the patient rehearse skills she was unsure of. In general, however, the therapist was more impressed with the cognitive distortion she presented than with her lack of social skill. As in most cases in which pervasive social avoidance is the presenting complaint, treatment was relatively lengthy. In this case it lasted for 32 months. However, improvement in the presenting symptoms was marked; the patient began to make friends, attend social gatherings, and eventually, to date.

SUMMARY

Social phobia, characterized by anxiety and social avoidance, is a commonly encountered clinical problem. The extent of avoidance may be relatively circumscribed (e.g., as in fear of writing in public), or it may involve extreme social isolation. While social phobia involves varying combinations of physiologic, cognitive and behavioral disturbance, cognitive errors (e.g., overestimations of the likelihood of rejection, embarrassment, or humiliation; catastrophic expectations regarding others' reactions to displays of anxiety) may play a particularly important role in its maintenance. Because social phobics frequently expose themselves to fear-evoking situations with little or no reduction in anxiety, it is important to combine exposure therapy with cognitive intervention to correct those cognitive errors instrumental in maintaining anxiety. In some cases, pharmacotherapy and social skills training may enhance treatment effects.

TEN

· · · · · · ·

Simple Phobias

· · · · · · · · · ·

Simple phobias are one of the most easily and effectively treated psychological problems, particularly by behavioral methods. A simple phobia is a persistent, irrational fear of some living thing, object, or situation and the desire to avoid it. A phobia consists of a fear and avoidance component. The fear can include all the features of anxiety and panic. Thus, when thinking about a feared object or situation, the patient may have subjective feelings of tension and anxiety, thoughts characteristic of anxiety, and psychophysiological arousal or even symptoms of panic attacks, including palpitations, shortness of breath and the other somatic symptoms, feelings of unreality, depersonalization, impending doom, dying, or going crazy. The panic attack symptoms are most likely to occur when the person is actually confronted with the phobic object or situation. The avoidance may be obvious, e.g., a person simply refuses to enter a situation where he or she may encounter the phobic stimulus, or subtle, e.g., the person afraid of large spiders never visits countries where they are to be found.

Simple phobias are different from agoraphobia and social phobia on a number of dimensions. Simple phobias are much more common than agoraphobia and social phobias, and they begin at a younger age. Unlike agoraphobics and social phobics, simple phobics generally are not anxious or depressed, nor do they score high on neuroticism measures or exhibit abnormally high readings on various physiologic and biochemical measures, except when confronted with the phobic object or situation. Thus, simple phobics are otherwise very normal. Yet the phobia may cause considerable disability. For instance, we received the following letter from a 34-year-old woman who requested treatment in one of our studies:

> Ever since I have been a small child I have had an irrational fear of spiders . . . . the fear has control of my entire life. I do not go camping, I

don't sit on the terrace by myself, I don't lie in the grass, I don't go into the cellar, I make sure I always lock the sunroof and close the windows of the car when I get out. I spray the house, attic, and basement every month and I feel extremely guilty because I am probably poisoning my family. . . . I . . . have spent thousands of dollars on unnecessary screens, double windows, door sealer, etc. I have research how to make DDT or obtain it illegally. . . . It takes only a picture in a magazine for me to develop itches and bumps and start dry-heaving along with hysteric crying fits. I turn on the lights three to four times a night just to look around the bedroom. When my husband is not there I sleep with the lights on and only after having a few brandies.

Another woman wrote as follows:

The other night I went into my bedroom to get a book. I turned on the bedroom light and screamed at the top of my lungs for my husband . . . there it was, a wolf spider about the size of a half dollar or larger. I ran out of the bedroom screaming and crying hysterically . . . jumped in the living room chair. . . . I sat crying, shaking and sweating, yet freezing cold at the same time. My husband came in the room and held me tight, but it didn't seem to help. I thought I was going to go crazy. I don't know if it was the sweat running down my body, or just my imagination, but twice I jumped up attacking myself, trying to get the crawling spiders off me. They felt so real, and I was scared to death.

Although simple phobias are very common and cause much distress, it is rare for patients to seek treatment for the phobia unless a change in their situation might cause them to encounter the feared object or situation. Examples of precipitating events that have caused patients to seek treatment in our clinic include the following: a spider phobic moves to a new house with many places where spiders can hide; another spider phobic is given the opportunity to do anthropological work in the Amazon; a height phobic wants to start skiing; an elevator phobic's business moves to the fourth floor of a new building; a jogger realizes that she is afraid of dogs. Flying phobias are particularly common and distressing, causing many people to avoid work and social opportunities.

Occasionally, with no change in a person's situation, a phobia under control becomes upsetting enough to move the patient to seek help; for example, a small-insect phobia begins to dominate a person's life. Illness or pregnancy can worsen a phobia or cause new phobias to develop; usually the distress is alleviated once the illness is resolved or the pregnancy ends. Occasionally, a traumatic event can cause a phobia. We have treated two patients who developed an acute flying phobia following a near crash (it is interesting that driving phobias rarely develop following near crashes).

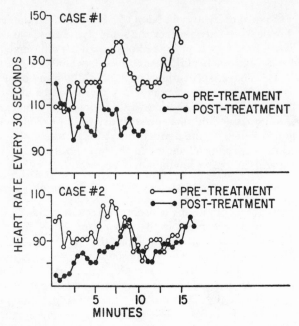

Figure 10.1 **Pre- to Post-Treatment Heart Rates in Spider-Phobic**
Patients

Figure 10.1   shows the heart rates in beats per minute averaged for every 30
seconds for two spider-phobic subjects encountering a series of spider-relat-
ed stimuli before and after treatment.

Reprinted with permission of publisher from: Taylor, C. B. Heart-rate
changes in improved spider-phobic patients. *Psychological Reports*, 1977, 41,
667–671. Fig. 2.

The peripheral physiologic response to a phobic situation has been
well characterized. Phobic stimuli cause autonomic responses similar to those induced by normal fear and greater than those elicited
by neutral stimuli (Mathews, 1971). When confronted with a phobic
image, phobics will show increased heart rate (usually 4–10 bpm)
and an increase in skin conductance fluctuation (Watson et al., 1972;
Stern & Marks 1973); however, measures of heart rate, skin conductance and subjective fear correlate poorly with one another. Forearm
blood flow, blood pressure, and electromyogram (EMG) also increase
when a person is confronted with the phobic situation. Many of these
responses habituate, that is, show a decrement in response as the
phobic stimuli are repeated. Figure 10.1 shows the heart rate response of two spider-phobic subjects undergoing exposure treatment.

Fear and simple phobias are accompanied by widespread changes in the neuroendocrine system, but these changes are not specific and can be elicited by any distressing experience. A recent study by Nesse et al. (1984) illustrates both the typical biochemical changes that occur when a phobic is exposed to a phobic stimulus and the patterns of change. In this study ten animal phobics were given two sessions of exposure. Each session lasted three hours. During exposure systolic blood pressure, diastolic blood pressure, epinephrine, nor-epinephrine, growth hormone, insulin, and cortisol all increased. Glucagon and pancreatic polypeptide did not change. These phys-iologic changes are controlled by both the hypothalamic-pituitary adrenal cortical system and the limbic adrenal medullary system.

We will now discuss some of the common phobias in more detail.

Animal Phobias

Animal phobias are characterized by a fear of small animals, in-cluding insects. The most common phobias involve snakes, insects, dogs, and birds. Most patients have only one small-animal phobia. Patients complain that the unpredictable characteristics of the ani-mal are most disturbing, e.g., the sudden flutter of a bird, dash of a spider, or rush of a dog. They are more afraid of their reaction to the animal than of actually suffering pain. Many patients dream of the animals they fear. Animal fears are a normal part of human develop-ment, arising between ages 2 and 4 and subsiding by about 20, al-though most adults have some mild fear of spiders, snakes, mice, dogs, or other species.

A frightening encounter with the animal was felt to produce the phobia in only 23 percent of patients in one series (McNally & Steketee, 1985). Adult-onset animal phobias are usually caused by a traumatic encounter with the animal.

Blood/Injury Phobias

Blood/injury phobias are those in which the sight of blood, injury, or gross deformity, or having blood drawn causes fear. Agras, Syl-vester, and Oliveau (1969) found 18 percent of a community sample to have injury phobias and about 15 percent to have injection pho-bias. In our experience, blood/injury phobias can be particularly se-rious. Patients with blood/injury phobias may faint when blood is being drawn, perhaps sustaining injury as a result, and may even avoid needed medical procedures. We have treated several patients who were refusing to continue with chemotherapy because of severe aversion to having blood drawn. Some people have decided not to pursue a career in health care because of blood/injury phobias. Blood/injury phobias differ from other simple phobias in three ways: they are associated with a diphasic cardiovascular response, nausea without fear, and a strong family history.

In contrast to most phobics, whose heart rates increase when encountering the phobic situation, blood/injury phobics show an initial rise in heart rate and blood pressure followed within a few seconds or minutes by slowing of the heart rate and drop in blood pressure. The patient feels nauseated and faint without feeling fear and may actually faint. This is, in fact, the same reaction seen in many normals who faint when blood is drawn and show evidence of sympathetic activity and vagal inhibition. In blood/injury phobics, fainting may even precipitate focal or generalized seizures.

Schraeder et al. (1983) reported the case of a 21-year-old student who fainted and developed a seizure while listening to the reading of a description of suffering from Fox's *Book of Martyrs*. Listening to the frightening passage while his EEG (electroencephalogram) and ECG (electrocardiogram) were being monitored, he had 25 seconds of no heart beat, ending in a silent EEG and another fit. Ambulatory monitoring revealed episodes of progressive sinus bradycardia (very slow heart rate) with PR-interval prolongation and atrioventricular block. A ventricular pacemaker was implanted, and there were no further symptoms over a one-year follow-up.

Another difference between blood/injury and other simple phobics is that the former have more relatives with a similar problem (Connolly et al., 1976; Yule & Fernando, 1980). Ost et al., (1984) found that among blood/injury phobics 68 percent had biological relatives who were blood phobic, a rate 3 to 6 times higher than the frequency of corresponding phobias in the families of agoraphobics, social, dental, or animal phobics. Marks (1987) speculates that the extreme autonomic responsivity of blood/injury phobias may be genetically determined and the degree of response normally distributed in the population. What would be the adaptive value of such responsivity? Fainting generally results in the head being lowered, which might restore circulation in a wounded organism that has lost blood. Others have speculated that the fainting reflex is akin to the tonic immobility evidenced in many species when approached by a potential predator.

Dental Phobias

Dental phobias are very common. In a representative sample of 784 women in Gothenburg, Sweden, from 38–54 years of age, point prevalence of dental phobias was 13 percent. About 40 percent of adults delay or avoid visits to the dentist unless they are having dental difficulties, but only about 5 percent have dental phobia (Gale & Ayer, 1969; Kleinknecht et al., 1973). Some dental phobics are actually suffering from a blood/injury phobia. Unlike other phobias, the dental phobia may be a conditioned phenomenon. Dental phobias seem to have diminished with modern dental procedures that have eliminated much of the discomfort.

Flying Phobias

Flying phobias are also common. The Boeing Company estimates that one of every six Americans is afraid to fly. About 20 percent of those who do fly have substantial anxiety during the flight (Greist & Greist, 1981).

Driving Phobias

Driving phobias are characterized by a fear of driving on busy streets, freeways, or in traffic. Driving phobics usually have some places where they are willing to drive; freeway driving is most frequently avoided. They state they are afraid of having a panic attack and being unable to move to the side of the road, or that they will lose control of the automobile. Most driving phobics have a history of having driven successfully and without fear; some have been in accidents long before the driving phobia developed. Driving phobias are very common with agoraphobics. In our survey, we found that 50 percent of 800 subjects requesting treatment in our center reported having a severe driving phobia. A principle components analysis of the Stanford Fear Inventory found that driving phobias could be separated from the other phobias and avoidances; that is, people who, for instance, avoided shopping were likely to avoid theaters but not necessarily driving. Many driving phobics meet the criteria for agoraphobia.

Sexual Phobias

Some sex therapists have pointed out that sex phobias are common in their clinical practice. In one sample of 373 patients who complained about sexual avoidance on the part of one or both partners, Kaplan (1987) found that 106 were phobic avoiders in the sense that they experienced panic or aversion in sexual situations, and 267 simply had no interest in sex but no apparent aversion when they engaged in sex. She claims that 25 percent of her patients with sexual avoidance also had panic disorder, a prevalence much greater than that estimated for the general population. Furthermore, another 38 percent had symptoms of atypical panic attacks, e.g., characterized by only a few symptoms or an atypical course.

Sexual phobias can involve any aspect of sex including sexual fantasies, sexual secretions and odors (semen, vaginal fluid), or sexual failure. Some patients with circumscribed sexual phobias may enjoy sex and function normally as long as they can manage to avoid their particular phobia. For example, women with penetration phobias panic only when they attempt intercourse. Kaplan (1987) notes that patients with sexual aversion or phobias develop ingenious and varied avoidance strategies. To avoid sex, they engage in prolonged telephone calls or excessive and late-night television watching, make themselves unattractive, complain of somatic symptoms, and employ a variety of other strategies.

Crenshaw (1985) identifies patients with primary and secondary sexual aversion. Primary sexual aversion is characterized by individuals who always find sex frightening or repulsive, and secondary sexual aversion by those who acquire the phobic response after enjoying a period of normal sexual functioning. Crenshaw reports that in her patient population, primary aversion is associated with more serious psychopathology, is more prevalent in men, and is more difficult to treat than secondary aversion. Kaplan (1987) has found that patients with panic disorder and sexual phobias, aversion, or avoidance seem to do worse with her treatment approach (which combines exposure to the feared sexual situation in order to extinguish the patient's irrational fear of sex with brief psychodynamically oriented therapy) than patients with the same sexual dysfunction but without panic disorder. She considers antipanic medication whenever patients do not progress satisfactorily in therapy, even when they fail to report spontaneous panic attacks. She may prescribe medication for patients who (1) have or have had one or more other phobias in addition to their sexual phobia or aversion, and (2) one of the following: atypical panic attack equivalents; more than one addiction to tranquilizers, stimulants, or alcohol, or an eating disorder; a history of excessive separation anxiety during childhood and/or evidence of significant separation problems in adult love relationships; or other features of panic attacks. She reports that such patients do very well with antipanic medication.

Kaplan has done an important service in identifying this syndrome. Even more importantly, she has outlined useful treatment strategies for sexual phobias and aversions. Because they are well described in her books on sexual therapy, we will not repeat them here except to note one caveat that fits our own, much more limited, experience in treating these problems:

> The sexual interactions that are prescribed in sex therapy are not simply mechanical exercise. They are highly charged erotic and intimate experiences which the patient has previously avoided because they are too threatening. . . .Behavioral prescriptions are extremely potent experiences that can rapidly strip away a patient's psychological defenses, and this can leave him or her feeling emotionally naked and vulnerable. While this is an excellent method for exposing important dynamic material and making this available for therapeutic exploration, the process can also be extremely threatening, especially in the context of conjoint therapy. For these reasons, the behavioral assignments should be devised with great sensitivity to their potential emotional effects on both spouses. (Kaplan, 1987, p. 104)

Other Specific Fears

Claustrophobia (fear of closed spaces) is often associated with agoraphobia but sometimes exists as an independent fear. Sufferers are afraid of being shut in elevators, tunnels, closets, or even small rooms. Such patients will rarely enter a situation where escape might be difficult. *Acrophobia* (fear of heights) often is associated with agoraphobia. Patients with acrophobia often have the irrational idea that they might jump off a high place. Others seem to "project themselves into space" and have vivid images of themselves falling.

Diagnosis

The diagnosis of a simple phobia is not difficult. DSM-III-R requires that the person have a persistent fear of a circumscribed stimulus other than having a panic attack (as in panic disorder), or a fear of humiliation or embarrassment in certain social situations (as in social phobia). Patients with agoraphobia avoid many situations: these should not be considered simple phobias if they are related in some way to the agoraphobia. During some phase of the disturbance, exposure to the specific phobic stimulus provokes an immediate anxiety response and the object or situation is avoided, or endured with intense anxiety. For DSM-III-R, the fear or the avoidant behavior must significantly interfere with the person's normal routine or with usual social activities or relationships with others, or there must be marked distress about having the fear. Finally, the person must recognize that his or her fear is excessive or unreasonable.

Incidence and Prevalence

Simple phobias are quite common. Agras, Sylvester, and Oliveau (1969) found a prevalence of 7.7/100 for any phobia but only 0.2/100 for disabling phobias. Before they are 6 months old, human infants show little fear. Thereafter they begin to fear strangers, separation, and unfamiliar toys and objects (Scarr & Salapatek, 1970). By 12 months about 50 percent of children show fear of strangers, 30 percent fear of pistol noise, and 70 percent fear of a visual cliff. Separation anxiety begins at about 8 months, peaking at 9 to 13 months (Kagan et al., 1978; Smith, 1979).

Fears are very common in children and seem related to development. MacFarlane et al. (1954) sampled 1096 children over 14 years. Based on their mother's reports (which appear to underestimate their children's fears), 90 percent of the children had at least one specific fear between the ages of 2 to 14. Incidence peaked at age 3 (56 percent of boys, 67 percent of girls) and declined slowly with age. Fears of animals increase at ages 2 to 4, and of darkness and imaginary creatures at ages 4 to 6 (Angelino et al., 1956; MacFarlane et al., 1954).

Genetics

Avoidance is a basic mechanism that helps determine the survivability of an organism that must learn which environments, foodstuffs, and situations are dangerous. Studies of various organisms have demonstrated the importance of genes in avoidance learning (Gould, 1982). For instance, one mutant type of fruitfly (called "dunce") cannot learn and also fails to habituate. These two functions are related to a single genetic defect. One type of mutant cricket fails to jump when puffed with compressed air; such crickets are caught by a vacuum cleaner whereas nonmutant crickets escape. The defect is related to a single gene affecting sensitive hairs in the tail. Rats tend to react to fright with defecation and urination. A breed of rats has been developed that shows little reactivity to fright. Of interest, this breed has very low fertility, requiring breeding from rats with slightly more reactivity for fertilization to occur. It is also more prone to seizures and has more benzodiazepine receptor binding sites in the brain (Robertson et al., 1978) than reactive rats. Studies on these rats have found that open-field inactivity and defecation are highly correlated, suggesting that they may be influenced by the same genes. These studies demonstrate the importance of genetic influence on behaviors related to fear.

Five studies have examined genetic effects in humans using fear survey schedules given to normals and their relatives. Monozygotic twins are more similar than dizygotic twins for specific fears (Rose et al., 1981; Rose & Ditto, 1983; Neale & Fulker, 1984; Torgersen, 1978; Carey & Gottesman, 1981). As mentioned above, blood/injury phobics are particularly likely to have relatives with the same problem (Connolly et al., 1976; Yule & Fernando, 1980). Twenty-one twin probands with phobic disorders were meticulously investigated by Carey (1982). Of these, 88 percent of the 8 MZ twins had either a phobic disorder or phobic features, compared with only 38 percent of the 13 DZ twins. Overall, the evidence favors a genetic predisposition to the development of specific fears. However, the nature of this predisposition is unknown.

Etiology

The etiology of simple phobias remains unknown. We assume that, as with other anxiety disorders, the cause of simple phobias is complicated and multidetermined. The evidence suggests that genetic, developmental, and environmental factors interact to determine the development of simple phobias. The neural systems modulating habituation, sensitization, classical conditioning, and other types of learning are particularly important in developing and maintaining fears. Yet the level of dysfunction in these neural systems determined by the genetic, developmental, and environmental factors is subtle and hardly differs from normals.

While early learning theorists argued that fears were simply learned, the difficulty of conditioning fearfulness to many things, as well as other observations, led to the "preparedness theory." This theory proposes that simple phobias involve classes of objects or situations that are dangerous to man in the natural environment (Marks, 1969). The theory allows for fears to be acquired in a single conditioning trial, to be selective to certain classes of objects, and to be resistant to extinction. A series of studies have provided evidence supporting this theory. Skin-conductance responses can be conditioned more easily and extinguished more slowly to stimuli such as spiders and snakes than to neutral stimuli like houses, flowers, or geometric figures (Ohman et al., 1974; Ohman, Fredrikson, & Hugdahl, 1978). After the acquisition of a fear response to prepared and unprepared stimuli, subjects told that the aversive stimulus would be discontinued immediately extinguished the response to irrelevant stimuli, while the response to the relevant stimuli continued. This finding is consistent with the irrationality of many phobias.

There are, however, a few cases of fears of objects of no biological threat (e.g., chocolate, leaves of vegetables, and plants; Rachman & Seligman, 1976), and such fears do not differ from relevant fears in treatment outcome, severity, degree of generalization, or other factors. Other evidence suggests that fears can be acquired through vicarious learning. For example, Meyer (discussed in Marks, 1987) reported the case of two sisters who developed a phobia of birds. During childhood, one of the two had been walking in the park and was brutally attacked by a bird. Her sister witnessed the event. Both girls thereafter developed phobias of flying birds suggesting both the traumatic and vicarious learning of fears. Yet only a few subjects can relate their fears to vicarious learning conditions (Rimm et al., 1977). Finally, cognitive theorists argue that intensive fears develop as a result of being told that the situation is dangerous. Borkovec and Sides (1979) have shown that individuals who think about avoiding the feared situation during imagined exposure maintain the physiologic fear. Overall, little data for or against the cognitive model exists. We assume that avoidance of the feared object or situation is the main factor in maintaining the fear. On the basis of this theory, exposure is the treatment of choice and should produce rather immediate and effective relief.

Assessment

Self-Report

Many fear inventories have been developed to measure phobias. These can be classified into two categories: general fear-assessment instruments that include a wide range of fears and instruments to measure fears in more detail.

The first general fear survey (FSS-I) was developed by Lang and Lazovick (1963). The survey listed 50 common fears to be rated by subjects on a seven-point scale. This was followed by a subsequent scale (Fear Survey Schedule-III) developed by Wolpe and Lang (1964), which consisted of 75 items. The items were derived from the fears that Wolpe saw most commonly in clinical practice and were subdivided into the following subcategories: animal, tissue damage and illness, death or associated stimuli, noises and miscellaneous. Geer (1965) added another fear survey (FSS-II), which consisted of 51 items. Many other general fear schedules have been devised by augmenting or combining some of the existing schedules.

The psychometric properties of these inventories have not been extensively studied, with the exception of FSS-II. With the FSS-II, Geer (1965) found the internal consistency reliability for college students to be an overall r of .94. However, the test-retest reliability for individual items is usually much lower. Also, general fear surveys have poor correlations with fear as measured by avoidance (Taylor & Agras, 1981). We use a version of the FSS-III as a screening instrument to identify potentially problematic fears (see Appendix 2). The most widely used general survey is the Marks-Mathews Fear Questionnaire (1979; see Appendix 1).

In general, fear inventories have demonstrated high internal consistency and test-retest reliability (Klorman et al., 1974). Interested readers can find examples of self-report measures for fear of snakes and spiders (Lang, Melamed, & Hart, 1970), mutilation (Hasting, 1971), and heights (Baker, Cohen & Saunders, 1973).

In addition to using the FSS-III for a general survey of patients' fears, and the FS as an outcome measure and for comparison with other studies, we also use a self-efficacy hierarchy with a particular phobia. Bandura (1977) has developed a number of such hierarchies, which allow individuals to rate their confidence in approaching a feared situation under very specific stimulus conditions.

Finally, some form of self-monitoring of self-directed practice should be used. Since most simple phobic subjects do not interact frequently with phobic situations, a very simple procedure, even the use of a diary, is sufficient.

Cognitive Measures

The measurement of cognitive factors has little utility in the treatment of simple phobias and there are no standardized instruments available for this purpose.

Behavior

Because a patient's self-report of fear may not reflect their behavior, direct measures of behavior are attractive but not always practical in the clinical setting. Many of the treatment approaches recommended below for specific phobias incorporate exposure to the feared object and situation and, essentially, represent behavioral avoidance tests.

Physiology and Biochemistry

While real or imagined contact with a phobic stimulus is associated with physiologic arousal and demonstrable changes in skin conductance, heart rate, and other measures, these have little usefulness as yet in clinical practice. However, a number of researchers are investigating the possibility that patients who continue to demonstrate arousal despite behavioral improvement may be more liable to relapse than those who don't.

TREATMENT OF SIMPLE PHOBIAS

Many years of outcome research have established that there are at least three effective treatments for simple phobia: systematic desensitization, in vivo flooding, and participant modeling.

Systematic Desensitization

Systematic desensitization is the oldest and most widely researched imagery-based approach for treating phobias. With systematic desensitization subjects create a hierarchy of their fearful situations. The top items on the hierarchy represent items that cause extreme fear in the patient. The bottom items represent those that cause only mild anxiety. For instance, one of our patients with an elevator phobia constructed the following hierarchy:

Item	Imagined Fear
Stand outside of building	5
Enter doors to building with elevator	10
Stand 100 feet from elevator	25
Stand 50 feet from elevator	30
Stand in front of elevator	55
Push elevator button	60
Enter elevator	90
Proceed to first floor	95
Proceed to fifth floor	95
Proceed to tenth floor	95

We asked him to create a hierarchy of about ten items and to break the steps into round figures. We also asked him to rate his fear when he imagined himself undertaking each of these steps on a scale from 0 to 100, where 0 equalled no fear and 100 equalled the worst fear that he could imagine. As can be seen from his hierarchy, he did not notice any difference in fear once he had entered the elevator.

Subjects begin the treatment by imagining the lowest item on the hierarchy while practicing deep muscle relaxation. When they can imagine that item without fear they move onto the next item, continuing to proceed up the hierarchy until they can complete the most difficult items without discomfort. Rachman (1966) advises therapists to check the durability of previously desensitized items at the beginning of each treatment session, since fear may return between sessions. In vivo desensitization is a variation of systematic desensitization in which the subject actually encounters the feared situation in a hierarchical fashion. This procedure has been essentially incorporated into participant modeling, except that efficacy ratings have replaced anxiety ratings. We find that efficacy ratings are a superior clinical tool for determining when to proceed with therapy.

In Vivo Exposure

In vivo exposure involves continued exposure to the stimulus that evokes fear until discomfort subsides. Exposure has come to be considered a critical component of treatment for phobias in only the last 10 to 15 years, following extensive studies demonstrating its effectiveness (see Table 10.1 on page 275). Although the way that exposure works has not been determined, it is generally assumed that it involves the same neural processes that effect habituation. Live exposure is generally superior to imaginary exposure, but the latter can be effective. Although Marks has long been an advocate of self-exposure (Ghosh & Marks, 1986) we find that relatively few simple phobics are willing to follow this procedure. There is evidence that long exposure is more effective than short exposure and that sessions massed together are better than sessions spaced apart. Preventing avoidance is also important. It is unimportant whether or not there is marked relaxation or high anxiety, except as the latter may make a subject unwilling to undergo the procedure.

It is also critical that the patient remain engaged in therapy. This is illustrated by catecholamine data from one of our studies. We found that efficacy levels were strongly associated with catecholamine response to the feared stimulus: catecholamine responses were diminished following efficacious treatment (Bandura et al., 1985). However, a few subjects with low efficacy also showed no evidence for arousal. These subjects said that they had simply decided that they couldn't do the task and hence were not trying. Patients have a variety of imaginative methods for altering the characteristics of the treatment. They may decide, for instance, that the particular spider they are asked to encounter differs from the spiders they are really afraid of. Or they may imagine that they are temporarily invulnerable or shielded from harm. Dissociation may represent one such engagement ritual. Hypothetically, patients would not habituate under such conditions. Physiologic arousal might be a good measure of engagement.

Participant Modeling

Participant modeling is a therapeutic approach developed by Bandura (1977) and the one we use with simple phobics. It combines features of in vivo desensitization and modeling and is an effective vehicle for increasing self-efficacy and producing exposure. To facilitate approach to the feared object, the therapist arranges the patient's environment in such a way that he is able to overcome his fear one small step at a time. With the therapist modeling the desired interaction with the feared object, patients rapidly begin to report less fear in the presence of a formerly feared object and at the same time show behavioral improvement. Participant modeling allows patients to experience success at each step in the treatment and gives them a sense of mastery of the feared object or situation. This, in turn, leads to a feeling of personal efficacy resulting in a reduction in defensive behavior. The steps in participant modeling are:

1. *Instruction.* Patients are given information about their feared object and its feared qualities in a way that shows the fear to be excessive and/or unrealistic.
2. *Response modeling.* The therapist handles the feared object and interacts with it, showing that the feared consequences don't materialize.
3. *Joint performance.* The patient is encouraged by the therapist to join with him in a series of interactions with the feared object, starting with situations that provoke relatively little anxiety and ending with the accomplishment of the feared activity. The substeps can include progressive physical approaches to the final task, increased length of time exposed to the feared object, the use of protective devices to attenuate the patient's fear (for example gloves with an insect or snake phobic) or exposure to a series of related, but much less fear-inducing, objects (for example, a small snake). Bandura calls these substeps "response-induction aids."
4. *Self-directed practice.* The patient is encouraged to practice his new-found fearlessness alone and in varied settings to ensure that he does not attribute his sudden bravery either to the therapist or to the therapeutic situation and that he generalizes his skill to the natural environment.

TABLE 10.1

Effects of Simple Phobia Treatment Strategies

Technique	Effective, Pre-to-Post Treatment			More Effective Than Control		
	Yes	No	?	Yes	No	=
Systematic desensitization	7	1	1	7	0	0
In vivo flooding	11	2	0	8	0	2
Participant modeling	5	0	0	2	0	0

Summarized from "Simple Phobia" by E. T. Sturgis and R. Scott, 1984. In *Behavioral Theories and Treatment of Anxiety* edited by S. M. Turner, pp. 108–123. New York: Plenum.

Table 10.1 represents a summary taken from Sturgis and Scott's (1984) review of studies that have used systematic desensitization, in vivo exposure, and/or participant modeling. The first part of the table lists pre–post results: all three treatments appear effective. The second part of the table lists comparisons with controls (the numbers differ in the two parts of the table because not all of the studies employed controls). All three treatments also appeared more effective than lack of treatment, as evidenced by the controls. Studies comparing in vivo flooding with systematic desensitization have found them to be equally effective. Thus the procedure that the therapist chooses can be based on convenience, patient accessibility, and cost; we prefer to use participant modeling whenever possible.

Cognitive Therapy

Cognitive therapies are based on the assumption that thoughts and cognitions mediate phobic and nonphobic behavior. They assume that cognitions must change for therapy to be effective. Outcome research lends little support for the specific effectiveness of cognitive therapy approaches for simple phobia. Marshall (1985) had 20 height phobics expose themselves to various heights with or without coping self-statements; the former did better at 4 week follow-up. Emmelkamp and Felten (1985) had 19 height phobic volunteers undergo exposure with or without cognitive therapy: the group with cognitive therapy had less anxiety than exposure alone. Four other studies have found no benefit from cognitive therapy (Brian & Wilson, 1981; Ladouceur, 1983; Girodo & Roehl, 1978, Klepac et al., 1984).

Other Psychotherapy Interventions

Many other psychotherapy approaches have been used to treat simple phobias. Freud presented case reports of phobias resolved with
psychoanalysis and many other case reports of successful treatment
of phobias appear in the psychoanalytic literature. Yet, psychoanalysis and interpretive therapy in general is an expensive and tedious way to approach a problem successfully resolved by simpler
means. Reassurance, bibliotherapy, paradoxical, and other approaches may also be helpful with some patients.

Medication

With the possible exception of flying phobias, there is little need for
the use of medication to treat simple phobics. Occasionally some
patients are so afraid of encountering any aspect of the phobic object
or situation that they may benefit from a benzodiazepine used at the
time of exposure. Animal studies would suggest that benzodiazepines
might block the effect of treatment, but at least one study has shown
this not to be the case (Stern & Marks, 1973). The use of medication to
treat flying phobics will be described below.

EXAMPLES OF THE TREATMENT OF SPECIFIC SIMPLE
PHOBIAS

We have treated over a hundred simple phobics, both research subjects and patients requesting therapy. Generally, as mentioned, we
use a participant modeling procedure, although with some simple
phobics, this is not possible. Our experience permits us to present the
treatment in a very optimistic light. We explain to patients that we
prefer to use a rapid treatment, generally not lasting more than three
sessions, and describe the participant modeling approach, if applica-
ble. We use self-efficacy instruments to guide treatment. In general,
patients will undertake a task if their efficacy exceeds 70 (on a scale of
0 to 100) for the particular step on a hierarchy.

Many patients will engage in a feared activity after simple reassurance and a thoughtful discussion of the procedures. The overall
strategy of participant modeling is to help the patient overcome his
fear a small step at a time, using graded fearful stimuli and the
therapist's modeled bravery along with instruction, encouragement,
and social reinforcement for each step taken. A word of caution: in
our experience, excessive or premature performance demands can

undermine patient self-confidence and reinstate fears that may have been partially eliminated, or increase the intensity of untreated fears.

To avoid this possibility, the patient should be asked if he is unduly frightened at each step of the procedure. If the answer is yes, the procedure is slowed or additional response-induction aids are used until the patient is calm. The problem can be avoided by carefully constructing a hierarchy of small steps that eventually include carrying out the feared activity. The use of response-induction aids and modeling of each step are important to the treatment. Once the immediate fear has been conquered, the patient should be encouraged to practice encountering the feared object in many situations to ensure that generalization of fearlessness to situations without the therapist takes place (Ferguson, Taylor, & Wermuth, 1978). Some imagination may be necessary to identify appropriate response aids.

Animal Phobia

A straightforward participant modeling approach is effective with most small animal phobics, as illustrated by the following case of a spider phobic.

P.Q. is a 20-year-old white female who called the clinic requesting treatment for her spider phobia. She stated that she had suffered from a spider phobia for as long as she could remember. She avoided areas of her household where she thought spiders might live (like a shed in her backyard) and experienced anxiety when cleaning behind curtains, opening garbage cans, or reaching into dark places. These fears severely restricted her behavior. After obtaining a brief history, the therapist conducted her on a spider phobic behavioral-avoidance course. She was unable to touch a web, uncover a rock where a spider might be "hiding," put her hand in a dark space, back toward a spider web, or touch a live spider. She shrieked when a spider darted out from under a rock.

Following the baseline assessment, the therapist first modeled a step in the treatment and then asked the patient to do the same when she was ready. The procedure involved successful performance of the following steps: looking at a drawing of an abstract spider; looking at sketches of progressively larger, darker, and hairier spiders; looking at colored pictures of large, hairy, dark tropical spiders; holding a jar containing a dead spider; holding a dead spider; holding a dead spider; holding a jar containing a live spider; having the live spider released ten, five, and 2 feet from her; and touching the live spider. When the subject reported no discomfort with one step, the next step was undertaken. She was able to progress through all the steps except that she initially dropped the dead spider when it touched her hand. She waited for a minute, then held the dead spider and proceeded to progress through the other steps without difficulty.

Following this forty-four minute procedure, she was able to complete all five items on the course and to complete the course in less time than during baseline. She was instructed to go home and return with a live spider. She returned two hours later with a dead spider, stating that she had tried to catch several live ones but was unsuccessful in doing so. At six months follow-up, she said that she still didn't like spiders but was now able to clean her house and enter her shed and no longer felt impaired by her spider phobia.

Blood/Injury Phobia

The following case, taken from Ferguson, Taylor and Wermuth (1978)* illustrates the use of participant modeling to eliminate a needle phobia in a surgery patient.

A 23-year-old white woman with Hodgkin's disease was admitted to a surgery service for a diagnostic staging laparotomy. Although the surgeons had explained the necessity for the operation to her and had attempted to allay her fears, she cried, screamed, and pulled away when approached by anyone with a hypodermic needle. Despite several hours of pleading and exhortation by the house staff and nurses, she would not allow blood to be drawn or an intravenous catheter to be placed in her arm. Because of the patient's lack of cooperation, the operation was postponed indefinitely and psychiatric consultation requested.

The patient remembered being afraid of needles as a child and reacting to all injections by crying. At age 13 she lost consciousness during an allergic response to an injection of penicillin. Although at age 18 she was able to tolerate the drawing of blood during a miscarriage of her first pregnancy, at age 20 during her second delivery she became acutely hysterical when an intravenous catheter was inserted into her arm. The anesthesiologist responded by removing it immediately. The patient was able to undergo a series of allergy shots over a 20-week period at age 22, but when Hodgkin's disease was diagnosed six months before the present admission, she began to experience an extreme fear of needles. Although her initial lymph node biopsy was conducted under general anesthesia, the patient was so fearful of this procedure that the anesthesiologist started the intravenous administration of anesthetic after she was unconscious, and removed the intravenous catheter before she was awake.

The patient had no additional significant psychiatric symptoms. She appeared to be an energetic, intelligent, sensitive young woman with an isolated fear of hypodermic needles and intravenous equipment.

A therapist met the patient on the surgery ward and obtained a brief

---

*From J. M. Ferguson, C. B. Taylor, and B. Wermuth, "Brief Communication—A Rapid Behavioral Treatment for Needle Phobics," *Journal of Nervous and Mental Disease*, 166 (4), 294–298, © by Williams & Wilkins, 1978.

history of the present disorder. He ascertained that the patient desired a staging laparotomy and treatment for Hodgkin's disease. He briefly explained the process of desensitization to her and told her it would take approximately one hour, during which time she would be asked to touch and experiment with some of the intravenous equipment. She was told that after this hour she would feel more comfortable with these items.

A Mayo stand with packaged tubing, syringes, tape, needles, gauze squares, medication vials, and a tourniquet was placed in the patient's room along with an intravenous apparatus pole. The patient was asked to sit as close to the assembled medical equipment as she felt comfortable, a distance of about one meter. The therapist picked up the packaged materials one at a time, identified them, and handed them to the patient, each time pausing until she was comfortable touching the packages. The patient was asked to remove the articles from the packaging, which she did very slowly. She helped the therapist connect the intravenous tubing to a bottle and hang it from the intravenous administration pole. The therapist then put an unexposed needle on a syringe, held it for a moment, and handed it to the patient. She held the syringe and needle and looked at them until she felt comfortable. At this point the therapist removed the cover from the needle.

When she signaled that she was no longer anxious holding the syringe with the bared needle, the therapist touched the needle to his own skin and held the needle between his fingers. The patient was able to copy these actions and she progressed to rubbing the needle on her own arm and the back of her hand. The hypodermic needle was taped to the back of her arm and left there for her to experience the feeling of the needle touching her skin. The therapist put a needle on a second syringe and filled it with procaine. The patient held the medication-filled syringe until she felt comfortable. The therapist then injected the procaine into an orange and asked the patient to copy his actions. She was able to inject the orange several times without undue anxiety.

At this point the patient and the therapist interviewed a second patient who had an intravenous catheter in his arm. She asked him some questions about how it felt and then watched the therapist remove this catheter. She was then handed a tourniquet, which she handled until she was comfortable. After the tourniquet was applied to her arm, her veins were identified and touched by both the therapist and the patient. Her skin was cleansed with alcohol, and procaine was injected over a vein with a 25-gauge (tuberculine) needle. The patient was asked to look at the small needle as it remained in her skin and watch as it was removed. Finally a large intravenous catheter was inserted into her vein without objection while she looked away. She was asked to look at the catheter taped in place and watch while the tubing was connected to a bottle of 5 percent dextrose and water solution.

Approximately one hour was needed for the entire procedure. The patient and the therapist talked about the catheter being in place, and about the therapeutic need to experience the catheter and intravenous apparatus until she felt comfortable with them. She was encouraged to walk around the room with the intravenous catheter in place to increase her sense of mastery over her feared objects. After 1½ hours, the catheter was removed and the patient was scheduled for a staging laparotomy later in the week. On the day of the operation, the patient tolerated multiple blood drawings and the placement of several intravenous catheters and needles both before and after the operation without incident. The patient reported a sense of pride in her accomplishment and felt more relaxed in the hospital. She felt more positively about both the operation and her doctors than she did before the desensitization procedure.

The patient completed a course of radiation and chemotherapy and one year after her surgery there was no evidence of recurrence of her tumor. She reported that she still cringed during blood-drawing procedures, but that she tolerated it far better than before her desensitization. To test her self-report, she was taken to a surgery ward and an intravenous infusion was started through a butterfly needle. Her behavioral response to the procedure was to turn her head to the side, close her eyes, and wince. She reported very little anxiety. The intravenous line was left in her arm during the hour-long follow-up interview without incident. The patient was pleased with her "cure," and the therapist felt that her reaction to the procedure was well within the normal limits. In the year since treatment, she developed no new fears or other psychiatric symptoms.

Fear of Flying

Because graded exposure to flying is difficult (people can't leave the airplane during takeoff) we rely more on cognitive and phar-macologic treatment for these problems than with other phobias. The outline for the treatment we use in the clinic (the protocol was devel-oped by Gunnar Götestam and Chris Hayward) is as follows:

Session 1

The patient is given information about the nature of flying phobia, the effects of anxiety on physiology, and the importance of substitut-ing positive for negative thoughts when flying. Relaxation training is introduced.

Session 2–3

Detailed instruction and training in progressive relaxation is given and the patient is encouraged to practice two times daily. The patient begins learning to apply cognitive coping strategies to assess the reality of his or her fears and the situation on the plane, to control his or her thoughts, to pay attention to arousal without becoming over-whelmed by it, to learn to cope with negative thoughts and cogni-tions, and to reinforce him- or herself with positive self-statements for using adequate coping techniques.

Sessions 4–5

The patient learns cue-controlled relaxation. Words like "calm" and "control" are verbalized while the patient is concentrating on breathing, and simultaneously with the expiration. The therapist repeats the procedure five times, synchronously with breathing. The patient trains 15 more times while focusing attention on relaxation sensations for 60 seconds. Twenty more repetitions are made and this is repeated weekly for the entire treatment period. Early bodily signs of arousal and anxiety should be used as cues in the conditioned relaxation. Every night, the patient has to rehearse the procedure 20 times after relaxation.

Sessions 6–9

The patient applies differential relaxation skills in role-play situations. The therapist coaches the patient to use relaxation skills systematically and discusses tension experienced during the role play after it is completed.

The patient is instructed to use these skills when confronting stimuli evoking fear of flying. For instance, he or she may be instructed to go to the local airport, enter the terminal and the waiting area, and watch planes take off while relaxing and monitoring his thoughts before actually taking a practice flight.

We are fortunate in the San Francisco Bay Area in having a short flight between the San Jose and San Francisco airports. This flight can be used as a practice flight for phobic subjects as can the shuttle between New York and Boston, New York and Washington, and other short flights.

The airlines and the Airline Pilot Association offer treatment programs in some of the larger cities. USAIR, for instance, has developed a seven-week program involving relaxation training and ways of coping with fears. The course teaches basic aviation principles, familiarization with the cabin and cockpit, and sessions that deal with turbulence and other flying conditions. The program also includes visits to the control tower and radar room, more relaxation exercises and, finally, a one-hour graduation flight. The program claims a better than 90 percent success rate. The Women Pilots Association sponsors a seminar that uses a combination of education and cognitive intervention. We have referred several patients to this program who benefited from it. Relaxation procedures may also be useful (Haug et al., 1987).

An alternative approach to the fear of flying is to use medication. The following case treated by one of our therapists involved the use of alprazolam. We have used this medication with similar success in about 10 patients.

Joan is a 41-year-old assistant manager in a small electronics company. She requested treatment for fear of flying because her job situation demanded more flying. She reported always having had a fear of flying, although the fear had become considerably worse over the past five years, to the point that she did not fly at the expense of missing a close family friend's funeral and two business meetings on the East Coast. She also experienced severe discomfort with spiders and snakes but had no disability from these phobias. She did not have spontaneous panic attacks, but the thought of flying caused her to experience palpitations, hot flushes, sweating, and "bowel upheaval." On several occasions, she was forced to fly and experienced these symptoms throughout the flight, only experiencing relief when she drank three vodka martinis on the flight and when the plane landed. She experienced extreme discomfort as soon as she left for the airport, and was not able to differentiate among the various other components of flying as the anxiety remained intense unless reduced by the martinis. Given the choice between a behavioral treatment and pharmacology she chose the later.

She was instructed to take a trial dose of medication, alprazolam 0.5 mg, to determine how this would make her feel and, if the medication did not cause her to become too drowsy, to take 0.5 mg on the night before the flight, 0.5 mg one hour before the flight, and to take 0.5 mg with her to be used on the flight if necessary. She was instructed not to use alcohol on the night before or the day of the flight and not to drive herself to the airport if she had taken alprazolam. Following this regimen, she was able to go on her next scheduled flight with only moderate anxiety. She continued to use alprazolam on subsequent flights over the next year and no longer experienced panic attacks or avoided flying. She did not use the medication at other times.

Driving Phobia

We presented the treatment of a driving phobia in our chapter on agoraphobia. The same approach is used for patients who have driving phobias independent of panic disorder or panic attacks. Such uncomplicated patients do exceptionally well with exposure-based treatments.

Claustrophobia

Claustrophobia occurs as a simple phobia but is also very common with agoraphobics. The following case illustrates the treatment of a 50-year-old woman who developed claustrophobia following a car accident.

Michelle was well until about age 47 when her husband died of cancer. Following his death, she became extremely depressed and withdrawn but because of lack of finances was forced to begin working as a secretary. On her way to work one morning about one year after her husband's death, she was hit head-on by another car that swerved in front of her. The impact of the accident caused her head to break through the windshield and she lost consciousness. When she recovered, she remembers feeling blood all over her face and seeing a strand of her hair and scalp on the broken windshield. She was taken via ambulance to an emergency room and developed acute claustrophobia while she was being X-rayed. She wanted desperately to get up from the cart she was on and to flee the emergency room but was much too weak to move.

The claustrophobia worsened while she was in the hospital, and the first night of her hospitalization she had a horrifying dream just as she was falling asleep. The dream seemed to begin when she heard a "hissing sound" like air leaving a tire and then felt as though she were being drawn into a small tunnel behind her. She began to hyperventilate and needed to rush to the window for air. The dream continued every night while she was in the hospital, gradually reducing in frequency over the next few months.

On presentation to the clinic she was severely avoidant of most situations. She was experiencing five to seven panic attacks per week, and was also severely depressed. She was started on imipramine 25 mg/day but experienced a "paradoxical response," so her dose was dropped to 5 mg/day, which she was able to tolerate. Over the next few weeks the dose was gradually increased to a total of 50 mg/day. At that dose, she began to notice a reduction in the frequency of her panic attacks and dreams. She was then started on intensive exposure treatment, beginning with her entering a dark, narrow hallway. She did so with great trepidation and fear (an anxiety of 9 on a 0–10 scale) and was able to remain in the hallway for about one hour on two separate occasions. The next day she was instructed to enter a smaller, darker hallway, which she again did, this time with less fear. Of interest, she had a nightmare that night, but the tunnel in her nightmare was lit with bright lights and the experience was not as suffocating as it had been. The next day she was instructed to enter a small room (4 X 4) and to remain there with the door closed, which she also accomplished. She felt exhausted and irritable after these attempts and had the first panic attack she had experienced in almost two months. The attack was precipitated by realizing that no one had picked up her son from school. Although the attack occurred with her typical symptoms, she reported being much less bothered by it.

Other Phobias

The principles we have described apply equally to many other phobias. It often requires imagination to construct a hierarchy and actual practice situations for patients. For instance, in developing exposure for one *acrophobic* patient, part of his treatment involved climbing onto the third floor of the medical center, one of the highest accessible buildings close to our clinic. Procedures for treating *dental phobics* are well described by Kleinknecht and Bernstein (1979), for *sexual phobias* by Kaplan (1979, 1987), and for driving and height phobics by Williams & Rappoport (1983) and Williams et al. (1985).

The treatment of simple phobias is often very gratifying. Patients can frequently overcome their impairment, quickly, economically, and effectively and are very appreciative of the help.

ELEVEN

. . . .

Psychopharmacology

. . . .

Effective treatment of anxiety disorders often involves the use of medication alone or in combination with psychotherapeutic treatments. In previous chapters we have reviewed the effectiveness of many of these agents and discussed their use in therapy. The basic pharmacology of the commonly used agents will be presented in this chapter. The drug groups used to treat anxiety disorders include the tricyclic antidepressants (e.g., imipramine, desipramine), the monoamine oxidase inhibitors (e.g., phenelzine), other antidepressants (e.g., trazodone), the benzodiazepines (e.g., diazepam; alprazolam), the beta-blockers (e.g., propanolol), and the azaspirodecanediones (e.g., buspirone).

Alcohol is the earliest and probably still the most widely used drug with antianxiety properties. Sedative-hypnotics with antianxiety properties were widely used during the 19th century. For instance, it is estimated that by the 1870s a single hospital in London specialized in nervous diseases might dispense several tons of bromides annually. Barbiturates, first synthesized in 1864, began to be widely used in medicine after 1900. Meprobamate, originally developed as a potential muscle relaxant in the 1950s, achieved rapid popularity and was widely prescribed until its addictive properties became apparent. The discovery of the effectiveness of the benzodiazepines was serendipitously made by Sternbach in 1957 who, when cleaning up his laboratory, decided to screen a group of compounds he had syn-

A NOTE OF CAUTION: The actual choice of a drug and dose administered to a patient should be considered carefully, and no recommendation in this volume or from any other source should be accepted unreservedly. The authors have attempted to ensure the accuracy of doses and dose ranges in this volume. However, errors are possible, and before prescribing any medication, the physician should take appropriate precautions, including referral to other sources.

thesized many years before (Sternbach, 1983). One compound, 1,4 benzodiazepine chlordiazepoxide, was two to five times more potent than meprobamate in producing relaxation in rats. Since then several hundred benzodiazepine derivatives (BZD) have been synthesized. Because of their clinical effectiveness and their low potential for fatal overdosage, BZDs have largely replaced other sedative hypnotics. In the early 1960s Klein reported that the monoamine oxidase inhibitors (MAOIs) and tricyclic antidepressants (TCAs) blocked anxiety attacks in patients prone to anxiety, even in those who were not depressed. Drugs that block the peripheral manifestations of anxiety, like the beta-blockers, have been used in some patients. More recently, drugs that increase serotonin levels in the brain amongst other effects, the azaspirodecanediones, have shown promise as antianxiety agents.

THE BENZODIAZEPINES

The names, initial dose, and dose range of the available benzodiazepines can be seen in Table 11.1

TABLE 11.1

Benzodiazepines

Generic	Representative Brand	Initial Oral Dose (mg)	Usual Dose Range (mg/day)
Longer Half-Life			
Chlordiazepoxide	Librium	5–25	15–200
Clonazepam	Klonopin	0.5–1	1.5–10
Clorazepate	Tranxene	7.5–15	15–60
Diazepam	Valium	2–10	2–40
Flurazepam	Dalmane	15–30	15–90
Halazepam	Paxipam	20–60	20–160
Prazepam	Centrax	10–30	10–80
Shorter Half-Life			
Alprazolam	Xanax	0.25–1	1–6
Oxazepam	Serax	10–20	15–120
Temazepam	Restoril	15–30	15–90
Triazolam	Halcion	0.125–0.5	0.125–1

Biological Effects and Mechanisms

BZDs have five clinically useful pharmacological effects: anxiolytic, sedative-hypnotic, anticonvulsant, muscle relaxant, and amnestic. This latter effect accounts in part for their use as a preanesthetic medication and as an adjunct to such procedures as endoscopy or electroconvulsive therapy. Animal models for these clinical effects provide the means for identifying biologically active members of this class of drugs and help in elucidating their mechanisms of action.

BZDs exert their pharmacological effects by stereospecific binding to a BZD receptor, which is widely distributed throughout the central nervous system. This BZD receptor is an integral part of the GABA receptor-chloride iron channel complex that functions as a major inhibitory system in the brains of vertebrates. BZDs function synergistically with GABA to increase the movement of chloride ions through the neural cell membrane and thus inhibit the neuron.

Onset and Duration of Action

The onset and duration of action of BZDs is determined by both the physico-chemical attributes and the metabolism of each drug. The majority of drugs in this class are absorbed readily and appear in the blood shortly after an oral dose. The rate of absorption through the gastrointestinal mucosa is most rapid for the highly lipophilic compounds diazepam and clorazepate, which reach peak plasma concentrations within an hour. Temazepam and oxazepam are absorbed more slowly, reaching maximum plasma concentrations in 2–3 hours. Some benzodiazepines must be transformed to an active metabolite before they become biologically active. Prazepam is slowly converted to the active substance desmethyldiazepam, which reaches a peak plasma level 4–8 hours after oral administration. A similar but slightly more rapid conversion occurs with halazepam.

Three BZDs are currently available in parenteral form: diazepam, chlordiazepoxide, and lorazepam. Onset of action following an intravenous dose is very rapid (30 seconds to 2 minutes), as all benzodiazepines are sufficiently lipophilic to cross the blood brain barrier readily once they are in the blood. When given intramuscularly, lorazepam is the most rapidly and reliably absorbed. This is probably because it is relatively hydrophilic and potent and, thus, more soluble in the injection vehicle at the milligram doses required.

When given in a single dose, the more lipophilic compounds, such as diazepam, have a shorter duration of psychopharmacological activity than the less lipophilic compounds such as lorazepam. This is due to the more rapid redistribution of the drug out of the blood and brain and into peripheral adipose tissue. This accounts for the shorter effective half-life of diazepam than lorazepam, even though the former has a longer metabolic half-life. This effect of redistribution is most evident following a single dose and is less important with continuous dose regimens.

When repeated doses of BZDs are given, the rate of accumulation of drug and active metabolites to a steady state depends primarily on the metabolic half-life of the drug. It is useful to divide the BZDs into those with long versus those with short metabolic half lives. Triazolam is the shortest acting drug in this class, with a half-life of 2–3 hours. Oxazepam, temezepam, alprazolam, and lorazepam have relatively short half-lives (6–16 hours). The remaining compounds have longer metabolic half-lives (up to 4 days).

With repeated doses, the accumulation of compounds with long half-lives is extensive. Steady state is reached only after about 5 half-lives. The clinical significance of this accumulation has been a subject of controversy. There is some evidence for more frequent occurrence of drowsiness, confusion, and impaired performance with long-acting than with short-acting BZDs. However, many studies reveal minimal impairment and no consistent differences between the various compounds. Typically, if these side effects occur, they present early in treatment and gradually subside while anxiolytic effects persist. Nonetheless, the clinician should be aware of the danger of increasing side effects with the slowly metabolized drugs, particularly in the elderly and the chronically ill.

Metabolism

Benzodiazepines are metabolized and eliminated by one of two routes. They are either conjugated to a glucuronide and excreted by the kidneys, or they are oxidized by the hepatic microsomal system. This latter pathway can be impaired by many factors, including old age, liver disease, or concurrent administration of drugs such as estrogens, cimetidine, disulfiram, and isoniazid. Such impairment of metabolism has been shown to increase drug half-life and may cause increased side effects and toxicity.

Tolerance, Dependence Abuse, and Withdrawal

All benzodiazepines have potential for tolerance, abuse, dependence, and withdrawal reactions, but they are less hazardous in this regard than barbiturates or alcohol. Tolerance is the tendency for a fixed dose of drug repeated over time to produce a progressively decreased effect. This sometimes leads to escalation of dosage. Tolerance clearly develops to the sedation and psychomotor impairment produced by BZDs. It is probable that some tolerance also develops to their anxiolytic effect, but it is not of such magnitude that it abolishes the therapeutic benefits of usual doses given for three to six months. In some patients, tolerance to anxiolytic effects may be more marked and lead to dose escalation and abuse. Abuse, or excessive use compromising health or social functioning is a particular risk in patients with a history of other substance abuse. Rapidly absorbed compounds, such as diazepam, produce more euphoria and thus more risk for abuse.

Dependence implies the development of a psychological or physical need for continued use of a drug. In the therapeutic setting, this is usually made evident by the emergence of withdrawal symptoms or drug seeking behavior when an attempt is made to decrease or discontinue drug treatment. Dependence and withdrawal do occur with chronic use of benzodiazepines, but less commonly and less severly than with barbiturates or alcohol. Use in excess of recommended doses or concurrently with other sedatives increases risk of dependence and withdrawal. Long-term use is also associated with greater withdrawal reactions. One study found patients treated with usual doses for less than 8 months had a 5 percent incidence of the withdrawal syndrome, while those treated for more than 8 months had a 43 percent incidence.

Risk of withdrawal is related to drug half-life. Very short-acting and very long-acting drugs pose lower risks. Triazolam, with a half-life of about 3 hours, is difficult to take often enough to produce the continuous receptor saturation necessary to produce withdrawal on termination of use. Prazepam, flurazepam, and other long-acting BZDs are eliminated slowly enough that serum levels are naturally "tapered" upon discontinuance of drug. This prevents the sudden decrease in receptor occupancy that predisposes to more severe withdrawal. Compounds with intermediate half-lives, such as alprazolam, oxazepam, and temezepam, can be taken often enough to sustain steady-state blood and tissue levels, but once discontinued, are eliminated from the body rapidly. These drugs are most likely to cause severe reactions on abrupt discontinuance. However, sudden termination of long-acting benzodiazepines can also cause severe withdrawal. Thus, all chronic regimens of BZDs must be tapered at termination of treatment. For diazepam, a typical tapering regimen would be decreasing the dose by 5 mg every 3–4 days (or the equivalent dose of another BZD). Slower tapering is indicated if the patient develops symptoms suggestive of withdrawal on this regimen. This is most likely to occur with the last few dosage decrements. If medically necessary, the medication can be tapered more quickly, as long as the patient is carefully monitored for the development of serious withdrawal phenomena. BZD withdrawal symptoms may include insomnia, irritability, increased anxiety, panic attacks, gastrointestinal disturbances, palpitations, headaches, muscle pains, sensory changes, depersonalization, confusion, and even psychotic episodes and grand mal seizures. Withdrawal begins more rapidly after discontinuance of shorter acting drugs, but generally peaks within 2–5 days and gradually subsides over 7–12 days. Most patients experience withdrawal as subjectively distinct from their usual anxiety, but it is not always possible to distinguish between the two. Recrudesence of clinical anxiety more typically will show a gradual increase over several weeks, if it occurs, rather than the more rapid peak and gradual decrease of the withdrawal syndrome.

Adverse Effects and Toxicity

The most common side effect of BZD is drowsiness. At higher doses, psychomotor impairment or ataxia may occur. Sedation may be minimized by starting with low doses and gradually increasing to a level that produces the desired anti-anxiety effect. Patients should be cautioned against activities requiring alertness, judgment, or coordination (such as driving or operating machinery) during the initial phase of treatment or following dosage increments. Tolerance to sedation usually develops fairly soon after dosage adjustments. Dizziness, headache, muscle weakness, fatigue, dry mouth, nausea, skin rash and fever may also occur. Depression may develop in patients on BZDs, and discontinuation will sometimes restore the normal mood. Paradoxical excitement, aggression and blood dyscrasias have been reported rarely. Occasionally patients may experience a distressing anterograde amnesia. Lorazepam appears to be most likely to produce this side effect. BZDs are the least toxic of all psychopharmacologic agents in common use. When taken alone in overdose, they are almost never fatal. When taken in combination with alcohol or other CNS depressants, fatalities are much more common, but it is unclear how much BZDs contribute to this increased toxicity.

Precautions and Interactions

The risk to the fetus of maternal BZD use has not been clearly established. BZD use during the first trimester of pregnancy has been associated with an increased incidence of cleft lip and palate, although follow-up studies have not confirmed this finding. A neonatal abstinence syndrome has been reported in mothers who took chlordiazepoxides in the last trimester of pregnancy. BZDs should be avoided during pregnancy and lactation.

Sedation and confusion with BZDs may be more pronounced in the elderly and in patients with organic brain disease. Thus treatment must be monitored more carefully in these patients. The clinician must be particularly alert for cumulative effects on chronic dose regimens.

Benzodiazepines do not significantly affect respiratory drive in patients with normal respiratory function, but they can occasionally cause serious respiratory depression in patients with COPD, sleep apnea, or other disorders of respiration. They should be used with caution in these patients or avoided altogether if respiratory dysfunction is severe.

Since lorazepam, oxazepam, and triazolam are eliminated by glucuronide formation, they are recommended for use in older patients, those with liver disease, and patients taking estrogens, cimetidine, disulfiram, or isoniazid. Diazepam must be used with caution in patients taking phenytoin or digoxin, as it may increase serum levels of these drugs. Antacids may impede absorption of oral benzodiazepines. Patients with renal disease can be treated with reduced doses if followed carefully for toxicity. BZDs may have added sedative effects in patients receiving other CNS depressants. Thus they should be used with caution in patients taking opiates, tricyclic antidepressants, antipsychotics, antihistamines, barbiturates, alcohol, or other sedatives.

Comparative Use

Although there are clear differences in milligram potency of the various benzodiazepines, there is no consistent evidence for any difference in anxiolytic potency among these agents (Maletsky, 1980). Alprazolam is effective in reducing the intensity and frequency of panic attacks. Other BZDs may also reduce panic attacks.

Alprazolam, like triazolam, is a benzodiazepine that contains a triazole ring. Alprazolam may be unique among the BZDs in having significant antidepressant actions. Alprazolam has pharmacological properties in animal models that are similar to traditional antidepressants. Clinical studies of the antidepressant efficacy of alprazolam, however, have produced mixed results and clarification of its role in the treatment of depression awaits further studies.

In some clinical situations, such as acute anxiety or preanesthesia, a rapid onset of action is desirable. This is best achieved with diazepam or chlorazepate. With patients at risk for substance abuse, however, rapid onset may be experienced as a "rush" or "high" and increase the abuse potential of the drug. When these patients need intermittent or continuous BZD treatment, a drug with a slow onset of action, such as prazepam, is recommended.

ANTIDEPRESSANTS

The Tricyclics

Chemistry

The tricyclic antidepressants (TCAs) are so named because of their chemical structure, which includes three three cylic rings. See Table 11.2 for initial and usual dose ranges.

TABLE 11.2

Antidepressants

Generic	Representative Brand	Initial Oral Dose (mg)	Usual Dose Range (mg/day)
Tricyclics			
Amitriptyline	Elavil, Endep	25–50	50–300
Desipramine	Norpramin, Pertofane	25–50	25–250
Doxepin	Adapin, Sinequan	25–75	75–150
Imipramine	Janimine, Sk-Pramine Tofranil	25–50	10–300
Nortriptyline	Aventyl, Pamelor	10–25	25–100
Protriptyline	Vivactil	10–20	20–60
Trimipramine	Surmontil	25–75	50–150
Non-Tricyclics			
Amoxapine	Ascendin	50–150	50–400
Maprotiline	Ludiomil	25–75	25–225
Trazodone	Desyrel	50–150	50–400
Monoamine Oxidase Inhibitors			
Isocarboxazid	Marplan	10–20	10–70
Phenelzine	Nardil	15–30	15–90
Tranylcypromine	Parnate	10–20	20–60

Biological Effects and Mechanisms

TCAs potentiate the action of biogenic amines (like dopamine) in the CNS by blocking the reuptake of these amines by the nerve terminals. The reuptake of biogenic amines is a major means of physiological inactivation, so by blocking this uptake, the TCAs increase the availability of amines at nerve terminals. Until recently, it was hypothesized that depression resulted from decreased availability of these amines, so that agents that increased amines resulted in lessened depression. But it is now apparent that the action of TCAs is complicated. Some TCAs are unable to potentiate the effects of biogenic amines, yet are effective antidepressants. Other agents that are potent inhibitors of amine uptake, notably amphetamine and cocaine, are poor antidepressants. Furthermore, some TCAs affect the reuptake of serotonin, while others have a greater effect on norepinephrine. TCAs also have strong anticholinergic effects manifest in blurred vision, dry mouth, constipation, and urinary retention.

Onset and Duration of Action

Imipramine and other tricyclic antidepressants are well absorbed after oral administration. They are lipophilic and strongly bound to plasma protein. Their relatively long half-lives permit a gradual transition toward a single daily dose given at bedtime. However, because of side effects, they are usually initially given in divided doses. The anticholinergic effects of some of the TCAs can slow gastrointestinal activity and gastric emptying time, resulting in slower or erratic absorption of these or other drugs taken concomitantly. This effect can complicate the management of acute overdosage. Concentrations in plasma typically peak within 2 to 8 hours. TCAs usually require two to three weeks to exert a therapeutic effects.

Metabolism

The TCAs are oxidized by hepatic microsomal enzymes, followed by conjugation with glucuronic acid. Imipramine is metabolized to desipramine, but it is not clear if the latter accounts for the activity of imipramine. Recently, there has been an attempt to relate the serum levels of these drugs to clinical response or toxicity. The half-lives of TCAs range from about 10–20 hours for imipramine to 80 hours for protriptyline. Therefore, most TCAs should be inactivated and excreted within a week after termination of treatment, except for protriptyline and overdosage. Cardiac arrhythmias have been reported for 20 days or longer following the acute intoxication with large doses of TCAs.

Tolerance, Dependence Abuse, and Withdrawal

Tolerance to the anticholinergic effects of TCAs tends to develop with continued use of the drug. Orthostatic hypotension may also occur initially. Patients rarely increase the use of the TCAs unless asked to do so by their physicians; more often patients are inclined to use less than prescribed. A withdrawal syndrome consisting of malaise, chills, coryza, and muscle aches has been reported to follow abrupt discontinuation of high doses of imipramine. The syndrome seems to occur if doses above 150 mg daily have been used for more than two months (Shatan, 1966). Other withdrawal reactions include gastrointestinal distress; sleep disturbance with initial and middle insomnia; and vivid, often terrifying, dreams, anxiety, agitation, jitteriness, and hypomania (Lawrence, 1985). Other TCAs probably produce the same effect and they should be withdrawn slowly at a rate of 10–25 percent every 3 or 4 days.

Adverse Effects and Toxicity

Adverse effects, particularly those related to anticholinergic activity, are common with TCAs. These side effects include: dry mouth, a sour or metallic taste, epigastric distress, constipation, dizziness, tachycardia, palpitations, blurred vision, urinary retention, cramps, edema, drowsiness, confusion, muscle tremor, excessive sweating, twitching, convulsions, dysarthria, paresthesias, peroneal palsies, sudden falls, ataxia, orthostatic hypotension, and weight gain. A fine tremor occurs in about 10 percent of patients receiving a tricyclic agent.

Imipramine, even at low doses, produces a paradoxical reaction in some patients with panic attacks. The following case describes this syndrome:

Sandy is a 34-year-old female with a four year history of panic attacks and agoraphobia. She was begun on imipramine 25 mg at bedtime. The following morning she felt anxious and irritable, "hyper" and restless. On physical examination she appeared flushed, was sweating profusely, and was tachycardic. She said the feeling was different from the anxiety she normally experienced. The dose was cut back to 10 mg yet she again experienced the same reaction. The dose was cut back to 5 mg, and she still had the same reaction. Finally, the dose was cut to about 2 mg which she was able to take with only mild discomfort. Even at that dose, she said that she felt her panic attacks were being partially blocked. Her dose was increased by about 5 mg a week to 25 mg, at which point she was panic attack free.

TCAs can create serious problems. Men with prostatic hypertrophy may develop acute urinary retention. The dizziness and orthostatic hypotension can lead to falls, particularly in the elderly. TCAs can precipitate narrow-angle type of glaucoma which, if left untreated, can result in loss of vision. TCAs can also cause jaundice, agranulocytosis, rashes, and orgasmic impotence.

A more common risk, particularly in patients with anxiety disorders, involves cardiovascular events. The cardiovascular effects of TCAs include: (1) increase in heart rate, (2) prolonged atrio-ventricular (A-V) conduction time, (3) orthostatic hypotension. These effects are manifest in the ECG by increased heart rate, increased QRS, PR interval and QTc interval, and nonspecific ST and T wave changes. The first effect is probably related to the anticholinergic effects of the drugs. TCAs routinely produce heart-rate increases of from 0–30 bpm.

Vhora et al., (1975) did not find correlations between serum levels and heart-rate changes; the heart-rate changes should be proportionate to anticholinergic effects of the drugs. Many patients are aware of the increased heart rate but rarely complain that it is bothersome to them. The long-term effects of the increased heart rate are not known. The Framingham longitudinal study of cardiovascular risk factors has established that higher heart rates are associated with increased risk of heart disease. However, it is generally assumed that the higher heart rates reflect individuals in poorer physical condition and that the lack of physical activity leading to the poor physical condition is the actual risk.

The second effect, decreased conduction, in the PR and HV interval reflecting decreased A-V conduction, is a potentially lethal effect. Vohra et al. (1975) found that TCAs prolong conduction in the His-Purkinje system and that this effect might be dangerous in patients with impaired ventricular conduction. These drugs should, therefore, be given with caution in patients with intraventricular conduction disturbance or A-V block as evidenced by prolonged QT or QRS intervals.

These effects do not per se preclude the use of TCAs in patients with preexisting cardiovascular disease. However, some studies have found a greater than expected sudden unexpected death rate in patients with cardiac disease taking amitriptyline (Moir et al., 1972). On follow-up, only patients over 70 were at increased risk, an effect evident only during the first six months of follow-up (Moir et al.,

1973). The Boston Collaborative Drug Surveillance Program reported on 80 patients with cardiovascular disease treated with TCAs compared to 3,994 cardiac patients not receiving TCAs. There was no difference between the two groups in the occurrence of arrhythmias, other cardiovascular complications, or death (Boston Collaborative Drug Surveillance Program, 1972).

Overall, TCAs can be safely used in most patients with cardiovascular disease. A cardiologic consultation should be obtained before prescribing TCAs in patients with preexisting A-V block, intraventricular conduction delay, or prolongation of ventricular repolarization. Such patients have, for instance, widened PR, QRS, or QT intervals (Hayward et al., 1987). The drugs should be used cautiously in older patients and, of course, suicidal patients should not be given potentially lethal quantities of pills. Baseline and serial ECGs can be used to monitor cardiovascular patients on TCAs.

Acute poisoning with TCAs is life-threatening and common. One regional center for treatment of drug overdoses reported that 10 percent of the 2,104 admissions in 1973 were attributed to TCAs (Newton, 1975). Deaths have been reported with doses of approximately 2,000 mg of imipramine (or the equivalent dosage of another drug), and severe intoxication can be expected at doses above 1,000 mg. Acutely depressed patients should not be given a lethal supply of imipramine; depression and suicidal tendencies must be frequently assessed in patients given these medications.

Drug Interactions

The effects of TCAs are potentiated by drugs that compete with binding to albumin like phenytoin, phenylbutazone, aspirin, scopolamine, and phenothiazines. TCA effects are also potentiated by drugs that interfere with their metabolism in the liver. This effect has been associated with neuroleptic drugs, methylphenidate, and certain steroids, including oral contraceptives. Lower doses of imipramine may be necessary in patients taking methylphenidate. Other drugs like barbiturates and certain other sedatives can increase the hepatic metabolism of the antidepressants by inducing microsomal enzyme systems. TCAs interact with a variety of other drugs, as listed in Table 11.3

Of particular note, antidepressants potentiate the effects of alcohol and other sedatives. The anticholinergic effects of TCAs are additive to those of other drugs. A particularly severe interaction has been reported following the concurrent administration of an MAO inhiband a TCA (Anath & Luchins, 1977). The resultant syndrome included severe CNS toxicity marked by hyperpyrexia, convulsions, and coma.

TABLE 11.3

TCA Interactions with Other Drugs

Drug	Effect
Alcohol	Increased effects
Anticholinergic	Combined effects
Biogenic amines (e.g., norepinephrine)	Potentiate—serious effect
Clonidine	May block central anti-hypertensive effect
CNS depressants	Increase effects
Guanethidine	May block effects
MAO inhibitors	Potentiate—serious effect

TCAs potentiate norepinephrine. Therefore, this drug should be given cautiously.

Treatment of Side Effects

The anticholinergic side effects are common with TCAs and can often be ameliorated. Some patients with dry mouth like to chew sugarless gum to increase saliva flow. Cholinergic drugs like oral pilocarpine or bethanechol chloride (Urecholine®) have been used in extreme cases. Similarly, pilocarpine or other local cholinergic agents can be used to ameliorate loss of visual accomodation (patients complain of blurred vision while reading). Constipation can be treated with water-retaining laxatives such as milk of magnesia, although patients should be advised not to use them in excess. Urinary retention occurs mostly frequently in men over 40, probably because subclinical prostate enlargement interacts with the anticholinergic effect on the urinary bladder detrusor muscle. Bethanechol chloride can be helpful with urinary retention or hesitancy; urologic consultation should be obtained in such cases. The drug should be stopped if there is more than mild difficulty urinating. We have found that some patients can restart the drug at a lower dose without difficulty and even be slowly increased back to the original dose without further difficulty.

Comparative Use

Of the many TCAs, imipramine has been most extensively studied in the treatment of panic disorder and agoraphobia. It is effective in

298 THE NATURE AND TREATMENT OF ANXIETY DISORDERS

reducing the frequency and intensity of panic attacks, facilitates exposure to feared situations, reduces anticipatory anxiety and depression. It has less effect on trait anxiety. The effects of other TCAs have been less intensively investigated but none seems superior to imipramine. There is limited evidence suggesting that desipramine (Rifkin et al., 1981), nortriptyline (Muskin & Fyer, 1981), maprotiline (Sheehan, 1982), doxepin (Lydiard & Ballenger, in press), and amitriptyline are all clinically effective and useful. Trazodone has been shown to be less effective than imipramine (Charney et al., 1986). Based on known effectiveness data, imipramine should be the first choice, followed by desipramine. Chlomipramine, an effective 5-HT reuptake inhibitor not approved for use in the U.S., has been shown to be effective in reducing panic attacks in several open and in three placebo-controlled trials (Escobar & Landbloom, 1976; Karabanow, 1977; Amin et al., 1977).

Cost should only be considered in choosing between agents when they are considered equal on other factors. Table 11.4 shows the average monthly cost for the antidepressants with some proven antipanic efficacy. The monthly cost was determined by multiplying the average daily dose with the lowest cost per milligram (Jurman & Davis, 1987). Furthermore, wholesale generic costs may be 1/10 those of brand costs. In fact, wholesale monthly drug costs for the average panic patient on generic imipramine can be less than $10.

TABLE 11.4

Cost of Antidepressants per Month

Drug Monthly	Brand	Cost/50mg	Average Daily Dose	Average Cost
Amitriptyline	Elavil	.007	150	$31.50
	Endep	.005	150	$22.50
Imipramine	Tofranil	.007	150	$31.50
Desipramine	Norpramin	.008	150	$33.90
	Pertofane	.006	150	$27.00
Doxepin	Adapin	.005	225	$33.80
	Sinequan	.008	225	$54.00
Maprotiline	Ludiomil	.008	125	$30.00
Nortriptyline	Pamelor	.009	150	$40.50
Trazodone	Desyrel	.006	300	$54.00

SOURCE: Adapted from "The Cost of Psychotropic Medication" by R. J. Jurman and J. M. Davis, 1987, *Psychiatric Annals*, 17, 173–177.

Side Effects and Patient Tolerance

Several reviews have reported that as many as 50 percent of patients refuse to take imipramine because of intolerable side effects (Aronson, 1987). Although these side effects can be minimized by reducing the dosage or using other medications concurrently, side effects are a significant problem with these drugs. Doxepin is reported to be less cardiotoxic than the others, but this is controversial. Patients showing intolerance to the anticholinergic side effects of imipramine might be switched to a TCA with lower effects.

MAO Inhibitors

The other group of antidepressants with significant antipanic effect are the MAO inhibitors. The monoamine oxidase (MAO) inhibitors comprise a heterogeneous group of drugs, which, as the name implies, block the enzyme monoamine oxidase. MAO inhibitors were first used to treat tuberculosis. Because the drugs seemed to have mood-elevating effects in tuberculosis patients, they were given to depressed psychiatric patients with favorable results. Klein (1964) was the first to report on their effect on reducing anxiety episodes in patients who would now be classified as having panic disorders.

There are only three MAO inhibitors now available, tranylcypromine, phenelzine, and isocarboxazid. The chemistry of the three drugs is quite different, although all inhibit MAO.

The antidepressant effects of MAO inhibitors are assumed to reflect the increased availability of one or more monoamines in the CNS or sympathetic nervous system. MAO is widely distributed throughout the body, although its important biological effects relate to its action within the mitrochondria. Norepinephrine and epinephrine released within the nerve terminal are deactivated by MAO; norepinephrine and epinephrine in other sites are largely unaffected by MAO inhibitors. MAO is also involved in serotonin degradation. Inhibition of MAO leads to increased effects mainly on organ systems influenced by sympathomimetic amines and serotonin.

MAO inhibitors are effective suppressors of REM sleep and they are effective antidepressants. They lower blood pressure and provide symptomatic relief in angina pectoris but are no longer used for these purposes.

All MAO inhibtors are readily absorbed when given by mouth. Maximal inhibition of MAO is usually achieved within 5 to 10 days, although the antidepressant effect may be delayed 2–3 weeks.

The hydrazine MAO inhibitors (phenelzine) are cleaved and are inactived by acetylation. Many people are "slow acetylators" of the hydrazine-type drugs and this may explain the exaggerated effects observed in some patients given conventional doses of phenelzine.

Patients do not develop tolerance for these drugs or dependence on them. However, increased anxiety, frontal headache, shivering, muscle weakness, paresthesias, tremulousness, and nightmares have been reported on discontinuation of phenelzine (Lawrence, 1985). The drugs should probably be discontinued at the rate of 10–25 percent every 3 or 4 days.

The MAO inhibitors are potentially very toxic agents. They can cause cellular damage to the hepatic parenchyma, an effect not related to dosage or duration of therapy. They can also cause excessive central stimulation, including convulsions. Orthostatic hypotension occurs with the use of all MAO inhibitors. One of the most serious adverse effects is related to the effect of MAO inhibitors in prolonging and intensifying the effects of other drugs and interfering with the metabolism of various naturally occurring substances.

The administration of precursors of biogenic amines may cause marked effects. Thus, the administration of levodopa or serotonin can be expected to produce agitation and hypertension. A hypertensive crisis, sometimes lethal, can result from MAOI interacting with other drugs. Foods containing tyramine and other monoamines are particularly dangerous. Presumably, tyramine and other monoamines in food, or produced by bacteria in the gut, enter the blood stream and are not metabolized in the liver due to the inhibition of hepatic MAO. They then release catecholamines that are present in supranormal amounts in nerve endings and the adrenal medulla, and the catecholamines cause the hypertensive crisis. Foods implicated in this syndrome include: natural or aged cheeses, beer, wine, pickled herring, snails, chicken liver, yeast, large quantities of coffee, citrus fruits, canned figs, broad beans, and chocolate and cream or their products (see Table 11.5). The tyramine effects are additive. A meal containing Stilton cheese, beer, and chicken liver combines the tyramine content of all three foods. Patients on MAOI need to be given lists of foods to avoid. Furthermore, because of the widespread effects on drug metabolism, patients on MAO inhibitors should be told not to use any other medications without permission.

Side effects from the MAOIs are similar to those of the antidepressants and the same approach can be taken. Patients should be told to call their physician at the first sign of a severe throbbing headache or to go to the emergency room if their physician is not immediately available to have their blood pressure monitored. Antiadrenergic drugs (e.g., phentolamine) can be used to reduce the blood pressure in a hypertensive crisis. Klein et al. (1980) report that these episodes last 1–3 hours. The cause of the increased hypertension must be as-

TABLE 11.5

Tyramine Concentrations of Various Foods

Foods and drinks		Tyramine (micrograms/gram)
Cheeses	Cheddar (U.S.)	1416
	Gruyere	516
	Stilton	466
	Emmenthal	225
	Brie	180
	Camembert	86
Dairy Products		
	Cream	<1
	Yogurt	<1
Beer		2–5
Wine	Chianti	25
	Sherry	4
	Riesling	1
	Sauterne	<1
	Port	<1

SOURCE: Adapted from "Monoamine Oxidase Inhibitors, Tyramine, and Cheese" by D. Horwitz, W. Lovenberg, K. Engelman, and A. Sjoerdsma, 1964, *Journal of the American Medical Association*, 188 (3), 1108–1110. Copyright 1964, American Medical Association.

certained. If the patient has forgotten and eaten a food that needs to be avoided, the MAOI can be restarted the next day. However, if the patient is not able to be compliant, the MAOI should be stopped.

The orthostatic hypotension frequently occurs early in treatment and can be managed with temporary dose reductions. Mineralcorticoids have been used to treat postural hypotension in patients taking MAOIs.

A number of authors have recommended the use of MAOIs and TCAs in patients with refractory depression. However, several authors have reported episodes of toxicity and death attributed to the combination. Klein et al. (1980) estimate that toxic interaction between MAOIs and TCAs is rare but that the drugs can be used in combination, with the exception of tranylcypromine and impiramine since toxic reactions are said to be more common when the combination includes either of these drugs. If TCAs and MAOIs are used in combination, Zisook (1985) recommends that the two drugs be started simultaneously (never give a TCA to a patient already on an MAOI without a drug free interval of at least two weeks). Initiate treatment at lower starting dosages of both agents and maintain doses below the upper therapeutic limits of either drug alone. Blood pressure and pulse readings should be obtained at least weekly for the first several weeks and whenever increases in the medications occur.

Drugs that should be avoided in patients treated with MAOIs include: amphetamine-like drugs, sympathomimetic drugs, some analgesics (e.g., meperidine and aspirin), barbiturates, methyldopa, ganglionic blocking agents, procaine and other anesthetic agents, chloral hydrate, dopamine, and norepinephrine.

The three available MAOIs appear to be equally effective for reducing panic and anxiety, but the most information is available on phenelzine. Jurman and Davis (1987) estimate that the average monthly cost for Parnate (tranylcypromine) of 40 mg/day is $23.36 compared to $29.70 for the monthly costs of 45 mg/day of Nardil (phenelzine). Toxicity and lethality are similar. Enzyme inhibition by tranylcypromine is reversed much more rapidly than the hydrazines or pargyline, so that another medication can be started sooner with patients on this drug.

Of the MAOIs, phenelzine has been most widely studied in anxiety disorders and is our drug of first choice on the basis of familarity. A variety of nontricyclic (and non-MAOI) antidepressants are now available. Although these drugs have the potential to be effective anti-anxiety agents, they have not been widely evaluated.

AZASPIRODECANEDIONES

Another group of drugs with quite different structures and pharmacologic effects than benzodiazepines have shown some promise in reducing anxiety. These agents offer the advantage of a low abuse potential and cause little psychomotor impairment. The most widely studied agent is called buspirone, a lipophilic, heterocyclic compound. These agents may offer some clinical advantages to the benzodiazepines, and the fact that they do not bind to benzodiazepine sites nor block GABA reuptake makes them of great theoretical interest, since the latter two effects are considered central to the anxiolytic effect of the benzodiazepines. Buspirone does not have hypnotic, anticonvulsant, or muscle relaxant properties.

The mechanism by which buspirone exerts its anxiolytic effect is unknown but appears to involve complex interactions among various central nervous system transmitters. It does not bind to benzodiazepine receptors or inhibit benzodiazepine binding in vitro (Eison & Temple, 1986). It also does not effect GABA binding or uptake. Also, in contrast to benzodiazepines, it increases noradrenergic metabolism, possible through noradrenergic receptor blockage. Some studies suggest that buspirone has a significant effect on serotonin neurotransmission. Buspirone binds with high affinity to serotonin receptors in the calf hippocampus. However, one study found that concentrations of serotonin and its major metabolite, 5-hydroxy-indole acetic acid (5-HIAA), were either decreased or unaffected by buspirone (Eison & Temple, 1986).

Unlike the benzodiazepines, buspirone does not appear to impair psychomotor skills. For instance, body sway and reactive and coordinative skills remained unaffected by doses 20 mg of buspirone (Mattilla et al., 1982). Buspirone combined with alcohol had no greater effects on psychomotor performance than alcohol alone, while lorazepam (a benzodiazepine) combined with alcohol severely impaired psychomotor performance. Interestingly, in this study buspirone was associated with greater reported sedation than lorazepam, although generally buspirone has been found to have less sedative effects than the benzodiazepines. Other studies have noted the paradox that subjects on buspirone may feel worse, even though their actual performance has not changed. In contrast, patients on benzodiazepines feel they are doing better on tasks despite objective evidence of impairment. The opposite effect on actual versus perceived impairment seen with buspirone compared to benzodiazepines may have important safety implications, particularly for subjects who might drink and drive while using an anxiolytic, i.e., buspirone would appear to be a much safer agent with such people.

Buspirone is well absorbed after oral administration and rapidly metabolized. "First pass" metabolism reduces the bioavailability of buspirone to less than 10 percent. It has a half-life of 2–11 hours, with a mean value of 2.4 hours in some studies (Mayol et al., 1985). Taking buspirone with food appears to reduce the rate of absorption, but it also appears to decrease the extent of "first pass" metabolism.

Buspirone does not have an effect in animals that is associated with abuse and physical dependence. In rhesus monkeys, buspirone did not substitute for cocaine. In drug discrimination studies in rats, it failed to act as a strong detectable cue, and in animals trained to discriminate, buspirone did not generalize to either pentobarbital or oxazepam. It also did not substitute for barbiturates after their chronic administration, evoke signs of dependence upon withdrawal following chronic administration, or signs of dependence upon precipitated withdrawal. The mean "street value" ratings assigned by users were $3.50 for methaqualone; $1.94 for diazepam (20 mg);

$0.68 for diazepam (10 mg), $0.24 for buspirone (10 mg), and $0.23 for placebo (Eison & Temple, 1986). Its low popularity with recreational users suggests that it may not produce a "high."

Buspirone has relatively few side effects. Compared to placebo, it seems to produce more nervousness, excitement, diarrhea, dizziness, light-headedness, paresthesias, headache, and sweating/clamminess. Compared to diazepam, buspirone produces much less drowsiness and fatigue but more tachycardia/palpitations, nervousness, nausea and diarrhea, and paresthesias. A composite suggests the following profile: dizziness (12 percent), nausea (8 percent), headache (6 percent), nervousness (5 percent), lightheadedness (3 percent), and excitement (2 percent). These side effects are generally mild; the mechanism for them is unknown.

Because buspirone can bind to central dopamine receptors, it has the potential to cause acute and chronic changes in dopamine-mediated neurological function. While this effect is unlikely, the long-term sequelae will become more apparent as the drugs gain wider and longer use. Toxicology studies of buspirone yielded lethal doses of 160–550 times the recommended human daily dose. Fatal overdoses have not been reported.

Buspirone in the therapeutic range does not appear to potentiate the sedative effect of CNS depressants. Buspirone increases haloperidol serum levels and should not be given concomitantly with this drug. One report suggested that the concomitant use of trazodone and buspirone may have caused 3- to 6-fold elevations of SGPT in a few patients. It is probably too early in the use of buspirone to be certain of drug interactions.

Little information is available on the comparative effects of these drugs, a number of which are now being investigated in clinical trials.

BETA-ADRENERGIC BLOCKING DRUGS

Beta-adrenergic blocking drugs have the effect of blocking the peripheral effects of the sympathetic nervous system. They have limited clinical usefulness for treating anxiety disorders (Noyes et al., 1984). However, some patients who are particularly bothered by peripheral anxiety symptoms, like tachycardia, may benefit from the concomitant use of beta-adrenergic blockers and other panic medications. Beta-adrenergic blockers are widely used to treat hypertension, angina pectoris, cardiac arrhythmias, migrane, hypertrophic subaortic stenosis, and pheochromocytoma, and reducing the risk of mortality in survivors of myocardial infarction. Because these agents have limited usefulness in treating anxiety disorder patients, only a few comments about other aspects of their pharmacology will be presented here.

As their name implies, beta-blockers block beta receptors, those responsible for effecting autonomic nervous system activity. There are two types of beta receptors; beta 1, which cause cardiac stimulation and fatty acid mobilization, and beta 2, which produce bronchodilation, vasodilation, decreased motility of the stomach and intestine, contraction of the spleen, glyconeogensis, increased insulin secretion, and other activities. B-blocking agents are partly classified on the basis of whether they are nonselective: i.e., they block both beta receptors; or cardioselective, i.e., they block beta 1 receptors.

Propanolol, is one of the earliest and still most widely used nonselective beta blockers—in fact, propanolol is one of the most widely prescribed of any drug. Propanolol decreases heart rate and cardiac output, prolongs mechanical systole, and slightly decreases blood pressure in resting subjects. Total coronary blood flow and myocardial oxygen consumption are also decreased as a result of these effects. As mentioned, propanolol is an effective antihypertensive agent, and it modifies carbohydrate and fat metabolism. It should not affect sweating or muscle tension. In addition, propanolol crosses the blood-brain barrier and produces a number of CNS effects. Fatigue, drowsiness, and depression are common side effects in people taking propanolol.

A withdrawal syndrome has been observed with patients stopping beta-adrenergic blocking agents. This syndrome is presumably due to supersensitivity of the beta-adrenergic receptor; the supersensitivity represents an accommodation to the blocked effect. Some patients may experience a severe exacerbation of anginal attacks. Myocardial infraction has occurred, and rebound hypertension may be life-threatening. Premonitory signs and symptoms, such as nervousness, sweating, and tachycardia may be interpreted as anxious symptoms. Patients should not decrease these medications on their own, and if therapy is stopped, it should be done gradually. These medications can cause bronchoconstriction and augment the hypoglycemic effect of insulin.

The cardioselective beta-blockers include atenolol, metoprolol, and practolol. Like the nonselective beta-blockers, they are effective anti-hypertensive agents, although this effect is mediated through reduction in cardiac output and through other effects on the heart as well as through reductions in plasma renin activity.

CENTRAL ADRENERGIC AGONISTS

Another group of theoretical importance in treating anxiety are central adrenergic agonists. On the assumption that central noradrenergic activity is increased, agents that reduce central noradrenergic activity should have antianxiety effects. One agent that has been evaluated for its antianxiety effects is clonidine, which reduces central sympathetic activity through potent agonistic activity on alpha-2 presynaptic receptors in the CNS. Clonidine has been found to be effective in the treatment of panic attacks (Liebowitz et al., 1981), anxiety experienced during opiate withdrawal, and anxiety accompanying depression (Uhde et al., 1984).

OTHER SEDATIVES

The benzodiazepines, antidepressants, and azaspirodecanediones have largely replaced the once widely prescribed barbiturates and propanediols. Barbiturates and propanediols (meprobamate and tybamate) are less effective anxiolytics than BZDs, have considerably more addiction potential, and are lethal in overdosage. There is little justification for their use. Chloral hydrate is also effective for mild anxiety, but frequent use of this short-acting drug increases risk of dependence and toxicity. Antihistamines such as hydroxyzine and diphenhydramine may also have some anxiolytic value as a result of their sedative effect, particularly in anxiety-related skin conditions. There is little abuse potential, but side effects such as visual disturbances, dry mouth, and paradoxical excitement limit their usefulness.

ANTIPSYCHOTIC DRUGS

Antipsychotic medications, like thioridazine, chlorpromazine, haldol, and mesoridazine have been advocated for the treatment of anxiety. Indeed, such agents are effective in reducing anxiety in patients with psychotic disorders. However, autonomic and extrapyramidal side effects and the risk of tardive dyskinesia make them generally inappropriate for patients with primary anxiety disorders. Patients with coexistent schizophrenia and panic disorder may benefit from antipsychotic medication and antipanic medications. Borderline patients with coexisting anxiety disorders unresponsive to first-line medications may be candidates for low doses of sedating antipsychotics, such as mesoridazine.

ETHYL ALCOHOL

Alcohol is the oldest and most widely used antianxiety agent. Although it is not a recommended prescribed treatment, it is so widely used by patients to reduce anxiety that the clinician should be aware of some of its pharmacologic effects. Alcohol acts like other general anesthetics as a primary and continuous depressant of the CNS. However, because it depresses some inhibitory mechanisms, resulting in less restrained activity in other parts of the brain, it is often considered to have a stimulating effect.

Alcohol is rapidly absorbed from the stomach, small intestine, and colon. After absorption, it is rapidly distributed throughout all tissues and all fluids of the body. Alcohol is metabolized through oxidation. The rate of metabolism is roughly proportional to body weight and probably to liver weight. Many other factors, such as diet, hormones, drug interactions, and enzyme mass affect alcohol metabolism. Alcohol use is also associated with tolerance, physical dependence and can lead to a life-threatening withdrawal reaction.

NEW NONBENZODIAZEPINE ANXIOLYTICS

Benzodiazepines remain the mainstay of anxiolytic treatment. However, benzodiazepines probably produce their effects by facilitating GABA neurotransmission, and GABA is found in almost every brain region. Drugs that affect the neuronal systems specifically involved with anxiety might be effective anxiolytics without having the undesirable side effects of the benzodiazepines. A number of substances, chemically unrelated to the benzodiazepines, possess preclinical profiles suggestive of anxiolytic effects (Gershon and Eison, 1987). One of these groups, the azaspirodecanediones was discussed before. Others, not yet available for clinical purposes, offer some insight into anxiety mechanisms.

Pyrazolopyradines display anxiolytic-like activity in animal models. These drugs seem to enhance benzodiazepine binding, but they have other pharmacological effects. They produce little sedation and do not interact with other CNS depressants. *Imidazole Derivatives.* Fenobam, an imidazole derivative, possesses anti-anxiety activity without muscle relaxant or sedative-hypnotic activity. It does not interact with CNS depressants. In clinical trials, fenobam has been found to be as effective as diazepam. *Quinoline* derivatives selectively inhibit diazepam binding. Unlike the benzodiazepines, they increase punished responses but do not antagonize convulsants. They also have little sedative effect.

New anxiolytics will be developed with hopes of affecting the various neural systems involved with anxiety. As mentioned, several lines of evidence suggest a role of *serotonergic (5HT)* mechanisms in anxiety. Drugs like mianserin, an antidepressant that binds to 5HT receptors and antagonizes 5HT-mediated responses, appears to have anxiolytic properties. Chlorimipramine, a potent inhibitor of 5HT reuptake has been reported to be effective in reducing panic attacks (Ballenger, 1986). Zimelidine, a selective 5HT uptake inhibitor was reported effective in treating phobic anxiety. Drugs that alter *noradrenergic function* might also reduce anxiety. We mentioned that clonidine appears to have antipanic effects. Drugs that affect the dopaminergic system and the septohippocampal system might also prove to have specific anxiolytic properties.

Anxiety disorders are caused by different mechanisms, and in the future, drugs may be available that have specific effects on the mechanism involved for a particular individual. Such agents might offer the advantage of reducing anxious symptoms without having the disadvantage of affecting a variety of systems that may cause other unnecessary and perhaps dangerous side effects.

TWELVE

· · · · · · · ·

Medical Problems Associated with Anxiety Disorders

· · · · · · · · · ·

Medical problems can initiate, maintain, or exacerbate anxiety disorders. In chapter 3 we provided a quick overview of medical problems that cause symptoms similar to anxiety and some differential characteristics. In this chapter, we discuss the medical conditions in more detail. A medical history and physical examination can identify most medical problems seen with anxiety disorder patients. We make recommendations at the end of each section as to when more extensive work-up is indicated.

CARDIOVASCULAR DISORDERS

Mitral Valve Prolapse

Mitral valve prolapse (MVP) is a disorder in which a portion of the mitral valve billows into the left atrium of the heart when blood is being ejected (see Figure 12.1). It is a common condition, occurring in 4 to 10 percent of the adult general population. Psychological symptoms have long been associated with the physical findings of MVP. Da Costa (1871) described the syndrome of "irritable heart" in American

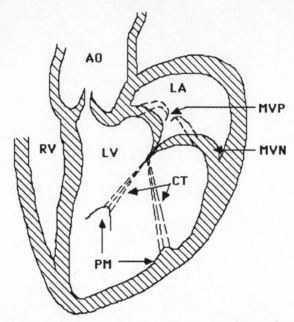

Figure 12.1 **Schematic Drawing of Mitral Valve Prolapse**

Solid lines show normal mitral valve; broken lines, prolapsed mitral valve.
AO = aorta, LA = left atrium, MVP = mitral valve prolapse, MVN = mitral
valve (normal), CT = chordae tendineae, PM = papillary muscles, LV = left
ventricle, RV = right ventricle.
Adapted from "Cardiovascular Aspects of Panic Disorder" by A. Ehlers et al. In
T. Elbert et al. (Eds.), *Behavioural Medicine in Cardiovascular Disorders* (in press).
Reprinted by permission of John Wiley & Sons, Ltd.

Civil War soldiers and reported hearing occasional clicks and apical
murmurs. His idea of irritability stemmed from the 18th century
view of organ fatigability also espoused by psychiatrists of the time
in the concept of "nervous exhaustion," a key feature of neurasthenia.
In 1941, Wood noted that Da Costa's syndrome was most common in
young women and described symptoms of palpitations, dyspnea,
chest pain, fatigue, and anxiety. In known MVP patients, palpitations
occur in 50 percent and chest pain in 30–50 percent. Such studies
raised the question as to whether or not there is an association between mitral valve disease and panic disorder and anxiety. Many
studies have addressed this issue in the past 10 years.

We recently combined seven studies reporting the occurrence of
MVP in patients with panic disorder or agoraphobia (Ehlers et al., in
press). Eighteen percent of these patients met criteria for definitive
MVP and 27 percent criteria for probable or definite MVP. The studies suggest that the prevalence of MVP is higher in patients with

panic or agoraphobia. However, MVP occurs for a variety of reasons. On one hand, pathological or structural MVP can result from connective tissue abnormality characterized by myxomatous infiltration of leaflets, elongation and attenuation of chordae, and dilation of the mitral annual. Such mitral valve problems are relatively rare. On the other hand, sophisticated cardiovascular diagnostic instruments can detect mitral valve prolapse that has no apparent pathophysiologic significance (Dager et al., 1987). It is likely that the high prevalence of MVP in panic disorder patients represents this benign MVP. Yet, it is interesting that an association between MVP and panic disorder or anxiety exists at all.

Gaffney et al. (1979) have argued that a subgroup of mitral valve prolapse patients may suffer from a primary abnormality affecting the autonomic nervous system. The MVP is a secondary phenomenon to this primary autonomic disorder. They postulate that in these patients, parasympathetic and alpha-adrenergic dysfunction may lead to excessive vasoconstriction and hypovolemia. On rising, the patient experiences a reduction in cardiac output that leads to further vasoconstriction and increased catecholamine release. The increased catecholamine release then leads to chronic vasoconstriction and further reduction in volume. A vicious cycle is thus established. The authors have observed that decreased ventricular filling in the upright position is a prominent feature in the pathophysiologic mechanisms of this syndrome. Consistent with Gaffney et al.'s observations, we have found that 11 of 39 panic patients had tachycardia on standing compared with 3 of 40 controls (Taylor et al., 1987). The tachycardia on standing could result from hypovolemia. Perhaps patients with panic disorder and patients with MVP have some adrenergic dysfunction, and in some patients, the dysfunction is manifested by both MVP and panic.

The diagnosis of MVP requires an expensive cardiologic examination and echocardiography. Furthermore, remember that most MVP is physiologic and not associated with increased morbidity and mortality. Jeresaty (1979), however, has identified a composite of the MVP candidate at risk for sudden death. The patient is a 40-year-old woman with a history of syncopal or presyncopal episodes, who has a late systolic murmur preceded by a click or a pansystolic murmur with late systolic accentuation. The electrocardiogram shows ST-T changes in the left precordial and inferior leads and multiple VPCs (ventricular premature contractions). Patients with such features should undergo further examination.

Recommendation. Anxiety patients with a history of fainting or of near fainting episodes should be evaluated by a physician. If these patients have the symptoms described above—a late systolic murmur preceded by a click, or a pansystolic murmur with late systolic accentuation, or ST-T changes in the left precordial and inferior leads and multiple VPCs—they should be evaluated by a cardiologist. Otherwise echocardiography does not seem indicated (Dager et al., 1986).

Hyperkinetic Heart Syndrome

The hyperkinetic heart, or high output, syndrome is a rare condition in which increased rate of ejection of blood with each cardiac beat occurs without increased output of blood per minute. The syndrome is associated with moderate exertional dypsnea, chest discomfort, and other cardiovascular symptoms. Such patients have a systolic ejection murmur, a "full and quick" pulse and an elevated resting heart rate (80–100 bpm). The cause of this syndrome is not known. Patients with high sustained heart rates need to be evaluated for this and other conditions that might cause a tachycardia.

Arrhythmias

A variety of arrhythmias have been reported to occur with anxiety. Arrhythmias are abnormalities of the rate and the rhythm of the pulse. In several studies we have shown that many panic attacks occur at heart rates disproportionate to physical activity (Taylor et al., 1983; 1986); maximum heart rates ranged between 115 and 148 bpm. A variety of pathological conditions can produce such high heart rates. In our studies of panic patients, six panic attacks occurred during simultaneous electrocardiogram monitoring (Taylor et al., 1986). When the heart rate was abnormally elevated, the rhythm represented a sinus tachycardia and not some other kind of arrhythmia. We have seen two patients in the clinic with abnormal tachycardias who had symptoms identical to those of panic patients.

Anxious patients may also have more irregular beats on ambulatory monitoring, although these are rarely of clinical significance (Shrear et al., 1986).

Recommendation. Patients with frequent panic episodes associated with heart rates greater than 125 bpm should be considered for evaluation with an ambulatory ECG monitor.

Chest Pain and Coronary Heart Disease (CHD)

About 60 percent of panic patients complain of chest pain, and chest pain may be a sign of serious heart disease. Angina pectoris occurs when cardiac work and the demand for myocardial oxygen exceed the ability of the coronary arterial system to supply oxygen.

The discomfort of angina pectoris, although highly variable in presentation, is most commonly felt beneath the sternum. It may be a vague, barely troublesome ache, or it may rapidly become a severe, intense crushing sensation. Pain may radiate to the left shoulder and down the inside of the left arm, even to the fingers. It may also radiate straight through to the back, into the throat, the jaw, the teeth, and occasionally down the right arm. It may be felt in the upper or lower abdomen. Angina pectoris is usually triggered by physical activity or intense emotion and usually persists no more than a few minutes, subsiding with rest. The pattern is usually similar from one episode to the next. Since the characteristics of angina are usually constant for a given individual, any change in the pattern of angina, e.g., increased intensity of attacks, decreased threshold of stimulus, longer duration, or occurrence when the patient is sedentary or awakening from sleep, should be viewed as a serious increase in symptoms. The heart rate and blood pressure usually rise during attacks. The diagnosis of angina is made on the basis of clinical signs and symptoms, ECG changes characteristic of ischemia, and rapid relief by taking sublingual nitroglycerin.

To complicate the picture, anxiety affects the self-report of angina. Costa et al. (1985) have found that "neuroticism" as defined by increased anxiety, hostility, and sensitivity to symptoms is associated with an increased report of angina but is not associated with an increased risk of morbidity and mortality from heart disease. Long-term self-monitoring of symptoms failed to find differentiating symptom patterns between angina in patients with demonstrable CHD from those with no disease. Beitman et al. (1987) have found that a third of patients with normal coronary arteries on angiography have features of panic disorder. This study suggests that anxiety, like pain, is a risk factor for angina but not for coronary artery disease. There is a large overlap in symptomology between patients with and without pathology identified on the coronary angiograms. The clinician must remain open to the possibility of angina in anxiety patients, listening for changes in complaint, and perhaps recommending less intrusive and inexpensive tests, like symptom-limited treadmill examinations, to help with the diagnosis before pursuing coronary angiography.

Recommendation. Patients with typical symptoms of angina, such as changes in presentation of chest pain symptoms, deserve further evaluation by their physician for angina.

Cardiovascular Risk Factors

There are two studies (Coryell et al., 1982; Coryell et al., 1986) which suggest that patients with panic disorder have increased cardiovascular mortality. Several authors have speculated that this increased mortality may be due to increased risk factors in patients with anxiety. An association between agoraphobia with panic attacks and alcoholism has been reported, and heavy alcoholism is associated with both hypertension and increased mortality from coronary heart disease (Dyer et al., 1977). Anxious patients also have higher rates of smoking (Hayward et al., submitted). Other risk factors are more controversial. Patients with anxiety disorders are often less fit, more hypertensive, and have higher LDL cholesterols, one of the cholesterol components associated with increased cardiovascular risk (Hayward et al., submitted). Of note, 45 percent of 53 anxious patients had serum cholesterol levels that fell above the 75th percentile of the Lipid Research Clinics Program. The NIH now recommends routine screening for cholesterol (NIH Consensus Conference, 1985). Given the apparent higher rates of at least some cholesterol fractions in patients with anxiety, it seems appropriate to do at least routine serum cholesterol levels in these patients.

Recommendation. Cardiovascular risk assessment (smoking history, blood pressure, total cholesterol, fitness by history, weight, alcohol consumption) should be undertaken in all anxious patients and treatment instituted as appropriate.

ENDOCRINE DISORDERS

Thyroid Disease

Excessive levels of thyroid hormones can produce severe anxiety symptoms. The excessive levels can occur because of various diseases or result from overtreatment of hypothyroidism. Lindemann et al. (1984) found 10.8 percent of patients with panic attacks reported a history of thyroid disease compared with less than 1 percent of the general population. Using a structured interview, Kathol et al. (1986) found that 23 of 29 consecutively evaluated hyperthyroid patients had symptoms of significant anxiety. Also 21 of the 23 patients with anxiety displayed complete resolution of these symptoms with antithyroid therapy.

The diagnosis of hyperthyroidism is usually straightforward and depends on a careful clinical history. A serum T4 assay and a T3 resin or serum are a highly accurate combination of initial tests for assessing thyroid status. The more common signs of hyperthyroidism are tachycardia; widened pulse pressure; warm, fine, moist skin; tremor; eye signs including lag, stare, lid retraction, and goiter. The most common symptoms include nervousness and increased activity, increased sweating, hypersensitivity to heat, palpitations, fatigue, tachycardia, and diarrhea. Many of these symptoms are probably related to increased adrenergic activity. Excessive levels of exogenous thyroid given to treat hypothyroidism may produce clinical signs and symptoms identical to thyroid disease.

Recommendation. Serum T3, T4, and TSH should be routinely obtained on anxious patients who have any signs or symptoms on history or clinical examination of thyroid disease.

Hypoglycemia

Hypoglycemia occurs when there is an abnormally low blood glucose level. The condition falls into two categories: reactive hypoglycemia, which occurs in response to a meal, specific nutrients, or drugs, and spontaneous hypoglycemia. In reactive hypoglycemia, most of the symptoms develop 2 to 4 hours after eating. Spontaneous hypoglycemia is rare and results either from excessive glucose utilization or deficient glucose production. The most common symptoms are faintness, weakness, tremulousness, palpitation, sweating, hunger, nervousness, headache, confusion, visual disturbances, motor weakness, muscle weakness, ataxia, and in several cases, loss of consciousness, convulsions, and coma. The diagnosis is made by a documented low plasma glucose (<50mg/dL), specifically associated with objective signs or subjective symptoms that are relieved by the ingestion of sugar or other food. Once the diagnosis is suspected, a series of subsequent tests can be performed to pinpoint the diagnosis. However, hypoglycemia is a rare condition and probably overdiagnosed (Permutt, 1980; Ford, Bray & Swerdloff, 1976).

Recommendation. The routine use of glucose tolerance tests is not recommended. Only when panic attacks are associated with hunger should a GTT be performed. In such cases, only a three-hour GTT is recommended (Stein, 1986).

Pheochromocytoma

Pheochromocytoma is a rare condition caused by a tumor of the cells that secrete catecholamines. The most prominent feature of a pheochromacytoma is hypertension that is paroxsymal in about half the cases and persistent in the other half. Pheochromocytomas have symptoms associated with catecholamine hormones release. Thus patients have tachycardia, diaphoresis, postural hypotension, rapid breathing, flushing of the skin, cold and clammy skin, severe headache, angina, palpitation, nausea, vomiting, epigastric pain, visual disturbances, shortness of breath, and a sense of impending doom.

The diagnosis is made by measurements of urinary metabolic products or epinephrine and norepinephrine, specifically metanephrines and vanillylmandelic acid (VMA). The diagnosis should be suspected in patients who are hypertensive and have the symptoms mentioned. Although pheochromocytomas are rare, missing the diagnosis may be catastrophic for the patient. Spot metanephrine determinations are satisfactory for initial testing.

Recommendation. Spot metanephrine determinations should be done in patients with symptoms or signs of phenochromacytoma and moderate or severe hypertension (e.g., diastolic pressure >110 mmHg) or poor therapeutic response to antihypertensive drugs.

Hypoparathyroidism

Hypoparathyroidism is a disease in which the parathyroid glands produce abnormally low amounts of parathyroid hormone. Parathyroid hormone controls calcium metabolism and low levels result in hypocalcemia and hyperphosphatemia. The low calcemia results in muscular cramps and paresthesias in the hand, feet, and around the mouth. Carpopedal spasm (spasm in the hands and feet) is a useful sign. Although hyperventilation may produce similar clinical features, muscle spasm is rarely one of them. The diagnosis is made by the determination of low levels of calcium in the presence of high levels of phosphate and normal renal function (Potts, 1980).

NEUROLOGIC DISORDERS

Vestibular Abnormalities

Vestibular abnormalities can produce symptoms that are identical to panic attacks. The most common symptoms are dizziness and vertigo, and these two symptoms usually dominate the clinical picture. The symptom of dizziness can be categorized into (1) rotational sensation, (2) loss of balance without head sensations (e.g., being pulled to the left), (3) feelings like fainting or losing consciousness, and (4) ill-defined "light-headedness" (Drachman and Hart, 1972). The first two symptoms more strongly implicate neurological or vestibular pathology, whereas the fainting variety usually signifies a vagal or cardiovascular origin (Jacob & Rapport, 1984). The most common vestibular abnormality is benign paroxysmal positional vertigo. This condition is characterized by sudden onset of vertigo triggered by head rotation or sometimes linear acceleration. Driving and even jogging can precipitate this problem. We have seen one patient with a middle ear infection that was associated with panic attacks. Resolution of the infection improved, but did not eliminate the panic attacks. Jacob et al. (1986) found significant vestibular dysfunction in 14 of 21 anxiety disorder patients who had sensations of dizziness, lightheadedness, or vertigo during their panic attacks.

Recommendation. Patients with a clinical history consistent with vertibular abnormalities should be worked up for the problem. Simple, in-office tests of autonomic dysfunction should be considered in patients with dizziness and postural instability and normal otological function.

Seizures

Two types of seizures have been associated with panic fear attacks: temporal lobe and partial seizures (Roth & Harper, 1962, Straus et al., 1982). Temporal lobe epilepsy is distinguished by episodes of dysphasia, motor automatisms and progression of attacks to unconsciousness (Roth and Harper, 1982).

Edlund et al. (1987) found that panic attack patients with abnormal EEGs differed from usual panic attack patients in several ways. First, the panic attacks were usually associated with severe derealization and sometimes with unusually severe autonomic symptoms, such as tachycardia with a heart rate over 125 bpm. Second, immediately before, during, or after the panic attacks, the patients became either highly irritable or overtly aggressive. In no case was the panic associated with avoidance or loss of consciousness. The EEG abnormalities involved the temporal lobes. For example:

Mr. B., 21-years-old, reported panic attacks "as long ago as I can remember." By his early teens he was experiencing circumscribed episodes of palpitations, sweating, increased respiration, feelings of impending doom, and marked depersonalization and derealization. He found that these attacks were made worse by marijuana and improved by alcohol. After some attacks he would "blow up" and smash things. Results of a neurological examination were normal; an EEG showed brief runs of left temporal sharp slowing. (From Edlund et al., 1987)

Partial seizures have also been associated with panic attacks. Partial seizures or focal seizures begin with specific motor, sensory, or psychomotor focal phenomena. Partial seizures leading to focal symptoms without involving motor movement are rare but have been reported.

In the absence of any of these features, the diagnosis of temporal lobe epilepsy is unlikely, and routine EEG studies are not warranted. The diagnosis of partial seizures requires an EEG.

The final case is that of hypogenic paroxysmal dystonia, a rare condition thought to be the result of abnormal epileptiform discharges in deep, mesial regions of the brain. Attacks occur at night usually during non-REM sleep and are characterized by the sudden onset of twisting, dystonic movements of the limbs that may last from 15 to 45 seconds.

A 22-year old single woman presented for evaluation of "anxiety attacks." Her first attack was spontaneous and occurred during the day, but six months after the first attack they became exclusively nocturnal. Each attack lasted 30–60 seconds, and she was having 3–4 attacks/night. There was no loss of consciousness nor any nightmares. A daytime EEG with nasopharyngeal leads was normal. However, the patient was started on carbamazepine, 400 mg at night, and the attacks were promptly relieved. Of interest, a trial of imipramine also relieved her panic attacks after 2 weeks of treatment. A videotape obtained during one of her episodes when she was off all medication showed "tonic extension of the left arm and hand, flexion of the right arm, and flexion of the right wrist in a 'drawn' position," suggesting the diagnosis of hypogenic paroxysmal dystonia. (Strovdemire et al., 1987)

This case suggests that the clinician should remain open to unusual seizure problems that might appear very similar to panic.

Recommendation. Patients with a history of altered consciousness, automatism, head injury, other seizures, characteristics of temporal lobe epilepsy, and neurological deficits on examination should be evaluated with a sleep-deprived EEG and possibly a CAT scan of the head (Raj & Sheehan, 1987).

APPENDIX ONE
· · · · · · · ·

Baseline
Assessment

· · · · · · · · · ·

Appendix 1 contains baseline assessment instruments used in the Stanford Anxiety Disorder Clinic. The Intake and Brief Medical History forms are self-explanatory. Section 1 is the Fear Questionnaire (Marks & Mathews, 1979). The column to the far right is used to create subscores for social fears (Soc), agoraphobia (AG) and blood/injury (BI). Section 2 is used to screen for panic attacks. Section 3 represents 13 of 14 items taken from Pilowsky's hypochondriasis questionnaire (Pilowsky, 1967). According to Pilowsky, patients answering yes on 8 or more items are likely to be hypochondriacal. Pilowsky also identified three factors on the scale: bodily preoccupation, represented by items 1 and 2; fear of illness, represented by items 3–6; and distrust/disease conviction, represented by items 7 and 8. Section 4 represents depression criteria taken from the DSM-III. Patients answering yes to item 1 and two or more of items 2–6 often meet the criteria for Major Depressive Episode. Section 5 represents the anxiety scale from the SCL-90 (Derogatis, Lipman, & Cove, 1973). Section 6 is a disability scale used in anxiety research outcome studies (Sheehan, 1983). These forms supplement the clinical interview and history-taking.

ANXIETY AND STRESS DISORDERS CLINIC

Intake Form

Name: (Last, First, MI) _____

Address: _____
          (Street)

          _____
          (City, State, Zip Code)

Telephone Number: (Home) (_ _ _)_ _ _-_ _ _ _
                  (Work) (_ _ _)_ _ _-_ _ _ _

Age: _____   Sex: ❏ Male, ❏ Female   Today's Date:_ _/_ _/_ _
                                         mo   day   year

Marital Status: ❏ Never Married, ❏ Married, ❏ Divorced/Separated/Widowed

Are you currently working? ❏ Yes, ❏ No.

If Yes, what is your current occupation? _____

Education: (Circle hightest level obtained)
          1 = Graduate or professional training.
          2 = College or university graduate
          3 = Partial college training
          4 = High school graduate
          5 = Did not complete high school

Living situation: (Circle appropriate number)
          1 = Lives alone
          2 = Lives with husband/wife
          3 = Single parent
          4 = Lives with parents
          5 = Other

Children:

Name	Sex	Age
_____	_____	_____
_____	_____	_____
_____	_____	_____
_____	_____	_____

BRIEF MEDICAL HISTORY

Please take a few minutes to answer the following questions about your general health:

Please circle the appropriate response.

1.	Have you ever had any pressure or heaviness in your chest?	Yes	No
2.	Have you ever had any discomfort or pain in your chest?	Yes	No
3.	Have you ever felt your heart turning over, skipping beats or pounding inappropriately?	Yes	No
4.	Do you get pain in either leg on walking?	Yes	No
5.	Do you have shortness of breath that occurs more easily than in others of your age/physical condition during physical activity?	Yes	No
6.	Do you have any difficulty breathing when you lie down?	Yes	No
7.	Do you have any swelling of your feet and ankles?	Yes	No
8.	Have you ever fainted or lost consciousness?	Yes	No
9.	Have you been told that you have:		

an enlarged heart	Yes	No
a heart murmur/abnormality	Yes	No
cardiac valve disease	Yes	No
rheumatic fever in childhood	Yes	No
high blood pressure	Yes	No
high cholesterol	Yes	No
diabetes	Yes	No
lung disease	Yes	No
thyroid problems	Yes	No
kidney problems	Yes	No
liver disease	Yes	No
gastrointestinal disease	Yes	No
gout	Yes	No
arthritis	Yes	No

10.	Have you ever been given a diagnosis of glaucoma (increased pressure in the eyeball)?	Yes	No
11.	Do you presently have trouble urinating?	Yes	No
12.	Please list, with dates, any serious medical disorder that you have had, or currently have.		

_____

_____

_____

_____

13.	Do you have any allergies?	Yes	No
14.	Have you ever been hospitalized?	Yes	No
15.	Have you had any operations?	Yes	No
16.	Do you have a family history of heart disease, hypertension, high cholesterol, diabetes, kidney disease, cancer or bleeding problems?	Yes	No
17.	Please list all medications that you are currently taking.		

_____

_____

_____

18.	If female, what was the date of your last period? _____		
19.	Do you smoke cigarettes?	Yes	No
20.	How much alcohol do you drink in a typical week? _____ (# drinks per week)		
21.	Do you currently have a drinking problem?	Yes	No
22.	Please list any previous medication you have taken.		

_____

_____

_____

_____

Section 1

FEAR QUESTIONNAIRE

Choose a number from the scale below to show how much you would avoid each of the situations listed below because of fear or other unpleasant feelings. Then write the number you have chosen on the line opposite each situation.

0	1	2	3	4	5	6	7	8
Would not avoid it		Slightly avoid it		Definitely avoid it		Markedly avoid it		Always avoid it

1. Main phobia you want treated (describe in your own words)
   _____
   _____   _____   **LEAVE THIS AREA BLANK**

2. Eating or drinking with other people.   _____
3. Being watched or stared at.   _____
4. Talking to people in authority.   _____
5. Being criticised.   _____
6. Speaking or acting to an audience.   _____
   _____ Soc

7. Travelling alone by bus or coach.   _____
8. Walking alone in busy streets.   _____
9. Going into crowded shops.   _____
10. Going alone far from home   _____
11. Large open spaces.   _____
   _____ AG

12. Injections or minor surgery.   _____
13. Hospitals.   _____
14. Sight of blood.   _____
15. Thought of injury or illness.   _____
16. Going to the dentist.   _____
   _____ BI

   TOTAL: _____

Section 2

1. Have you ever had attacks of extreme anxiety or panic that seem to come on suddenly in situations or places that pose no "real" danger?   ☐ Yes, ☐ No

2. If yes, please check each of the symptoms below that you experienced during your last bad panic attack.

   ☐ Shortness of breath
   ☐ Choking or smothering sensations
   ☐ Palpitations (heart racing or pounding)
   ☐ Chest pain, pressure, tightness, or discomfort
   ☐ Sweating
   ☐ Feeling faint (doesn't mean you have to actually faint)

322

- ☐ Dizziness, unsteadyness
- ☐ Nausea or abdominal distress
- ☐ Depersonalization, derealization (things seem unreal, or you feel detached from your body)
- ☐ Numbness or tingling in any part of your body
- ☐ Hot or cold flashes
- ☐ Trembling or shaking
- ☐ Fear of dying
- ☐ Fear of going crazy or doing something uncontrolled
- ☐ Other. (Please describe)_____
  _____
  _____

3. How many panic attacks (including milder ones) have you had in the last seven days?   _____

4. How many panic attacks (including milder ones) have you had in the last month?   _____

5. Do some of your panic attacks occur "out of the blue" in "safe" situations like being at home?   ☐ Yes, ☐ No

Section 3

		Yes	No
1.	Are you bothered by many different symptoms?	☐	☐
2.	Do you find that you are often aware of various things happening in your body?	☐	☐
3.	If a disease is brought to your attention through the radio, television, newspaper or someone you know, do you worry about getting it yourself?	☐	☐
4.	Is it easy for you to forget about yourself and think about all sorts of other things?	☐	☐
5.	Do you think that you worry about your health more than most people?	☐	☐
6.	Are you afraid of illness?	☐	☐
7.	Is it hard for you to believe the doctor when he tells you there is nothing for you to worry about?	☐	☐
8.	Do you get the feeling that people are not taking your illness seriously enough?	☐	☐
9.	I've always had one thing or another wrong with my health.	☐	☐
10.	Others have told me that I spend too much time talking about my health.	☐	☐
11.	I am sure something is wrong with my health that the doctors still haven't been able to find.	☐	☐
12.	I find myself worrying about my health.	☐	☐
13.	I feel like I need to see my physician even though I am not always able to.	☐	☐

323

Section 4

		Yes	No
1.	Have you been depressed or down in your mood or lost interest in most things every day for the past two weeks?	❏	❏
2.	Do you have a poor appetite or significant weight loss?	❏	❏
3.	Have you had trouble falling asleep, waking frequently, trouble staying asleep, waking too early or sleeping too much?	❏	❏
4.	Have you lost interest or pleasure in your usual activities?	❏	❏
5.	Have you been having trouble thinking or concentrating?	❏	❏
6.	Have you been thinking about death or hurting yourself?	❏	❏
7.	Have you had some kind of pain in your body for nearly every day for the last six months?	❏	❏

Section 5

Below is a list of problems and complaints that people sometimes have. Check one of the spaces to the right that best describes how much that problem bothered or distressed you during the last week, including today.

	Not at All	A little Bit	Moder- ately	Quite A Bit	Extremely
Nervousness or shakiness inside	❏	❏	❏	❏	❏
Trembling	❏	❏	❏	❏	❏
Suddenly scared for no reason	❏	❏	❏	❏	❏
Feeling fearful	❏	❏	❏	❏	❏
Heart pounding or racing	❏	❏	❏	❏	❏
Feeling tense or keyed up	❏	❏	❏	❏	❏
Spells of terror or panic	❏	❏	❏	❏	❏
Feeling so restless you couldn't sit still	❏	❏	❏	❏	❏
The feeling that something bad is going to happen to you	❏	❏	❏	❏	❏
Thoughts and images of a frightening nature	❏	❏	❏	❏	❏

Section 6

Circle a number that best describes your situation now.

WORK

Because of my problems my work is impaired.

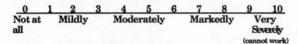

0 1 2 3 4 5 6 7 8 9 10
Not at   Mildly   Moderately   Markedly   Very
all   Severely
                                                               (cannot work)

SOCIAL LIFE/LEISURE ACTIVITIES
(With other people at parties, socializing, visiting, dating, outings,
clubs, and entertaining)

Because of my problems my social life/leisure is impaired.

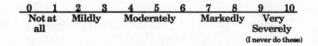

0 1 2 3 4 5 6 7 8 9 10
Not at   Mildly   Moderately   Markedly   Very
all   Severely
                                                               (I never do these)

FAMILY LIFE/HOME RESPONSIBILITIES
(For example, relating to family members, paying bills,
managing home, shopping and cleaning.)

Because of my problems my family life/home
responsibilities are impaired.

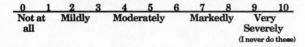

0 1 2 3 4 5 6 7 8 9 10
Not at   Mildly   Moderately   Markedly   Very
all   Severely
                                                               (I never do these)

325

APPENDIX TWO

. . . .

Additional Assessment Instruments

. . . .

Appendix 2 contains additional assessment instruments used to further quantify patients' problems and to monitor treatment. The Hamilton Anxiety Rating Scale (Hamilton, 1959) is the standard pharmacology outcome rating scale for anxiety. It is designed to be completed by an interviewer. The Stanford Panic Appraisal Inventory (Telch, 1985) was designed to assess patients' panic cognitions. The Common Fears and Phobias questionnaire is an adaption of the Fear Survey (Wolpe & Lang, 1964). The Stanford Panic Diary is used to collect information on the intensity, symptomotology, place of occurrence, cognition, and patient response to panic attacks. Patients should be given a sufficient number of forms for them to be able to record this information on all the panic attacks they may experience from one visit to another. The Panic Attack Self-Efficacy form is used to monitor treatment. Patients need to be taught how to use the form. Finally, the Phobic Avoidance Inventory, developed by Michael Telch, Ph.D., for the Stanford Agoraphobia Avoidance Research Projects, is a useful clinical tool. Some of the items will need to be changed if the form is used in geographic locations other than the San Francisco Bay area. For instance, the "Driving an Automobile" section refers to Route 280 and Highway 101.

Panic Attack Self-Efficacy Form

Instructions: Please indicate your level of confidence in your ability to cope effectively with the panic attacks listed below. By cope effectively, we refer to your ability to continue functioning, without running away or avoiding the situation you are in. For each item, rate your confidence using this scale:

0	10	20	30	40	50	60	70	80	90	100
Definitely Cannot Do			Probably Cannot Do			Maybe Can Do		Probably Can Do		Definitely Can Do

Part I.

A. Spontaneous Attacks. **Please rate your confidence in being able to tolerate or cope with spontaneous attacks (those that come out of the blue):**

	% Confidence
1. Mild intensity	_____
2. Moderate intensity	_____
3. Severe intensity	_____

B. Situational Attacks. **Please rate your confidence in being able to tolerate or cope with situational attacks (those that are related to predictable situations):**

	% Confidence
1. Mild intensity	_____
2. Moderate intensity	_____
3. Severe intensity	_____

Part II.

Panic attacks consist of a number of different components. Now we would like you to rate your confidence to:

% Confidence

A. cope with the beginning of a panic, that is thoughts, feelings, events, or situations that signal you are about to have a panic attack.   _____

B. cope with the rapid build-up phase of the panic attack, that is the phase when the symptoms and intensity begin to increase.   _____

C. cope with the somatic feelings, like heart pounding, sweating, chest pain, and feeling like you can't breathe.   _____

D. cope with the thought that you might die or some other catastrophic event might occur to you.   _____

E. cope with the urge to run away from the situation where the panic attack is occuring.   _____

Part III.

Panic attacks occur in a variety of situations. Please rate your confidence to handle, cope with or tolerate panic attacks in these situations:
(Please note that you need to make three ratings for each question.)

	Mild Panic Attack %Confidence	Moderate Panic Attack %Confidence	Severe Panic Attack %Confidence
1. Driving on the freeway.	____	____	____
2. Shopping in the supermarket, or being in a department store.	____	____	____
3. Sitting in a closed space, like a movie theater or elevator.	____	____	____
4. Eating in a restaurant, being at a party.	____	____	____
5. Riding in an airplane.	____	____	____
6. Walking alone outside a mile or more from home.	____	____	____

Part IV. We would now like you to rate your confidence to apply various therapeutic procedures when you are having a moderate to severe panic attack.

% Confidence

1. Timing the course of the panic attack from beginning to end. _____

2. Letting the panic attack "peak and pass." _____

3. Putting the panic attack in perspective, that is, not letting it dent your functioning. _____

4. Engage in controlled breathing. _____

5. Use "positive thoughts" during the panic attack. _____

Part V.

Yes   No

Are you now taking any medication for your panic attacks? _____   _____

% Confidence

If you are taking medication how confident are you that you can cope with, handle or tolerate panic attacks without medication? _____

STANFORD PANIC DIARY INSTRUCTIONS

On the attached form, please record each panic attack and its associated symptoms by carefully following the steps below. Complete a panic attack description for each attack you have between now and when I see you again.

STEP 1: Next to "**Date**," note the date when you have the panic attack.

STEP 2: Next to "**Level**," note your level of panic using the scale below:

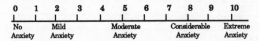

STEP 3: Next to "**Symptoms**", record the symptoms you experienced during the attack. Please use the following code numbers to record your symptoms:

1. Shortness of breath or smothering sensations.
2. Palpitations (pounding heart) or accelerated heart rate (heart racing).
3. Sweating.
4. Choking or difficulty in swallowing.
5. Faintness.
6. Dizziness, lightheadedness, or unsteady feelings.
7. Chest pain or discomfort.
8. Trembling or shaking.
9. Fear of dying.
10. Numbness or tingling sensations.
11. Fear of going crazy or doing something uncontrolled.
12. Flushes (hot flashes or chills).
13. Nausea or abdominal distress.
14. Feelings of unreality or being detached from parts of body or things around you.
15. Other (if other, specify): _____

STEP 4. Next to "**Time Began**" and "**Time Ended**", record when the attack started and when it ended. (Be sure to look at your watch or a clock when the attack begins and when it ends.)

STEP 5. Next to "**Type**," classify your panic attack using the system below:

1. **SPONTANEOUS ATTACK.** A sudden panic attack that comes on "**out of the blue**." (In order to classify an attack as "**Spontaneous**," you must not be in a feared situation nor thinking about or anticipating something fearful.)

2. **ANTICIPATORY PANIC.** A panic attack that occurred in anticipation of (before) facing a feared situation or thinking about something fearful.

3. **SITUATIONAL PANIC.** A panic attack that occurred while you were in a feared situation.

NOTE: Each attack should have only one classification (1, 2, or 3).

STEP 6: Next to "**Where Were You**" and "**What Were You Doing**," record this information in the assigned boxes.

STEP 7. Note any thoughts you had during the panic attack.

STEP 8. What did you do in response to the panic attacks?

STANFORD PANIC ATTACK DIARY

Panic Attack Description

Date	
Level (0-10)	
Symptoms:	
Time beg250:gan:	
Time ended:	
What type?	
Where were you?	
What were you doing?	
Thoughts:	
Comments:	

Panic Attack Description

Date	
Level (0-10)	
Symptoms:	
Time began:	
Time ended:	
What type?	
Where were you?	
What were you doing?	
Thoughts:	
Comments:	

330

HAMILTON ANXIETY RATING SCALE

MILD - OCCURS IRREGULARLY AND FOR SHORT
    PERIODS OF TIME

SEVERE - CONTINUOUS AND DOMINATES
    PATIENT'S LIFE

MODERATE - OCCURS MORE CONSTANTLY AND
    OF LONGER DURATION

VERY SEVERE - INCAPACITATING

		Not Present 0	Mild 1	Moderate 2	Severe 3	Very Severe 4
1. ANXIOUS MOOD	Worries, anticipation of the worst, fearful anticipation, irritability					
2. TENSION	Feelings of tension, fatigability, moved to tears easily, trembling feelings of restlessness, startle response, inability to relax.					
3. FEARS	Of dark, of strangers, of being left alone, of animals, of traffic, of crowds					
4. INSOMNIA	Difficulty in falling asleep, night terrors, unsatisfying sleep, fatigue on waking, dreams, nightmares					
5. INTELLECTUAL (cognition)	Difficulty in concentration, poor memory					
6. DEPRESSED MOOD	Loss of interest, lack of pleasure in hobbies, depression, early waking, diurnal swing					
7. SOMATIC (muscular)	Pains and aches, twitchings, stiffness, myoclonic jerks, grinding of teeth, unsteady voice, increased muscle tone					
8. SOMATIC	Tinnitus, blurring of vision, hot and cold flashes, feelings of weakness, prickling sensation					
9. CARDIOVASCULAR SYMPTOMS	Tachycardia, palpitations, pain in chest, throbbing of vessels, feeling faint, missed beat					
10. RESPIRATORY SYMPTOMS	Pressure or constriction in chest, choking feelings, sighing, dyspnea					
11. GASTROINTESTINAL SYMPTOMS	Difficulty in swallowing, wind, burning sensations, abdominal pain, nausea, vomiting, looseness of bowels loss of weight, constipation.					
12. GENITOURINARY	Frequency and urgency of urination, amenorrhea, menorrhagia, frigidity, loss of libido, impotence, premature ejaculation					
13. AUTONOMIC SYMPTOMS	Dry mouth, flushing, pallor, sweating, giddiness, tension headache					
14. BEHAVIOR AT INTERVIEW	Fidgeting, restlessness or pacing, tremor, furrowed brow, strained face, sighing or rapid respiration, facial pallor, swallowing, belching					
					TOTAL	

COMMON FEARS AND PHOBIAS

Name_____Date_____ID_____

<u>Directions</u>:

Please indicate how fearful you are of each of the following objects and situations by putting an "X" in the appropriate column.

	No fear	Mild discomfort	Moderate discomfort, but can face it if I must	Extreme fear, avoid at all costs
1. Sharp objects, such as a knife	___	___	___	___
2. Dead bodies	___	___	___	___
3. Traveling on an airplane	___	___	___	___
4. Traveling across a bridge	___	___	___	___
5. Walking across a main street alone	___	___	___	___
6. Rats and/or mice	___	___	___	___
7. Injections	___	___	___	___
8. Being criticized	___	___	___	___
9. Meeting a stranger	___	___	___	___
10. Being alone at home	___	___	___	___
11. Thoughts of death	___	___	___	___
12. Going to visit a friend's home alone	___	___	___	___
13. Crowds	___	___	___	___
14. Sight of blood	___	___	___	___
15. Heights	___	___	___	___
16. Traveling alone by train	___	___	___	___
17. Thought of injury or illness	___	___	___	___
18. Driving an automobile alone	___	___	___	___
19. Talking to people in authority	___	___	___	___
20. Closed places, such as a small room	___	___	___	___
21. Boating	___	___	___	___
22. Spiders	___	___	___	___
23. The sound of a thunderstorm	___	___	___	___
24. Walking away from home by yourself for 15 minutes	___	___	___	___
25. Harmless snakes	___	___	___	___
26. Visiting a cemetary	___	___	___	___

	No fear	Mild discomfort	Moderate discomfort, but can face it if I must	Extreme fear, avoid at all costs
27. Speaking or acting to an audience	___	___	___	___
28. Dogs	___	___	___	___
29. Traveling by bus by yourself for 15 minutes	___	___	___	___
30. Going to a crowded department store alone	___	___	___	___
31. Traveling through a tunnel alone	___	___	___	___
32. Deep water	___	___	___	___
33. The sight of an accident	___	___	___	___
34. Being in a new place	___	___	___	___
35. Answering the door bell	___	___	___	___
36. Talking to a neighbor in the street	___	___	___	___
37. Loud noises	___	___	___	___
38. Sitting in a hall alone	___	___	___	___
39. Going to the dentist	___	___	___	___
40. Walking round the nearest large shopping center	___	___	___	___
41. Entering large open spaces alone	___	___	___	___
42. Sirens	___	___	___	___
43. Crowded rooms	___	___	___	___
44. Bats	___	___	___	___
45. Flying insects	___	___	___	___
46. Sudden noises	___	___	___	___
47. Cats	___	___	___	___
48. Birds	___	___	___	___
49. Dead animals	___	___	___	___
50. Guns	___	___	___	___
51. Dirt	___	___	___	___
52. Eating or drinking with other people	___	___	___	___
53. Hospitals	___	___	___	___
54. Walking alone in a busy street	___	___	___	___
55. Being watched or stared at	___	___	___	___
56. Crawling insects	___	___	___	___
57. Sick people	___	___	___	___
58. Elevators	___	___	___	___

	No fear	Mild discomfort	Moderate discomfort, but can face it if I must	Extreme fear, avoid at all costs
59. Feeling rejected	——	——	——	——
60. Feeling disapproved of	——	——	——	——
61. Losing control	——	——	——	——
62. Mental illness	——	——	——	——
63. Going alone far from home	——	——	——	——

STANFORD PANIC APPRAISAL INVENTORY

Listed below are 20 statements reflecting some common feelings and thoughts that people report during sudden attacks of panic or extreme anxiety. Read each item carefully and then choose the number from the scale which best describes the degree to which you are troubled by the feeling or thought. Then write the number on the line opposite each statement.

0 1	2 3	4 5	6 7 8	9 10
Not at all troubling	Mildly troubling	Moderately troubling	Markedly troubling	Extremely troubling

1. I may faint. ____
2. People will stare at me. ____
3. I may become hysterical. ____
4. I may have a heart attack. ____
5. I may drive off the road and crash. ____
6. I may do something uncontrollable like jump out a window. ____
7. I may scream. ____
8. I may not be able to move from one spot. ____
9. I may be put into a mental hospital. ____
10. I may get sick to my stomach. ____
11. People will laugh at me. ____
12. I may lose my balance and fall. ____
13. I may suffocate. ____
14. I will be an embarrasment to my family and friends. ____
15. I may die. ____
16. I may go insane. ____
17. I may lose control of my bowels. ____
18. I will be trapped. ____
19. Others will think I am weird. ____
20. I may have a brain tumor. ____

PHOBIC AVOIDANCE INVENTORY

INSTRUCTIONS: Listed on the following pages are behaviors that people with agoraphobia sometimes have difficulty performing. For most of the behaviors listed you are asked both whether you can perform the behavior alone and perform the behavior with a companion. However, some of the items only ask whether you can perform the behavior alone.

For each behavior category listed, place a check (√) in the CAN DO column labeled "With Someone" if you can perform the behavior with a companion and place a check (√) in the column "Alone" if you can perform the behavior by yourself. If you do not place a check next to an item it means that you don't think that you can perform the behavior. Make your judgments as though you were asked to perform the behaviors right now.

Below is an example to show you how the scale works. This is how one person completed the form about her ability to lift boxes of various weights:

SAMPLE

A. LIFTING BOXES. Can you:

		CAN DO	
		Alone	With Someone
1.	lift a 15 pound box	√	√
2.	lift a 30 pound box	√	√
3.	lift a 45 pound box	√	√
4.	lift a 60 pound box	√	√
5.	lift a 75 pound box	√	√
6.	lift a 100 pound box	___	√
7.	lift a 125 pound box	___	√
8.	lift a 150 pound box	___	√
9.	lift a 200 pound box	___	√

A. BE ALONE. Can you remain alone in your home for:

		CAN DO
		Alone
1.	10 minutes	___
2.	30 minutes	___
3.	one hour	___
4.	two hours	___
5.	four hours	___
6.	six hours	___
7.	all day (10 hours)	___
8.	all day and all night	___
9.	week-end	___
10.	one week	___

B. WALKING AWAY FROM YOUR HOME.

Can you:

		CAN DO	
		Alone	With Someone
1.	walk out the front door, close it behind you, and walk five steps away from it	___	___
2.	walk out to the sidewalk	___	___
3.	walk away from your home for a distance of half a block	___	___
4.	walk away from your home for a distance of 1 block	___	___

335

Can you:	Alone	With Someone

5. walk away from your home for a distance of 2 blocks ___ ___

6. walk away from your home for a distance of 3 blocks ___ ___

7. walk away from your home for a distance of 5 blocks ___ ___

8. walk away from your home for a distance of 7 blocks ___ ___

9. walk away from your home for a distance of 10 blocks (1 mile) ___ ___

10. walk away from your home for a distance of 20 blocks (2 miles) ___ ___

C. RIDING AN ELEVATOR.

CAN DO

Can you:	Alone	With Someone

1. walk into an elevator with the door open and then walk right out ___ ___

2. walk into an elevator, close the door part way, then open it and walk out ___ ___

3. ride an elevator up one floor in a twelve story apartment building ___ ___

4. ride an elevator up 2 floors in a twelve story apartment building ___ ___

5. ride an elevator up 3 floors in a twelve story apartment building ___ ___

6. ride an elevator up 4 floors in a twelve story apartment building ___ ___

7. ride an elevator up 6 floors in a twelve story apartment building ___ ___

8. ride an elevator up 8 floors in a twelve story apartment building ___ ___

9. ride an elevator up 10 floors in a twelve story apartment building ___ ___

10. ride an elevator up to the top of a twelve story apartment building ___ ___

D. BE IN A LARGE COFFEE SHOP (LIKE DENNY'S)

Can you:

1. step inside the door of the coffee shop then walk right out ___ ___

2. have a cup of coffee while sitting near the exit ___ ___

3. have a cup of coffee while sitting far from the exit ___ ___

336

Can you:	Alone	With Someone

4. eat an entire meal while sitting near the exit — —

5. eat an entire meal while sitting far from the exit — —

E. GOING UP TO HIGH PLACES. Imagine a tall residential building with a staircase going up one side of it. In this staircase the ground is visible from each floor.

CAN DO

	Alone	With Someone

Can you:

1. walk up to the second floor and look over the railing at the ground for 1 minute — —

2. walk up to the third floor and look over the railing at the ground for 1 minute — —

3. walk up to the fourth floor and look over the railing at the ground for 1 minute — —

4. walk up to the fifth floor and look over the railing at the ground for 1 minute — —

5. walk up to the sixth floor and look over the railing at the ground for 1 minute — —

6. walk up to the seventh floor and look over the railing at the ground for 1 minute — —

7. walk up to the eighth floor and look over the railing at the ground for 1 minute — —

8. walk up to the ninth floor and look over the railing at the ground for 1 minute — —

9. walk up to the tenth floor and look over the railing at the ground for 1 minute — —

10. walk up to the twelfth floor and look over the railing at the ground for 1 minute — —

F. TOLERATING CLOSED-IN PLACES.

CAN DO

Can you go into a small office (8' X 8') without windows and:	Alone	With Someone

1. close the door and then walk right out — —

2. close the door and stay for 15 seconds — —

3. close the door and stay for 1 minute — —

337

Can you:

4. close the door and stay for 5 minutes   ___   ___

5. close the door and stay for 15 minutes   ___   ___

G. DRIVING ACROSS BRIDGES.

Can you:

1. drive across a short freeway overpass (distance = 1 block)   ___   ___

2. drive across a long freeway overpass (distance = 2 blocks)   ___   ___

3. drive across a bridge over a river (distance = half a mile)   ___   ___

4. drive across a mile long low bridge close to the water (e.g., Dumbarton)   ___   ___

5. drive across a mile long bridge high over the water (e.g., Golden Gate)   ___   ___

H. DISTANCE AWAY FROM HOME.
(In answering this question, assume you are able to get to each of the distances listed below)

Can you:

1. be 1 block from home   ___   ___

2. be one half mile from home   ___   ___

3. be 1 mile from home   ___   ___

4. be 5 miles from home   ___   ___

5. be 20 miles from home   ___   ___

6. be 60 miles from home   ___   ___

7. be 100 miles from home   ___   ___

8. be in Los Angeles   ___   ___

9. be on the East Coast   ___   ___

10. be in Europe   ___   ___

I. SHOPPING AT THE GROCERY STORE.

Can you:

1. walk inside the front door and then immediately leave   ___   ___

2. walk all the way to the back of the store and then immediately leave   ___   ___

3. walk all the way to the back of the store, select one item, and then go buy it without having to wait in line   ___   ___

338

Can you:

4. buy 10 items while having to wait behind two people who were each buying ten items ___ ___

5. buy an entire shopping cart full of groceries while having to wait behind 8 people who were each buying full carts of groceries ___ ___

J. FLYING IN AIRPLANES.
(In answering this question, assume you have no trouble being away from home)

CAN DO

Alone   With Someone

Can you:

1. enter a terminal, go to a passenger boarding area and stay there for 15 minutes ___ ___

2. walk onto an airplane and then walk right off ___ ___

3. sit in an airplane at the airport for 5 minutes and then get off ___ ___

4. sit in an airplane at the airport for 15 minutes and then get off ___ ___

5. sit in an airplane and taxi around the runway and then return to the terminal ___ ___

6. fly in an airplane from Oakland to San Francisco ___ ___

7. fly in an airplane from San Francisco to Los Angeles ___ ___

8. fly in an airplane from San Francisco to the East Coast (direct flight) ___ ___

9. fly in an airplane from San Francisco to the East Coast with a stop-over ___ ___

10. fly in an airplane from San Francisco to Hawaii ___ ___

K. RIDING CITY BUSES.

Can you:

1. ride one block in a fairly empty city bus ___ ___

2. ride one block in a crowded city bus ___ ___

3. ride 3 blocks in a crowded city bus ___ ___

4. ride one mile in a crowded city bus ___ ___

5. ride 5 miles in a crowded city bus ___ ___

339

L. WALKING THROUGH A CROWDED DEPARTMENT STORE (e.g., MACYS).

Can you: Alone   With Someone

1. walk inside the front door and then immediately leave ___ ___

2. walk 30 steps into the store and then leave ___ ___

3. walk to the middle of the ground floor and then leave ___ ___

4. browse on the ground floor for 15 minutes ___ ___

5. purchase an item on the ground floor (assuming no line) ___

6. take escalator up to the second floor and browse for 15 minutes ___

7. take escalator up to the second floor and purchase an item (assuming 2 people ahead of you in line) ___ ___

8. take escalator up to third floor and browse for 15 minutes ___ ___

9. take escalator up to third floor and purchase several items (assuming 5 people ahead of you in line) ___

10. take escalator up to third floor and try on several articles of clothing in the dressing room. ___ ___

M. GOING INTO A CROWDED MOVIE THEATRE. Can you:

1. sit in the back row near the aisle for 5 minutes ___ ___

2. sit halfway toward the front of the theatre near the aisle for 10 minutes ___ ___

3. sit halfway toward the front of the theatre away from the aisle for 30 minutes ___ ___

4. sit near the front of the theatre away from the aisle for one hour ___ ___

5. sit near the front of the theatre away from the aisle for an entire 3-hour movie ___ ___

N. DRIVING AN AUTOMOBILE.

Can you: Alone   With Someone

1. sit in a parked car for two minutes ___ ___

2. drive in a quiet, residential area 1 block ___ ___

3. drive in a quiet, residential area 10 blocks with traffic signals and turns ___ ___

4. drive a minor thoroughfare 5 blocks with traffic signals and turns ___ ___

340

Can you:	Alone	With Someone
5. drive a minor thoroughfare 10 blocks with traffic signals and turns	——	——
6. drive a major thoroughfare 5 blocks with traffic signals and turns	——	——
7. drive a major thoroughfare 10 blocks (1 mile) with traffic signals and turns	——	——
8. drive a lightly traveled freeway (such as Route 280) one exit in the right lane	——	——
9. drive a lightly traveled freeway (such as Route 280) 2 exits changing lanes	——	——
10. drive a heavily traveled freeway (such as Hwy. 101) 5 exits changing lanes	——	——

O. ATTEND SOCIAL GATHERINGS

CAN DO

Can you:	Alone	With Someone
1. attend a small dinner get together at a close friend's house (no more than 4 people)	——	——
2. attend a small office Christmas party (about 15 people)	——	——
3. attend a medium size birthday party (about 25 people)	——	——
4. attend a dance with live music (about 50 people)	——	——
5. attend a wedding (about 100 people)	——	——
6. attend a large high school graduation ceremony (about 500 people)	——	——
7. attend an amusement park like Great America (about 5,000 people)	——	——
8. attend a college basketball game (about 10,000 people)	——	——
9. attend a large outdoor political rally (about 50,000)	——	——
10. attend the Superbowl at Stanford Stadium	——	——

P. WORK AT A JOB

Can you:		
1. work at a job out of your home	——	——
2. work at a job near your home for 10 hours per week	——	——
3. work at a job near your home for 20 hours per week	——	——
4. work at a full-time job near your home	——	——
5. work at a full-time job far from your home (i.e., 25 minute drive in one direction)	——	——

341

APPENDIX THREE

· · · · · · · · ·

The Stanford
Agoraphobia
Exposure
Protocol

· · · · · · · · · ·

Mary Brouillard
Michael Telch, Ph.D.

INTRODUCTION

This appendix summarizes the main features of the exposure treatment protocol used in a large study designed to evaluate the relative
contributions of imipramine and exposure in reducing avoidance and
panic attack intensity and frequency in patients with agoraphobia.
One hundred and four patients have been randomized to a 1-year
trial of imipramine or placebo with either behavioral exposure instructions or intensive group exposure therapy with a follow-up at 2
years. Although designed for research, the protocol conveys the essential features and methods of intensive group exposure therapy. We
have also included a case example, drawn from a variety of patients,

to illustrate what happens to the typical patient in the course of treatment.

The treatment protocol was developed by Mike Telch, Ph.D. with Mary Brouillard, Stewart Agras, M.D., and Barr Taylor, M.D., and other members of the Stanford Anxiety Research group. An expanded version with forms can be obtained for $15 from Mary Brouillard, Laboratory for the Study of Behavioral Medicine, Stanford Medical Center, Stanford, CA 94305.

This treatment program has four important components: education, therapist-directed in vivo exposure, cognitive therapy, and group-supported self-directed exposure. The overall format for the treatment is a group approach, but the exposure is conducted individually. This design allows the patient to benefit from the therapeutic aspects of both group and individual treatment: the supportive, interactive benefits of the group and the personalized attention of individual treatment. Basic educational information about panic and agoraphobia is given in the group setting and general exposure goals are set and reviewed there. In this way, all the patients receive the same basic information. Further, they can benefit from hearing about other patients' progress and problems and can discuss their own concerns, triumphs, and frustrations with others who "really understand." The educational information is elaborated upon by the therapist during the individualized exposure. This insures that each patient receives a highly individualized educational and therapeutic exposure experience.

Structure of the Program

The program is 6 weeks long and is divided into an *intensive phase* and a *transition phase*. The intensive phase consists of six 3-hour sessions over a 2-week period. It gives the patient 18 hours of intensive integrated education, cognitive therapy, and therapist-assisted exposure therapy. The transition phase consists of four 1½-hour weekly sessions with both the patients and their partners. It is designed to educate the partners, to assist in goal-setting for self-directed home practice, and to transfer the principles learned in the intensive phase to the "real world." In general, the patients are taught the principles and receive exposure therapy during the intensive phase and then move on to practice on their own with the help of the group during the 4-week transition phase. By the end of the 6 weeks, the patients should be prepared to continue exposure practice on their own with periodic guidance and support from a therapist. The program moves the patients progressively from intensive exposure to assisted practice to self-directed mastery practice.

Intensive Phase

The intensive phase is divided into six 3-hour sessions. The sessions are organized around the following themes:

1. Agoraphobia and behavior change principles
2. Tips for effective practice
3. Cognitions in panic
4. Rules for coping with panic
5. Relapse prevention
6. Relationships and recovery

Typically, the sessions are held on Tuesday, Wednesday, and Thursday mornings at the clinic. The 3 consecutive days are chosen to maximize the effects of the intensive practice. The patients then have 4 days to rest and to begin some self-directed practice, the results of which are reported back to the group. Thus, any potential problems in the home environment that may impede practice and recovery later can be identified early. Our groups are usually comprised of three to four patients with one therapist for every one to two patients. We find these groups large enough for the patients to benefit from a variety of experiences and yet small enough for each one to be able to ask questions and voice their concerns.

Each session is divided into 3 parts as follows:

1. One-half to 1 hr	group education and discussion of goals, obstacles, concerns, etc.
2. 1 and one-half to 2 hrs	individual therapist-directed in vivo exposure
3. One-half hr	group review of exposure practice with feedback and discussion.

The group meets for an education and discussion session and then disperses for the exposure therapy. Each patient-therapist team sets specific goals for the day and then leaves the clinic for the exposure practice for 2 hours. The educational information is elaborated upon by the therapist during the fieldwork in whatever way is most appropriate for the patient.

For purposes of illustration, we will follow the exposure treatments of a fictitious patient named Joyce, who typifies the problems individuals encounter during exposure therapy. Joyce is a 37-year-old white female who is married with two children ages 6 and 7. She had her first panic attack 5 years ago, shortly after she and her husband moved to the area from another state. At the time of the move, her husband had just finished business school and was starting a job in the area. Her first attack occurred in the grocery store about 2 months after the move. She became very frightened, thinking that she was seriously ill, and left her groceries and returned home quickly. The next day she went to a local doctor who assured her that she was healthy and had probably experienced anxiety. Two weeks later she had another attack in the drug store and one while standing in line at the bank. From that point, the attacks began to occur at least weekly and Joyce became quite concerned. She began avoiding all shopping unless her husband was with her. She also became afraid to drive out of her local neighborhood for fear a panic episode would render her helpless and unable to return home. The only place she felt completely safe was at home and then only if her husband and children were nearby. Joyce describes herself as a happy, energetic woman who can't understand what is happening to her. She is showing signs of depression that have developed as her condition has worsened.

Joyce was diagnosed as having agoraphobia with panic attacks. Her Beck Depression Inventory score was 18, and the agoraphobia subscale on the Fear Questionnaire was 38. She was unable to complete the behavioral test walk that involved walking along a city street and through a local department store.

SESSION 1

Education Component

Summary of the Lecture

I. The sessions begin with each person recounting his or her history of panic attacks and agoraphobia. They are also asked what brought them to treatment at this time.

II. The therapist gives an overview of agoraphobia, defining it as a "fear of fear." Patients are told that:

1. *Agoraphobia develops in stages.* The first stage is the experience of the spontaneous panic attack. In the second phase, the anticipatory anxiety phase, the person begins to anticipate the occurrence of the next attack with dread. In the third phase, the person decides to try to cope with panic by avoiding the situations where they have occurred or are likely to occur. In the fourth phase, some people experience depression and loss of self-esteem as a consequence of being disabled and dependent on others.

2. *Panic disorder and agoraphobia are not the same.* The differences are discussed.

3. *Panic disorder may have a biological basis.*

III. Roles of medication and behavior therapy in the treatment of panic and agoraphobia. The simplest explanation is that panic-blocking medication is used to control the spontaneous panic attacks and that the purpose of the behavior therapy is to help the patient overcome the avoidance behavior.

IV. Principles of exposure therapy. It is essential that patients understand these principles:

1. *Confront the feared situation to learn to deal with the "fear of fear" and overcome avoidance.* The therapy involves repeated ventures into anxiety-provoking situations using techniques designed to help the patient overcome the fear.

2. *Let the anxiety peak and pass.* Anxiety will not continue to increase indefinitely. It will eventually reach a peak and then begin to decrease regardless of where the person is. If the person feels anxious in a situation and leaves as the anxiety is increasing, this sensitizes the person to that situation and reinforces the idea that the situation caused the anxiety and escape caused it to decrease. It is likely that the anxiety will be higher the next time the person goes into that situation. Staying in the situation, however, until the anxiety begins to subside will lead to habituation—the anxiety will be less every time the person returns. Leaving reinforces avoidance; staying leads to recovery.

3. *Accept the panic; bring it on.* This is a critical change in attitude. Panic is viewed not as dangerous, only very uncomfortable. It may be helpful to think of it as an exaggeration of the body's stress response. The consequences of panic that are so frightening will in all likelihood not occur. Because panic is so frightening the person exerts considerable energy trying to push it down or avoid it, which impairs his/her ability to function normally and creates even more anxiety. The way to recover is to stop fearing the panic—to actually allow it to happen in order to learn to deal with it.

4. *Use a graduated hierarchy of exposure.* Confronting a task, such as going into the grocery store, may be too difficult to attempt all at once. The most useful practice is one in which the person experiences a moderate level of anxiety and learns to deal with it. Going into the store may generate too much anxiety and be counterproductive. Any task can be broken down into a series of smaller, more manageable steps that the person can do progressively with moderate anxiety. It is desirable to experience a moderate level of anxiety and to learn to deal with it in a new way, without fear and avoidance.

5. *Response aids or induction aids can help to get the exposure behavior started.* Sometimes it helps a person to use something or

someone to make it easier to enter a situation the first time. Examples of some response aids are another person, carrying a "safe" object like a purse, or smoking a cigarette. These things are used only to get the behavior started and are gradually phased out over the course of practice until the person can function completely without them.

6. *Return to the anxiety-provoking situation repeatedly to decrease anxiety.* During practice (repeated trials), it is best to reenter the situation several times in order to clearly see the anxiety decreasing with each trial. A good rule of thumb is that if a situation evokes an anxiety level of 4 or above, repeat the practice in that situation until the task can be performed with an anxiety level of 3 or less. These ratings are based on a 10 point scale, the SUDS (Subjective Units of Distress Scale) where 0 indicates no anxiety, 1 to 3 is mild, 4 to 6 is moderate, 7 to 9 is severe, and 10 is full-blown panic.

7. *Focus on behavior, not on feelings.* The most effective way to cope with this problem is to concentrate on what you do, not on how you feel. The bodily sensations that are associated with anxiety can be experienced without the subjective feeling of anxiety. In fact, these physical sensations often take longer to resolve than the affective reactions. The sensations of light-headedness, palpitations, tingling, etc. are physical feelings—they do not have to be labeled as anxiety. Rather than focusing on these symptoms, it is more productive to focus on behavior. Whether a person leaves the house alone or goes shopping is more important than whether s/he feels sweaty, tingly, or dizzy while doing it.

V. Obstacles to practice—These are common experiences that may make it more difficult to return for the next therapy session. Telling the patients about these ahead of time can decrease their impact.

1. *Fatigue—exposure practice is exhausting.* It is common to feel quite tired after practice and to sleep a lot or even to have difficulty sleeping. This is expected. It is an indication that the person has worked hard.

2. *Anticipatory anxiety—this is the worry about what will happen the next day.* It can take a number of forms. For example, we commonly have patients think that they are "coming down with something" and shouldn't come in. If they do not have a fever, we urge them to come in anyway; almost always they find that it was anxiety. This is a valuable learning experience about the effect anxiety has on their lives. We also remind patients that they will be able to go at their own pace. The therapy is a collaborative

venture and we will work together to set goals that are manageable and not overwhelming.

3. *Good days and bad days—we all have some days that are harder than others*. It is important to realize this and practice less if necessary on a bad day and work harder on a good day.

VI. Identitifying areas for practice—Using the Avoidance Form have the patients rate the degree to which they avoid each of the situations listed. The Avoidance Form is a worksheet that can be used to design exposure experiences during the fieldwork.

VII. Description of the fieldwork—Every day there will be approximately 2 hours of field practice. Each patient will go with one therapist to some of the places that create anxiety and avoidance and will practice confronting these situations using the principles that have just been discussed. The goal is to confront and conquer some difficult situations, to learn to overcome the fear of panic, and to learn the behavior therapy principles, so that self-directed practice can continue after this phase of the program is completed.

VIII. Confidence Form—Patients are given a form on which to estimate their confidence in coping with panic and the associated cognitions.

Handouts

1. The Agenda—outline of the topics to be covered in the session.
2. Avoidance Rating Form—patients rate the degree to which they avoid doing various activities, using a 0–4 avoidance scale. The exposure therapy will be based on this information.
3. Confidence Form—see above. (This form is undergoing revision and will be available from Dr. Telch at University of Texas at Austin.)
4. Behavior Therapy Progress Record—a form for patients to chart their practice sessions.

In Vivo Exposure Component

Choose an initial practice session task that can be broken into smaller steps easily and one in which the patient is likely to experience only a moderate level of anxiety (about 4–5+ on the 10-point SUDS scale). A situation that the patient rated 2 on the Avoidance Form is usually a good place to start. Have the patient go into the situation, rate the anxiety, and stay in the situation until the anxiety begins to decrease. Point out that staying until the anxiety decreases

Agoraphobia Treatment Program
Agenda

- Introductions

- What is Agoraphobia

- Overview of Behavioral Treatment Program

- Principles of Effective Behavioral Treatment

  - Learning to Confront Feared Situations
  - Letting the Anxiety Peak and Pass
  - Learning to Use Response Aids Effectively
  - Importance of Repeated Trials
  - Learning to Fade Out Response Aids
  - Self-Directed Mastery Practice

- Obstacles to Watch Out For

- Identifying Areas for Practice

  - Going into Crowded Stores
  - Walking Along Busy Streets
  - Waiting in Lines at Banks, Stores, etc.
  - Riding Buses
  - Eating in Restaurants
  - Grocery Shopping
  - Heights
  - Using Elevators
  - Using Escalators
  - Driving
  - Other(s)_____

- Individualized Field Work

is part of the process of overcoming anxiety. Leaving before the anxiety decreases will only reinforce the avoidance and will not lead to recovery. Have the patients repeat the situation several times to show how anxiety diminishes with every successive trial. This demonstrates the principle of repeated trials. By the end of the session the patient should have a better understanding of breaking a task into smaller, more manageable steps, rating the anxiety, letting it peak and pass, and repeating the trial to further overcome the anxiety.

Case Example

On the Avoidance Form, Joyce rated walking alone on a busy street as causing her severe anxiety, yet she can do it. We take her to a nearby small busy downtown street and park on a neighboring street.

The task "walking alone on a busy street" can be broken down into several smaller tasks. First, Joyce can walk to the corner but stay within sight of the car. A second step would be to have Joyce turn the corner and walk toward stores down the block. In this step, she will be on the busy street and out of sight of the car and therapist. A third step could be to have her walk around the corner and down a full block. These are among many possible ways that the task could be broken down; usually the therapist and patient together decide on the steps to use.

AVOIDANCE FORM

For each of the following circumstances, use the scale below to rate how you behave **ALONE.** Use the Comments area to describe each situation more specifically.

DO WITH NO ANXIETY	DO WITH MILD ANXIETY	DO WITH SEVERE ANXIETY	DO ONLY WITH TERROR	WILL NOT DO UNDER ANY CONDITION
0	1	2	3	4

Situation	Rating	Comments
1. Going into crowded store	_____	_____
2. Walking along busy streets	_____	_____
3. Waiting in line	_____	_____
4. Riding buses	_____	_____
5. Eating in restaurants	_____	_____
6. Grocery shopping	_____	_____
7. Heights	_____	_____
8. Using elevators	_____	_____
9. Using escalators	_____	_____
10. Driving local streets	_____	_____
11. Driving freeways	_____	_____
12. Driving far from home	_____	_____
13. Walking away from home	_____	_____
14. Being home alone	_____	_____
15. Sitting in a movie theater	_____	_____
16. Going to church	_____	_____
17. Crossing bridges	_____	_____
18. Walking in open places	_____	_____
19. Attending a class	_____	_____
20. Riding BART	_____	_____
21. Other_____	_____	_____
22. Other _____	_____	_____

Name: _____   Date: _____   Problem Area: _____

BEHAVIOR THERAPY PROGRESS RECORD

Description of Activities	Time Started/ Completed	Maximum Anxiety (0-10)	Ending Anxiety (0-10)	Comments

Now Joyce is ready to try step 1. We remind her that the purpose of exposure therapy is to experience some anxiety and to remain in the situation until it begins to pass. We have Joyce rate her anxiety on the 0 to 10 SUDS scale before starting and write down the rating and the time on the Progress Record. Joyce walks to the corner, pauses, and returns. She reports that her anxiety stayed at a 2 the whole time. This tells us that she is ready for a more difficult step.

Next, Joyce is to go around the corner and past two stores. She rates her beginning anxiety as a 2 and records the time. She returns 5 minutes later and reports that her anxiety reached a 5 when she went around the corner but that she stayed until it came down to a 3 before coming back. She is delighted—she didn't really believe that the anxiety would come down unless she left. In keeping with the principle of repeated trials, we have Joyce complete the same step again. This time she experiences an anxiety level of 3 when she rounds the corner and returns with a level of 1. We have her repeat it once again and she leaves with a level of 1.

We will then have Joyce do Step 3, walking around the corner to the end of the block. She will repeat this step as she did with Step 2 until she can perform the step with minimal anxiety. This has been a positive experience

TIPS FOR EFFECTIVE PRACTICE

- BREAK YOUR GOALS INTO SMALLER BEHAVIORAL STEPS

- CHOOSE PRACTICE TARGETS THAT PRODUCE MODERATE ANXIETY NOT FULL-BLOWN PANIC

- USE AIDS EFFECTIVELY
  If necessary, use aids to get a behavior started. As you are able to perform the behavior with less anxiety, begin to fade the aids until you can perform the behavior independently (without aids).

- PERFORM EACH STEP OVER AND OVER UNTIL THE ANXIETY GOES DOWN

- ONCE YOU HAVE MASTERED A PARTICULAR STEP MOVE ON TO A MORE CHALLENGING ONE

- LONGER PRACTICE SESSIONS (90 MINUTES OR LONGER) ARE MORE EFFECTIVE THAN SHORTER ONES

- PROGRAM REGULAR PRACTICE INTO YOUR ROUTINE

for Joyce. She now has an idea of how to break up a task, how to rate her anxiety, how to let the anxiety peak and pass, and how to repeat a step until the anxiety decreases. She tells you that this is the first time she has been on a downtown street alone without being very anxious in 5 years.

Group Review Component

Topics to Discuss

The general topics for discussion are as follows:

1. Each patient discusses his/her activities during the exposure using the Progress Record as a guideline.
2. Congratulate each patient's progress or attempts.
3. Constructively evaluate situations where the behavior therapy principles were not utilized or could have been used differently.
4. Reiterate the principles used by each patient and how these worked.
5. Remind patients of the obstacles to returning the next day— fatigue, anticipatory anxiety, etc.
6. Discuss the feelings and individual appraisals of the day's activities.

Example

Joyce comes back to the group and describes her fieldwork in detail. The rest of the group and the therapists share in her excitement about her progress and reiterate to her how she successfully utilized the behavior therapy principles. We remind her that even though she feels happy and optimistic now she should not be surprised if she feels quite tired tonight and possibly has trouble sleeping. Also she may have some anticipatory anxiety in the morning and not want to return. She may even feel as though she is "coming down with something." If she remembers that these obstacles are common and expected, she will not give in to them. Once again we congratulate her on her successful efforts.

SESSION 2

Education Component

Summary of the Lecture

I. Discussion about experiences since yesterday's session. Patients are encouraged to talk about their physical and emotional experiences since the previous day's session. Were they tired? Did they sleep more or less than usual? Did they have any anticipatory anxiety last night or this morning? Did they notice any physical symptoms of anxiety? Did they talk with anyone about yesterday? What was the interaction like? How did the other person/s react? Do they have any questions, thoughts, or concerns about anything that was covered in the first session? Questions such as these can be used to stimulate discussion. The point of the discussion is to encourage participation and group interaction and to get the patients to begin to recognize their particular symptoms of anxiety and its effects on their lives. II. Tips for Effective Practice. The behavior change principles covered yesterday are reviewed.

1. *Break your goals into smaller behavioral steps.* Every task can be broken down into several smaller, progressively more difficult tasks.

2. *Choose practice targets that produce moderate anxiety, not full-blown panic*—tasks that produce anxiety in the 4 to 7 range are best. This allows the patient to experience anxiety and practice coping techniques but not to a point where he/she becomes overwhelmed. This is not flooding! If a task seems easy, practice it to be sure it is mastered and then move on to a more challenging task. If something is too difficult, break it into smaller steps and begin to practice those.

3. *Using aids effectively*—use response aids to help begin the task and then fade away the aids. Response aids are things or people that allow the task to be performed with less anxiety. As the task becomes easier, systematically withdraw the aid until it is no longer used. For example, patients often feel better carrying a "safe" object such as their keys. If the task is to cross the street, the patient may first cross the street carrying the keys in his or her hand. Once this is mastered, s/he could cross the street with keys in his or her pocket. Finally, s/he would cross without the keys.

4. *Perform each step over and over until the anxiety goes down.* This is the principle of repeated trials. Repeat each step within one practice session until the anxiety is less than 4.

5. *Once you have mastered a particular step, move on to a more challenging one.*

6. *Longer practice sessions (90 minutes or longer) are more effective than shorter ones.* A longer session allows time to practice more steps and perform more repeated trials. Also a minimum of two practice sessions per week is recommended.

7. *Program regular practice into your routine.*

Handout

Tips For Effective Practice—reviews the principles of behavior change.

In Vivo Exposure Component

This session incorporates all behavior therapy principles in a more intensive practice session.

Case Example

This morning Joyce awoke with an upset stomach, but she remembered what we had said about anticipatory anxiety symptoms and began to relax. After a small breakfast, she felt fine.

In reviewing Joyce's Avoidance Form, we see that she rated both riding elevators and standing in lines as 3. She has further specified on her form that elevators which are crowded and lines with more than three people are particularly difficult for her. Joyce agrees that entering these situations is so hard for her that she usually, but not always, avoids them. Her recent attempts to enter elevators or lines has evoked significant anxiety. Because these situations are strongly feared but not completely avoided, they are good choices for this practice session.

Joyce feels that she would like to begin working on elevators since this phobia really hinders her life. Before we start the actual practice, we talk to Joyce about the most frightening aspects of elevators. We want to know what it is about riding the elevators that triggers the anxiety. This information will help us design the exposure so that the tasks she practices have some of the anxiety-provoking features. She tells us that the movement of the elevator and the feeling of being trapped with other people for a long time are the most frightening things. She is not bothered by the number of floors that the elevator rises, only the amount of time that she is in it. This is important information—Joyce is not afraid of heights. If her fear of elevators was complicated with a height phobia, we might need to work on the height phobia first.

We surmise that the most frightening scenario for Joyce would be a long ride in a crowded rickety elevator. She agrees (with a shudder), and so we begin to break this down into simple tasks beginning with an empty, stable elevator. We decide to practice on the elevator in the clinic first, since she has no fear of the clinic building itself. This way we know that the anxiety Joyce experiences is most likely due to being in the elevator. We first have her walk into the elevator and stand inside while holding the door open for 1 minute. Her anxiety starts at 1 and is unchanged by this exercise. Next, we have her ride the elevator one floor and we meet her at the second floor. Her anxiety went from 1 to 3 on this ride. We have her ride back to the first floor and we meet her again. Her anxiety remained at 1 this time.

To provoke a higher level of anxiety we have Joyce ride up two floors, get out, go back in, and return to the ground floor alone. She has a 6 on the ride up and a 5 on the ride down. We congratulate her for raising her level of anxiety. You want to bring it on in order to deal with it, we remind her. She repeats the same exercise, this time with a 4 going up and a 3 coming down. A third repetition results in an anxiety level of 2 both going up and coming down. We point out how she has conquered this task with repeated trials.

Next we have her ride up three floors with another person, get off, and come back down when someone else does. She reports a 7 on the way up and a 4 on the way down. We ask her what she thinks, and she says that she should repeat it again. This time, she has a 3 going up and coming down and feels quite excited about her progress. She suggests that the next step be a ride up five floors alone and a ride down with another person. She does this with a 4 and a 6, respectively. She repeats it twice until she has a 3 on both rides.

We move to an elevator in another building that has more traffic. We have her ride up five floors alone first since this is a new elevator, but her anxiety is only 3. Next she rides up and down five floors with three people. She reports a 6 on both rides. She repeats this 4 times until her anxiety is 3 on each ride. Finally she rides five floors with five people until her anxiety is consistently 3. She says she is thrilled and can't wait to tell her husband. We review with her the principles that she used and the effects of each.

Group Review Component

Joyce reviews her fieldwork progress with enthusiasm. The group congratulates her on her success in "bringing on" the anxiety and repeating each step until she could perform it with minimal anxiety. She says again that she cannot wait to tell her husband and will maybe even try to ride an elevator with him. We tell her that this would be fine but to remember her principles if she does. She also says that she is surprised at how tired she feels and is looking forward to a nap. We remind her that this is a positive sign that she has really worked hard.

SESSION 3

Education Component

Summary of the Lecture

I. Review of events since previous meeting and discussion of questions or concerns.

II. The role of cognitions in panic. It is the thoughts that we have about situations that influence how we act. If we think something is fun, we are likely to stay and enjoy it. If we think a situation is dangerous, we are likely to avoid it. Similarly, it is what we think about panic attacks that influence how we respond to them. The person who views panic attacks as harmful and dangerous is going to fear them and try to prevent them, but the person who sees them as an uncomfortable inconvenience will react differently. It is important to look at what it is about panic that makes it so frightening; what we think will happen as a result of a panic attack constitutes the fear that maintains it.

III. Assessment of individual categories of cognitions. Panic cognitions seem to fall into three categories: social concerns, physical concerns, and concerns about loss of control. The Stanford Panic Appraisal Inventory assesses the relative importance of these categories for an individual. Each patient will complete and score this instrument during the session and then discuss with the group the most salient concerns.

IV. Cognitive restructuring. In order to recover from agoraphobia, it is necessary to work on the beliefs about panic that maintain it. First, we must decide if these beliefs are valid. Often we think things are true without testing them. We can test these ideas about panic and see if they are true. The evidence against physical concerns can come from the experience of the patient and from information supplied by the therapist. For example, a patient who is afraid of fainting can be asked how many times she has actually fainted during a panic attack. The other patients can be polled also for fainting episodes. The therapist can explain that it is unlikely for a person to faint during a panic attack because fainting is caused by a decrease in blood supply to the brain and in a panic attack there is actually more blood, because the heart is beating faster. Evidence against concerns about loss of control can also come from the patient's experience, such as the number of times s/he has actually become hysterical during a panic attack. It can also be useful to ask "So what? What would really happen if you screamed when you were anxious?" Finally, evidence contrary to social concerns can often be gained during the fieldwork by having the patient or therapist role-play a feared scenario and observe the reactions of people in the area. Also, discussing the consequences of social fears can be helpful—"What if people noticed that you are anxious?"

Second, if these beliefs are not true, we must develop a new way to think about panic and the consequences that we have come to associate with it. Part of the exposure practice will begin to focus on the fearful thoughts that occur when the anxiety increases, the ways that these thoughts contribute to the anxiety, and some new thoughts that can help lower the anxiety.

Handout

Stanford Panic Appraisal Inventory—assesses the salience of thoughts in the physical, social, and loss of control categories. (This form is undergoing revision and will be available from Dr. Telch at the University of Texas at Austin.)

IN VIVO EXPOSURE COMPONENT

From this session on, the fieldwork will integrate both behavioral and cognitive components. While the patient is practicing using the behavior change principles, the therapist will also help the patient identify the thoughts that occur along with the anxiety. The exposure should be designed to collect disconfirming evidence regarding the particular thoughts and beliefs that are associated with the anxiety. Also the therapist can continue to offer explanations about the likelihood of some of the feared consequences.

Case Example

In the group, Joyce is excited and smiling. She took a nap yesterday and slept well last night. She had some anticipatory anxiety on the way into the clinic but was able to reassure herself. She said that her husband was very supportive when she told him about her elevator success but that they did not have the chance to go out so she could show him.

Joyce's most troublesome cognitions concern the reaction other people will have when she panics. To address this fear and to practice the behavior change principles, we go to a local department store. Joyce rated department stores as 4 on her Avoidance Form. Since she also has most trouble with stores that are crowded or have shiny floors, the store we first choose has carpeting and has a moderate number of shoppers. We only want to deal with one feared situation at a time. Joyce says that she is most frightened of being in the store alone and has not been in a department store for a long time. She buys most of her clothes from a catalogue or goes with her husband to small specialty shops.

We decide to use the therapist as a response aid to make going into the store more manageable. The first step is going inside the door of the store with the therapist for 1 minute and then leaving. Time is also being used as a response aid, since being in the store for 1 minute is easier than staying indefinitely. As we go in, Joyce rates her anxiety a 4. Inside it rises to a 7, and she is reminded that this is great, not to fight it, and just to allow it to peak and pass. By the end of 1 minute, Joyce's anxiety has come down to a 5 so we leave the store. (Had it stayed at 7 we would have stayed in the store until it began to come down before leaving.)

When we are outside we ask her what was going through her mind, what was she frightened of. She replies that she is afraid that the anxiety is going to get worse and she will do something to draw attention to herself. She is afraid that she will lose control of herself, people will notice, and she will be terribly embarrassed. We ask her how often this has heppened to her, and she replies that it never has but that she is always afraid of it. We ask her what is so terrible about being embarrassed or having someone notice that she is anxious. Do people really take that much notice of others? Will they rush down to the newspaper and have a story published about the woman who got anxious in the department store? Will she or anyone else die or lose their credit rating if she gets shaky and leaves the store? By using a little humor we try to help Joyce put the possible consequences of her anxiety into perspective. The most important question is whether these consequences are so serious that they warrant completely restructuring one's life to prevent them.

She goes into the store four more times with the therapist until her anxiety is a 3. We suggest that she pay attention to her thoughts during each practice and to ask herself what the worst outcome might be. Next she goes in alone and is told to stay until her anxiety diminishes. As before, Joyce's level of anxiety rises to 7 then comes down to 5 before she leaves. She repeats this step three times. We repeat this practice having her walk half way down the aisle, then to the escalator, and, finally, across the store to the other door. After 90 minutes of practice she is able to walk around the ground floor of the store alone in the main aisle with minimal anxiety.

To address the social concerns associated with fear of fainting, we go into the store with Joyce to do a role play. The therapist will pretend to faint and Joyce is to stand in an out-of-the-way spot and observe the reaction of the other shoppers. Joyce stands behind a rack of clothes. The therapist walks midway down the aisle and pretends to faint. One man comes over to see if she needs any help, and the therapist asks for some water and says she is okay, just a little shaky. A couple of other people look over but continue with their shopping when they see the man come to help. No one stops to stare or points and laughs. Afterward Joyce says that she is amazed that no one did any of the things of which she was afraid. In fact, she is touched and reassured that someone came to offer help in such a nonjudgmental way.

Group Review Component

Topics to Discuss

1. Review and discuss the fieldwork progress.
2. Discuss any work that was done with cognitions during practice.
3. Set goals for self-directed practice over the weekend.
4. Discuss reactions to the day.

Example

Joyce recounts her experience in the department store for the group. She says that she has never realized how worried she was about what other people think.

Joyce is particularly impressed with the fainting role play in the store. She says that really showed her that even if she did faint, the worst thing she imagined would probably not happen. The rest of the group is amazed, too. Another patient says that she has the same fear and listening to Joyce's experience will help her the next time she is anxious.

Since this is the last session this week, we spend some time talking about the 4-day period of time until next week's sessions. We recommend that each patient do one 90-minute practice session over the weekend. This will give them some experience practicing exposure on their own. This is a good way to identify any problems that may arise when the phase of treatment involving therapist-assisted exposure ends and patients must rely on their ability to practice self-exposure. Joyce wants to practice going into a local grocery store alone. She usually does her shopping there with her husband or one of her children but never alone. This seems like an appropriate goal for the weekend and we discuss breaking this down into smaller steps. She will first go inside the door, then midway down an aisle, and finally to the back of the store. She will progressively increase the amount of time at each step until she is able to walk around the back of the store indefinitely with minimal anxiety. We decide to avoid having her purchase any items alone at this point, since this might also include standing in lines, which she has not worked on. She will record her practice on her Progress Record and tell the group about it next week. We also encourage her to pay attention to the thoughts that she has when she is anxious and possibly even keep a record of them. Also we encourage her to notice and record anything that she says to herself to help her deal with the anxiety.

SESSION 4

Education Component

Summary of the Lecture

I. Review of the weekend practice—Each patient discusses in detail the practice done over the weekend. Any problems or concerns are discussed with the group.

II. "Ten Rules For Coping With Panic"—This handout excerpted from *Agoraphobia: Nature and Treatment* (1981) by A. M. Mathews, M. G. Gelder, and D. W. Johnston lists ten things to remember when anxious. It has two formats. In one, the "rules" are written in sentence form; the second format has short reminder phrases. The patients are encouraged to use these rules in their daily life. We usually suggest that patients carry the short form of the rules with them in their purse or wallet so they can take them out and read them any time that they get anxious. The long form can be put at home someplace where it can be read frequently. Using the rules gives the patients a plan for coping with panic when it occurs.

Handout

Ten Rules For Coping with Panic—a long and a short version of ideas to remember when feeling anxious.

In Vivo Exposure Component

Practice

The fieldwork on Days 4, 5, and 6 continues to integrate the cognitive and behavioral aspects of exposure therapy. Patients continue to confront feared situations using the behavior change principles and focus on the cognitions that maintain the anxiety. They are encouraged to use their Panic Rules as a way of cognitively coping with panic and to develop their own positive self-talk to decrease the anxiety. Finally, the exposure is structured so that they can continue to gain disconfirming evidence regarding their fears.

Over the next three sessions, the therapist will play a progressively less directive role in designing the exposure. The patient will be encouraged to set goals, design the steps of practice, and make decisions about dealing with difficult situations. This helps prepare the patient for the self-directed practice that begins after the intensive phase.

Case Example

Joyce is 15 minutes late for the meeting today. When she comes in, she seems subdued and quiet. When the other patients urge her to talk, she bursts into tears and says that she had a panic attack while practicing in the grocery store over the weekend. She is very upset, saying that all her work was wasted and that she is never going to get any better. She had been so excited and optimistic last week thinking that she was really recovering, and now she has had a panic attack.

We ask her to recount the events leading up to the panic attack. She says that she had gone to the store to practice alone on Sunday morning when she knew it would not be crowded. She went inside the door and stayed for 2 minutes without any anxiety. She felt so good about this that she decided to go straight to the back of the store without any intermediate steps. She went back in and walked to the back of the store to the meat department. She had been there with an anxiety of about 4 for 2 minutes when suddenly she had "a full blown #10 panic." She was surprised and frightened and ran out of the store. She went straight home and went to bed for the rest of the day and didn't do any other practicing on Monday. She said she had to force herself to get out of bed this morning to come to the meeting.

We ask Joyce to think back to the situation and to try to remember the thoughts she was having just before the attack. Upon reflection, she says she remembers thinking that she was a long way from the door and that she might get trapped if she saw someone she knew and had to talk to them. She also was afraid that someone would notice that she was just standing around and would ask her what she was doing. We point out that these thoughts may have had a lot to do with provoking the attack. We also point out that in skipping a step in the practicing, she may have moved too quickly to a more anxiety-producing step.

This episode with Joyce triggers an important discussion in the group. Does having a panic attack mean that you are not recovered from agoraphobia? The answer is no. We remind the group that panic disorder and agoraphobia are separate although associated conditions and it is the avoidance behavior, not the panic attacks, that define agoraphobia. A person who is recovered from agoraphobia may continue to have panic attacks occasionally because the panic disorder is still present, but s/he does not have to avoid any situations because of it. This recovered person is no longer afraid of the attacks knowing that they are not dangerous, only uncomfortable, and that they will pass in a short time. A recovered agoraphobic is one who can say, "I can have a panic attack and it is no big deal. I don't avoid anything in my life because of them."

In reviewing Joyce's situation, we identify three difficulties. First, she skipped a step in the practice going on to a more difficult one. Second, she did not notice the anxiety-provoking thoughts that she was having in the back of the store. Third, she ran away from the panic situation rather than staying and letting it pass. Keeping these points in mind, we encourage Joyce and the group to "rewrite" the back of the store scenario. They decide that first of all Joyce should have stayed until the panic passed and then walked slowly out of the store. Then she should have gone back to a less difficult step and practiced that several times rather than going home.

Our final comment to Joyce is to remind her that she made considerable progress last week and to remember that. We suggest that she look at the episode in the store as an important learning experience rather than a failure. She says that she really sees how important the principles are and that she is going to pay much more attention to her thoughts now.

In the fieldwork session we decide with Joyce that it is important for her to go back to the store where she had the panic attack and practice there. She is also instructed to record her thoughts during the practice. After an hour of exposure, Joyce is able to walk around the entire store with minimal anxiety and even stop to talk with one of the butchers about a special cut of meat. By tracking her thoughts, she is more aware of them and finds that she can lower her anxiety by countering each frightening thought with a reassuring one. During the second hour Joyce elects to practice standing in lines. We go to a local large post office and have her practice standing in progressively longer lines using the behavior change principles and recording her thoughts. This practice goes quite smoothly, and by the end of the fieldwork, Joyce is again feeling pleased and enthusiastic.

Group Review Component

Case Example

Joyce reviews her progress with enthusiasm and the group is supportive and happy for her. We ask her to reiterate the principles that she used in dealing with the grocery store, and she is able to do this accurately.

SESSION 5

Education Component

Summary of the Lecture

I. Discussion of concerns or questions.
II. Setbacks and relapse. An individual with agoraphobia may have a setback or a relapse at any time. It is important to know the difference between the two and to be aware of some common circumstances that can increase the risk of setback or relapse.

    1. *Setback versus relapse—A setback is more than just a bad day.* It is a consistent pattern or shift in what the patient is able to do but involves less impairment than a relapse. The patient may become unable to do something that s/he could before or may find that some of the things that s/he is continuing to do are creating more anxiety. A relapse is much more severe. It is an almost complete return of the phobias. The person is back to avoiding almost all of the situations that s/he had before the treatment started. It is important to see the setback as a *temporary* slip and to take steps to prevent it from leading to a relapse.

    2. *When a setback occurs—Two things are important to remember when faced with a setback.* First, setbacks are quite common; it is how the person deals with them that determines their potency. One needs to be aware that setbacks may happen, to know the circumstances that put him/her at risk, and to view them as manageable. Giving up leads to relapse. If a person has a setback and

deals with it successfully, this can be a powerful learning aid to prevent it from happening again. Second, remember that it is what you do, not how you feel, that is the yardstick of improvement. Continue to confront the anxiety-producing situations using the behavior change principles that have been taught. It may be necessary to break a situation that has been previously mastered down into smaller steps and begin practicing them again. Perhaps some repeated trials of the troublesome situation is all that is necessary. Confronting and dealing with the anxiety is the key. Do not let the avoidance increase!

3. *Risk factors for a setback*—Some common circumstances that may make a person more vulnerable for a setback are:

(a). Panic attacks

(b). Stress such as job pressure or relationship conflict

(c). Physical illness especially if it immobilizes the person for a while

(d). Depression

(e). Lack of practice

(f). Allowing irrational thoughts to return

(g). Complacency—the feeling that the person has come far enough results in a loss of enthusiasm about bringing on panic and facing it.

The golden rule for dealing with setbacks and preventing relapse is to be aware of the risk factors, work on the anxiety-provoking thoughts, and continue to try to take on the courageous attitude that feeling anxious presents opportunities for managing the anxiety differently. This shift in attitude leads to recovery.

In Vivo Exposure Component

Case Example

To begin this fieldwork session we decide to return to the grocery store where Joyce had her panic attack and where she practiced yesterday. We want to show Joyce how anxiety can build up in a situation when you have been away from it for a period of time and how to handle it. Joyce finds that when she goes into the back of the store, she has an anxiety level of 5 whereas she had none yesterday. Since we had discussed it beforehand, she was not surprised and thought that she should practice this task a few more times. This indicates to us that Joyce is beginning to use the behavior change principles appropriately on her own. After three practices, she can again walk around the store with minimal anxiety.

Next, we decide to have her practice standing in line by having her buy some items in this store. This task could be broken down into several steps, such as picking up a few items and standing in line but not purchasing them, standing in progressively longer lines without making a purchase, purchasing a few items in progressively longer lines, and purchasing many items in a long line. Joyce chooses to buy several items in a line with five people. She does this with an anxiety level of 3. Next she collects several items and stands in a line with seven people. After 5 minutes in the line she rates her anxiety a 7, but she reminds herself of the benefits of learning to cope with anxiety more effectively. She notices that she is thinking about whether the checker will realize that she has been through another line before and is worried what he will think. She tells herself that he probably won't notice, but even if he does her health is more important to her than what he thinks. She also thinks that she could just tell him that standing in line is hard for her and she is practicing.

Joyce is using cognitive coping strategies that she has created which work well in her particular situation. She also takes out her Panic Rules to remind her of points that she has forgotten. By the time she reaches the front of the line, her anxiety is at 2. The checker seems unaware that she has been through another line and she realizes that the thing she was most afraid of, which increased her anxiety, did not happen. This is more evidence for her that her beliefs about the anxiety are irrational.

For the remainder of the session, we have Joyce practice going into several stores that have shiny floors. We start with a small store and eventually move on to larger stores. She practices each task using a series of small steps and repeated trials with good success.

Group Review Component

Case Example

Joyce reviews her fieldwork and receives special congratulations from the group for handling her anxiety in the grocery line so well. We reiterate both the cognitive and behavioral coping strategies that she used and point out that she seems to have really adopted the spirit of getting anxious and dealing with it.

SESSION 6

Education Component

Summary of the Lecture

I. Review of concerns and questions.
II. Recovery and relationships. A person's recovery can affect his or her significant relationships, and the relationships can influence the recovery. First, recovering from agoraphobia creates change in a rela-

tionship, and for some relationships this change can be a stressor. For example, it is not uncommon for a significant other to worry that the patient will recover so much that s/he won't be needed any more. These feelings can create stress in the relationship, and this stress may have an impact on the recovery, possibly making a setback more likely. On the other hand, a significant other can be an important help in the patient's recovery. By encouraging, praising, and supporting the patient's practice efforts, the partner can facilitate the recovery process. Alternatively, the patient's recovery may free up the couple to engage in activities together (or apart) that they have not been able to do for a long time. This may improve a relationship that had been strained by the restrictions of the patient.

In Vivo Exposure Component

Case Example

Since this is the final session in the intensive fieldwork, we ask Joyce to direct this session herself with minimal input from us. She elects to work on riding escalators in a local department store. Before starting on the escalators she wants to practice walking around inside the store in case this generates some anxiety. The first time through the store she rates her anxiety a 5, but after two more practices she can walk throughout the first floor without anxiety. She also practices riding the store elevator two floors, which she is delighted to find causes no anxiety.

In practicing on the escalator, she decides to ride up one floor on the elevator and ride down on the escalator. She feels it will be easier to come down knowing that we are waiting on the first floor. On the first trial she rates her anxiety a 5 but this decreases to a 2 with two more trials. Next she rides the elevator to the second floor and rides down on the escalator. Finally she rides the escalator up and down one floor and then two. She practices each step repeatedly until she achieves the appropriate reduction in anxiety.

As a last step, Joyce asks us to leave the store and go to a unspecified place outside. This way she will not know exactly where we are if she has trouble. She is fading us away as response aids and practicing riding the escalator, the elevator, and being in the store without an aid. She practices for 30 minutes alone in the store and then finds us outside. She recounts having an anxiety level of 8 on the second floor of the store when she realized where she was and that she was alone. However, she said she was glad this happened because it gave her an opportunity to deal with the anxiety and do her thinking completely on her own. She feels quite confident that she can deal with her anxiety in almost any situation without panicking and running out.

Group Review Component

Topics to Discuss

1. Review of fieldwork.
2. Set goals for self-directed practice for the next week.
3. Administer Confidence Form to show patients the progress that they have made in the intensive phase.
4. Negotiate meeting time for the next week.

Case Example

Joyce is enthusiastic about practicing on her own. She decides that she would like to practice going to church alone and possibly going to a movie. She feels that she can work on the church alone but would like to go to the movie with her husband or a friend and try sitting in different parts of the theater progressively further from the door. The group agrees that these are appropriate goals and we help her outline the specific practice steps using the Goal Worksheet.

Joyce also fills out the Confidence Form. At the first session Joyce's total confidence rating was 130 out of a possible 800. Now her total rating is 670. This is a remarkable improvement in Joyce's confidence in her ability to handle panic without avoidance. She is impressed with her progress and says that the biggest difference is in the way she thinks about panic—it is not nearly as frightening as it used to be.

DESCRIPTION OF THE TRANSITION PHASE

This phase of the program is designed to help the patient make the transition from the intensive therapist-directed exposure therapy to independent self-directed exposure practice in the "real world." The patients will be practicing on their own during the week and will come to the clinic for a 1½-hour weekly meeting with the group to discuss their progress and to set goals for the next week. These meetings provide a forum for obtaining group support and for getting help in setting and achieving practice goals.

Spouses or significant others are encouraged to attend these meetings also. The educational information from the intensive phase will be presented in condensed form for their benefit and as a refresher for the patients. The role of the spouse in supporting and praising the patient's progress and in not reinforcing avoidance behavior will be emphasized. The purpose is to help spouses become more aware of the nature of agoraphobia and of the steps that the patients are taking to overcome it. It is important to emphasize that these sessions are for education and consultation about the exposure practice and not for marital counseling.

OUTLINE OF EDUCATION TOPICS

Session 1   Etiology of agoraphobia and the principles of behavior change.

Session 2   Review of practice principles and goal setting.

Session 3   Prevention of setbacks and relapse.

Session 4   Planning for the future: continuing to practice on your own.

References

. . . .

Achenbach, T. (1985). Assessment of anxiety in children. In A. H. Tuma & J. D. Maser (Eds.), *Anxiety and the anxiety disorders*. Hillsdale, NJ: LEA.

Aden, G. C., & Thein, S. G. (1980). Alprazolam compared to diazepam and placebo in the treatment of anxiety. *Journal of Clinical Psychiatry, 41*, 245–248.

Ader, R., & Friedman, S. B. (1968). Plasma corticosterone response to environmental stimulation: Effects of duration of stimulation and the 24-hour adrenocortical rhythm. *Neuroendocrinology, 3*, 378–386.

Agras, W. S. (1985). *Panic: Facing fears, phobias and anxiety*. New York: W. H. Freeman.

Agras, W. S., & Jacob, R. (1980). Phobia: Nature and measurement. In M. Mavissakalian & D. H. Barlow (Eds.), *Phobia: psychological and pharmacological treatment*. New York: Guilford Press.

Agras, W. S., Sylvester, D., & Oliveau, D. C. (1969). The epidemiology of common fears and phobias. *Comprehensive Psychiatry, 10*, 151–156.

Ainsworth, M. D., & Bell, S. M. (1970). Attachment, exploratory behavior and separation: Illustrated by the behavior of one-year-olds in a strange situation. *Child Development, 41*, 49–67.

Ainsworth, M. D., Blehar, M., Water, E., & Wall, S. (1978). *Patterns of Attachment. A psychological study of the stranger situation*. Hillsdale, NJ: LEA.

Alden, L., & Cappe, R. (1981). Nonassertiveness: Skill deficit or selective self-evaluation? *Behavior Therapy, 12*, 107–114.

Alden, L., & Safran, J. (1978). Irrational beliefs and nonassertive behavior. *Cognitive Therapy and Research, 2*, 357–364.

Alström, J. E., Nordlund, C. L., Persson, G., Harding, M. & Ljungqvist, C. (1984). Four treatment methods in social phobic patients. *Acta Psychiatrica Scandinavica, 70*, 97–110.

American Psychiatric Association. (1952). *Diagnostic and statistical manual of mental disorders*. Washington, D.C.: American Psychiatric Association.

American Psychiatric Association. (1968). *Diagnostic and statistical manual of mental disorders (DSM-II)*. Washington, D.C.: American Psychiatric Association.

American Psychiatric Association. (1980). *Diagnostic and statistical manual of mental disorders (DSM-III)*. Washington, D.C.: American Psychiatric Association.

American Psychiatric Association. (1987). *Diagnostic and statistical manual of mental disorders (DSM-III-R)*. Washington, D.C.: American Psychiatric Association.

Amies, P. L., Gelder, M. G., & Shaw, P. M. (1983). Social phobia: A comparative clinical study. *British Journal of Psychiatry, 142,* 174–179.

Amin, M. M., Ban, T. A., Pecknold, J. C., Klingner, A. (1977). Chlorimipramine (Anafranil) and behavior therapy in obsessive–compulsive and phobic disorders. *Journal of International Medical Research, 5*(Suppl. 5), 33–37.

Anath, J., & Luchins, D. (1977). A review of combined tricyclic and MAOI therapy. *Comprehensive Psychiatry, 18,* 221–230.

Angelino, H., Dollins, J., & Mech, E. V. (1956). Trends in the fears and worries of school children. *Journal of Genetic Psychology, 89,* 263–267.

Angst, J., & Dobler-Mikola, A. (1983). Anxiety states, panic and phobia in a young general population. In *World Psychiatry Congress Proceedings, Vienna.* New York: Plenum Press.

Annau, Z., Kamin, L. J. (1961). The conditioned emotional response as a function of intensity of the US. *Journal of Comparative and Physiological Psychology, 54,* 428–432.

Arieti, S. (1978). *On schizophrenia, phobias, depression, psychotherapy, and the farther shores of psychiatry: Selected papers of Silvano Arieti.* New York: Brunner/Mazel.

Arnow, B. A. (1984). *Enhancing agoraphobia treatment by changing couple communication patterns: An experimental study.* Unpublished doctoral dissertation, Stanford University, Stanford, CA.

Arnow, B. A., Taylor, C. B., Agras, W. S., & Telch, M. J. (1985). Enhancing agoraphobia treatment outcome by changing couple communication patterns. *Behavior Therapy, 16,* 452–467.

Aronson, T. A. (1987). A naturalistic study of imipramine in panic disorder and agoraphobia. *American Journal of Psychiatry, 144,* 1014–1019.

Arrindell, W. A., & Emmelkamp, P. M. (1985a). Psychological profile of the spouse of the female agoraphobic patient. *British Journal of Psychiatry, 146,* 405–414.

Arrindell, W. A., & Emmelkamp, P. M. (1985b). A test of the repression hypothesis in agoraphobics. *Psychological Medicine, 15,* 125–129.

Arrindell, W. A., & Emmelkamp, P. M. (1986). Marital adjustment, intimacy and needs in female agoraphobics and their partners. *British Journal of Psychiatry, 149,* 592–602.

Arrindell, W. A., Emmelkamp, P. M., Monsma, A., & Brilman, E. (1983). The role of perceived parental rearing practices in the aetiology of phobic disorders: A controlled study. *British Journal of Psychiatry, 143,* 183–187.

Ascher, L. M. (1980). Paradoxical intention. In A. Goldstein & E. B. Foa (Eds.), *Handbook of behavioral interventions: A clinical guide*. New York: Wiley.

Ascher, L. M. (1981). Paradoxical intention for agoraphobia. *Behaviour and Research Therapy, 19*, 533–542.

Ascher, L. M., Schotte, D. E., & Grayson, J. B. (1986). Enhancing effectiveness of paradoxical intention in treating travel restriction in agoraphobia. *Behavior Therapy, 17*, 124–130.

Ashton, H. (1984). Benzodiazepine withdrawal: An unfinished story. *British Medical Journal, 288*, 1135–1140.

Ax, A. F. (1953). The physiological differentiation between fear and anger in humans. *Psychosomatic Medicine, 15*, 433–442.

Ayd, F. J. (1980). Social issues: Misuse and abuse. *Psychosomatics, 21* (Suppl.), 21–25.

Baker, B. L., Cohen, D. C., & Saunders, J. T. (1973). Self-directed desensitization for acrophobia. *Behavior Research and Therapy, 11*, 79–89.

Ballenger, J. C. (1986). Pharmacotherapy of the panic disorders. *Journal of Clinical Psychiatry, 47*(Suppl.), 27–32.

Bandura, A. (1969). *Principles of behavior modification*. New York: Holt, Rinehart & Winston.

Bandura, A. (1977). Self-efficacy: Toward a unifying theory of behavioral change. *Psychological Review, 84*, 191–215.

Bandura, A. (1982). Self-efficacy mechanisms in human agency. *American Psychologist, 37*, 122–147.

Bandura, A. (1983). Self-efficacy determinants of anticipated fears and calamities. *Journal of Personal and Social Psychology, 45*, 464–469.

Bandura, A. (1986). *Social foundations of thought and action: A social cognitive theory*. Englewood Cliffs, NJ: Prentice-Hall.

Bandura, A., Blanchard, E. B., & Ritter, B. (1969). Relative efficacy of desensitization and modeling approaches for inducing behavioral, affective, and attitudinal changes. *Journal of Personality and Social Psychology, 13*, 173–199.

Bandura, A., & Rosenthal, T. (1966). Vicarious classical conditioning as a function of arousal level. *Journal of Personality and Social Psychology, 3*, 54–62.

Bandura, A., Taylor, C. B., Williams, S. L., Mefford, I. Y., & Barchas, J. D. (1985). Catecholamine secretion as a function of perceived coping self-efficacy. *Journal of Consulting and Clinical Psychology, 53*, 406–414.

Barlow, D. H. (1988). *Anxiety and its disorders: The nature and treatment of anxiety and panic*. New York: Guilford Press.

Barlow, D. H., Agras, W. S., Leitenberg, J., & Wincze, J. P. (1970). An experimental analysis of the effectiveness of "shaping" in reducing maladaptive avoidance behavior: An analogue study. *Behaviour Research and Therapy, 8*, 165–173.

Barlow, D. H., Cohen, A. S., Waddell, M. T., Vermilyea, B. B., Klosko, J. S., Blanchard, E. B., & DiNardo, P. A. (in press). Panic and generalized anxiety disorders: Nature and treatment. *Behavior Therapy*.

Barlow, D. H., Leitenberg, J., Agras, W. S., & Wincze, J. P. (1969). The transfer gap in systematic desensitization: An analogue study. *Behaviour Research and Therapy, 7,* 191–196.

Barlow, D. H., Mavissakalian, M., & Schofield, L. (1980). Patterns of desynchrony in agoraphobia: A preliminary report. *Behaviour Research and Therapy, 18,* 441–448.

Barlow, D. H., O'Brien, G. T., & Last, C. G. (1984). Couples treatment of agoraphobia. *Behavior Therapy, 15,* 41–58.

Barlow, D. H., Vermilyea, J., Blanchard, E. B., Vermilyea, B. B., DiNardo, P. A., & Cerny, J. A. (1985). The phenomenon of panic. *Journal of Abnormal Psychology, 94,* 320–328.

Barlow, D. H., & Wolfe, B. (1981). Behavioral approaches to anxiety disorders: A report on the NIMH–SUNY research conference. *Journal of Consulting and Clinical Psychology, 49,* 448–454.

Barlow, J. B. & Bosman, C. K. (1966). Aneurysmal protrusion of the posterior leaflet of the mitral valve. *American Heart Journal, 71,* 166–168.

Bateson, G. (1961). The biosocial integration of behavior in the schizophrenic family. In N. Ackerman, F. Beatmen, & S. Sherman (Eds.), *Exploring the base for family therapy.* New York: Family Service Association of America.

Beaumont, G. (1977). A large open multi-center trial of chlorimipramine (Anafranil) in the management of phobic disorders. *Journal of International Medical Research, 5,* 116–123.

Beck, A. T. (1976). *Cognitive therapy and the emotional disorders.* New York: International Universities Press.

Beck, A. T., & Emery, G. (1985). *Anxiety disorders and phobias: A cognitive perspective.* New York; Basic Books.

Beck. A. T., Laude, R., & Bohnert, M. (1974). Ideational components of anxiety neurosis. *Archives of General Psychiatry, 31,* 319–325.

Beck, A. T., Rush, A. J., Shaw, B. F., & Emery, G. (1979). *Cognitive therapy of depression.* New York: Guilford Press.

Beck, A. T., Ward, C. H., Mendelson, M., Mock, J., & Erbaugh, J. (1961). An inventory for measuring depression. *Archives of General Psychiatry, 4,* 561–571.

Beidel, D. C., Turner, S. M., & Dancu, C. V. (1985). Physiological, cognitive and behavioral aspects of social anxiety. *Behaviour Research and Therapy, 23,* 109–117.

Beitman, B. D., Basha, I. M., DeRosear, L., Flaker, G., & Mukerji, V. (1987a). Panic disorder uncomplicated and panic disorder with agoraphobia in cardiology patients with atypical or non-anginal chest pain. *Journal of Anxiety Disorders, 1,* 301–312.

Beitman, B. D., Lamberti, J. W., Mukerji, V., DeRosear, L., Basha, I., & Schmid, L. (1987b). Panic disorder in chest pain patients with angiographically normal coronary arteries: A pilot study. *Psychosomatics, 28,* 480–484.

Bellak, L. (1984). Intensive brief and emergency psychotherapy. In L. Grinspoon (Ed.), *Psychiatry Update* (Vol. 3). Washington: APA Press.

Benson, H. (1975). *The relaxation response*. New York: Morrow.

Berg, I., Butler, A., & Pritchard, J. (1974). Psychiatric illness in the mothers of school phobic adolescents. *British Journal of Psychiatry, 125*, 466–467.

Bergman, H., Borg, S., & Holm, L. (1980). Neuropsychological impairment and exclusive abuse of sedatives or hypnotics. *American Journal of Psychiatry, 137*, 215–217.

Bernadt, M. W., Silverstone, T., & Singleton, W. (1980). Behavioural and subjective effects of beta-adrenergic blockage in phobic subjects. *British Journal of Psychiatry, 137*, 452–457.

Bernstein, D. (1973). Situational factors in behavioral fear assessment: A progress report. *Behavior Therapy, 4*, 41–48.

Bernstein, D., & Borkovec, T. D. (1973). *Progressive relaxation training*. Champaign, IL: Research Press.

Bertalanffy, L. von. (1950). An outline of general system theory. *British Journal of the Philosophy of Science, 1*, 136–165.

Bertalanffy, L. von. (1967). *Robots, men and minds*. New York: George Braziller.

Biamino, G., Fenner, H., Schüren, K., Meye, J., Ramdohr; B., & Lohmann, F. (1975). Cardiovascular effects of tricyclic antidepressants—a risk in the use of these drugs. *International Journal of Clinical Pharmacology, 22*, 253–261.

Bianchi, G. N. (1972). A comparative trial of doxepin and diazepam in anxiety states. *Psychopharmacologia, 25*, 86–95.

Bibb, J. L., & Chambless, D. L. (1986). Alcohol use and abuse among diagnosed agoraphobics. *Behaviour and Research Therapy, 24*, 49–58.

Bland, K., & Hallam, R. S. (1981). Relationship between response to graded exposure and marital satisfaction in agoraphobics. *Behaviour Research and Therapy, 19*, 335–338.

Blanchard, E. B., & Hersen, M. (1976). Behavioral treatment of hysterical neurosis: Symptom substitution and symptom return. *Psychiatry, 39*, 118–129.

Bohus, B. (1982). Anxiety: Dysfunction of transmission or modulation. *Behavioral and Brain Sciences, 5*, 482.

Bolles, R. C. & Fanselow, M. D. (1980). A perceptual-defensive-recuperative model of fear and pain. *Behavior and Brain Sciences, 3*, 291–323.

Bonn, J. A., Harrison, J., and Rees, L. (1973). Lactate infusion in the treatment of "free-floating" anxiety. *Canadian Journal of Psychiatry, 18*, 41–46.

Bordin, E. S. (1979). The generalizability of the psychoanalytic concept of working alliance. *Psychotherapy: Theory, Research and Practice, 16*, 252–260.

Borkovec, T. D., & Sides, J. (1979). Relaxation and expectance in fear reduction via graded imaginal exposure to feared stimuli. *Behaviour and Research Therapy, 17*, 529–540.

Boston Collaborative Drug Surveillance Program. (1972). Adverse reaction to the tricyclic antidepressant drugs. *Lancet, 2*, 529–531.

Boulenger, J.-P., & Uhde, T. W. (1982). Caffeine consumption and anxiety: Preliminary results of a survey comparing patients with anxiety disorders and normal controls. *Psychopharmacology Bulletin, 18*, 53–57.

Boulenger, J.-P., Uhde, T. W., Wolff, E. A., & Post, R. M. (1984). Increased sensitivity to caffeine in patients with panic disorders: Preliminary evidence. *Archives of General Psychiatry, 41*, 1067–1071.

Boulougouris, J. C., Marks, I. M., & Marset, P. (1971). Superiority of flooding (implosion) to desensitization for reducing pathological fear. *Behaviour Research and Therapy, 9*, 7–16.

Bowen, R. C., Cipywnyk, D., & Keegan, D. (1984). Alcoholism, anxiety disorders, and agoraphobia. *Alcoholism: Clinical Experimental Research, 8*, 48–50.

Bowlby, J. (1969). *Attachment and loss: Vol 1. Attachment*. New York: Basic Books.

Bowlby, J. (1973). *Attachment and loss: Vol 2. Separation*. New York: Basic Books.

Bradley, G. W. (1978). Self-serving biases in the attribution process: A reexamination of the fact or fiction question. *Journal of Personality and Social Psychology, 36*, 56–71.

Brady, J. P. (1984a). Social skills training for psychiatric patients, I: Concepts, methods, and clinical results. *American Journal of Psychiatry, 141*, 333–340.

Brady, J. P. (1984b). Social skills training for psychiatric patients, II: Clinical outcome studies. *American Journal of Psychiatry, 141*, 491–498.

Braestrup, C., Honore, T., Nielsen, M., Petersen, E. N., & Jensen, L. H. (1983). Benzodiazepine receptor ligands with negative efficacy: Chloride channel coupling. *Advances in Biochemistry and Psychopharmacology, 38*, 248–254.

Braestrup, C., & Squires, R. F. (1977). Specific benzodiazepine receptors in rat brain characterized by high affinity 3H-diazepam binding. *Proceedings of the National Academy of Sciences, U.S.A., 74*, 3805–3809.

Braestrup, C., & Squires, R. F. (1978). Brain specific benzodiazepine receptors. *British Journal of Psychiatry, 133*, 249–260.

Brantigan, C., Brantigan, T., & Joseph, N. (1982). Effect of beta blockade and beta stimulation on stage fright. *American Journal of Medicine, 72*, 88–94.

Bregman, E. (1934). An attempt to modify the emotional attitudes of infants by the conditioned response technique. *Journal of Genetic Psychology, 45*, 169–198.

Breier, A., Charney, D. S., & Heninger, G. R. (1986). Agoraphobia with panic attacks: Development, diagnostic stability and course of illness. *Archives of General Psychiatry, 43,* 1029–1036.

Brenner, C. (1953). An addendum to Freud's theory of anxiety. *International Journal of Psycho-analysis, 34,* 18–24.

Breton, S. (1986). *Don't panic.* New York: Facts on File.

Brian, M., & Wilson, G. T. (1981). Treatment of phobic disorders using cognitive and exposure methods: A self-efficacy analysis. *Journal of Consulting and Clinical Psychology, 49,* 886–899.

Brown, W. A., & Heninger, G. (1975). Cortisol, growth hormone, free fatty acids, and experimentally evoked affective arousal. *American Journal of Psychiatry, 132,* 1172–1176.

Bryant, B., & Trower, P. E. (1974). Social difficulty in a student sample. *British Journal of Educational Psychology, 44,* 13–21.

Buglass, D., Clarke, J., Henderson, A. S., Krietman, N., & Presley, A. S. (1977). A study of agoraphobic housewives. *Psychological Medicine, 7,* 73–86.

Bulges, J., & Vallejo, J. (1987). Therapeutic response to phenelzine in patients with panic disorder and agoraphobia with panic attacks. *Journal of Clinical Psychiatry, 48,* 55–59.

Buss, A. H. (1980). *Self-consciousness and social anxiety.* San Francisco: W. H. Freeman.

Busto, U., Sellers, E. M., Naranjo, C. A., Cappell, H., Sanchez-Craig, M., & Sykora, K. (1986). Withdrawal reaction after long-term therapeutic use of benzodiazepines. *New England Journal of Medicine, 315,* 854–859.

Butcher, J. N., & Koss, M. P. (1978). Research on brief and crisis-oriented therapies. In S. L. Garfield & A. E. Bergin (Eds.), *Handbook of psychotherapy and behavior change* (2nd ed.). New York: Wiley.

Butler, G. (1985). Exposure as a treatment for social phobia: Some instructive difficulties. *Behaviour Research and Therapy, 23,* 651–657.

Butler, G., Cullington, A., Munby, M., Amies, P., & Gelder, M. (1984). Exposure and anxiety management in the treatment of social phobia. *Journal of Consulting and Clinical Psychology, 52,* 642–650.

Butler, G., & Matthews, A. (1983). Cognitive processes in anxiety. *Advances in Behavior Research and Therapy, 5,* 51–62.

Cannon, W. B. (1929). *Bodily changes in pain, hunger, fear and rage: An account of recent research into the function of emotional excitement* (2nd ed.). New York: Appleton-Century-Crofts.

Caplan, G. (1964). *Principles of preventive psychiatry.* New York: Basic Books.

Carey, G. (1982). Genetic influences on anxiety neurosis and agoraphobia. In R. J. Mathew (Ed.), *The biology of anxiety.* New York: Brunner/Mazel.

Carey, G. (1987). Big genes, little genes, affective disorder, and anxiety. *Archives of General Psychiatry, 44,* 486–491.

Carey, G., & Gottesman, I. I. (1981). Twin and family studies of anxiety, phobic, and obsessive disorders. In D. K. Klein & J. Rabkin (Eds.), *Anxiety: New research and changing concepts.* New York: Raven Press.

Carlson, R. J. (1986). Longitudinal observations of two cases of organic anxiety syndrome. *Psychosomatics, 27*, 529–531.

Carr, A. T. (1979). The psychopathology of fear. In W. Sluckin (Ed.), *Fear in animals and man*. New York: Van Nostrand Rheinhold.

Carr, D. B., Sheehan, D. V. (1984). Panic anxiety: A new biological model. *Journal of Clinical Psychiatry, 45*, 323–330.

Carr, D. B., Sheehan, D. V., Surman, O. S., Coleman, J. H., Greenblatt, D. J., Heninger, G. R., Jones, K. J., Levine, P. H., & Watkins, W. D. (1986). Neuroendocrine correlates of lactate-induced anxiety and their response to chronic alprazolam therapy. *American Journal of Psychiatry, 143*, 483–494.

Carver, C. S. (1979). A cybernetic model of self-attention processes. *Journal of Personality and Social Psychology, 37*, 1251–1281.

Catalan, J., & Gath, D. H. (1985). Benzodiazepines in general practice: Time for a decision. *British Journal of Medicine, 290*, 1374–1376.

Cattell, R. B., & Scheier, I. H. (1958). The nature of anxiety: A review of thirteen multi-variate analyses comprising 814 variables. *Psychological Reports, 4*, 351–388.

Cattell, R. B., & Scheier, I. H. (1961). *The meaning and measurement of neuroticism and anxiety*. New York: Ronald Press.

Chambless, D. L. (1985). The relationship of severity of agoraphobia to associated psychopathology. *Behaviour and Research Therapy, 23*, 305–310.

Chambless, D. L., Caputo, G. C., Bright, P., & Gallagher, R. (1984). Assessment of fear of fear in agoraphobics: The body sensations questionnaire and the agoraphobic cognitions questionnaire. *Journal of Consulting and Clinical Psychology, 52*, 1090–1097.

Chambless, D. L., Caputo, G. C., Jasin, S. E., Gracely, E. J., & Williams, C. (1985). The mobility inventory for agoraphobia. *Behaviour Research and Therapy, 23*, 35–44.

Chambless, D. L., Foa, E., Groves, G., & Goldstein, A. (1979). Flooding with Brevital in the treatment of agoraphobia: Countereffective? *Behaviour Research and Therapy, 17*, 243–251.

Chambless, D. L., & Goldstein, A. J. (1981). Clinical treatment of agoraphobia. In M. R. Mavissakalian & D. H. Barlow (Eds.), *Phobia: Psychological and pharmacological treatment*. New York: Guilford Press.

Charney, D. S., Heninger, G. R., & Redmond, D. E., Jr. (1983). Yohimbine-induced anxiety and increased noradrenergic function in humans: Effects of diazepam and clonidine. *Life Sciences, 33*, 19–29.

Charney, D. S., Heninger, G. R., & Breier, A. (1984). Noradrenergic function in panic anxiety; Effects of yohimbine in healthy subjects and patients with agoraphobia and panic disorder. *Archives of General Psychiatry, 41*, 751–763.

Charney, D. S., & Redmond, D. E., Jr. (1983). Neurobiological mechanisms in human anxiety. *Neuropharmacology, 22*, 1531–1536.

Charney, D. S., Woods, S. W., Goodman, W. K., Rifkin, B., Kinch, M., Aiken, B., Quardino, L. M., & Heninger, G. R. (1986). Drug treatment of panic disorder: The comparative efficacy of imipramine, alprazolam, and trazodone. *Journal of Clinical Psychiatry, 47*, 580–586.

Chiles, J. A., Carlin, A. S., & Beitman, B. D. (1984). A physician, a nonmedical psychotherapist, and a patient: The pharmacotherapy–psychotherapy triangle. In B. D. Beitman & G. L. Klerman (Eds.), *Combining psychotherapy and drug therapy in clinical practice.* New York: Spectrum Publications.

Ciba Foundation. (1978). *Functions of the septo-hippocampal system.* Ciba Foundation Symposium New Series, No. 58. Amsterdam: Elsevier.

Clark, D. M. (1986). A cognitive approach to panic. *Behaviour Research and Therapy, 24*, 461–470.

Clark, D. A., & de Silva, P. (1985). The nature of depressive and anxious intrusive thoughts: Distinct or uniform phenomena? *Behaviour and Research Therapy, 23*, 383–393.

Clark, D. M., Salkovskis, P. M., & Chalkley, A. J. (1985). Respiratory control as a treatment for panic attacks. *Journal of Behavioral Therapy and Experimental Psychiatry, 16*, 23–30.

Clayton, P. J., Herjanic, M., Murphy, G. E., & Woodruff, R. (1974). Mourning and depression: Their similarities and differences. *Journal of the Canadian Psychiatric Association, 19*, 309–312.

Clevenger, S. W. (1890). Heart disease in insanity and a case of panphobia. *Alienist and Neurologist, 11*, 535–543.

Clinthorne, J. K., Cisin, I. R., Balter, M. B., Mellinger, G. D., & Uhlenhuth, E. H. (1986). Changes in popular attitudes and beliefs about tranquilizers, *Archives of General Psychiatry, 43*, 527–532.

Cloninger, C. R., Martin, R. L., Clayton, P., & Guze, S. B. (1981). A blind follow-up and family study of anxiety neurosis: Preliminary analysis of the St. Louis 500. In D. F. Klein & J. G. Rabkin (Eds.), *Anxiety: New research and changing concepts.* New York: Raven Press.

Cohen, S., Montiero, W., & Marks, I. M. (1984). Two-year follow-up of agoraphobia after exposure and imipramine. *British Journal of Psychiatry, 144*, 276–281.

Cohn, J. B. (1981). Multicenter double-blind efficacy and safety study comparing alprazolam, diazepam and placebo in clinically anxious patients. *Journal of Clinical Psychiatry, 42*, 347–351.

Coleman, R. E. (1981). Cognitive–behavioral treatment of agoraphobia. In G. Emery, S. D. Hollon, R. C. Bedrosian (Eds.), *New directions in cognitive therapy.* New York: Guilford Press.

Compton, A. (1972a). A study of the psychoanalytic theory of anxiety, I. The development of Freud's theory of anxiety. *Journal of the American Psychoanalytic Association, 20*, 3–44.

Compton, A. (1972b). A study of the psychoanalytic theory of anxiety, II. Developments in the theory of anxiety since 1926. *Journal of the American Psychoanalytic Association, 20*, 341–394.

Connolly, J. C., Hallam, R. S., & Marks, I. M. (1976). Selective association of fainting with blood-injury-illness fear. *Behavioral Therapy, 7*, 8–13.

Cooper, B., & Sylph, J. (1973). Life events in the onset of neurotic illness: An investigation in general practice. *Psychological Medicine, 3*, 421–435.

Cormack, M. A., & Sinnott, A. (1983). Psychological alternatives to long-term benzodiazepine use. *Journal of the Royal College of General Practice, 33*, 279–281.

Coryell, W., Noyes, R., & Clancy, J. (1982). Excess mortality in panic disorder: A comparison with primary unipolar depression. *Archives of General Psychiatry, 39*, 701–703.

Coryell, W., Noyes, R., & House, J. D. (1986). Mortality among outpatients with anxiety disorder. *American Journal of Psychiatry, 143*, 508–510.

Costa, E., Guidotti, A., & Toffano, G. (1978). Molecular mechanisms mediating the action of benzodiazepines on GABA receptors. *British Journal of Psychiatry, 133*, 239–248.

Costa, E., Guidotti, S., Mao, C. C. (1975). Evidence for involvement of GABA in the action of benzodiazepines: Studies on rat cerebellum. In E. Costa & P. Greengard (Eds.), *Mechanism of action of benzodiazepines*. New York: Raven Press.

Costa, P. T. (1987). Influence of the normal personality dimension of neuroticism on chest pain symptoms and coronary artery disease. *American Journal of Cardiology, 60*, 20J–26J.

Costa, P. T., & McCrae, R. R. (1985). Hypochondriasis, neuroticism, and aging: When are somatic complaints unfounded? *American Psychologist, 40*, 19–28.

Costa, P. T., Zonderman, A. B., Engel, B. T., Bail, W. F., Brimlow, D. L., & Brinker, J. (1985). The relation of chest-pain symptoms to angiographic findings of coronary artery stenosis and neuroticism. *Psychosomatic Medicine, 47*, 285–293.

Crasilneck, H. D., & Hall, J. A. (1985). *Clinical hypnosis: Principles and applications* (2nd ed.). New York: Grune & Stratton.

Crenshaw, T. (1985). The sexual aversion syndrome. *Journal of Sex and Marital Therapy, 11*, 285–292.

Crisp, A. H. (1966). "Transference," "symptom emergence," and "social repercussion" in behavior therapy. *British Journal of Medical Psychology, 39*, 179–196.

Crits-Christoph, P. (1986). The factor structure of the cognitive–somatic anxiety questionnaire. *Journal of Psychosomatic Research, 30*, 685–690.

Crowe, M. J., Marks, I. M., Agras, W. S., & Leitenberg, H. (1972). Time-limited desensitization implosion and shaping for phobic patients: A cross-over study. *Behaviour Research and Therapy, 10*, 319–328.

Crowe, R. R., Noyes, R. J., Pauls, D. L., & Slyman, D. (1983). A family study of panic disorder. *Archives of General Psychiatry, 40,* 1065–1069.

Crowe, R. R., Pauls, D. L., Slyman, D. J., & Noyes, R. J. (1980). A family study of anxiety neurosis. *Archives of General Psychiatry, 37,* 77–79.

Curran, J. P. (1977). Skills training as an approach to the treatment of heterosexual-social anxiety: A review. *Psychological Bulletin, 84,* 140–157.

Da Costa, J. M. (1871). On irritable heart: A clinical study of a functional cardiac disorder and its consequences. *American Journal of Medical Science, 61,* 17–52.

Dager, S. R., Comess, K. A., & Dunner, D. L. (1986). Differentiation of anxious patients by two-dimensional echocardiographic evaluation of the mitral valve. *American Journal of Psychiatry, 143,* 533–535.

Dager, S. R., Cowley, D. S., & Dunner, D. L. (1987). Biological markers in panic states: Lactate-induced panic and mitral valve prolapse. *Biological Psychiatry, 22,* 339–359.

Dahlstrom, W. G., Welsh, G. S., & Dahlstrom, L. E. (1972). *An MMPI handbook* (Vol. 1), *Clinical Interpretation.* Minneapolis: University of Minnesota Press.

Darwin, C. (1965). *The expression of the emotions in man and animals.* Chicago: University of Chicago Press.

Delgado, J. M. R. (1972). Physical control of the mind. In E. M. Karlins, & L. M. Andrews (Eds.), *Man controlled: Readings in the psychology of behaviour control.* New York: The Free Press.

Delprato, D. (1980). Heredity determinants of fears and phobias. *Behavior Therapy, 11,* 79–103.

Delprato, D., & McGlynn, F. D. (1984). Behavioral theories of anxiety disorders. In S. M. Turner (Ed.), *Behavioral treatment of anxiety disorders.* New York: Plenum Press.

Dembroski, T. M., MacDougall, J. M., & Shields, J. M. (1977). Physiologic reactions to social challenge in persons evidencing the Type A coronary prone behavior pattern. *Journal of Human Stress, 3,* 2–10.

Derogatis, L. R., Klerman, G. L., & Lipman, R. S. (1972). Anxiety states and depressive neuroses: Issues in nosological discrimination. *Journal of Nervous and Mental Disease, 155,* 392–403.

Derogatis, L. R., Lipman, R. S., & Cove, L. (1973). The SCL-90: An outpatient psychiatric rating scale: Preliminary report. *Psychopharmacological Bulletin, 9,* 13–28.

Deutsch, H. (1929). The genesis of agoraphobia. *International Journal of Psychoanalysis, 10,* 51–69.

Dickinson, A. (1980). *Contemporary animal learning theory.* Cambridge: Cambridge University Press.

Dimsdale, J. (1977). Emotional causes of sudden death. *American Journal of Psychiatry, 134,* 1361–1366.

Dimsdale, J., & Herd, J. A. (1982). Variability of plasma lipids in response to emotional arousal. *Psychosomatic Medicine, 44*, 413–430.

Dimsdale, J. E., & Moss, J. (1980). Short-term catecholamine response to psychological stress. *Psychosomatic Medicine, 42*, 493–497.

DiNardo, P. A., O'Brien, G. T., Barlow, D. H., Waddell, M. T., & Blanchard, E. B. (1983). Reliability of DSM-III anxiety disorder categories using a new structured interview. *Archives of General Psychiatry, 40*, 1070–1074.

DiNardo, P. A., Barlow, D. H., Cerny, J. A., Vermilyea, J. A., Vermilyea, D. D., Himadi, W., Waddell, M. T. (1985). *The Anxiety Disorders Interview Schedule* (Rev.). New York: Center for Stress and Anxiety Disorders.

Dobson, K. S. (1985). An analysis of anxiety and depression scales. *Journal of Personality Assessment, 49*, 523–527.

Dohrenwend, B. S., & Dohrenwend, B. D. (Eds.), (1981). *Stressful life events and their contexts*. New York: Prodist.

Dollard, J., & Miller, N. E. (1950). *Personality and Psychotherapy*. New York: McGraw-Hill.

Drachman, D. A., & Hart, C. W. (1972). An approach to the dizzy patient. *Neurology, 22*, 323–334.

Dunner, D. L., Ishiki, D., Avery, D. H., Wilson, L. G., & Hyde, T. S. (1986). Effect of alprazolam and diazepam on anxiety and panic attacks in panic disorder: A controlled study. *Journal of Clinical Psychiatry, 47*, 458–460.

Dyer, A. R., Stamler, J., Paul, O., Berkson, D. M., Lepper, M. H., McKean, H., Shekelle, R. B., Lindberg, H. A., & Garside, D. (1977). Cardiovascular risk factors and mortality in two Chicago epidemiologic studies. *Circulation, 56*, 1067–1074.

Edlund, J. E., Swan, A. C., & Clothier, J. (1987). Patients with panic attacks and abnormal EEG results. *American Journal of Psychiatry, 144*, 508–509.

Ehlers, A., Margraf, J., & Roth, W. T. (1986). Experimental induction of panic attacks. In I. Hand & H. J. Wittchen (Eds.), *Panic and Phobias*. Berlin: Springer-Verlag.

Ehlers, A., Margraf, J., Roth, W. T., Taylor, C. B., & Birbaumer, N. (1988). Anxiety induced by false heart rate feedback in patients with panic disorder. *Behaviour Research and Therapy, 26*, 1–11.

Ehlers, A., Margraf, J., Roth, W. T., Taylor, C. B., Maddock, R. J., & Kopell, B. S. (1985). *CO_2 as a trigger for panic in panic patients*. Paper presented at the annual meeting of the American Psychiatric Asociation, Dallas, TX.

Ehlers, A., Margraf, J., Roth, W. T., Taylor, C. B., Maddock, R. J., Sheikh, J., & Kopell, M. L. (1986). Lactate infusions and panic attacks: Do patients and controls respond differently? *Psychiatry Research, 17*, 295–308.

Ehlers, A., Margraf, J., Taylor, C. B. & Roth, W. T. (in press). Cardiovascular aspects of panic disorder. In T. Elbert, W. Langosch, A. Steptoe, & D. Vaitl (Eds.), *Behavioural medicine in cardiovascular disorders*. Chichester, England: Wiley.

Eison, A. S., & Temple, D. L. (1986). Buspirone: Review of its pharmacology and current perspectives on its mechanism of action. *The American Journal of Medicine, 80* (Suppl. 3B), 1–9.

Elam, M., Yao, T., Svensson, T. H., & Thoren, P. (1984). Regulation of locus coeruleus neurons and splanchnic, sympathetic nerves by cardiovascular afferents. *Brain Research, 290,* 281–287.

Elam, M., Yao, T., Thoren, P., & Svensson, T. H. (1981). Hypercapnia and hypoxia: Chemoreceptor-mediated control of locus coeruleus neurons and splanchnic, sympathetic nerves. *Brain Research, 222,* 373–381.

Ellis, A. (1962). *Reason and emotion in psychotherapy.* New York: Lyle Stuart.

Emde, R. N. (1981). Changing models of infancy and the nature of early development. *Journal of the American Psychoanalytic Association, 29,* 179–219.

Emde, R. N. (1985). Early development and opportunities for research on anxiety. In A. H. Tuma & J. D. Maser (Eds.). *Anxiety and the anxiety disorders.* Hillsdale, NJ: LEA.

Emde, R. N., Gaensbauer, T. J. and Harmon, R. J. (1976). Emotional expression in infancy. In *Psychological Issues Monograph 37.* New York: International Universities Press.

Emmelkamp, P. M. G. (1974). Self-observation versus flooding in the treatment of agoraphobia. *Behaviour Research and Therapy, 12,* 229–237.

Emmelkamp, P. M. G. (1982). Anxiety and fear. In A. Bellack, M. Hersen, & A. Kazdin (Eds.), *International Handbook of Behavior and Therapy.* New York: Plenum Press.

Emmelkamp, P. M. G., Brilman, E., Kuiper, H., & Mersch, P.-P. (1985). The treatment of agoraphobia: A comparison of self-instructional training, rational emotive therapy, and exposure in vivo. *Behavior Modification, 10,* 37–53.

Emmelkamp, P. M. G., & Felten, M. (1985). Cognitive and physiological changes during exposure in vivo treatment of acrophobia. *Behaviour Research and Therapy, 23,* 219–223.

Emmelkamp, P. M. G., & Kraanen, J. (1977). Therapist controlled exposure in vivo versus self-controlled exposure in vivo: A comparison with obsessive-compulsive patients. *Behaviour Research and Therapy, 15,* 491–495.

Emmelkamp, P. M. G., & Kuipers, A. C. M. (1979). Agoraphobia: A follow-up study four years after treatment. *British Journal of Psychiatry, 134,* 352–355.

Emmelkamp, P. M. G., Kuipers, A. C., & Eggeraat, J. B. (1978). Cognitive modification versus prolonged exposure in vivo: A comparison with agoraphobics as subjects. *Behaviour Research and Therapy, 16,* 33–41.

Emmelkamp, P. M. G., & Mersch, P. (1982). Cognition and exposure in vivo in the treatment of agoraphobia. Short term and delayed effects. *Cognitive Therapy and Research, 6,* 77–78.

Emmelkamp, P. M. G., & Mersch, P. (1985). Case histories and shorter communications. *Behaviour Research and Therapy, 23,* 365–369.

Emmelkamp, P. M. G., Mersch, P., Vissia, E., & van der Helm, M. (1985).

Social phobia: A comparative evaluation of cognitive and behavioral interventions. *Behaviour Research and Therapy, 23,* 365–369.

Emmelkamp, P. M. G., van der Helm, H., van Zanten, B., & Plochg, I. (1980). Contributions of self-instructional training to the effectiveness of exposure in vivo: A comparison with obsessive-compulsive patients. *Behaviour Research and Therapy, 18,* 61–66.

Emmelkamp, P. M. G., & Ultee, K. A. (1974). A comparison of successive approximation and self-observation in the treatment of agoraphobia. *Behavior Therapy, 5,* 605–613.

Emmelkamp, P. M. G., & Wessels, H. (1975). Flooding in imagination vs. flooding in vivo. A comparison with agoraphobics. *Behaviour Research and Therapy, 13,* 7–16.

Endicott, J., & Spitzer, R. L. (1979). Use of the research diagnostic criteria and the schedule for affective disorders and schizophrenia to study affective disorders. *American Journal of Psychiatry, 136,* 52–56.

Endicott, J. E., Spitzer, R. L., & Fleiss, J. L. (1975). Mental status examination record (MSER). Reliability and validity. *Comparative Psychiatry, 16,* 285–301.

English, H. B. (1929). Three cases of the "conditioned fear response." *Journal of Abnormal Social Psychology, 34,* 221–225.

Escobar, J. I., & Landbloom, R. P. (1976). Treatment of phobic neurosis with chlorimipramine: A controlled clinical trial. *Current Therapy & Research, 20,* 680–685.

Evans, A. J., King, A. C., Albright, C., Haskell, W. L., DeBusk, R. F., & Taylor, C. B. (1986). Resting heart rate vs average daily heart rate: Relationships to measures of physical reactivity and state anxiety. *Proceedings of the Society of Behavioral Medicine,* p. 58.

Eysenck, H. J. (1976). The learning theory model of neurosis—a new approach. *Behaviour Research and Therapy, 14,* 251–267.

Eysenck, H. J. (1979). The conditioning model of neurosis. *Behavioral and Brain Sciences, 2,* 155–199.

Eysenck, H. J., & Eysenck, S. B. (1969). *Manual of the Eysenck Personality Questionnaire.* London: Hodder & Stroughton.

Eysenck, H. J., & Rachman, S. (1965). *The causes and cures of neurosis.* San Diego: Robert R. Knapp.

Falloon, I. R. H., Lloyd, G. G., & Harpin, R. E. (1981). Real-life rehearsal with nonprofessional therapists. *Journal of Nervous and Mental Disorders, 169,* 180–184.

Faucheux, B. A., Baulon, A., Poitrenaud, J., Lille, F., Moreaux, C., Dupuis, C., & Bourlieve, F. (1983). Heart rate, urinary catecholamines and anxiety during mental stress in men. *Age and Ageing, 12,* 144–150.

Feigler, J. P. (1987). Buspirone in the long-term treatment of generalized anxiety disorder. *Journal of Clinical Psychiatry, 48,* 3–6.

Feighner, J., Merideth, C., & Hendrickson, G. (1982). A double blind comparison of buspirone and diazepam in outpatients with generalized anxiety disorder. *Journal of Clinical Psychiatry, 43* (12, section 2), 103–107.

Fenichel, O. (1945). *The psychoanalytic theory of neurosis.* New York: Norton.

Fenigstein, A. (1979). Self-consciousness, self-attention, and social interaction. *Journal of Personality and Social Psychology, 37,* 75–86.

Ferguson, J. M., Marquis, J., & Taylor, C. B. (1977). A script for deep muscle relaxation. *Diseases of the Nervous System, 38,* 703–708.

Ferguson, J. M., Taylor, C. B., & Wermuth, B. (1978). Rapid behavioral treatment for needle phobics. *Journal of Nervous and Mental Diseases, 166,* 294–298.

Finlay-Jones, R., & Brown, G. W. (1981). Types of stressful life events and the onset of anxiety-depressive disorder. *Psychological Medicine, 11,* 803–815.

Fisher, L. M., & Wilson, G. T. (1985). A study of the psychology of agoraphobia. *Behaviour and Research Therapy, 23,* 97–107.

Fishman, S. M., Sheehan, S. V., & Carr, D. B. (1985). Thyroid indices in panic disorder. *Journal of Clinical Psychiatry, 46,* 432–433.

Fleischhacker, W. W., Barnas, C., & Hackenberg, B. (1986). Epidemiology of benzodiazepine dependence. *Acta Psychiatric Scandinavica, 74,* 80–83.

Flescher, J. (1955). A dualistic viewpoint on anxiety. *Journal of the American Psychoanalytic Association, 3,* 415–446.

Foa, E. B., Jameson, J. S., Turner, R. M., & Payne, L. L. (1980). Massed vs. spaced exposure sessions in the treatment of agoraphobia. *Behaviour Research and Therapy, 18,* 333–338.

Ford, C. V., Bray, G. A., & Swerdloff, R. S. (1976). A psychiatric study of patients referred with a diagnosis of hypoglycemia. *American Journal of Psychiatry, 133,* 290–294.

Fowles, D. C. (1980). The three arousal model: Implications of Gray's two-factor learning theory for heart rate, electrodermal activity, and psychopathy. *Psychophysiology, 17,* 87–104.

Frankenhauser, M. (1978). Psychoneuroendocrine approaches to the study of emotion as related to stress and coping. *Nebraska Symposium on Motivation, 26,* 123–161.

Frankenhauser, M. (1983). Catecholamines and emotion. In L. Levi (Ed.), *Emotions—their parameters and measurement.* New York: Raven Press.

Freedman, A. M. (1986). Psychopharmacology and psychotherapy in the treatment of anxiety. *Current Psychiatric Therapies: 1986.* New York: Grune & Stratton.

Freud, A. (1946). *The ego and the mechanisms of defence.* New York: International University Press.

Freud, S. (1894). On the grounds for detaching a particular syndrome for neurasthenia under the description "anxiety neurosis." In *Standard edition of the complete psychological works of Sigmund Freud* (Vol. 3). London: Hogarth Press.

Freud, S. (1895). Obsessions and phobias; their psychical mechanisms and their aetiology. In *Sigmund Freud collected papers* (Vol. 1) (J. Riviere, trans.) New York: Basic Books.

Freud, S. (1909). Analysis of a phobia in a five-year-old boy. In *Standard edition of the complete psychological works of Sigmund Freud*. London: Hogarth Press.

Freud, S. (1917). New introductory lectures on psychoanalysis. In *Standard edition of the complete psychological works of Sigmund Freud*. London: Hogarth Press. (Also, New York: Norton, 1933).

Freud, S. (1924). Obsessions and phobias. Reprinted as Chapter 7 in *Collected papers* (Vol. 1). London: Hogarth Press.

Freud, S. (1926). Inhibition, symptoms, and anxiety. In *Standard edition of the complete psychological works of Sigmund Freud* (Vol. 20). London: Hogarth Press.

Freud, S. (1936). *The problem of anxiety*. New York: Norton.

Freud, S. (1943). *A general introduction to psychoanalysis*. Garden City, NY: Doubleday.

Freud, S., & Breuer, J. (1966). *Studies on hysteria*. New York: Avon.

Frohlich, E. D., Dustan, H. P. & Page, I. H. (1966). Hyperdynamic beta-adrenergic circulatory state. *Archives of Internal Medicine, 117*, 614–619.

Fry, W. F. (1962). The marital context of an anxiety syndrome. *Family Process, 1*, 245–252.

Fuller, J. L., & Thompson, W. R. (1978). *Foundations of behavior genetics*. St. Louis: Mosby.

Funkenstein, D. H. (1955). The physiology of fear and anger. *Scientific American, 192*, 74–80.

Gaffney, F. A., Karlsson, E. S., Campbell, W., Schutte, J. E., Nixon, J. V., Willerson, J. T., & Blomqvist, C. G. (1979). Autonomic dysfunction in women with mitral valve prolapse syndrome. *Circulation, 59*, 894–901.

Gale, E. N. & Ayer, W. A. (1969). Treatment of dental phobias. *Journal of the American Dental Association, 78*, 1304–1307.

Garakani, H., Zitrin, C. M., & Klein, D. F. (1984). Treatment of panic disorder with imipramine alone. *American Journal of Psychiatry, 141*, 446–448.

Gardin, J. M., Isner, J., Ronana, J. A., & Fox, S. M. (1980). Pseudoischemia "false positive" S-T segment changes induced by hyperventilation in patients with mitral prolapse. *American Journal of Cardiology, 45*, 952–957.

Garfield, S., Gershon, S., Sletten, I., Sunland, D. M., & Ballou, S. (1967). Chemically induced anxiety. *International Journal of Neuropsychiatry, 3*, 426–433.

Gath, D., & Catalan, J. (1986). The treatment of emotional disorders in general practice: Psychological methods versus medication. *Journal of Psychosomatic Research, 30*, 381–386.

Geer, J. H. (1965). The development of a scale to measure fear. *Behaviour Research and Therapy, 3*, 45–53.

Geer, J. H. (1966). Fear and autonomic arousal. *Journal of Abnormal Psychology, 71*, 253–255.

Gelder, M. G., Bancroft, J. H. J., Gath, D. H., Johnston, D. W., Mathews, A. M., & Shaw, P. M. (1973). Specific and non-specific factors in behaviour therapy. *British Journal of Psychiatry, 123*, 445–462.

Gelder, M. G., & Marks, I. M. (1966). Severe agoraphobia: A controlled prospective trial of behaviour therapy. *British Journal of Psychiatry, 112*, 309–319.

Gelder, M. G., & Marks, I. M. (1968). Desensitization and phobias: A crossover study. *British Journal of Psychiatry, 114*, 323–328.

Gelder, M. G., Marks, I. M., & Wolff, H. H. (1967). Desensitization and psychotherapy in the treatment of phobic states: A controlled enquiry. *British Journal of Psychiatry, 113*, 53–73.

Gelhorn, E. (1965). The neurophysiological basis of anxiety: A hypothesis. *Perspectives in Biology and Medicine, 8*, 488–515.

Gershon, S., & Elson, A. S. (1987). The ideal anxiolytic. *Psychiatric Annals, 17*, 156–170.

Ghosh, A., & Marks, I. M. (1987). Self-directed exposure for agoraphobia: A controlled trial. *Behavior Therapy, 18*(1), 3–16.

Girodo, M., & Roehl, J. (1978). Coping preparation and coping self-talk during the stress of flying. *Journal of Consulting and Clinical Psychology, 46*, 978–989.

Gittelman, R., & Klein, D. F. (1985). Childhood separation anxiety and adult agoraphobia. In A. H. Tuma & J. D. Maser (Eds.), *Anxiety and the anxiety disorders*. Hillsdale, NJ: LEA.

Gittelman-Klein, R., & Klein, D. F. (1971). Controlled imipramine treatment of school phobia. *Archives of General Psychiatry, 25*, 204–207.

Gittelman-Klein, R., & Klein, D. F. (1980). Separation anxiety in school refusal and its treatment with drugs. In L. Hersov & I. Berg (Eds.), *Out of School*. New York: Wiley.

Gladstone, W. H. (1962). A multidimensional study of facial expressions of emotion. *Australian Journal of Psychology, 14*, 95–100.

Glass, C. R., Merluzzi, T. V., Biever, J. L., & Larsen, K. H. (1982). Cognitive assessment of social anxiety: Development and validation of a self-statement questionnaire. *Cognitive Therapy and Research, 6*, 37–55.

Gloger, S., Grunhaus, L., Birmacher, B., & Troudart, T. (1981). Treatment of spontaneous panic attacks with chlorimipramine. *American Journal of Psychiatry, 138*, 1215–1217.

Gloor, P., Olivier, A., Quesney, L. F., Andermann, F., & Horowitz, S. (1982). The role of the limbic system in experiential phenomena of temporal lobe epilepsy. *Annals of Neurology, 12*, 129–144.

Goldberg, R. J., Capone, R. J., & Hunt, J. D. (1985). Cardiac complications following tricyclic antidepressant overdose: Issues for monitoring policy. *Journal of the American Medical Association, 254*, 1772–1775.

Goldfried, M. R. (1977). The use of relaxation and cognitive relabeling as coping skills. In R. B. Stuart (Ed.), *Behavioral self-management*. New York: Brunner/Mazel.

Goldfried, M. R., & Sobocinski, D. (1975). Effect of irrational beliefs on emotional arousal. *Journal of Consulting and Clinical Psychology, 43,* 504–510.

Goldfried, M. R., & Trier, C. S. (1974). Effectiveness of relaxation as an active coping skill. *Journal of Abnormal Psychology, 83,* 348–355.

Goldstein, A. J., & Chambless, D. L. (1978). A re-analysis of agoraphobia. *Behavior Therapy, 9,* 47–59.

Gorman, J. M., Askanazi, J., Liebowitz, M. R., Fyer, A., Stein, J., Kinney, J. M., & Klein, D. F. (1984). Response to hyperventilation in a group of patients with panic disorder. *American Journal of Psychiatry, 141,* 857–861.

Gorman, J. M., Fyer, A. F., Glicklich, J., King, D., & Klein, D. F. (1981). Effects of sodium lactate on patients with panic disorder and mitral valve prolapse. *American Journal of Psychiatry, 138,* 247–249.

Gorman, J. M., Fyer, M. R., Goetz, R., Askanazi, J., Leibowitz, M. R., Fyer, A. J., Kinney, J., & Klein, D. F. (1988). Ventilatory physiology of patients with panic disorder. *Archives of General Psychiatry, 45,* 531–61.

Gorman, J. M., Levy, G. F., Liebowitz, M. R., McGrath, P., Appleby, I. L., Dillon, D. J., Davies, S. O., & Klein, D. F. (1983). Effect of acute beta-adrenergic blockade on lactate-induced panic. *Archives of General Psychiatry, 40,* 1079–1082.

Gottschalk, L. A., Stone, W. N., & Gleser, C. G., (1974). Peripheral versus central mechanisms accounting for anti-anxiety effects of propranolol. *Psychosomatic Medicine, 36,* 47–56.

Gould, J. L. (1982). *Ethology.* New York: Norton.

Gray, J. A. (1979). A neuropsychology of anxiety. In C. Izard (Ed.), *Emotions in personality and psychopathology.* New York: Plenum Press.

Gray, J. A. (1982). Précis of the neuropsychology of anxiety: An enquiry into the functions of the septo-hippocampal system. *Behavioral and Brain Sciences, 5,* 469–534.

Gray, J. A. (1985). Issues in the neuropsychology of anxiety. In A. H. Tuma & J. D. Maser (Eds.), *Anxiety and the anxiety disorders.* Hillsdale, NJ: LEA.

Grayson, J. B., & Borkovec, T. D. (1978). The effects of expectancy and imagined response to phobic stimuli on fear reduction. *Cognitive Therapy and Research, 20,* 323–328.

Grayson, J. B., Foa, E. B., & Steketee, G. (1982). Habituation during exposure treatment: Distraction vs. attention-focusing. *Behaviour Research and Therapy, 20,* 323–328.

Greden, J. F. (1974). Anxiety or caffeinism: A diagnostic dilemma. *American Journal of Psychiatry, 131,* 1089–1092.

Greenberg, D., & Stravynski, A. (1983). Social phobia. *British Journal of Psychiatry, 143,* 526.

Greenblatt, D. J., & Shader, R. I. (1974). *Benzodiazepines in clinical practice.* New York: Raven Press.

Greenblatt, D. J., & Shader, R. I. (1978). Pharmacotherapy of anxiety with benzodiazepines and B-adrenergic blockers. In M. A. Lipton, A. Di-

Mascio, & A. F. Killam (Eds.), *Psychopharmacology: A generation of progress.* New York: Raven Press.

Greenblatt, D. J., Shader, R. I., & Abernathy, D. R. (1983). Current status of benzodiazepines (Pt. I & Pt. II). *New England Journal of Medicine, 309,* 354–358; 410–416.

Greenson, R. (1965). The working alliance and transference neurosis. *Psychoanalytic Quarterly, 34,* 158–181.

Greenson, R. (1967). *The technique and practice of psychoanalysis* (Vol. 1). New York: International Universities Press.

Greist, J. H., & Greist, G. L. (1981). *Fearless flying: A passenger guide to modern airline travel.* Chicago: Nelson Hall.

Greist, J., Marks, I. M., Berlin, F., & Noshirvani, H. (1980). Avoidance versus confrontation of fear. *Behavior Therapy, 11,* 1–14.

Grey, S. J., Sartory, G., & Rachman, S. (1979). Synchronous and desynchronous changes during fear reduction. *Behaviour Research and Therapy, 17,* 137–148.

Griez, E., & van den Hout, M. A. (1983). Treatment of phobophobia by exposure to CO_2-induced anxiety symptoms. *Journal of Nervous and Mental Diseases, 171,* 506–508.

Griez, E., & van den Hout, M. A. (1984). Carbon dioxide and anxiety. Joint doctoral dissertation. Riuksuniversiteit Limburg, Maastricht: The Netherlands.

Guidano, V. F., and Liotti, G., (1983). *Cognitive processes and emotional disorders.* New York & London: Guilford Press.

Guttmacher, L. B., & Nelles, C. (1984). In vivo desensitization alteration of lactate-induced panic: A case study. *Behavior Therapy, 15,* 369–372.

Haefely, W., Kulcsar, A., Mohler, H., Pierl, L., Polc, P., & Schaffner, R. (1975). Possible involvement of GABA in the central action of benzodiazepines. In E. Costa & P. Greengard (Eds.), *Mechanism of action of benzodiazepines.* New York: Raven Press.

Hafner, R. J. (1976). Fresh symptom emergence after intensive behaviour therapy. *British Journal of Psychiatry, 129,* 378–383.

Hafner, R. J. (1977). The husbands of agoraphobic women and their influence on treatment outcome. *British Journal of Psychiatry, 131,* 289–294.

Hafner, R. J. (1979). Agoraphobic women married to abnormally jealous men. *British Journal of Medical Psychology, 52,* 99–104.

Hafner, R. J., & Marks, I. M. (1976). Exposure in vivo of agoraphobics: Contributions of diazepam, group exposure, and anxiety evocation. *Psychological Medicine, 6,* 71–88.

Hafner, R. J. & Milton, F. (1977). The influence of propranolol on the exposure in vivo of agoraphobics. *Psychological Medicine, 7,* 419–425.

Haley, J. (1963). *Strategies of psychotherapy.* New York: Grune & Stratton.

Haley, J. (1980). *Leaving home.* San Francisco: Jossey-Bass.

Hamilton, M. (1959). The assessment of anxiety states by rating. *British Journal of Medical Psychology, 32,* 50–55.

Hamilton, M. (1960). A rating scale for depression. *Journal of Neurology, Neurosurgery and Psychiatry, 23*, 56–62.

Hancock, E. W., & Cohn, K. (1966). The syndrome associated with mid-systolic click and late systolic murmur. *American Journal of Medicine, 41*, 183–196.

Hand, I., Angenendt, J., Fischer, M., & Wilke, C. (1986). Exposure in vivo with panic management for agoraphobia: Treatment rationale and longterm outcome. In I. Hand & H. Wittchen (Eds.), *Panic and phobias: Empirical evidence of theoretical models and longterm effects of behavioral treatments.* Berlin: Springer-Verlag.

Hand, I., Lamontagne, Y., & Marks, I. M. (1974). Group exposure (flooding) in vivo for agoraphobics. *British Journal of Psychiatry, 124*, 588–602.

Handly, R., & Neff, P. (1985). *Anxiety and panic attacks.* New York: Rawson.

Hansell, N. (1976). *The person in distress.* New York: Human Sciences Press.

Harris, S. L., & Ferrari, M. (1983). Developmental factors in child behavior therapy. *Behavior Therapy, 14*, 54–72.

Harris, E. L., Noyes, R., Jr., Crowe, R. R., & Chaudhry, D. R. (1983). Family study of agoraphobia: Report of a pilot study. *Archives of General Psychiatry, 40*, 1061–1064.

Harrison, M., Busto, U., Naranjo, C. A., Kaplan, H. L., & Sellers, E. M. (1984). Diazepam tapering in detoxification for high-dose benzodiazepine abusers. *Clinical Pharmacology and Therapeutics, 36*, 527–533.

Hartley, L. R., Ungapen, S., Davie, I., Spencer, D. J. (1983). The effect of beta adrenergic blocking drugs on speakers' performance and memory. *British Journal of Psychiatry, 142*, 512–517.

Haskell, D., Cole, J. O., Schniebolk, S., & Lieberman, B. (1986). A survey of diazepam patients. *Psychopharmacology Bulletin, 22*, 434–438.

Hastings, J. E. (1971). *Cardiac and cortical responses to affective stimuli in a reaction time task.* Unpublished doctoral dissertation, University of Wisconsin.

Haug, T., Brenne, L., Johnsen, B. H., Berntzen, D., Götestam, K. G., Hugdahl, K. (1987). A three-system analysis of fear of flying: a comparison of a consonant vs a non-consonant treatment method. *Behavioral Research Therapy, 25*, 187–194.

Hayward, C., Taylor, C. B., Roth, W. T., King, R., & Agras, W. S. (submitted). Cardiovascular risk factors in women with panic disorder.

Hebb, D. O. (1946). On the nature of fear. *Psychological Review, 53*, 259–276.

Heider, F. (1958). The psychology of interpersonal relations. New York: Wiley.

Hendler, N., Cimini, C., Terrence, M. A., & Long, D. (1980). A comparison of cognitive impairment due to benzodiazepines and to narcotics. *American Journal of Psychiatry, 137*, 828–830.

Helzer, J. E., Robins, L. N., & McEvoy, L. (1987). Post-traumatic stress disorder in the general population. *New England Journal of Medicine, 317*, 1630–1634.

Herman, J. B., Rosenbaum, J. F., & Brotman, A. W. (1987). The alprazolam to clonazepam switch for the treatment of panic disorder. *Journal of Clinical Psychopharmacology, 7*, 175–178.

Hibbert, G. N. (1984). Ideational components of anxiety: Their origin and content. *British Journal of Psychiatry, 144*, 618–624.

Himadi, W. G., Cerny, J. A., Barlow, D. H., Cohen, S. L., & O'Brien, G. T. (1986). The relationship of marital adjustment to agoraphobia treatment outcome. *Behaviour Research and Therapy, 24*, 107–115.

Hodgson, R. J., & Rachman, S. (1974). Desynchrony in measures of fear. *Behaviour Research and Therapy, 12*, 319–326.

Hoehn-Saric, R. (1982). Comparison of generalized anxiety disorder with panic disorder patients. *Psychopharmacology Bulletin, 18*, 104–108.

Hoehn-Saric, R., Merchant, A. F., Keyser, M. L., & Smith, V. K. (1981). Effects of clonidine on anxiety disorders. *Archives of General Psychiatry, 38*, 1278–1282.

Hofer, M. A. (1970). Cardiac and respiratory function during sudden prolonged immobility in young rodents. *Psychosomatic Medicine, 32*, 633–647.

Hoff, L. A. (1984). *People in crisis: Understanding and helping* (2nd ed.). Menlo Park, CA: Addison-Wesley.

Hoffman, L. (1971). Deviation-amplifying processes in natural groups. In J. Haley (Ed.), *Changing families.* New York: Grune & Stratton.

Horowitz, M. J. (1975). Intrusive and repetitive thought after experimental stress: A summary. *Archives of General Psychiatry, 32*, 1457–1463.

Horowitz, M. J. (1976). *Stress response syndromes.* New York: Jason Aronson.

Horowitz, M. J. (1979). *States of mind.* New York: Plenum Press.

Horwitz, D., Lovenberg, W., Engelman, K., & Sjoerdsma, A. (1964). Monoamine oxidase inhibitors, tyramine, and cheese. *Journal of the American Medical Association, 188*, 1108–1110.

Hudson, B. (1974). The families of agoraphobics treated by behaviour therapy. *British Journal of Social Work, 4*, 51–59.

Hyman, S. E. (1984). *Manual of psychiatric emergencies.* Boston: Little, Brown.

International Classification of Diseases, 9th Revision (ICD-9). (1979). Ann Arbor: Commission on Professional and Hospital Activities.

Isaacson, R. L., (1974). *The limbic system.* New York: Plenum Press.

Iverson, S. D. (1982). Integrating the literature on anxiety, memory and the hippocampus. *Behavioral and Brain Sciences, 5*, 487–488.

Jablensky, A. (1985). Approaches to the definition and classification of anxiety and related disorders in European psychiatry. In A. H. Tuma & J. P. Maser (Eds.), *Anxiety and the anxiety disorders.* Hillsdale, NJ: LEA.

Jackson, D. D. (1957). The question of family homeostasis. *Psychiatric Quarterly Supplement, 31*, (Pt. 1), 79–90.

Jackson, D. D., & Weakland, J. (1959). Schizophrenic symptoms and family interaction. *Archives of General Psychiatry, 1*, 618–621.

Jacob, R. G., & Rapport, M. D. (1984). Panic disorder: Medical and psychological parameters. In S. M. Turner (Ed.), *Behavioral theories and treatment of anxiety*. New York: Plenum Press.

Jacob, R. G., Moller, M. B., Turner, S. M., & Wall, C., III. (1986). Otoneurological dysfunction in patients with panic disorder or agoraphobia with panic attacks. *American Journal of Psychiatry, 143*, 807–808.

Jacobson, E. (1939). *Progressive relaxation*. Chicago: University of Chicago Press.

James, I., Griffith, D., Pearson, R., & Newbury, P. (1977). Effect of oxprenolol on stage fright in musicians. *Lancet, 2*, 952–954.

James, I. M., Burgoyne, W., Savage, I. T. (1983). Effect of pindilol on stress-related disturbances of musical performance: Preliminary communication. *Journal of Research and Social Medicine, 76*, 194–196.

Jannoun, L., Munby, M., Catalan, J., & Gelder, M. (1980). A home-based treatment programme for agoraphobia: Replication and controlled evaluation. *Behavior Therapy, 11*, 294–305.

Jenkins, C. D. (1982). Psychosocial risk factors for coronary heart disease. *Acta Medica Scandinavica, 660*(Suppl.), 123–136.

Jeresaty, R. M. (1979). *Mitral valve prolapse*. New York: Raven Press.

Johnston, D. W., Lancashire, M., Mathews, A. M., Munby, M., Shaw, P. M., & Gelder, M. G. (1976). Imaginal flooding and exposure to real phobic situations: Changes during treatment. *British Journal of Psychiatry, 129*, 372–377.

Johnston, M., Johnston, D. W., Wilkes, H., Burns, L. E., & Thorpe, G. L. (1984). Cumulative scales for the measurement of agoraphobia. *British Journal of Clinical Psychology, 23*, 133–143.

Jones, E. E., & Nisbett, R. E. (1971). *The actor and the observer: Divergent perceptions of the causes of behavior*. Morristown, NJ: General Learning.

Jones, M. C. (1924). A laboratory study of fear: The case of Peter. *Pedegogical Seminary, 31*, 308–315.

Juneau, M., Rogers, F., De Santos, V., Yee, M., Evans, A., Bohn, A., Haskell, W. L., Taylor, C. B., & DeBusk, R. F. (1987). Effectiveness of self-monitored home-based moderate-intensity exercise training in middle-aged men and women. *American Journal of Cardiology, 60*, 66–70.

Jurman, R. J. & Davis, J. M. (1987). The cost of psychotropic medication. *Psychiatric Annals, 17*, 173–177.

Kagan, J., Kearsley, R., & Zelaso, P. (1978). *Infancy: Its place in human development*. Cambridge: Harvard University Press.

Kagan, J., & Moss, H. A. (1962). *Birth of maturity*. New York: Wiley.

Kahn, R. J., McNair, D. M., Lipman, R. S., Covi, L., Rickels, K., Downing, R., Fisher, S., & Frankenthaler, L. M. (1986). Imipramine and chlordiazepoxide in depressive and anxiety disorders: II. Efficacy in anxious outpatients. *Archives of General Psychiatry, 43*, 79–85.

Kales, A., Sharp, N. B., & Kales, J. D. (1978). Rebound insomnia: A new clinical syndrome. *Science, 201*, 1039–1041.

Kamin, L. J., Brimer, C. J., & Black, A. H. (1963). Conditioned suppression as a monitor of fear of the CS in the course of avoidance training. *Journal of Comparative and Physiological Psychology, 56*, 497–501.

Kandel, E. (1983). From metapsychology to molecular biology: Explorations into the nature of anxiety. *American Journal of Psychiatry, 140*, 1277–1292.

Kaplan, H. S. (1979). *Disorders of sexual desire.* New York: Brunner/Mazel.

Kaplan, H. S. (1987). *Sexual aversion, sexual phobias, and panic disorder.* New York: Brunner/Mazel.

Kaplan, P. M., Smith, A., Grobstein, R., & Fischman, S. E. (1973). Family mediation of stress. *Social Work, 18*, 60–69.

Karabanow, O. (1977). Double-blind controlled study in phobias and obsessions. *International Journal of Medical Research, 5*, 42–48.

Kathol, R. G., Turner, R., & Delahunt, J. (1986). Depression and anxiety associated with hyperthyroidism: Response to antithyroid therapy. *Psychosomatics, 7*, 501–505.

Katon, W. (1986). Panic disorder: Epidemiology, diagnosis, and treatment in primary care. *Journal of Clinical Psychiatry, 47*(10, Suppl.), 21–27.

Kazdin, A. E. (1984). Integration of psychodynamic and behavioral psychotherapies. Conceptual versus empirical syntheses. In H. Arkowitz & S. B. Messer (Eds.), *Psychoanalytic therapy and behavior therapy: Is integration possible?* New York: Plenum Press.

Kelly, D., Guirguis, W., Frommer, E., Mitchell-Heggs, N., & Sargant, W. (1970). Treatment of phobic states with antidepressants: A retrospective study of 245 patients. *Journal of Psychiatry, 116*, 387–389.

Kelly, D., Mitchell-Heggs, N., & Sherman, D. (1971). Anxiety and the effects of sodium lactate assessed clinically and physiologically. *British Journal of Psychiatry, 119*, 129–141.

Kendler, K. S., Heath, A. C., Martin, N. G., & Eaves, L. J. (1987). Symptoms of anxiety and symptoms of depression. *Archives of General Psychiatry, 44*, 451–457.

Kendrick, M. J., Craig, K. D., Lawson, D. M., & Davidson, P. O. (1982). Cognitive and behavioral therapy for musical-performance anxiety. *Journal of Consulting and Clinical Psychology, 50*, 353–362.

Kenyon, F. E. (1976). Hypochondriacal states. *British Journal of Psychiatry, 129*, 1–14.

Killen, J., Maccoby, N., Taylor, C. B. (1984). Nicotine gum and self-regulation training in smoking relapse prevention. *Behavior Therapy, 15*, 234–248.

Kimmel, H. D. (Ed.). (1979). *Biofeedback and self-regulation.* Hillsdale, NJ: LEA.

Kirsch, I. (1985). Self-efficacy and expectancy: Old wine with new labels. *Journal of Personal and Social Psychology, 42*, 132–136.

Klein, D. F. (1964). Delineation of two drug-responsive anxiety syndromes. *Psychopharmacologia, 5*, 397–408.

Klein, D. F., & Davis, J. (1969). *The diagnosis and treatment of psychiatric disorders.* Baltimore: Williams & Wilkins.

Klein, D. F., & Fink, M. (1962). Psychiatric reaction patterns to imipramine. *Journal of Psychiatry, 119,* 432–438.

Klein, D. F., Gittelman, R., Quitken, F., & Rifkin, A. (1980). *Diagnosis and drug treatment of psychiatry disorders: Adults and children* (2nd ed.). Baltimore: Williams and Wilkins.

Klein, D. F., & Gittelman-Klein, R. (1978). Drug treatment of separation anxious and depressive illness in children. In J. Mendlewicz & H. M. van Praag (Eds.), *Advances in biological psychiatry* (Vol. 2). Basel: Karger.

Klein, D. F., Ross, D. C., & Cohen, P. (1987). Panic and avoidance in agoraphobia. *Archives of General Psychiatry, 44,* 377–385.

Klein, D. F., Zitrin, C. M., & Woerner, M. G. (1977). Imipramine and phobia. *Psychopharmacological Bulletin, 13,* 24–27.

Klein, D. F., Zitrin, C. M., & Woerner, M. (1978). Antidepressants, anxiety, panic and phobia. In M. A. Lipton, A. DiMascio, & R. F. Killam (Eds.), *Psychopharmacology: A generation of progress.* New York: Raven Press.

Klein, D. F., Zitrin, C. M., Woerner, M. G., & Ross, D. C. (1983). Treatment of phobias: Are there any specific ingredients? *Archives of General Psychiatry, 40,* 139–145.

Klein, M. (1952). On the theory of anxiety and guilt. In J. Riviere (Ed.), *Developments in psychoanalysis.* London: Hogarth Press.

Kleinknecht, R. A., & Bernstein, D. A. (1979). Short term treatment of dental avoidance. *Journal of Behavior Therapy and Experimental Psychiatry, 10,* 311–331.

Kleinknecht, R. A., Klepac, R. K., & Alexander, L. D. (1973). Origin and characteristics of fear of dentistry. *Journal of the American Dental Association, 86,* 842–847.

Kleinman, A. (1977). Depression, somatization and the new cross-cultural psychiatry. *Social Science and Medicine, 11,* 3–10.

Klepac, R. K., Lander, E. M., & Smith, G. R. (1984). *Graduated Exposure and Two Forms of Stress Inoculation for Dental Fear.* Paper presented at the November meeting of the Association for the Advancement of Behavior Therapy, Washington, DC.

Klorman, R., Weerts, T. C., Hastings, J. E., Melamed, B. G., & Lang, P. J. (1974). Psychometric description of some specific fear questionnaires. *Behavior Therapy, 5,* 401–409.

Kohut, H. (1971). *Analysis of the self.* New York: International Universities Press.

Kripke, D. F., & Garfinkel, L. (1984). Excess nocturnal deaths related to sleeping pill and tranquilizer use. *Lancet, 1,* 99.

Krishnan, G. (1975). Oxprenolol in the treatment of examination nerves. *ScotMed Journal, 20,* 288–289.

Krope, P., Kohrs, A., Ott, H., Wagner, W., & Fichts, K. (1982). Evaluating mepindolol in a test model of examination anxiety in students. *Pharmacopsychiatria, 15*, 41–47.

Lader, M. H. (1982). Biological differentiation of anxiety, arousal, and stress. In R. J. Matthew (Ed.), *The biology of anxiety*. New York: Brunner/Mazel.

Lader, M. H. (1985). Benzodiazepines, anxiety, and catecholamines: A commentary. In Tuma, A. H., Maser, J. D. (Eds.), *Anxiety and the anxiety disorders*. Hillsdale, New Jersey: LEA.

Lader, M. H. (1987). Assessing the potential for buspirone dependence or abuse and effects of its withdrawal. *American Journal of Medicine, 82* (Suppl. 5A), 20–26.

Lader, M. H., & Marks, I. (1971). *Clinical anxiety*. New York: Grune & Stratton.

Lader, M. H., & Olajide, D. (1987). A comparison of buspirone and placebo in relieving benzodiazepine withdrawal symptoms. *Journal of Clinical Psychopharmacology, 7*, 11–15.

Lader, M. H., Ron, M., & Petursson, H. (1984). Computer axial brain tomography in long-term benzodiazepine users. *Psychological Medicine, 14*, 203–206.

Lader, M. H. & Wing, L. (1966). *Physiological measures, sedative drugs and morbid anxiety* (Maudsley Monograph No. 14). London: Oxford University Press.

Ladouceur, R. L. (1983). Participant modeling with or without cognitive treatment for phobias. *Journal of Consulting and Clinical Psychology, 51*, 942–944.

Lang, P., Melamed, B. H., & Hart, J. (1970). Psychophysiological analysis of fear modification with automated desensitization. *Journal of Abnormal Psychology, 76*, 220–234.

Lang, P. J. (1964). Experimental studies of desensitization psychotherapy. In J. Wolpe (Ed.), *The conditioning therapies*. New York: Holt, Rhinehart & Winston.

Lang, P. J. (1984). Cognition in emotion: Concept and action. In C. E. Izard, J. Kagan, & R. Zajonc (Eds.), *Emotion, cognition and behavior*. New York: Cambridge University Press.

Lang, P. J. (1985). The cognitive psychophysiology of emotion: Fear and anxiety. In A. H. Tuma & J. O. Maser (Eds.), *Anxiety and the anxiety disorders*. Hillsdale, NJ: LEA.

Lang, P. J., & Lazovik, A. D. (1963). Experimental desensitization of a phobia. *Journal of Abnormal and Social Psychology, 66*, 519–525.

Lang, P. J., Levin, D. N., Miller, G. A., & Kozak, M. (1983). Fear behavior, fear imagery, and the psychophysiology of emotion: The problem of affective response integration. *Journal of Abnormal Psychology, 92*, 276–306.

Lapierre, Y. D., Knott, V. J., & Gray, R. (1984). Psychophysiological correlates of sodium lactate. *Psychopharmacology Bulletin, 20*, 50–57.

Lazarus, A. A. (1961). Group therapy of phobic disorders by systematic desensitization. *Journal of Abnormal Social Psychology, 63*, 504–510.

Lazarus, A. A. (1966). Behavior rehearsal versus non-directive therapy versus advice in effecting behavior change. *Behaviour Research and Therapy, 4*, 209–212.

Lazarus, A. A. (1971). *Behavior therapy and beyond.* New York: McGraw-Hill.

Lazarus, A. A. (1976). *Multimodal therapy.* New York: Springer.

Lawrence, J. M. (1985). Reactions to withdrawal of antidepressants, antiparkinsonian drugs and lithium. *Psychosomatics, 26*, 869–874.

Leckman, J. F., Weissman, M. M., Merikangas, K. R., Pauls, D. L., & Prusoff, B. A. (1983). Panic disorder and major depression: Increased risk of depression, alcoholism, panic, and phobic disorders in families of depressed probands with panic disorder. *Archives of General Psychiatry, 403*, 1055–1060.

Ledwidge, B. (1978). Cognitive behavior modification: A step in the wrong direction? *Psychological Bulletin, 85*, 353–375.

Lennane, J. K. (1986). Treatment of benzodiazepine dependence. *Medical Journal of Australia, 144*, 594–597.

Lewis, Sir A. J. (1970). The ambiguous word "anxiety." *International Journal of Psychiatry, 9*, 62–79.

Lewis, B. I. (1954). Chronic hyperventilation syndrome. *Journal of the American Medical Association, 155*, 1204–1207.

Lewis, M., & Brooks, J. (1974). Self, other and fear: Infants' reactions to people. In M. Lewis & L. A. Rosenblum (Eds.), *The origins of fear.* New York: Wiley.

Lewis, M., Feiring, C., McGuffey, C., & Jaskir, J. (1984). Predicting psychopathology in six-year-olds from early social relations. *Child Development, 55*, 123–136.

Ley, R. (1985). Agoraphobia, the panic attack and the hyperventilation syndrome. *Behaviour and Research Therapy, 23*, 79–81.

Liden, S., & Gottfries, C. (1974). Beta-blocking agents in the treatment of catecholamine-induced symptoms in musicians. *Lancet, 2*, 529.

Liebowitz, M. R., Campeas, R., Levin, A., Sandberg, D., Hollander, E., & Papp, L. (1987). Pharmacotherapy of social phobia. *Psychosomatics, 28*, 305–308.

Liebowitz, M. R., Fyer, A. J., Gorman, J. M., Campeas, R., Levin, A., Davies, S. R., Goetz, D., & Klein, D. F. (1986a). Alprazolam in the treatment of anxiety disorders. *Journal of Clinical Psychopharmacology, 6*, 13–20.

Liebowitz, M. R., Fyer, A. J., Gorman, J. M., Campeas, R., & Levin, A. (1986b). Phenelzine in social phobia. *Journal of Clinical Psychopharmacology, 6*, 93–98.

Liebowitz, M. R., Gorman, J. M., Fyer, A. J., Klein, D. F. (1985a). Social phobia: Review of a neglected anxiety disorder. *Archives of General Psychiatry, 42*, 729–736.

Liebowitz, M. R., Gorman, J. M., Fyer, A. J., Levitt, M., Dillon, D., Levy, G., Appleby, I. L., Anderson, S., Palij, M., Davies, S., & Klein, D. F. (1985b). Lactate provocation of panic attacks: II. Biochemical and physiological findings. *Archives of General Psychiatry, 42,* 709–719.

Liebowitz, M. R., Fyer, A. J., Gorman, J. M., Dillon, D., Davies, S., Stein, J. M., Cohen, B., & Klein, D. F. (1985c). Specificity of lactate infusions in social phobia vs panic disorders. *American Journal of Psychiatry, 142,* 947–949.

Liebowitz, M. R., Quitkin, F. M., Stewart, J. W., et al. (1984). Phenelzine versus imipramine in atypical depression: A preliminary report. *Archives of General Psychiatry, 41,* 669–677.

Liebowitz, M., Fyer, A., McGrath, P., & Klein, D. (1981). Clonidine treatment of panic disorder. *Psychopharmacology Bulletin, 17,* 122–123.

Lindemann, C. G., Zitrin, C. M., & Klein, D. F. (1984). Thyroid dysfunction in phobic patients. *Psychosomatics, 25,* 603–606.

Lipsedge, M., Hajioff, J., Huggins, P., Napier, L., Pearce, J., Pike, D. J., & Rich, M. (1973). Iproniazid and systematic desensitization for severe agoraphobia. *Psychopharmacologia, 32,* 67–80.

Logue, P. E., Gentry, W. D., Linnoila, M., & Erwin, C. W. (1978). Effect of alcohol consumption on state anxiety changes in nonalcoholics. *American Journal of Psychiatry, 135,* 1079–1081.

Lorr, M., & McNair, D. (1982). *Profile of mood states: Bi-polar form (POMS-BI).* San Diego: Educational and Industrial Testing Service.

Lucki, I., & Rickels, K. (1986). The behavioral effects of benzodiazepines following long-term use. *Psychopharmacology Bulletin, 22,* 424–433.

Lukas, S. E. & Griffiths, R. R. (1982). Precipitated withdrawal by a benzodiazepine receptor antagonist after 7 days of diazepam. *Science, 217,* 1161–1163.

Lum, L. C. (1976). The syndrome of chronic habitual hyperventilation. In O. W. Hill (Ed.), *Modern Trends in Psychosomatic Medicine.* London: Butterworth.

Luria, A. (1961). *The role of speech in the regulation of normal and abnormal behaviors.* New York: Liveright.

Lydiard, R. B. (1987). Desipramine in agoraphobia with panic attacks: An open, fixed-dose study. *Journal of Clinical Psychopharmacology, 7,* 258–260.

Lydiard, R. B., & Ballenger, J. C. (in press). Antidepressants in panic disorder and agoraphobia. *Psychiatric Medicine.*

Macfarlane, J. W., Allen, L., & Honzik, M. P. (1954). *Behaviour problems of normal children between 21 months and 14 years.* Berkeley: University of California Press.

Magarian, G. J. (1982). Hyperventilation syndromes: Infrequently recognized common expressions of anxiety and stress. *Medicine, 61,* 219–236.

Malan, D. H. (1976). *The frontier of brief psychotherapy: An example of the convergence of research and clinical practice.* New York: Plenum Press.

Maletzky, B. M. (1980). Anxiolytic efficacy of alprazolam compared to diazepam and placebo. *Journal of International Medical Research, 8,* 139–143.

Malleson, N. (1959). Panic and phobia: A possible method of treatment. *Lancet,* i, 225–227.

Mann, J. (1984). Time-limited psychotherapy. In L. Grinspoon (Ed.), *Psychiatry Update* (Vol. III). Washington: American Psychiatric Press.

Margraf, J., Ehlers, A., & Roth, W. T. (1986). Sodium lactate infusions and panic attacks: A review and critique. *Psychosomatic Medicine, 48,* 23–51.

Margraf, J., Taylor, C. B., Arnow, B., Ehlers, A., & Roth, W. T. (submitted). Guttman scaling in agoraphobia: Cross cultural replication and prediction of treatment response patterns.

Margraf, J., Taylor, C. B., Ehlers, A., Roth, W. T., & Agras, W. S. (1987). Panic attacks in the natural environment. *Journal of nervous and mental disorders, 175,* 558–565.

Marks, I. M. (1969). *Fears and phobias.* New York: Academic Press.

Marks, I. M. (1970). The classification of phobic disorders. *British Journal of Psychiatry, 116,* 377–386.

Marks, I. M. (1978). Exposure treatments. In W. S. Agras (Ed.), *Behavior modification* (2nd ed.), Boston: Little, Brown.

Marks, I. M. (1987). *Fears, phobias and rituals.* New York: Oxford University Press.

Marks, I. M., Boulougouris, J. C., & Marset, P. (1971). Flooding versus desensitization in the treatment of phobic patients: A cross-over study. *British Journal of Psychiatry, 119,* 353–375.

Marks, I. M., & Gelder, M. G. (1965). A controlled retrospective study of behavior therapy in phobic patients. *British Journal of Psychiatry, 111,* 571–573.

Marks, I. M., & Gelder, M. G. (1966). Different ages of onset in varieties of phobias. *American Journal of Psychiatry, 123,* 218–221.

Marks, I. M., Gray, S., Cohen, D., Hill, R., Mawson, D., Ramm, R., & Stern, R. S. (1983). Imipramine and brief therapist aided exposure in agoraphobics having self-exposure homework. *Archives of General Psychiatry, 40,* 153–162.

Marks, I. M., & Herst, E. R. (1970). A survey of 1200 agoraphobics in Britain. *Social Psychiatry, 5,* 16–24.

Marks, I. M., & Lader, M. H. (1973). Anxiety states (anxiety neurosis): A review. *Journal of Nervous and Mental Diseases, 156,* 3–18.

Marks, I. M., & Mathews, A. M. (1979). Brief standard self-rating for phobic patients. *Behaviour Research and Therapy, 17,* 263–267.

Marlatt, G. A., & Gordon, J. R. (1985). *Relapse prevention.* New York: Guilford Press.

Marmor, J. (1980). Dynamic psychotherapy and behavior therapy: Are they irreconcilable? In J. Marmor & S. M. Woods (Eds.), *The interface between the psychodynamic and behavioral therapies*. New York: Plenum Press.

Marshall, D. W., Westmoreland, B. F., & Sharbrough, F. W. (1983). Ictal tachycardia during temporal lobe seizures. *Mayo Clinic Proceedings, 58*, 443–446.

Marshall, W. L. (1985). Variable exposure in flooding. *Behaviour Research and Therapy, 16*, 117–135.

Masserman, J. H. (1943). *Behavior and neurosis: An experimental psychoanalytic approach to psychobiologic principles*. Chicago: University of Chicago Press.

Mathews, A., Teasdale, J., Munby, M., Johnston, D., & Shaw, P. (1977). A home-based treatment program for agoraphobia. *Behavior Therapy, 8*, 915–924.

Mathews, A. M. (1971). Psychophysiological approaches to the investigation of desensitization. *Psychological Bulletin, 76*, 73–91.

Mathews, A. M., Gelder, M. G., & Johnston, D. W. (1981). *Agoraphobia: Nature and treatment*. New York: Guilford Press.

Mathews, A. M., Johnston, D. W., Lancashire, M., Munby, D., Shaw, P. M., & Gelder, M. G. (1976). Imaginal flooding and exposure to real phobic situations: Treatment outcome with agoraphobic patients. *British Journal of Psychiatry, 129*, 362–371.

Mathews, A. M., Johnston, D. W., Shaw, P. M., & Gelder, M. G. (1974). Process variables and the prediction of outcome in behaviour therapy. *British Journal of Psychiatry, 125*, 256–264.

Mathews, A. M., & Shaw, P. M. (1977). Cognitions related to anxiety: A pilot study of treatment. *Behaviour and Research Therapy, 15*, 503–505.

Mattila, M. J., Aranko, K., & Seppala, T. (1982). Acute effects of buspirone and alcohol on psychomotor skills. *Journal of Clinical Psychiatry, 43*, 56–60.

Mavissakalian, M. (1986). Clinically significant improvement in agoraphobia research. *Behaviour Research and Therapy, 24*, 369–370.

Mavissakalian, M., & Barlow, D. H. (1981). Phobia: An overview. In M. Mavissakalian & D. H. Barlow (Eds.), *Phobia: Psychological and pharmacological treatment*. New York: Guilford Press.

Mavissakalian, M., & Hamann, M. S. (1986). DSM-III personality disorder in agoraphobia. *Comprehensive Psychiatry, 27*, 471–479.

Mavissakalian, M., Michelson, L., & Dealy, R. S. (1983). Pharmacological treatment of agoraphobia: Imipramine versus imipramine with programmed practice. *British Journal of Psychiatry, 143*, 348–355.

Mavissakalian, M., Michelson, L., Greenwald, D., Kornblith, S., & Greenwald, M. (1983a). Paradoxical intention vs. self-statement training of agoraphobia. *Behaviour and Research Therapy, 21*, 75–80.

Mavissakalian, M., Perel, J. M., & Michelson, L. (1984). The relationship of plasma imipramine and N-desmethylimipramine to improvement in agoraphobia. *Journal of Clinical Psychopharmacology, 4,* 36–40.

May, R. (1950). *The meaning of anxiety.* New York: Ronald Press.

Mayol, R. F., Adamson, D. S., Gammans, R. E., & LaBudde, J. A. (1985). Pharmacokinetics and disposition of 14C-buspirone HCl after intravenous and oral dosing in man. *Clinical Pharmacology and Therapeutics, 37,* 210 (abstract).

McCrae, R. R., & Costa, P. T., Jr. (1985). Updating Norman's "adequate taxonomy": Intelligence and personality dimensions in natural language and in questionnaires. *Journal of Personality and Social Psychology, 49,* 710–721.

McDonald, R., Sartory, G., Grey, S. J., Cobb, J., Stern, R., & Marks, I. (1979). The effects of self-exposure instructions on agoraphobic outpatients. *Behaviour Research and Therapy, 17,* 83–85.

McEwan, K. L., & Devins, G. M. (1983). Is increased arousal in social anxiety noticed by others? *Journal of Abnormal Psychology, 92,* 417–421.

McNair, D. M., & Kahn, R. J. (1981). Imipramine and chlordiazepoxide for agoraphobia. In D. F. Klein & J. G. Rabin (Eds.), *Anxiety: New research and changing concepts.* New York: Raven Press.

McNair, D. M., & Lorr, M. (1964). An analysis of mood in neurotics. *Journal of Abnormal and Social Psychology, 69,* 620–627.

McNair, D. M., Lorr, M., & Droppleman, L. F. (1971). *Manual: Profile of mood states.* San Diego: Educational and Industrial Testing Services.

McNally, R. J., & Reiss, S. (1983). The preparedness theory of phobias and human safety-signal conditioning. *Behaviour Research and Therapy, 20,* 153–159.

McNally, R. J., & Steketee, G. S. (1985). Etiology and maintenance of severe animal phobias. *Behaviour Research and Therapy, 23,* 431–435.

McPherson, F. M., Brougham, L., & McLaren, S. (1980). Maintenance of improvement in agoraphobic patients treated by behavioral methods—a four-year follow-up. *Behaviour Research and Therapy, 18,* 150–152.

Mehrabian, A., & Russell, J. A. (1974). *An approach to environmental psychology.* Cambridge: MIT Press.

Meichenbaum, D. (1974). *Cognitive behavior modification.* Morristown, NJ: General Learning Press.

Meichenbaum, D. (1977). *Cognitive Behavior Modification: An integrative approach.* New York: Plenum Press.

Meichenbaum, D. (1979). Cognitive behavior modification: The need for a fairer assessment. *Cognitive Therapy and Research, 3,* 127–132.

Meichenbaum, D., & Turk, D. (1976). The cognitive-behavioral management of anxiety, anger, and pain. In P. O. Davison (Ed.), *The behavioral management of anxiety, depression, and pain.* New York: Brunner/Mazel.

Michels, R., Frances, A., & Shear, M. K. (1985). Psychodynamic models of anxiety. In A. H. Tuma & J. D. Maser (Eds.), *Anxiety and the anxiety disorders*. Hillsdale, NJ: LEA.

Michelson, L., & Ascher, L. M. (1984). Paradoxical intention for agoraphobia and other anxiety disorders. *Journal of Behavior Therapy and Experimental Psychiatry, 15*, 215–220.

Michelson, L., Mavissakalian, M., & Marchione, K. (1985). Cognitive and behavioral treatments of agoraphobia: Clinical, behavioral, and psychophysiological outcomes. *Journal of Consulting and Clinical Psychology, 53*, 913–925.

Michelson, L., Mavissakalian, M., & Menninger, S. (1983). Prognostic utility of locus of control in treatment of agoraphobia. *Behaviour Research and Therapy, 21*, 309–314.

Milton, F., & Hafner, J. (1979). Outcome of behavior therapy for agoraphobia in relation to marital adjustment. *Archives of General Psychiatry, 36*, 807–811.

Mineka, S. (1986). The frightful complexity of the origins of fears. In J. B. Overmier & F. R. Brush (Eds.), *Affect, conditioning, and cognition: Essays on the determinants of behavior*. Hillsdale, NJ: LEA.

Minuchin, S. (1974). *Families and family therapy*. Cambridge: Harvard University Press.

Minuchin, S., Rosman, B., & Baker, L. (1978). *Psychosomatic families: Anorexia nervosa in context*. Cambridge: Harvard University Press.

Mohler, H., & Okada, T. (1977). Properties of H-3 diazepam binding to benzodiazepine receptors in rat cortex. *Life Sciences, 20*, 2101–2110.

Moir, D. C., Crooks, J., Cornwell, W. B., O'Malley, K., Dingwall-Fordyce, I., Turnbull, M. J., & Weir, R. D. (1972). Cardiotoxicity of amitriptyline. *Lancet, 2*, 561–564.

Moir, D. C., Dingwall-Fordyce, I., & Weir, R. D. (1973). A follow-up study of cardiac patients receiving amitriptyline. *European Journal of Clinical Pharmacology, 6*, 98–101.

Montgomery, G. T., & Crowder, J. E. (1972). The symptom substitution hypothesis and the evidence. *Psychotherapy: Theory, Research and Practice, 9*, 98–102.

Mountjoy, C. Q., Roth, M., Garside, R. F., & Leitch, I. M. (1977). Phenelzine in anxiety, depression and phobic neurosis. *British Journal of Psychiatry, 13*, 486–492.

Mowrer, O. H. (1939). A stimulus-response analysis of anxiety and its role as a reinforcing agent. *Psychological review, 46*, 553–565.

Mowrer, O. H. (1947). On the dual nature of learning: A reinterpretation of "conditioning" and "problem solving." *Harvard Educational Review, 17*, 102–148.

Mowrer, O. H. (1960). *Learning theory and behavior*. New York: Wiley.

Mullaney, J. A., & Trippett, C. J. (1979). Alcohol dependence and phobias: Clinical description and relevance. *British Journal of Psychiatry, 135*, 565–573.

400   *References*

Munby, M., & Johnston, D. W. (1980). Agoraphobia: The long-term follow-up of behavioural treatment. *British Journal of Psychiatry, 137*, 418–427.

Munjack, D. J., & Moss, H. B. (1981). Affective disorders and alcoholism in families of agoraphobics. *Archives of General Psychiatry, 38*, 869–871.

Munjack, D. J., Rebal, R., Shaner, R., Staples, F., Braun, R., & Leonard, M. (1985). Imipramine versus propranolol for the treatment of panic attacks: A pilot study. *Comprehensive Psychiatry, 26*, 80–88.

Muskin, P. R. & Fyer, A. J. (1981). Treatment of panic disorder. *Journal of Clinical Psychopharmacology, 1*, 81–90.

Myers, J. K., Weissman, M. M., Tischer, G. L., Holzer, C. E., Leaf, P. J., Orvaschel, H., Anthony, J. C., Boyd, J. H., Burke, J. D., Kramer, M., & Stoltzman, R. (1984). Six-month prevalence of psychiatric disorders in three communities. *Archives of General Psychiatry, 41*, 959–967.

National Institutes of Health Consensus Conference. (1985). Lowering blood cholesterol to prevent heart disease. *Journal of the American Medical Association, 253*, 2080–2086.

Neale, M. C., & Fulker, D. W. (1984). A bivariate path analysis of fear data on twins and their parents. *Acta Genetical Medicae et Gemellologiae, 33*, 273–286.

Neftel, K., Adler, R., Kappeli, L., Rossi, M., Dolder, M., Kaser, H., Bruggesser, H., & Vorkauf, H. (1982). Stage fright in musicians: A model illustrating the effect of beta blockers. *Psychosomatic Medicine, 44*, 461–469.

Nemiah, J. L. (1975). Obsessive-compulsive neurosis. In A. M. Freedman & H. I. Kaplan (Eds.), *A Comprehensive textbook of psychiatry*. Baltimore: Williams & Wilkins.

Nemiah, J. L. (1981). The psychoanalytic view of anxiety. In D. P. Klein & J. G. Rabkin (Eds.), *Anxiety: New research and changing concepts*. New York: Raven Press.

Nesse, R. M., Cameron, O. G., Curtis, G. C., McCann, D. S., & Huber-Smith, M. J. (1984a). Adrenergic function in patients with panic anxiety. *Archives of General Psychiatry, 41*, 771–776.

Nesse, R. M., Curtis, G. C., Thyer, B. A., McCann, D. S. (1984b). Endocrine and cardiovascular responses during phobic anxiety. *Psychosomatic Medicine, 7*, 320–332.

Newton, R. W. (1975). Physostigmine salicylate in the treatment of tricyclic antidepressant overdose. *Journal of the American Medical Association, 231*, 941–944.

Nichols, K. A. (1974). Severe social anxiety. *British Journal of Medical Psychology, 47*, 301–306.

Nies, A., Howard, D., & Robinson, D. S. (1982). Antianxiety effects of MAO inhibitors. In R. J. Mathew (Ed.), *The biology of anxiety*. New York: Brunner/Mazel.

Norton, G. R., Harrison, B., Hauch, J., & Rhodes, L. (1985). Characteristics of people with infrequent panic attacks. *Journal of Abnormal Psychology, 94*, 216–221.

Noyes, R., Jr. (1985). Beta-adrenergic blocking drugs in anxiety and stress. *Psychiatric Clinics of North America, 8,* 119–132.

Noyes, R., Jr., Anderson, D. J., Clancy, J., Crowe, R. R., Slymen, D. J., Ghoneim, M. M., & Hinrichs, J. V. (1984). Diazepam and propranolol in panic disorder and agoraphobia. *Archives of General Psychiatry, 41,* 287–292.

Noyes, R., Jr., Clancy, J., Crowe, R., Hoenk, P. R., & Slymen, D. J. (1978). The familial prevalence of anxiety neurosis. *Archives of General Psychiatry, 35,* 1057–1059.

Noyes, R., Jr., Clancy, J., Hoenk, P. R., & Slymen, D. J. (1980). Prognosis of anxiety neurosis. *Archives of General Psychiatry, 37,* 173–178.

Noyes, R., Jr., Clarkson, C., Crowe, R. R., Yeats, W. R., & McChesney, C. M. (1987). A family study of generalized anxiety disorder. *American Journal of Psychiatry, 144,* 1019–1024.

Noyes, R., Jr., Perry, P. J., Crowe, R., Coryell, W. H., Clancy, J., Yamada, T., & Gabel, J. (1986). Seizures following the withdrawal of alprazolam. *Journal of Nervous and Mental Diseases, 174,* 50–52.

O'Brien, G. T., & Barlow, D. H. (1984). Agoraphobia. In S. M. Turner (Ed.), *Behavioral theories and treatment of anxiety.* New York: Plenum Press.

Öhman, A., Eriksson, A., Fredrikson, M., Hugdahl, K., & Olofsson, C. (1974). Habituation of the electrodermal orienting reaction to potentially phobic and supposedly neutral stimuli in normal human subjects. *Biological Psychology, 2,* 85–92.

Öhman, A., Fredrikson, M., Hugdahl, K. (1978). Orienting and defensive responding in the electrodermal system: Palmar-dorsal differences and recovery rate during conditioning to potentially phobic stimuli. *Psychophysiology, 15,* 93–101.

Öhman, A., Fredrikson, M., & Hugdahl, K. (1978). Towards an experimental model for simple phobic reactions. *Behavioral Analysis and Modification, 2,* 97–114.

Öst, L.-G. (1978). Behavioral treatment of thunder and lightning phobias. *Behaviour Research and Therapy, 16,* 197–207.

Öst, L.-G., & Hugdahl, K. (1981). Acquisition of phobias and anxiety response patterns in clinical patients. *Behaviour Research and Therapy, 19,* 439–447.

Öst, L.-G., & Hugdahl, K. (1983). Acquisition of agoraphobia, mode of onset and anxiety response patterns. *Behaviour Research and Therapy, 21,* 623–631.

Öst, L.-G., & Jerremalm, A. J. J. (1981). Individual response patterns and the effects of differential behavioral methods in the treatment of social phobia. *Behaviour Research and Therapy, 19,* 1–16.

Öst, L.-G., Jerremalm, A. J. J., & Jansson, L. (1984). Individual response patterns and different behavioral treatments of agoraphobia. *Behaviour Research and Therapy, 22,* 697–707.

Oster, G., Russell, M. W., Huse, D. M., Adams, S. F., & Imbimbo, J. (1987).

Accident- and injury-related health-care utilization among benzodiazepine users and nonusers. *Journal of Clinical Psychiatry, 48,* 17–21.

Owen, R. T., & Tyrer, P. (1983). Benzodiazepine dependence: A review of the evidence. *Drugs, 25,* 385–398.

Pappas, D. G., Crawford, W., & Coghlan, H. C. (1986). Dizziness and the autonomic dysfunction syndrome. *Otolaryngology, 94,* 186–194.

Papez, J. W. (1937). A proposed mechanism of emotion. *Archives of Neurology and Psychiatry, 38,* 725–743.

Parker, G. (1979). Reported parental characteristics of agoraphobics and social phobics. *British Journal of Psychiatry, 135,* 555–560.

Parker, G., Tupling, H., & Brown, L. B. (1979). A parental bonding instrument. *British Journal of Medical Psychology, 52,* 1–11.

Parkinson, P., & Rachman, S. (1980). Are intrusive thoughts subject to habituation? *Behaviour Research and Therapy, 28,* 409–418.

Parry, H. J., Balter, M. B., Millinger, G. D., Cisin, I. H., & Manheimer, D. I. (1973). National pattern of psychotropic drug use. *Archives of General Psychiatry, 28,* 769–783.

Paul, S. M., Syapin, P. J., Paugh, B. A., Moncada, V., & Skolnick, P. (1979). Correlation between benzodiazepine receptor occupation and anticonvulsant effects of diazepam. *Nature, 281,* 688–689.

Pavlov, I. P. (1927). *Conditioned reflexes.* London: Oxford University Press.

Peck, R. E. (1966). Observations on salivation and palmar sweating in anxiety and other psychiatric conditions. *Psychosomatics, 7,* 343–348.

Permutt, M. A. (1980). Is it really hypoglycemia? If so, what should you do. *Medical Times, 108,* 35–43.

Petursson, H., & Lader, M. (1984). *Dependence on tranquillisers.* London: Oxford University Press.

Peveler, R. C., & Johnston, D. W. (1986). Subjective and cognitive effects of relaxation. *Behaviour Research and Therapy, 24,* 413–419.

Pfeffer, J. M. (1978). The aetiology of the hyperventilation syndrome. *Psychotherapy and Psychosomatics, 30,* 47–56.

Pilowsky, I. (1967). Dimensions of hypochondriasis. *British Journal of Psychiatry, 113,* 89–93.

Pitts, F. M., & McClure, J. N. (1967). Lactate metabolism in anxiety neurosis. *New England Journal of Medicine, 277,* 1329.

Piesiur-Strehlow, B., Strehlow, U., & Poser, W. (1986). Mortality of patients on benzodiazepines. *Acta Psychiatric Scandinavia, 73,* 330–335.

Plomin, R., & Rowe, D. C. (1979). Genetic and environmental etiology of social behavior in infancy. *Developmental Psychology, 15,* 62–72.

Pomerleau, O. F., & Pomerleau, C. S. (1984). Neuroregulators and the reinforcement of smoking: Towards a biobehavioral explanation. *Neuroscience and Biobehavioral Review, 8,* 503–513.

Potts, J. T. (1980). Disorders of parathyroid glands. In K. J. Isselbacher, R. D. Adams, E. Braunwald, R. G. Petersdorf, & J. D. Wilson (Eds.), *Harrison's Principles of Internal Medicine* (9th ed.). New York: McGraw-Hill.

Putman, F. W., Guroff, J. J., Silberman, E. K., Barban, L., & Post, R. M. (1986). The clinical phenomenology of multiple personality disorder: Review of 100 recent cases. *Journal of Clinical Psychiatry, 47*, 285–293.

Rachman, E., & DeSilva, P. (1978). Abnormal and normal obsessions. *Behaviour Research and Therapy, 16*, 233–248.

Rachman, E., & Seligman, M. (1976). Unprepared phobias: Be prepared. *Behaviour Research and Therapy, 14*, 333–338.

Rachman, S. (1966). Studies in desensitization—III: Speed of desensitization. *Behaviour Research and Therapy, 4*, 7–15.

Rachman, S. (1977). The conditioning theory of fear-acquisition. A critical examination. *Behaviour Research and Therapy, 15*, 375–384.

Rachman, S. (1981). Part 1. Unwanted intrusive cognitions. *Advances in Behavior Research and Therapy, 3*, 89–99.

Rachman, S. (1984). Agoraphobia: A safety signal perspective. *Behaviour Research and Therapy, 22*, 59–70.

Rachman, S., & Levitt, K. (1985). Panics and their consequences. *Behaviour Research and Therapy, 23*, 585–600.

Raj, A., Sheehan, D. V. (1987). Medical evaluation of panic attacks. *Journal of Clinical Psychiatry, 48*, 309–313.

Rapee, R. (1986). Differential response to hyperventilation in panic disorder and generalized anxiety disorder. *Journal of Abnormal Psychology, 95*, 24–28.

Raskin, M., Johnson, G., & Rondestvedt, J. W. (1973). Chronic anxiety treated by feedback-induced muscle relaxation. *Archives of General Psychiatry, 28*, 263–267.

Raskin, M., Peeke, H. V. S., Dickman, W., & Pinkster, H. (1982). Panic and generalized anxiety disorders: Developmental antecedents and precipitants. *Archives of General Psychiatry, 39*, 687–689.

Redmond, D. E., Jr., (1985). Neurochemical basis for anxiety and anxiety disorders: Evidence from drugs which decrease human fear or anxiety. A. H. Tuma & J. D. Maser (Eds.), *Anxiety and the anxiety disorders*. Hillsdale, NJ: LEA.

Redmond, D. E., Jr., Huang, Y. H., Snyder, D. R., & Maas, J. W. (1976). Behavioral effects of stimulation of the nucleus locus coeruleus in the stump-tailed monkey (*Macaca arctoides*). *Brain Research, 116*, 502–510.

Reiman, E. M., Raichle, M. E., Butler, K. F., Herscovitch, P., & Robins, E. (1984). A focal brain abnormality in panic disorder, a severe form of anxiety. *Nature, 310*, 683–685.

Riccio, D. C., & Silvestri, R. (1973). Extinction of avoidance behavior and the problem of residual fear. *Behaviour Research and Therapy, 11*, 1–9.

Rickels, K. (1981). Recent advances in anxiolytic therapy. *Journal of Clinical Psychiatry, 42*, 40–44.

Rickels, K., Case, G., Downing, R. W., & Winokur, A. (1983). Long-term diazepam therapy and clinical outcome. *Journal of the American Medical Association, 250*, 767–771.

Rickels, K., Case, W. G., Schweizer, E. E., Swenson, C., & Friedman, R. B. (1986). Low-dose dependence in chronic benzodiazepine users: A preliminary report on 119 patients. *Psychopharmacology Bulletin, 22,* 407–415.

Rickels, K., & Schweizer, E. E. (1986). Benzodiazepines for treatment of panic attacks: A new look. *Psychopharmacology Bulletin, 22,* 93–99.

Rickels, K., & Schweizer, E. E. (1987). Treatment of benzodiazepine dependence. *Lancet, 1,* 78–79.

Rickels, K., Weisman, K., Norstad, N., Singer, M., Stoltz, D., Brown, A., & Danton, J. (1982). Buspirone and diazepam in anxiety: A controlled study. *Journal of Clinical Psychiatry, 43, 12* (Pt. 2), 81–86.

Rickels, K., Weisse, C., Feldman, H., Fee, E. M., & Wiswesser, G. (1978). Loxapine in neurotic anxiety: Some modifiers of treatment response. *Journal of International Medical Research, 6,* 180–185.

Rifkin, A., Klein, D. F., Dillon, D., & Levitt, M. (1981). Blockade by imipramine or desipramine of panic induced by sodium lactate. *American Journal of Psychiatry, 138,* 676–677.

Rimm, D. C., Janda, L. H., Lancaster, D. W., Nahl, M., & Dittmar, K. (1977). The origin and maintenance of phobias. *Behaviour Research and Therapy, 15,* 231–238.

Robertson, H. A., Martin, I. L., & Candy, J. M. (1978). Differences in bz receptor binding in Maudsley reactive and non-reactive rats. *European Journal of Pharmacology, 50,* 455–457.

Rohsenow, D. J. (1982). Social anxiety, daily moods, and alcohol use over time among heavy social drinking men. *Addictive Behavior, 7,* 311–315.

Rose, R. J., & Ditto, W. B. (1983). A developmental genetic analysis of common fears from early adolescence to early childhood. *Child Development, 54,* 361–368.

Rose, R. J., Miller, J. Z., Pogue-Geile, M. F., & Cardwell, G. F. (1981). Twin-family studies of common fears and phobias. In *Twin Research 3: Intelligence, Personality and Development,* 169–174.

Rosenbaum, J. F. (1987). Limited-symptom panic attacks. *Psychosomatics, 28,* 407–412.

Rosenthal, S., & Bowden, C. L. (1973). A double-blind comparison of thioridazine (Mellaril) versus diazepam (Valium) in patients with chronic mixed anxiety and depressive symptoms. *Current Therapeutic Research, 15,* 261–267.

Roth, M. (1984). Agoraphobia, panic disorder and generalized anxiety disorder: Some implications of recent advances. *Psychiatric Developments, 2,* 31–52.

Roth, M., Gurney, C., Garside, R. F., & Kerr, T. A. (1972). Studies in the classification of affective disorder. The relationship between anxiety states and depressive illnesses. *British Journal of Psychiatry, 121,* 147–161.

Roth, M., & Harper, M. (1962). Temporal lobe epilepsy and the phobic anxiety depersonalization syndrome. Part II. Practical and theoretical considerations. *Comprehensive Psychiatry, 23,* 215–226.

Roth, W. T., Telch, M. J., Taylor, C. B., Sachitano, J. A., Gallen, C. C., Kopell, M. L., McClenahan, K. L., Agras, W. S., & Pfefferbaum, A. (1986). Autonomic characteristics of agoraphobia with panic attacks. *Biological Psychiatry, 21*, 1133–1154.

Roth, W. T., Telch, M. J., Taylor, C. B., & Agras, W. S. (in press). Autonomic changes after treatment of agoraphobia with panic attacks. *Psychiatric Research*.

Roth, W. T., Tinklenberg, J., Doyle, C. M., Horvath, T. B., & Koppel, B. S. (1976). Mood states and twenty-four-hour cardiac monitoring. *Journal of Psychosomatic Research, 20*, 179–186.

Russell, J. A. (1980). A circumplex model of affect. *Journal of Personality and Social Psychology, 39*, 1161–1178.

Sachs, D. P. (1986). Cigarette smoking: Health effects and cessation strategies. *Clinics in Geratric Medicine, 2*, 337–362.

Salkovskis, S. P., & Harrison, J. (1984). Abnormal and normal obsessions. *Behaviour Research and Therapy, 22*, 549–552.

Salkovskis, P. M., Jones, D. R. O., & Clark, D. M. (1986). Respiratory control in the treatment of panic attacks: Replication. *British Journal of Psychiatry, 148*, 526–532.

Sanchez-Craig, M., Kay, G., Busto, U., & Cappell, H. (1986). Cognitive-behavioural treatment for benzodiazepine dependence. *Lancet, i, 388*.

Sanderson, W. C., & Barlow, D. H. (1986). *Domains of worry within the proposed DSM-III-revised generalized anxiety disorder category: Reliability and description*. Paper presented at the annual meeting of the Association for Advancement of Behavior Therapy, Chicago, November 1986.

Sanderson, W. C., Rapee, R. M., & Barlow, D. H. (1987). The DSM-III-R anxiety disorder categories: Description and patterns of comorbidity. Paper presented at the annual meeting of the Association for the Advancement of Behavior Therapy, Boston, MA.

Sargant, W. (1960). Some newer drugs in the treatment of depression and their relation to other somatic treatments. *Psychosomatics, 1*, 14–17.

Scarr, S., & Salapatek, P. (1970). Patterns of fear development during infancy. *Merrill-Palmer Quarterly, 26*, 53–90.

Schlenker, B. R., & Leary, M. R. (1982). Social anxiety and self-presentation: A conceptualization and model. *Psychological Bulletin, 92*, 641–669.

Schneider, J. A., Allen, R. A., Agras, W. S., Taylor, C. B., & Southam, M. A. (1980). Stanford behavioral medicine relaxation procedures. Stanford: Laboratory for the Study of Behavioral Medicine.

Schoenfeld, M. (1984). Meeting of the Psychoanalytic Association of New York, October 18, 1982. *Psychoanalytic Quarterly, 53*, 498–501.

Schraeder, P. L., Pontzer, R., & Engel, T. R. (1983). A case of being scared to death. *Archives of International Medicine, 143*, 1793–1794.

Schwarz, G., Davidson, R. J., & Goleman, D. (1978). Patterning of cognitive and somatic processes in the self-regulating of anxiety: Effects of medication versus exercise. *Psychosomatic Medicine, 40*, 321–328.

Schwarz, R. M., Burkhart, B. R., & Green, S. B. (1982). Sensation-seeking and anxiety as factors in social drinking by men. *Journal of Studies in Alcohol, 43*, 1108–1114.

Schweitzer, E., Winokur, A., & Rickels, K. (1986). Insulin-induced hypoglycemia and panic atacks. *American Journal of Psychiatry, 141*, 1451–1463.

Sewitch, T. S., & Kirsch, I. (1984). The cognitive content of anxiety: Naturalistic evidence for the predominance of threat-related thoughts. *Cognitive Therapy and Research, 8*, 49–58.

Shapiro, K., Roth, M., Kerr, T. A., & Gurney, C. (1972). The prognosis of affective disorders: The differentiation of anxiety from depressive illness. *British Journal of Psychiatry, 121*, 175–181.

Shatan, C. (1966). Withdrawal symptoms after abrupt termination of imipramine. *Canadian Psychiatry Association Journal, 22* (Suppl.), S150–S158.

Shaw, P. (1976). The nature of social phobia. Paper delivered at the Annual Conference of the British Psychological Society, York, England.

Shaw, P. (1979). A comparison of three behaviour therapies in the treatment of social phobia. *British Journal of Psychiatry, 134*, 620–623.

Shrear, M. K. (1986). Pathophysiology of panic: A review of pharmacologic provocative tests and naturalistic monitoring data. *Journal of Clinical Psychiatry, 47*, 18–26.

Sheehan, D. (1983). *The anxiety disease.* New York: Scribner's.

Sheehan, D. V. (1982). Current concepts in psychiatry: Panic attacks and phobias. *New England Journal of Medicine. 307*, 156–158.

Sheehan, D. V., Ballenger, J., & Jacobson, G. (1980). Treatment of endogenous anxiety with phobic, hysterical and hypochondriacal symptoms. *Archives of General Psychiatry, 37*, 51–59.

Sheehan, D. V., Ballenger, J., & Jacobson, G. (1981). Relative efficacy of monoamine oxidase inhibitors and tricyclic antidepressants in the treatment of endogenous anxiety. In D. Klein & J. Rabkin (Eds.), *Anxiety: New research and changing concepts.* New York: Raven Press.

Sheehan, D. V., Coleman, J. H., Greenblatt, D. J., Jones, K. J., Levine, P. H., Orsulak, P. J., Peterson, M., Schildkraut, J. J., Uzogara, E., & Watkins, D. (1984). Some biochemical correlates of panic attacks with agoraphobia and their response to a new treatment. *Journal of Clinical Psychopharmacology, 4*, 66–75.

Sherman, A. R., & Plummer, I. L. (1973). Training in relaxation as a behavioral self-management skill: An exploratory investigation. *Behavior Therapy, 4*, 543–550.

Sidman, M. (1960). *Tactics of scientific research.* New York: Basic Books.

Sifneos, P. M. (1972). *Short-term psychotherapy and emotional crisis.* Cambridge: Harvard University Press.

Siltonen, L., & Janne, J. (1976). Effect of beta-blockade during bowling competitions. *Annual Clinical Research, 8*, 393–398.

Silber, A. (1984). Meeting of the Psychoanalytic Association of New York. *Psychoanalytic Quarterly, 53*, 498–501.

Skinner, B. F. (1953). *Science and human behavior.* New York: Macmillan.

Skolnick, P., Syapin, P. J., Paugh, B. A., Monacada, V., Marangos, P. J., & Paul, S. M. (1979). Inosine, an endogeneous ligand of the brain benzodiazepine receptor, antagonizes pentylenetetrazole-evoked seizures. *Proceedings of the National Academy of Sciences, U.S.A., 76,* 1515–1518.

Sluzki, C. E. (1981). Process of symptom production and patterns of symptom maintenance. *Journal of Marital and Family Therapy, 7,* 273–280.

Smith, P. K. (1979). The ontogeny of fear in children. In W. Sluckin (Ed.), *Fear in animals and man.* London: Van Nostrand/Reinhold.

Solyom, L., Beck, P., Solyom, C., & Hugel, R. (1974). Some etiological factors in phobic neuroses. *Journal of the Canadian Psychiatric Association, 19,* 69–78.

Solyom, L., Ledwidge, B., & Solyom, C. (1986). Delineating social phobia. *British Journal of Psychiatry, 149,* 464–470.

Solyom, L., Solyom, C., LaPierre, Y., Pecknold, J., & Morton, L., (1981). Phenelzine and exposure in the treatment of phobias. *Biological Psychiatry, 16,* 239–247.

Speth, R. C., Bresolin, N., & Yamamura, I. (1979). Acute diazepam administration produces rapid increases in brain benzodiazepine receptor density. *European Journal of Pharmacology, 59,* 159–160.

Spiegel, D., Detrick, D., & Frischholz, E. (1982). Hypnotizability and psychopathology. *American Journal of Psychiatry, 139,* 431–437.

Spielberger, C. D. (1966). Theory and research on anxiety. In C. D. Spielberger (Ed.), *Anxiety and behavior.* New York: Academic Press.

Spielberger, C. D. (1972). Conceptual and methodological issues in anxiety research. In C. D. Spielberger (Ed.), *Anxiety: Current trends in theory and research* (Vol. 2). New York: Academic Press.

Spielberger, C. D. (1975). The measurement of state and trait anxiety: Conceptual and methodological issues. In L. Levi (Ed.), *Emotions—their parameters and measurement.* New York: Raven Press.

Spielberger, C. D. (1983). *Manual for the state-trait anxiety inventory (STAI Form Y).* Palo Alto, CA: Consulting Psychologists Press.

Spier, S. A., Tesar, G. E., Rosenbaum, J. F., & Woods, S. W. (1986). Treatment of panic disorder and agoraphobia with clonazepam. *Journal of Clinical Psychiatry, 47,* 238–242.

Spitz, R. A. (1950). Anxiety in infancy: A study of its manifestations in the first year of life. *International Journal of Psychoanalysis, 31,* 138–143.

Spitzer, R. L., Endicott, J., & Robins, E. (1978). *Research diagnostic criteria (RDC) for a selected group of functional disorders* (3rd ed.). New York: Biometrics Research, New York State Psychiatric Institute.

Spitzer, R. L., Fleiss, J. L., Endicott, J., & Cohen, J. (1967). Mental status schedule: Properties of factor analytically derived scales. *Archives of General Psychiatry, 16,* 479–491.

Spitzer, R. L., Williams, J. B. W., & Gibbon, M. (1987). Structured clinical interview for DSM-III-R. New York: New York State Psychiatric Institute.

Sroufe, L. A. (1979). The coherence of individual development. *American Psychologist, 34*, 834–841.

Squires, R. F., & Braestrup, C. (1977). Benzodiazepine receptors in rat brain. *Nature, 266*, 732–734.

Stein, M. B. (1986). Panic disorder and medical illness. *Psychosomatics, 27*, 833–838.

Stern, R. S., & Marks, I. M. (1973). Brief and prolonged flooding: A comparison in agoraphobic patients. *Archives of General Psychiatry, 28*, 270–276.

Sternbach, L. H. (1983). The discovery of CNS active 1,4 benzodiazepines. In E. Costa (Ed.), *The benzodiazepines: From molecular biology to clinical practice*. New York: Raven Press.

Stevenson, J., Burrows, G., & Chiu, E. (1976). Comparison of low doses of haloperidol and diazepam in anxiety states. *Medical Journal of Australia, 1*, 451–459.

Stockwell, T., Smail, P., Hodgson, R., & Canter, S. (1984). Alcohol dependence and phobic anxiety states: II. A retrospective study. *British Journal of Psychiatry, 144*, 58–63.

Stone, W. N., Gleser, G. C., & Gottschalk, L. A. (1973). Anxiety and beta-adrenergic blockade. *Archives of General Psychiatry, 29*, 620–622.

Stoyva, J. M. (1979). Guidelines in the training of general relaxation. In J. V. Basmajian (Ed.), *Biofeedback—principles and practice for clinicians*. Baltimore: Williams & Wilkins.

Strauss, E., Risser, A., & Jones, M. W. (1982). Fear responses in patients with epilepsy. *Archives of Neurology, 39*, 626–630.

Stravynski, A., & Shahar, A. (1983). The treatment of social dysfunction in nonpsychotic outpatients: A review. *Journal of Nervous and Mental Disease, 171*, 721–728.

Stroudemire, A., Ninan, P. T., & Wooten, V. (1987). Hypogenic paroxysmal dystonia with panic attacks responsive to drug therapy. *Psychosomatics, 28*, 280–281.

Strupp, H. H., & Binder, J. L. (1984). *Psychotherapy in a new key: A guide to time-limited dynamic psychotherapy*. New York: Basic Books.

Sturgis, E. T., & Scott, R. (1984). Simple phobia. In S. M. Turner (Ed.), *Behavioral theories and treatment of anxiety*. New York: Plenum Press.

Suinn, R. M. (1984). Generalized anxiety disorder. In S. M. Turner (Ed.), *Behavioral theories and treatment of anxiety*. New York: Plenum Press.

Suinn, R. M., & Richardson, F., (1971). Anxiety management training: A nonspecific behavior therapy program for anxiety control. *Behavior Therapy, 2*, 498–510.

Sullivan, H. S. (1953). *The interpersonal theory of psychiatry*. New York: Norton.

Sussman, N. (1986). Diazepam, alprazolam, and buspirone: Review of comparative pharmacology, efficacy, and safety. *Hospital Formula, 21*, 1110–1122.

Suzman, M. M. (1976). Propranolol in the treatment of anxiety. *Postgraduate Medicine Journal, 52,* 168–174.

Svensson, T. H. (1987). Peripheral, autonomic regulation of locus coeruleus noradrenergic neurons in brain: Putative implications for psychiatry and psychopharmacology. *Psychopharmacology, 92,* 1–7.

Tallman, J. F., Paul, S. M., Skolnick, P., & Gallager, D. W. (1980). Receptors for the age of anxiety. *Science, 207,* 274–281.

Tallman, J. F., Thomas, J. W., & Gallager, D. W. (1978). GABAergic modulation of benzodiazepine binding site sensitivity. *Nature, 274,* 383–385.

Taylor, C. B. (1977). Heart-rate changes in improved spider-phobic patients. *Psychological Reports, 41,* 667–671.

Taylor, C. B. (1982). Adult medical disorders. In M. Hersen, A. S. Bellak, & A. E. Kazdin (Eds.), *International handbook of behavior modification and therapy.* New York: Plenum Press.

Taylor, C. B., & Agras, W. S. (1981). Assessment of phobia. In D. H. Barlow (Ed.), *Behavioral assessment of adult disorders.* New York: Guilford Press.

Taylor, C. B., Kenigsberg, M. L., & Robinson, J. M. (1982). A controlled comparison of relaxation and diazepam in panic disorder. *Journal of Clinical Psychiatry, 43:10,* 423–425.

Taylor, C. B., King, R., Ehlers, A., Margraf, J., Clark, D., Hayward, C., Roth, W. T., & Agras, S. (1987). Treadmill exercise test and ambulatory measures in panic attacks. *American Journal of Cardiology, 60,* 48J–52J.

Taylor, C. B., Sallis, J. M., & Needle, R. (1985). The relationship of exercise and physical activity to mental health. *Public Health Reports, 100,* 195–202.

Taylor, C. B., Sheikh, J., Agras, W. S., Roth, W. T., Margraf, J., Ehlers, A., Maddock, R., & Gossard, D. (1986). Self-report of panic attacks: Agreement with heart rate changes. *American Journal of Psychiatry, 143,* 478–482.

Taylor, C. B., Telch, M. J., & Haavik, D. (1983). Ambulatory heart rate changes during panic attacks. *Journal of Psychiatric Research, 17,* 201–206.

Taylor, J. A. (1951). The relationship of anxiety to the conditioned eyelid response. *Journal of Experimental Psychology, 42,* 183–188.

Teasdale, J. D., Walsh, P. A., Lancashire, M., & Mathews, A. M. (1977). Group exposure for agoraphobia: A replication study. *British Journal of Psychiatry, 130,* 186–193.

Telch, M., Agras, W. S., Taylor, C. B., Roth, W. T., Gallen, C. C. (1985). Combined pharmacological and behavioral treatment for agoraphobia. *Behaviour Research and Therapy, 23,* 325–335.

Telch, M., Tearnan, B., & Taylor, C. B. (1983). Antidepressant medication in the treatment of agoraphobia. *Behaviour Research and Therapy, 21,* 505–518.

Telch, M. J. (1985). Stanford panic appraisal inventory, (SPAI), phobic avoidance inventory and Stanford agoraphobia severity scale. Stanford, CA: Laboratory for the Study of Behavioral Medicine, unpublished.

Telch, M. J., Brouillard, M., Telch, C. S., Agras, W. S., Taylor, C. B. (submitted). Role of cognitive appraisal in panic-related avoidance.

Tennant, C., Hurry, J., & Bebbington, P. (1981). Demographic and clinical predictors of remission of neurotic disorders in the community. *Australian and New Zealand Journal of Psychiatry, 15*, 111–116.

Thomas, A., & Chess, S. (1977). *Temperament and development.* New York: Brunner/Mazel.

Thorndike, E. (1932). *Fundamentals of learning.* New York: Teachers College Press.

Thorpe, G. K., Burns, L. E. (1983). *The agoraphobic syndrome.* New York: Wiley.

Thurstone, L. L., & Thurstone, T. G. (1930). A neurotic inventory. *Journal of Social Psychology, 1*, 3–30.

Thyer, B. A., & Himle, J. (1985a). Temporal relationship between panic attack onset and phobic avoidance in agoraphobia. *Behaviour Research and Therapy, 23*, 607–608.

Thyer, B. A., Himle, J., Curtis, G. C., Cameron, O. G., & Nesse, R. M. (1985b). A comparison of panic disorder and agoraphobia with panic attacks. *Comprehensive Psychiatry, 26*, 208–214.

Thyer, B. A., Nesse, R. M., Cameron, O. G., & Curtis, G. C. (1985c). Agoraphobia: A test of the separation anxiety hypothesis. *Behaviour Research and Therapy, 23*, 75–78.

Thyer, B. A., Parrish, R. T., Curtis, G. C., Nesse, R. M., & Cameron, O. G. (1985d). Ages of onset of DSM-III anxiety disorders. *Comprehensive Psychiatry, 26*, 113–122.

Torgersen, S. (1978). The contribution of twin studies to psychiatric nosology. In W. E. Hance, G. Allen, & P. Parisi (Eds.), *Twin Research.* New York: Lisse.

Torgersen, S. (1979). The nature and origin of common phobic fears. *British Journal Psychiatry, 134*, 343–351.

Torgersen, S. (1983). Genetic factors in anxiety disorders. *Archives of General Psychiatry, 40*, 1085–1089.

Torgersen, S. (1985). Hereditary differentiation of anxiety and affective neuroses. *British Journal of Psychiatry, 146*, 530–534.

Trower, P., & Turland, D. (1984). Social phobia. In S. Turner (Ed.), *Behavioral theories and treatment of anxiety.* New York: Plenum.

Trower, P., Bryant, B., & Argyle, M. (1978). *Social skills and mental health.* Pittsburgh: University of Pittsburgh Press.

Trower, P., Yardley, K., Bryant, B. M., & Shaw, P. (1978). The treatment of social failure: A comparison of anxiety-reduction and skills acquisition procedures on two social problems. *Behavior Modification, 2*, 41–60.

Tryer, P. J., & Lader, M. H. (1974). Response to propranolol and diazepam in somatic and psychic anxiety. *British Medical Journal, 2*, 14–16.

Tyrer, P., Candy, J., & Kelly, D. (1973). Phenelzine in phobic anxiety: A controlled trial. *Psychopharmacologia, 32*, 237–254.

Tyrer, P., Murphy, S., Oates, G., & Kingdon, D. (1985). Psychological treatment for benzodiazepine dependence. *Lancet, i,* 1042–1043.

Tyrer, P., Owen, R., & Dawlin, S. (1983). Gradual withdrawal of diazepam after long-term therapy. *Lancet, ii,* 1402–1406.

Tyrer, P., & Steinberg, D. (1975). Symptomatic treatment of agoraphobia and social phobias: A followup. *British Journal of Psychiatry, 127,* 163–168.

Tuma, A. H., & Maser, J. D. (Eds.). (1985). *Anxiety and the anxiety disorders.* Hillsdale, NJ: LEA.

Turner, R. M., DiTomasso, R., & Murray, M. R. (1980). Psychometric analysis of the Willoughby Personality Schedule. *Journal of Behavior Therapy in Experimental Psychiatry, 11,* 185–195.

Turner, R. M., Meles, D., & DiTomasso, R. (1983). Assessment of social anxiety: A controlled comparison among social phobics, obsessive-compulsives, agoraphobics, sexual disorder and simple phobics. *Behaviour Research and Therapy, 21,* 181–183.

Turner, S. M. & Beidel, D. C. (1985). Empirically derived subtypes of social anxiety. *Behavior Therapy, 16,* 384–392.

Turner, S. M., McCanna, M., & Beidel, D. C. (1987). Validity of the social avoidance and distress and fear of negative evaluation scales. *Behaviour Research and Therapy, 25,* 113–115.

Uhde, T. W., Boulenger, J.-P., Jimerson, D. C., & Post, R. M. (1984). Caffeine: Relationship to human anxiety, plasma MHPG and cortisol. *Psychopharmacology Bulletin, 20,* 426–430.

Uhde, T. W., Boulenger, J.-P., Roy-Byrne, P. P., Geraci, M. F., Vittone, B. J., & Post, R. M. (in press). Longitudinal course of panic disorder: Clinical and biological considerations. *Progress in Neuro-Psychopharmacology and Biological Psychiatry.*

Uhde, T. W., Boulenger, J.-P., Post, R. M., Siever, L. J., Vittone, B. J., Jimerson, D. C., & Roy-Byrne, P. O. (1984). Fear and anxiety: Relationship to noradrenergic function. *Psychopathology, 17,* (Suppl. 3), 8–23.

Uhde, T. W., Roy-Byrne, P. P., Vittone, B. J., Boulenger, J.-P., Post, R. M. (1985). Phenomenology and neurobiology of panic disorder. In A. H. Tuma & J. D. Maser, (Eds.), *Anxiety and the anxiety disorders.* Hillsdale, NJ: LEA.

Uhlenhuth, E. H., Balter, M. B., & Lipman, R. S. (1978). Minor tranquilizers: clinical correlations of use in an urban population. *Archives of General Psychiatry, 35,* 650–665.

Uhlenhuth, E. H., Balter, M. B., Mellinger, G. D., Cisin, I. H., & Clinthorne, J. (1983). Symptom checklist syndromes in the general population: Correlations with psychotherapeutic drug use. *Archives of General Psychiatry, 40,* 1167–1173.

Valentine, C. W. (1930). The innate bases of fear. *Journal of Genetic Psychology, 37,* 394–419.

Valentino, R. J., Foote, S. L., & Aston-Jones, G. (1983). Corticotropin-releasing factor activates noradrenergic neurons of the locus coeruleus. *Brain Research, 270,* 363–367.

van den Hout, M. A., & Griez, E. (1984). Panic symptoms after inhalation of carbon dioxide. *British Journal of Psychiatry, 144,* 503–507.

van den Hout, M. A., & Griez, E. (1985). Peripheral panic symptoms occur during changes in alveolar carbon dioxide. *Comprehensive Psychiatry, 26,* 381–387.

Van Valkenburg, C., Akiskal, H. S., Puzantian, V., & Rosenthal, T. (1984). Anxious depression: Clinical, family history, and naturalistic outcome comparisons with panic and major depressive disorders. *Journal of Affective Disorders, 6,* 67–82.

Vohra, J., Burrows, G. D., & Sioman, G. (1975). Assessment of cardiovascular side effects of therapeutic doses of tricyclic antidepressant drugs. *Australia-New Zealand Journal of Medicine, 5,* 7–11.

Vygotsky, L. (1962). *Thought and language.* New York: Wiley.

Wachtel, P. L. (1977). *Psychoanalysis and behavior therapy: Toward an integration.* New York: Basic Books.

Waddell, M. T., Barlow, D. H., & O'Brien, G. T. (1984). A preliminary investigation of cognitive and relaxation treatment of panic disorder: Effects on intense anxiety versus "background" anxiety. *Behaviour Research and Therapy, 22,* 393–402.

Wade, T. C., Baker, T. B., & Hartmann, D. P. (1979). Behavior therapists: Self-reported views and practices. *The Behavior Therapist, 2,* 3–6.

Waldron, S. (1976). The significance of childhood neurosis for adult mental health: A follow-up study. *American Journal of Psychiatry, 133,* 532–538.

Wallerstein, R. S. (1986). *Forty-two lives in treatment: A study of psychoanalysis and psychotherapy.* New York: Guilford Press.

Walters, E. T., Carew, T. J., & Kandel, E. R. (1981). Associative learning in aplysia: Evidence for conditioned fear in an invertebrate. *Science, 211,* 504–506.

Watson, D., & Friend, R. (1969). Measurement of social-evaluative anxiety. *Journal of Consulting and Clinical Psychology, 33,* 448–457.

Watson, J. B., & Morgan, J. B. (1917). Emotional reactions and psychological experimentation. *American Journal of Psychology, 28,* 163–174.

Watson, J. B., & Rayner, R. (1920). Conditioned emotional reactions. *Journal of Experimental Psychology, 3,* 1–14.

Watson, J. P., Gaind, R., & Marks, I. M. (1972). Physiological habituation to continuous phobic stimulation. *Behaviour Research and Therapy, 20,* 269–278.

Watson, J. P., Mullett, G. E., & Pillay, H. (1973). The effects of prolonged exposure to phobic situations upon agoraphobic patients treated in groups. *Behaviour Research and Therapy, 11,* 531–545.

Watson, S. J., Khachaturian, H., Lewis, M. E., & Akil, H. (1986). Chemical neuroanatomy as a basis for biological psychiatry. In P. A. Berger & H. K. Brodie (Eds.), *American handbook of psychiatry,* (Vol. 8). New York: Basic Books.

Watts, F. N. (1979). Habituation model of systematic desensitization. *Psychological Bulletin, 86,* 627–637.

Watzlawick, P., Beavin, J. H., & Jackson, D. D. (1967). *Pragmatics of human communication: A study of interactional patterns, pathologies, and paradoxes.* New York: Norton.

Weeks, C. (1984). *Peace form nervous suffering.* New York: Bantam.

Weiner, I. B. (1975). *Principles of Psychotherapy.* New York: Wiley.

Weissman, M. M. The Epidemiology of anxiety disorders: Rates, risks, and familial patterns. (1985). In A. H. Tuma & J. D. Maser (Eds.), *Anxiety and the anxiety disorders.* Hillsdale, NJ: LEA.

Weissman, M. M., Gershon, E. S., Kidd, K. K., Prusoff, B. A., Leckman, J. F., Dibble, E., Hamovit, J., Thompson, W. D., Pauls, D. S., & Guroff, J. J. (1984). Psychiatric disorders in the relatives of probands with affective disorders: With Yale-NIMH collaborative family study. *Archives of General Psychiatry, 41,* 13–21.

Weissman, M. M., Myers, J. K., & Harding, P. S. (1978). Psychiatric disorders in a U.S. urban community. *American Journal of Psychiatry, 135,* 459–462.

Weissman, M. M., & Klerman, G. (1978). Epidemiology of Mental Disorders. *Archives of General Psychiatry, 35,* 705–712.

Werman, D. S. (1984). *The practice of supportive psychotherapy.* New York: Brunner/Mazel.

Westphal, C. (1871). Die agarophobie, eine neuropathische erscheinung. *Archiv für Psychiatrie und Nervenkrankheiten, 3,* 138–161.

Wiener, N. (1948). *Cybernetics.* New York: Wiley.

Williams, S. L., & Rappoport, A. (1983). Cognitive treatment in the natural environment for agoraphobics. *Behavior Therapy, 14,* 299–313.

Williams, S. L., Turner, S. M., & Peer, D. (1985). Guided mastery and performance desensitization treatments for severe acrophobia. *Journal of Consulting and Clinical Psychology, 53,* 237–247.

Willoughby, R. R. (1932). Some properties of the Thurstone Personality Schedule and a suggested revision. *Journal of Social Psychology, 3,* 401–424.

Willoughby, R. R. (1934). Norms for the Clark-Thurstone Inventory. *Journal of Social Psychology, 5,* 91–97.

Wilson, G. T., & Davison, G. (1971). Processes of fear reduction in systematic desensitization. *Psychological Bulletin, 76,* 1–14.

Winkle, R. A., Lopes, M. G., Goodman, D. J., Fitzgerald, J. W., Schroeder, J. S., & Harrison, D. C. (1977). Arrhythmias in patients with mitral valve prolapse. *American Heart Journal, 93,* 422–427.

Wolberg, L. R. (1967). *The technique of psychotherapy* (2nd ed.). New York: Grune & Stratton.

Wolberg, L. R. (Ed.). (1965). *Short-term psychotherapy.* New York: Grune & Stratton.

Wolpe, J. (1958). *Psychotherapy by reciprocal inhibition.* Stanford: Stanford University Press.

Wolpe, J. (1970). Identifying the antecedents of an agoraphobic reaction: A transcript. *Journal of Behavior Therapy and Experimental Psychiatry, 1,* 299–304.

Wolpe, J. (1973). *The practice of behavior therapy.* New York: Pergamon Press.

Wolpe, J., & Lang, P. G. (1964). A fear survey schedule for use in behavior therapy. *Behaviour Research and Therapy, 2,* 27–30.

Wolpe, J., & Lazarus, A. A. (1966). *Behavior therapy techniques.* New York: Pergamon Press.

Woodruff, R. H., Guze, S. B., & Clayton, P. J. (1972). Anxiety neurosis among psychiatric outpatients. *Comprehensive Psychiatry, 23,* 165–170.

Wood, P. W. (1941). Da Costa's syndrome (or effort syndrome). *British Medical Journal, i,* 845–851.

Woods, S. W., Charney, D. S., Loke, K. J., Goodman, W. K., Redmond, D. E., & Heninger, G. R. (1985). CO_2 chemoceptor sensitivity in panic patients. Paper presented at the meeting of the American Psychiatric Association, Dallas, May 1985.

Woods, S. W., Charney, D. S., Loke, J., Goodman, W. K., Redmond, D. E., Jr., & Heninger, G. R. (1986). Carbon dioxide sensitivity in panic anxiety. *Archives of General Psychiatry, 43,* 900–909.

Woods, S. W., Charney, D. S., McPherson, C. A., Gradman, A. H., & Heninger, G. R. (1987). Situational panic attacks. *Archives of General Psychiatry, 44,* 365–375.

Woodward, R., & Jones, R. B. (1980). Cognitive restructuring treatment: A controlled trial with anxious patients. *Behaviour Research and Therapy, 18,* 401–407.

Yamamoto, J., Kline, F., & Burgoyne, R. (1973). The treatment of severe anxiety in outpatients: A controlled study comparing chlordiazepoxide and chlorpromazine. *Psychosomatics, 14,* 46–51.

Yule, W., & Fernando, P. (1980). Case histories and shorter communications: Blood phobia—beware. *Behaviour Research and Therapy, 28,* 587–590.

Zane, M. D., & Milt, H. (1984). *Your phobia.* Washington, D.C.: American Psychiatry Press.

Zetzel, E. R. (1958). The concept of anxiety in relation to the development of psychoanalysis. *Journal of the American Psychoanalytic Association, 3,* 369–388.

Zisook, S. (1985). A clinical overview of monoamine oxidase inhibitors. *Psychosomatics, 26,* 240–246.

Zitrin, C. M. (1981). Combined pharmacologic and psychotherapeutic treatment of phobias. In M. R. Mavissakalian & D. H. Barlow (Eds.), *Phobia: Psychological and pharmacological treatment.* New York: Guilford Press.

Zitrin, C. M., Klein, D. F., & Woerner, M. G. (1978). Behavior therapy, supportive psychotherapy, imipramine, and phobias. *Archives of General Psychiatry, 35,* 307–316.

Zitrin, C. M., Klein, D. F., & Woerner, M. G. (1980). Treatment of agoraphobia with group exposure in vivo and imipramine. *Archives of General Psychiatry, 37,* 63–72.

Zitrin, C. M., Klein, D. F., Woerner, M. G., & Ross, D. C. (1983). Treatment of phobias: I. Comparison of imipramine hydrochloride and placebo. *Archives of General Psychiatry, 40,* 125–138.

Zucker, D., Taylor, C. B., Brouillard, M., Margraf, J., Ehlers, A., Telch, M., Roth, W. T., & Agras, W. S. (Submitted). Cognitive aspects of panic attacks: Content, course, and relationship to laboratory stressors.

Zuckerman, M. (1960). The Development of an affect adjective check list for the measurement of anxiety. *Journal of Consulting Psychology, 24,* 475–482.

Zuckerman, M., & Lubin, B. (1965). *Manual for the multiple affect adjective check list.* San Diego: Educational and Industrial Testing Service.

Zung, W. W. K. (1965). A rating instrument for anxiety disorders. *Psychosomatics, 12,* 371–379.

Index

. . . .

Fear Survey Schedules (I, II, III), 270–271
Fearful face, 12
Fenobam, 307
Fieldwork, description of, 348
Fight/flight, 10–12, 38
First pass metabolism, 303
Flooding, 26
Flowchart for Clinical Diagnosis, 56–58, 68
Flurazepam, 289
Flying phobia, 265
  case illustration of, 282
  treatment of, 280–281
Freezing, 12

GABA (Gamma-aminobutryic acid), 37
GABA-benzodiazepine system, 37, 41, 110–111
Galvanic skin response, 115
Generalization, 214
Generalized anxiety disorder (GAD), 4, 22, 24, 43, 45, 46, 67, 102–103, 122, 125, 143
  course of, 110
  description of and criteria for, 53–54, 55
  diagnosis of, 107–109
  etiology of, 110–111
  examples of, 104–105
  family studies of, 109–110
  prevalence of, 109
  treatment of, 116–136
    case illustrations of, 133–135
    premises regarding, 135–136
    techniques in, 117
Glutethimide, 100
Graduated exposure, 158, 159
Growth hormone, 28

Habituation, 111, 181, 219
Halazepam, 287
Half-life of drugs, 288
Haloperidol (Haldol®), 306
Hamilton Anxiety Interview, 114, 116
Hamilton Anxiety Rating Scale, 326, 331
Hamilton Depression Interview, 151
Hamilton Depression Inventory, 63, 116
Heart-healthy life-style, 125
Heights, fear of, 22
Hippocampus, 33
Hormones, 35
Hydroxyzine, 306
HYPAC (hypothalamic-pituitary-adrenal cortical) system, 106
Hypertension, 300
Hyperventilation, 31, 147, 148, 149, 171, 159–160, 176
Hypnosis, 118, 121
Hypochondriasis, 64
Hypochrondiasis questionnaire, 319
Hypochrondriasis scale, 153
Hypogenic paroxysmal dystonia, 318
Hypoglycemia, 315
Hypothalamus, 33, 34, 36, 41
Hypoparathyroidism, 316

Illness, fear of, 319
Imaginal flooding, 155, 197
Imidazole derivatives, 307
Imipramine, 23, 39, 163, 166–168, 198, 203, 285, 293, 294, 296–299, 301, 342
Immobility, 12, 13
Implosion therapy, 26
Imprinting, 21
In vivo desensitization, 273
In vivo exposure, 155–157, 171, 180, 197–199, 206, 252, 273, 275. *See also* Exposure therapy
Inhibitions, 17
  behavioral, 37, 38
Instincts, 21
Instructions that produce fear, 26
Insulin, 28
International Classification of Diseases (ICD), 56
Interpersonal relationships, importance of, 19
Involutional melancholia, 194
Isocarboxazid, 299

Lactate infusion, 243
Lactate-induced panic attacks, 145–148
Learning theories, 24–30, 192
  treatment implications of, 31
Life circumstance problem, 56, 58, 89
Life-style changes, 125
Limbic system, 33, 36
Limited-symptom panic attacks, 51, 141, 184
Lipophilic compounds, 287, 288
Locus coeruleus (LC), 33, 34, 36, 41, 111
Lorazepam, 287, 288, 290, 291
Loss of love, fear of, 18

Manifest Anxiety Scale, 112, 116
Maprotiline, 298
Marital therapy, 125, 199–200
Medical conditions, 59–61
Medication, 346
  abuse of, 289
  failure to properly use, 75
Medications and drugs, 61–62. *See also* Pharmacotherapy; Psychopharmacology
Meditation, 118
Meprobamate, 100, 285, 306
Mesoridazine (Serentil®), 306
Methyprylon, 100
Metoprolol, 305
Mianserin, 308
Mild anxiety and depression, 44
Mild episodic anxiety, 44
Misdiagnosis, 75
Mitral valve prolapse, 309–311
MAOIs (monoamine oxidase inhibitors), 100, 165, 169, 246, 285, 286, 299–302. *See also* Isocarboxazid; Phenelzine; Tranylcypromine
Mobility Inventory, 66, 116, 195, 196, 206